Science and the Beauty Business

Companion volume by the same author

Science and the Beauty Business —
VOLUME 2 The Beauty Salon and its Equipment

Science and the Beauty Business

VOLUME 1
The Science of Cosmetics

John V. Simmons
BSc (Hons) C Biol MI Biol
Member of the Society of Cosmetic Scientists

M
MACMILLAN

First published 1989

Published by
MACMILLAN EDUCATION LTD
Houndmills, Basingstoke, Hampshire RG21 2XS
and London
Companies and representatives
throughout the world

Printed in Hong Kong

British Library Cataloguing in Publication Data
Simmons, John V.
Science and the beauty business.
V.1: The science of cosmetics
1. Beauty culture
I. Title
646.7′2 TT958

ISBN 0-333-43844-2
ISBN 0-333-43845-0 Pbk

Contents

Preface

The scientific principles of Beauty Therapy divide quite naturally into two distinct areas: the science of cosmetics and toiletries which is the subject of this volume, and the science of the salon and its equipment which is dealt with in Volume 2.

Together, the two volumes are primarily intended for students of Beauty Therapy studying for the major examinations offered by BTEC, the City and Guilds of London Institute and the professional beauty therapy organisations.

The content is however deliberately not limited by the examination syllabuses. Instead it examines the scientific principles of all aspects of the beauty industry and as such it will be valuable to all who seek a good general insight into the subject.

Cosmetics & toiletries

Cosmetics are products to be applied to improve the appearance and instil a feeling of self-confidence – to LOOK GOOD, SMELL GOOD and FEEL GOOD.

There are actually two groups of products, *cosmetics* and *toiletries*. Until recently the two terms were ill-defined. Some products were called cosmetics, some were toiletries and others could be either. Legislation has now clarified the matter:

Cosmetics – are skin care and decorative products; that is, skin creams and lotions and make-up.

Toiletries – are cleansing products and 'active' products such as anti-perspirants and depilatories.

There remains, however, a 'grey' area in distinguishing between certain active cosmetics and pharmaceuticals. To be effective some products must actually affect the *physiology* of the part of the body to which they are applied. This brings them rather close to being products applied for a medicinal purpose.

The sequence of the book

The early chapters consider the theoretical and practical aspects of the formulation of cosmetics and toiletries. Next there follow chapters on the skin and skin care products, the hands, the feet and the nails, the hair and hair care products, and the teeth. Finally the book deals with perfumery, product safety and the packaging of products.

The formulations

Although it is by no means an exhaustive 'recipe book', many formulations for products are given. Mostly, they have been selected from the technical literature. They have been chosen with two main considerations in mind:

1 that they are representative of the particular type of product – though it is unlikely that they will exactly copy any market brand;
2 that, as far as possible, the raw materials used are obtainable from the usual laboratory suppliers, although this is not always possible and certain materials will have to be obtained from specialist suppliers or even from the manufacturers.

The legal considerations

As far as possible, the suggested formulations comply with the current legislation regarding cosmetics and toiletries as laid down in the *EEC Cosmetics Directive* of 1972 and enacted in the UK by the *Cosmetic Product Regulations* of 1978 which are part of the Consumer Protection Act of 1961.

This legislation is under constant review and is frequently updated, so the intending manufacturer must ascertain the legal position current at the time regarding the materials and methods it is intended to use. He must also appreciate that the manufacturers and suppliers of raw materials ACCEPT NO RESPONSIBILITY for the way in which their materials are used.

When innovative materials and formulations are introduced it is customary for the innovators to *patent* their ideas. If it is intended to manufacture any published formulation *for sale*, the manufacturer must ascertain the patent situation regarding that formulation.

Acknowledgements

I wish to express my gratitude to my many friends and colleagues in the Cosmetics Industry and in the Beauty Profession, and in particular to fellow members of the Society of Cosmetic Scientists who have both knowingly and unknowingly contributed to the content of this Volume. I also offer my most grateful thanks to beauty therapist Teresa Zajac for her tremendous assistance in preparing and checking the text and the illustrations.

JOHN V. SIMMONS
1988

1 Weighing & Measuring in Laboratory & Salon

Metric system – Système International; conversion between metric and Imperial; weighing and measuring in the beauty salon; weighing and measuring equipment in the laboratory; density and relative density; temperature

Weights and measures

In the quest for beauty, health and fitness, people are made to feel constantly aware of their personal weight and measurements.

It has been customary in the United Kingdom and much of the English-speaking world to use the Imperial System of weights and measures – stones and pounds, feet and inches. In the modern international world we should however be using the international metric system, *Système International* or SI for short.

Science has used the metric system for many years, but in the UK we have been most reluctant to use it, either in industry or in our everyday lives.

SI tables for length, volume and weight

Length – standard unit, the **metre.**
10 millimetres (mm) = 1 centimetre (cm)
100 centimetres (cm) = 1 metre (m)

Volume – standard unit, the **decimetre cubed** or **litre.**
1000 centimetres cubed (cm^3) = 1 decimetre cubed (dm^3)
or millilitres (ml), or litre (l)

Weight – standard unit, the **gram.**
1000 milligrams (mg) = 1 gram (g)
1000 grams (g) = 1 kilogram (kg)

Conversions between SI and imperial units

Until one is familiar with the 'size' of metric units, it is useful to compare them with Imperial units. Here are some typical conversions:

For *length:*	1 inch	= 2.54 centimetres
	1 centimetre	= 0.39 inches
	1 metre	= 39.4 inches

Very approximately, an inch is about 2½ centimetres and a metre is 3 inches more than a yard.

For *volume:*	1 fluid ounce	= 28.4 centimetres cubed
	1 pint	= 568 centimetres cubed
	1 litre	= 1.76 pints

Approximately, a fluid ounce can be compared with 30 centimetres cubed and a litre is 1¾ pints.

For *weight:*	1 pound	= 454 grams
	1 kilogram	= 2.2 pounds
	1 ounce	= 28.4 grams
	1 stone	= 6.35 kilograms

Approximately, 30 grams are equivalent to an ounce and a stone is 6⅓ kilograms.

Weighing and measuring in the beauty salon

Ideally, the personal measurements of clients should be taken and recorded in *metric* units. For this purpose measuring tapes, height gauges and personal scales are all available, calibrated in metric units. Frequently they show Imperial units as well, so it is easy to compare measurements in the two systems (see figures 1.1, 1.2, 1.3 and 1.4).

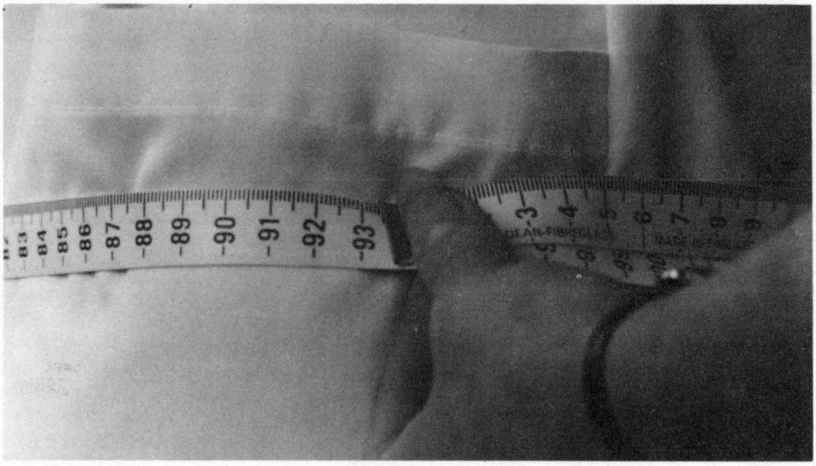

Figure 1.1 Using a metric tape to take personal measurements

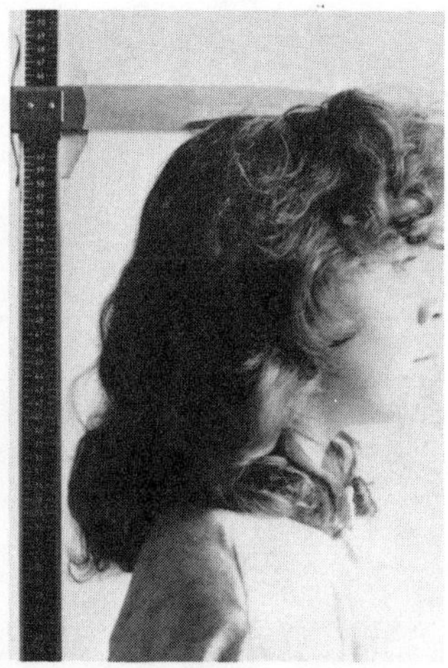

Figure 1.2 A personal height gauge

Figure 1.3 A personal weighing scale

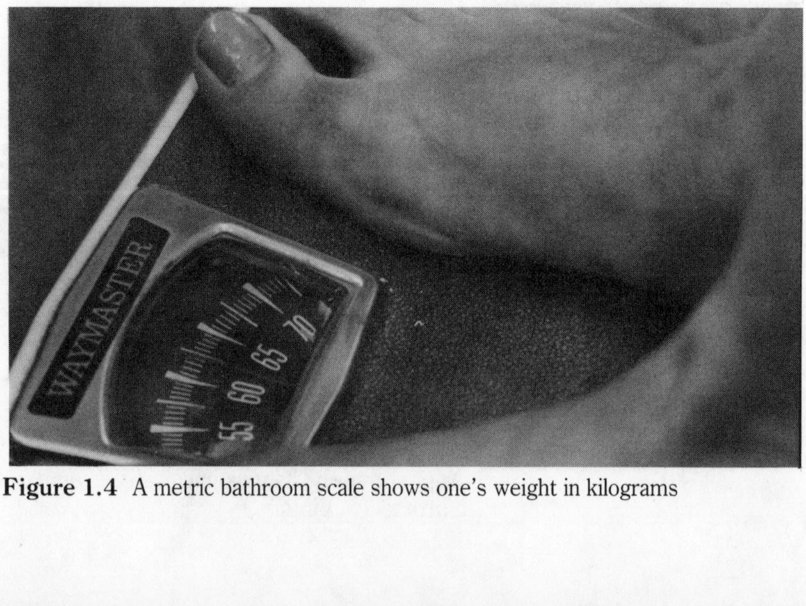

Figure 1.4 A metric bathroom scale shows one's weight in kilograms

In practice, though, you will find that metric units will mean little to most of your clients. An amazing 50 kilograms is barely 8 stone. Even the winner of a beauty contest might be alarmed to know her 'vital statistics' are 91, 61, 91 – the centimetre equivalent of 36, 26, 36!

Weighing and measuring in the laboratory

For most purposes in the laboratory, such as the making of samples of cosmetics, weighing may be done on a simple laboratory balance such as the 'sliding mass' type so long as it is accurate to within 0.1 g (see figure 1.5).

For more accurate weighings where small amounts of materials are required, a modern electric or electronic balance is desirable (see figure 1.6).

Figure 1.5 Using a sliding mass balance to weigh materials for a sample of a cosmetic

Figure 1.6 An electronic top-pan balance

Such a balance is accurate to within 0.01 g or even 0.001 g. Remember that a balance is an expensive precision instrument and should be treated with great care.

Materials should always be weighed in a container and *never* directly on to the balance pan. To take account of the weight of the container, a '*tare*' facility is very useful. This enables you to place the empty container on the balance and reset the scale to zero before weighing the material. Do not forget to reset this facility for each container.

In most cases the measuring of volumes of liquids can be done in *measuring cylinders*. These are accurate enough for larger quantities (see figure 1.7). To dispense small volumes of liquids more accurately, a suitable *pipette* or even a *burette* could be used (see figures 1.8 and 1.9). Always remember to use a pipette filler. Never suck up liquid into it by mouth.

Note that the liquid surface in a measuring device is *not* level, but curves where it meets the glass. This curved surface is called a *meniscus*. When reading a volume of liquid, the *bottom* of the curve is adjusted to the line on the scale (see figure 1.10).

Viscous liquids such as oils or glycerol are not easy to measure by volume. Even if you succeed in pouring the correct quantity into a measuring cylinder, you will have great difficulty pouring it all out again. It is much better to *weigh* such liquids directly into the mixing vessel.

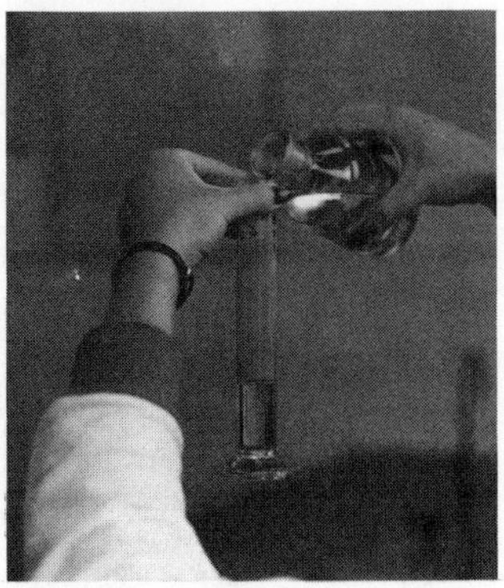

Figure 1.7 How to use a measuring cylinder

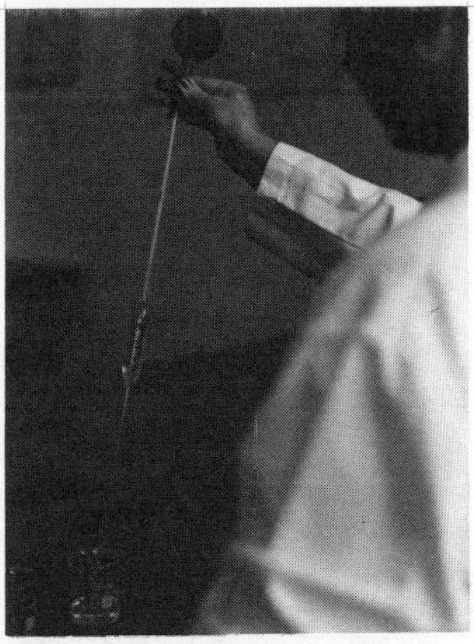

Figure 1.8 Using a pipette with a safety filter

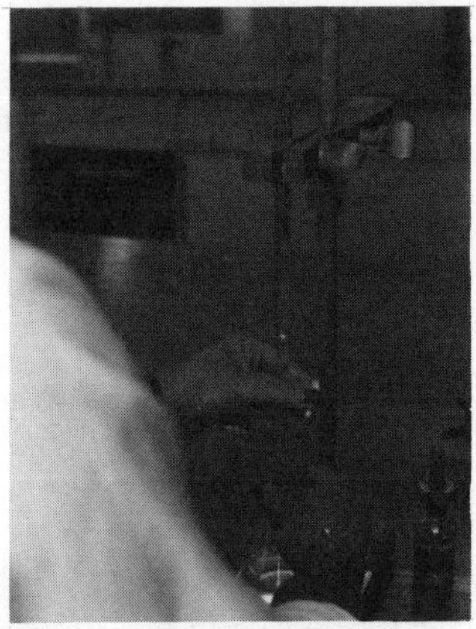

Figure 1.9 Using a burette

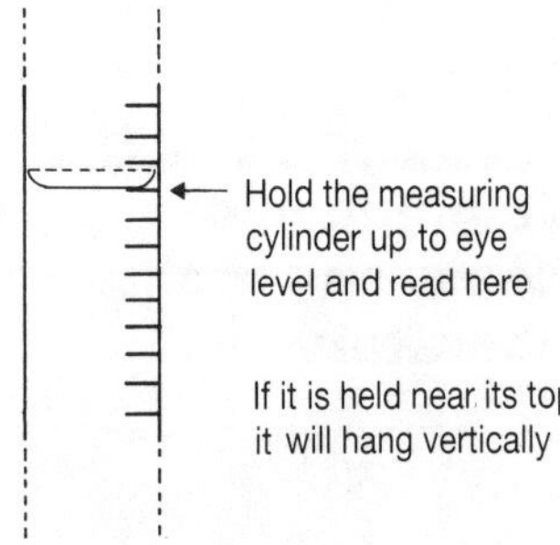

Figure 1.10 Reading the level of liquid in a measuring cylinder

Density

In the 'recipe' or *formulation* for a cosmetic product it is usual to show the relative quantity of each raw material in *parts by weight* out of 100.

Formulation for a traditional cold cream	
White beeswax – 16.0	Borax – 0.8
Mineral oil – 50.0	Water – 33.2

The beeswax and borax are solids. They can be weighed out. The water and mineral oil are liquids, so it might be more convenient to measure them by volume.

To find the volume of a certain weight of a substance we need to know its *density*. Density is the relationship between the weight or *mass* of a substance and its volume: that is, whether a substance is 'light' like air or 'heavy' like lead.

Density is the mass in grams of 1 cm^3 of a substance.

To find the density of a substance, weigh a sample of it and find its volume. Then:

$$\text{Density} = \frac{\text{Mass}}{\text{Volume}} \ g/cm^3$$

For example, to find the density of the rectangular block of iron shown in figure 1.11:

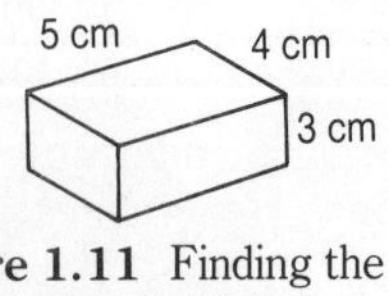

Figure 1.11 Finding the density of an iron block

$$\text{Volume} = 5\ cm \times 4\ cm \times 3\ cm$$
$$= 60\ cm^3$$
$$\text{Weight} = 470\ g$$
$$\text{Density} = \frac{470}{60}$$
$$\text{Density of iron} = 7.83\ g/cm^3$$

Density of liquids

The density of a liquid may be found by carefully measuring out, say, a 100 cm^3 sample and weighing it. Here are some useful examples:

100 cm^3 of WATER weighs 100 g.

The *density of water* is, therefore, $\frac{100}{100}$ or 1 g/cm^3.

100 cm^3 of MINERAL OIL weighs 86 g.

The *density* of *mineral oil* is $\frac{86}{100}$ or 0.86 g/cm^3.

100 cm^3 of ALCOHOL weighs 86 g.

The *density of alcohol* is $\frac{80}{100}$ or 0.80 g/cm^3.

Finding the volume of a liquid in a formulation

Water is easy. Because its density is 1 g/cm^3, each gram of water is also 1 cm^3. So if the formulation requires a certain number of grams of water, just measure out that number of cm^3. To make a 100 g sample of the cold cream requires 33.2 g – that is, 33.2 cm^3 of water.

The mineral oil is not quite so easy. Each gram is *not* 1 cm^3. The cold cream requires 50 g of mineral oil. Let us work out its volume.

$$\text{If Density} = \frac{\text{Mass (Weight)}}{\text{Volume}}$$

by transposing

$$\text{Volume} = \frac{\text{Weight}}{\text{Density}}$$

So if we divide the required weight of a liquid by its density we get its volume. The density of mineral oil is 0.86 g/cm^3 and we require 50 g:

$$\frac{50}{0.86} = 58$$

We must measure out 58 cm^3 of mineral oil. But remember mineral oil is a *viscous* liquid – it is not very 'runny'. In practice it is easier to *weigh* it into the mixing vessel rather than measure it by volume.

Alcohol is frequently used in cosmetic products. Being free flowing it is more convenient to measure it by volume than weigh it. Again we must be aware that each gram is *not* 1 cm^3.

In this simple formulation for a hair setting lotion, the setting agent, polyvinyl pyrrolidone is dissolved in a mixture of alcohol and water.

Formulation for a hair setting lotion

Polyvinyl pyrrolidone	– 2.0
Alcohol	– 48.0
Water	– 50.0

We require 48 g of alcohol. Its density is 0.80 g/cm^3 so we divide the weight by the density:

$$\frac{48}{0.80} = 60$$

We must measure out 60 cm^3 of alcohol.

Relative density or specific gravity

For liquids the term *relative density* is frequently used instead of density. Relative density is the density of a liquid compared with that of water. In effect, it is the number of times a liquid is 'heavier' than water. Water is 'as heavy as itself'! Its relative density is 1.

To find the relative density of a liquid, weigh a sample of the liquid then weigh an equal volume of water.

$$\text{Relative density} = \frac{\text{Weight of sample of liquid}}{\text{Weight of equal volume of water}}$$

An example:

100 cm^3 of alcohol weighs 80 g

100 cm^3 of water weighs 100 g

$$\text{Relative density of alcohol} = \frac{80}{100} \text{ or } 0.80$$

Relative density is numerically the same as density but it is just a number. It has no units.

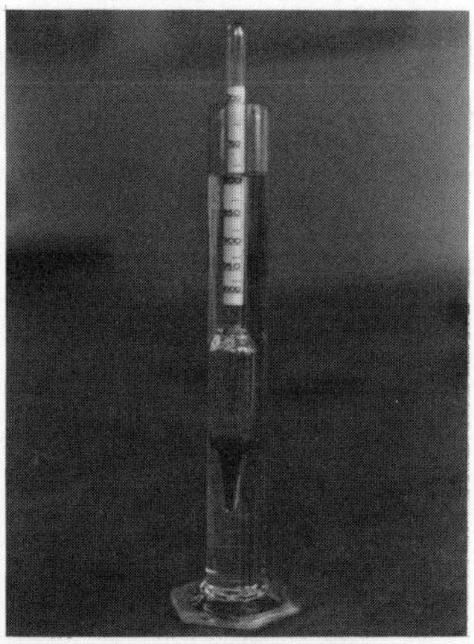

Figure 1.12 Using a hydrometer to measure the relative density of a liquid

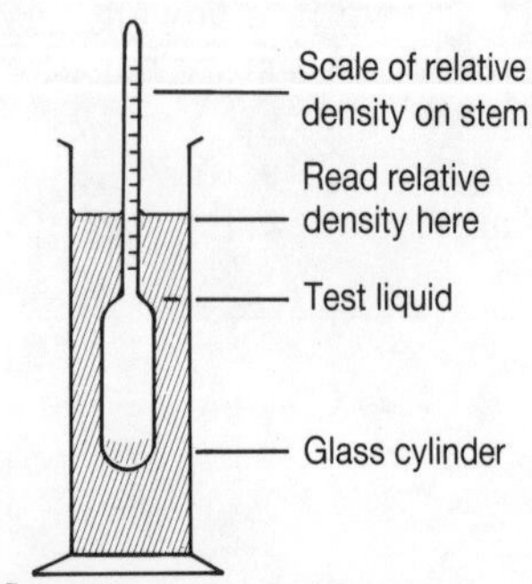

Figure 1.13 Reading a hydrometer

Hydrometer

A simple way to measure the relative density of a liquid is to use a floating device called a *hydrometer*. This floats to a greater or lesser depth in a liquid, depending on its relative density. The reading is taken at the point on the scale at liquid surface level (see figures 1.12 and 1.13).

Remember to handle a hydrometer carefully. It is made of glass. It is very fragile and good ones are quite expensive.

The main use made of relative density measurements is to check the strength of solutions. A solution of a particular substance of a certain strength always has the same relative density.

Solutions of *hydrogen peroxide* are used a great deal by hairdressers and to some extent by beauty therapists. It is vitally important that the correct strength of solution is used.

Table 1.1 shows how the percentage strength, the 'volume strength' and the relative density are related.

Table 1.1 Relative Density of Hydrogen Peroxide Solutions

% Strength	*'Volume Strength'*	*Relative Density*
3%	10 volume	1.010
6%	20 volume	1.020
9%	30 volume	1.030
12%	40 volume	1.040
18%	60 volume	1.060
30%	100 volume	1.100
	↑ Note the coincidence ↑	

A hairdresser may have a *peroxometer* to check hydrogen peroxide solutions. This is simply a hydrometer with a scale which reads directly 'volume' or percentage strength.

Temperature

Temperatures may be measured with a *thermometer* on one of two common scales: *Fahrenheit* and *Celsius*. In the metric system, *Celsius* is used, though most people in the UK have been brought up with Fahrenheit temperatures. They know what a temperature 'feels like' in the more familiar Fahrenheit.

Normal Body Temperature is 37°C or 98.4°F

A comfortable salon temperature is 21°C or 70°F

Conversion of temperature scales

Should it be necessary to convert a temperature from one scale to the other, there are two procedures to follow (see figure 1.14).

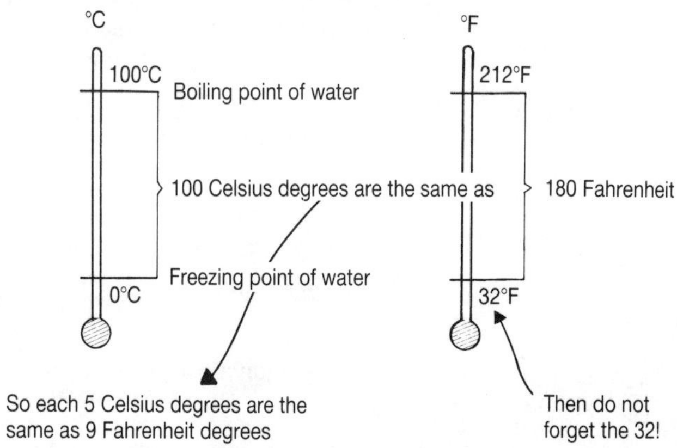

Figure 1.14 Comparison of Celsius and Fahrenheit temperature scales

To convert a Celsius temperature to its Fahrenheit equivalent:

Multiply by 9

Divide by 5

Add 32

Here is an example. Convert 20°C to Fahrenheit:

$20 \times 9 = 180$

$180 \div 5 = 36$

$36 + 32 = 68$

$20°C = 68°F$

To convert a Fahrenheit temperature to its Celsius equivalent:

Subtract 32

Multiply by 5

Divide by 9

Here is an example. Convert 68°F to Celsius:

$$68 - 32 = 36$$
$$36 \times 5 = 180$$
$$180 \div 9 = 20$$
$$68°F = 20°C$$

Things to do

1 To familiarise yourself with the 'size' of metric units, look at the weight or volume of the contents stated on the containers of cosmetics, toiletries and food items.

2 Fill in a figure diagnosis record card for yourself, entering your weight and measurements in metric units.

3 Look at the formulations for cosmetics and toiletries both in this book and others. Note how the materials are listed in parts by weight.

4 Practise weighing and measuring in the laboratory and make up samples of some of the easier formulations shown in this book. A talcum powder (chapter 11) or a hair setting lotion (chapter 18) are suitable products to try.

5 Use a hydrometer to check the relative density of a variety of liquids.

Self-assessment questions

1 What are the standard metric units of (a) volume and (b) weight?

2 Work out the equivalent in inches of a waist measurement of 65 cm. (25.35 inches)

3 What is the equivalent in stones and pounds of a body weight of 55 kg? (8 st. 9 lb)

4 A perfume cologne requires 85 g of alcohol. It has a relative density of 0.80. What volume of alcohol is required? (106.25 cm^3)

5 A hydrometer check on a sample of old 40 volume hydrogen peroxide shows 1.035. What does this tell you about the hydrogen peroxide?

6 A sauna is operating at 80°C. What is the Fahrenheit equivalent of this temperature? (176°F)

2 An Introduction to Chemistry

Substances; states of matter; elements and compounds; acids and alkalis; indicators and pH; the pH of the skin and its significance

Substances

Cosmetics and toiletries are made from a great variety of *substances* which are called raw materials. Each raw material is used because it has specific characteristics or properties which it imparts on the finished product. In this chapter and the next, we will consider some of the properties of substances.

Pure substances and mixtures

Many of the things around us are *mixtures* of more than one substance. The air is a mixture of gases. A cosmetic is a mixture of raw materials. Our bodies are mixtures of literally thousands of different substances. Other things are *pure substances*: the distilled water used for making solutions, the copper used for electrical wiring.

A *pure substance* is one of which all the parts are chemically identical and all samples, however made, have the same composition.

Composition of substances: atoms and molecules

If a piece of a substance were to be divided into two, then into two again and so on, it appears that one could go on forever, getting smaller and smaller pieces. However, there will come a point, far beyond the capability of even the most powerful microscope to see, when a piece of a substance can be divided no further into smaller pieces of the *same* substance.

The smallest particle of a substance is a *molecule*.

If a single molecule were to be further divided it would be into particles called *atoms*. Such a division would have to tear the molecule apart. A chemical change or a *chemical reaction* would have occurred.

An *atom* is the smallest particle of matter capable of taking part in a chemical reaction.

The three states of matter

All the substances of which ourselves and everything around us are made are called *matter*. Matter can have only three basic forms or states: solid, liquid and gas. Every substance is either a *solid*, a *liquid* or a *gas*.

Solids

In a solid substance the molecules are in close proximity and *attract* each other strongly. This enables a solid to hold together. Because the molecules are so closely packed, they cannot easily change places so the solid keeps its *shape*.

A *solid* has a definite volume and a definite shape. It has closely packed molecules and a comparatively high density.

The molecules of a substance possess *energy* and, because of this, they are in constant motion. In a solid, because of the tight packing, the motion can be no more than a *vibration*.

Expansion

If a substance is heated, its molecules gain more energy. This makes them vibrate more vigorously. They push each other further apart and the substance in consequence *expands*.

A substance *expands* when it is heated. It *contracts* when it cools. This is *thermal expansion*.

As a solid is heated and its molecules push further apart, it becomes easier for them to be forced past each other. While a *cold* solid tends to be *hard* and *brittle*, a *warm* solid tends to be *softer* and *pliable*; a warm wax can be moulded and a hot metal can more easily be bent.

Melting

Eventually, at a certain temperature, the molecules are far enough apart to pass easily. The substance can no longer keep its shape. This temperature is the *melting point*. The solid becomes a *liquid*; it *melts*.

For most substances this takes place at a sharp, definite temperature, but the long, spaghetti-like molecules of fats and waxes unravel themselves more gradually and for them melting is a gradual softening process which takes place over a temperature span of several degrees.

Liquids

A *liquid* has a definite volume but no definite shape. It takes the shape of its container. It is usually *less dense* than the solid substance.

The usual conception of a liquid is of a free-flowing, runny or *mobile* substance like water or alcohol, but many liquids do not flow freely: they are *viscous*. Viscosity may occur because the molecules of the liquid have a strong chemical attraction for each other. If this is the case, such liquids have similar attractions for other substances too and they are sticky or *adhesive*.

Liquids may also be viscous if their long, spaghetti-like molecules tend to tangle with each other. If such a liquid is stirred, this disentangles the molecules and the liquid becomes quite runny, but let it stand and it will set again. A liquid with variable viscosity is *thixotropic*.

Further increasing the temperature will cause a liquid to expand. As the greater energy and activity of its molecules more nearly counteracts the forces of attraction between them, the liquid becomes less *cohesive* and less able to hold itself together, so it will flow more easily or separate into droplets.

Take care not to overfill bottles with liquid. Should they become hot, the pressure exerted by the expanding liquid could burst the bottle.

Evaporation

Not all the molecules in a liquid have the same level of energy. It may be that those which have a greater than average level of energy will be moving so fast that they overcome the attractive forces between the molecules and escape from the liquid completely. They will have become molecules of *gas*. *Evaporation* will have occurred.

Evaporation is the change from liquid to gas at a temperature below its boiling point. It takes place from the *surface* of the liquid.

Evaporation is the important process in drying both of water and other solvents. Liquids which evaporate easily are *volatile*. Liquids evaporate more easily if they are *warm*.

Evaporation and cooling

Because the more energetic, faster molecules escape, the average energy level of those left behind is less. The remaining liquid is therefore *cooler*.

Evaporation has a *cooling effect*.

The cooling effect of evaporation is useful in a number of ways:

Evaporation of *sweat* cools the body.
The water content of a *cold cream* evaporates, cooling the skin.
The water evaporates from a *face pack* giving a cool sensation.
The alcohol from a *cologne* or *after-shave* cools and refreshes by evaporation.

Boiling

Heating a liquid continues to expand it until the molecules become so energetic that the attractive forces between them are completely overcome. The molecules fly apart to become a *gas*: this is *boiling*. It takes place at a definite temperature, the *boiling point*.

Gases

A *gas* has *no* definite shape or volume. It will spread to 'fill' the available space. Because the molecules are widely spaced a gas has a *low density*.

The molecules of different gases easily intermingle to form mixtures. The air is a mixture of many gases.

Gases too expand when heated. If however a gas is enclosed in a container, it will instead increase its *pressure* as it gets hotter. An aerosol can contains gas already under pressure. If an aerosol is subjected to extreme heat, the extra pressure could burst the can.

Physical changes

Expansion and contraction, melting, evaporation and boiling are examples of *physical changes* which can happen to substances. In these, although the substance might change its character, the individual molecules remain intact. Later in this chapter we will consider *chemical changes* in which molecules of substances are torn apart and reassembled to form molecules of different substances.

Other important physical changes include *condensation* in which a gas on cooling changes to a liquid and *solidifying* or *freezing* which is the change from liquid to solid.

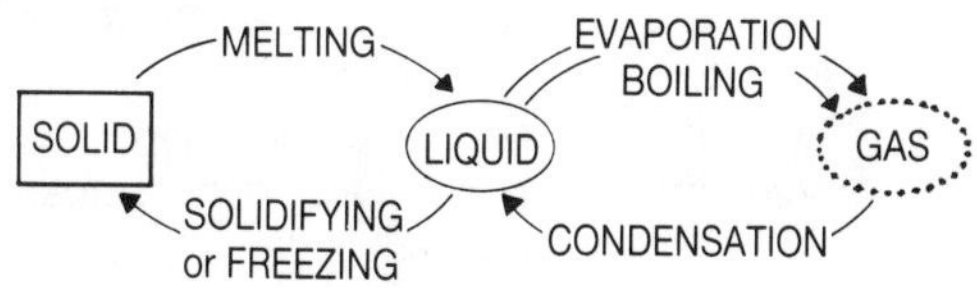

Figure 2.1 The changes of state of matter

Classification of substances

Substances can be classified according to the atoms and molecules of which they are composed into three categories: elements, compounds and mixtures.

Elements are the simplest substances. An element is composed of *one* kind of atom only.
Compounds. All the molecules of a compound are alike but each molecule is made of the atoms of *two* or more elements.
Mixtures are made of the molecules of *two* or more different elements or compounds.

Elements and compounds are *pure substances* – mixtures are not.

Elements

There are some 103 different elements, each with its own kind of atom. How the atoms differ from each other is detailed in chapter 3. A beauty therapist does not need to know all the elements; some are extremely rare. A selection of the more common ones is listed below. Alongside each is its chemical shorthand *symbol*. Elements may be divided into two categories: *metals* and *non-metals* (see table 2.1).

Table 2.1 Some Common Elements

Some Common Metals		*Some Common Non-metals*		
Sodium	Na	Hydrogen	H	gases
Potassium	K	Oxygen	O	gases
Calcium	Ca	Nitrogen	N	gases
Magnesium	Mg	Chlorine	Cl	– gas but easily liquefied
Zinc	Zn			
Copper	Cu			
Lead	Pb	Carbon	C	solids
Iron	Fe	Silicon	Si	solids
Aluminium	Al	Phosphorus	P	solids
Silver	Ag	Sulphur	S	solids
Mercury	Hg			

All metals except mercury which is liquid, are solid at ordinary temperatures. They are hard. They have a characteristic shine or *lustre*. They can be bent, rolled or drawn; they are *malleable* and *ductile*.

Some *non-metals* are solids, some liquids and some gases. Solid non-metals tend to be powdery and dull and are much less dense than metals.

Compounds

A molecule of a compound is formed by linking together the atoms of its constituent elements. By combining 103 different elements there are obviously many thousands of different compounds.

Valency

When the atoms of elements combine to form molecules, each type of atom can and indeed *must* make a definite number of connections or *bonds* to other atoms. The number of bonds an atom must form is the *valency* number of that element.

A hydrogen atom can make only *one* connection. Its valency is *one*. An oxygen atom can make *two* connections. Its valency is *two*.

In hydrogen, the molecules are made of two atoms each joined by their single bond. In oxygen, the molecules are also made of two atoms but this time joined by two bonds (see figure 2.2).

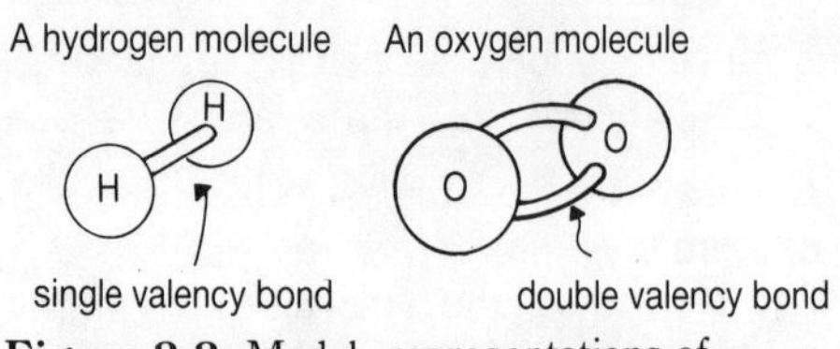

Figure 2.2 Model representations of hydrogen and oxygen molecules

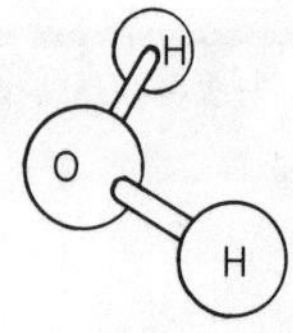

Figure 2.3 Model of a water molecule

Water is a compound of hydrogen and oxygen. Each water molecule consists of two hydrogen atoms and one of oxygen (figure 2.3).

Chemical formulae

In chemical shorthand water is written as H_2O. This is the *formula* for water. The shorthand translates: 'Water is a compound of hydrogen and oxygen. Each molecule consists of two atoms of hydrogen and one atom of oxygen'.

Hydrogen peroxide is also a compound of hydrogen and oxygen. Its formula is H_2O_2. Its molecules consist of two hydrogen and *two* oxygen atoms. To obey the valency rules, they must be linked as shown in figure 2.4.

Common salt, sodium chloride is a compound of sodium, a metal, and chlorine, a non-metal. Both have a valency of one, so the molecule consists of one atom of each (see figure 2.5).

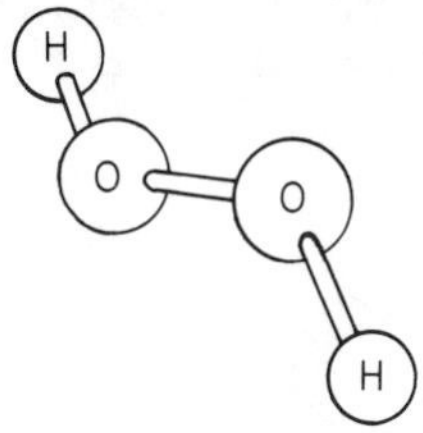

Figure 2.4 Model of a hydrogen peroxide molecule

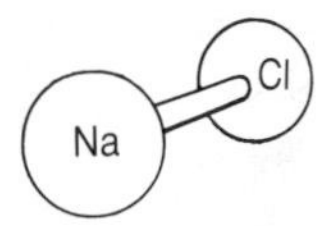

Figure 2.5 Model of a sodium chloride molecule

Compounds

Compounds are of two main categories: *inorganic* and *organic*. Inorganic compounds are mostly of mineral origin; they are the substances of the earth and the air. Organic compounds are so called because in the main they are the substances of living things. They contain a high proportion of the element *carbon* and the term 'organic' is now used to refer to the compounds of carbon, whatever their origin. Because many of the raw materials used to make cosmetics and toiletries are organic, they are dealt with separately in chapter 4.

Inorganic compounds

The main categories of inorganic compounds are oxides, bases and alkalis, acids and salts. Each of the elements is to a greater or lesser extent able to combine with *oxygen* to form an *oxide*. The process is one form of *oxidation*.

Bases and alkalis

If a metallic element combines with oxygen it forms a *metallic oxide*. Most metallic oxides can be reacted upon by acids to form salts. If this is so, the metallic oxide is called a *base*. Some bases are able to dissolve in water. A soluble base is called an *alkali*.

Magnesium is a metal which will easily form an oxide, a base, which will dissolve (slightly) in water to form an alkali.

Some 5 cm lengths of magnesium ribbon may be burned in air and will form a white ash of magnesium oxide. Magnesium plus oxygen forms magnesium oxide.

This is a *chemical change*. Molecules of magnesium and oxygen are rearranged to form molecules of magnesium oxide. The reaction may be shown in chemical shorthand in a *chemical equation*:

$$Mg + O \longrightarrow MgO$$

The magnesium oxide may then be stirred in a little distilled water. Some will dissolve and react with the water to form magnesium hydroxide, an alkali:

$$MgO + H_2O \longrightarrow Mg(OH)_2$$

The presence of the alkali can be shown by testing with an *indicator* such as *litmus*. Put a piece of red and a piece of blue litmus paper in the magnesium hydroxide solution. The red litmus will turn *blue* to indicate the presence of the alkali.

A variety of metallic oxides are used as cosmetic raw materials. Magnesium oxide, zinc oxide and titanium dioxide are all dense white powders and are used as white pigments. There are a number of different iron oxides which are coloured and are used as pigments in make up.

Alkalis used in cosmetics include potassium hydroxide in cuticle removers. Ammonium hydroxide is an ingredient of hair bleaches and permanent waving lotions, and sodium hydroxide is used in the manufacture of soaps and shaving creams.

Acidic oxides and acids

If a non-metallic element combines with oxygen, the oxide produced is quite likely to be a gas. If the gas is collected and dissolved in water, the result is an *acid*. For this reason non-metal oxides are called *acidic oxides*.

Sulphur is a non-metal which will burn easily in air to form a gas with an unpleasant choking smell, sulphur dioxide. This will dissolve in water to form sulphuric (IV) acid.

A little sulphur may be burned on a combustion spoon within the confines of a gas jar. If there is a little distilled water in the jar, the dense fumes of sulphur dioxide will soon dissolve and in a litmus test, the blue litmus will turn red to confirm the presence of an acid.

$$\underset{\text{sulphur}}{S} + \underset{\text{oxygen}}{O_2} \rightarrow \underset{\text{sulphur dioxide}}{SO_2}$$

$$\underset{\text{sulphur dioxide}}{SO_2} + \underset{\text{water}}{H_2O} \rightarrow \underset{\text{sulphuric (IV) acid}}{H_2SO_3}$$

Sulphuric, nitric, hydrochloric and phosphoric are examples of inorganic or *mineral* acids. They are far too strong for use in cosmetics. A variety of *organic* acids such as citric, tartaric, stearic and thioglycollic are used as cosmetic raw materials. Organic acids are described in chapter 4.

Acids, alkalis and salts

An acid and an alkali or base are in a sense chemical opposites, and if put together they will react with each other. If they are mixed in appropriate proportions they will reach a state which is neither acidic nor alkaline. This state is *neutral*. The reaction between an acid and an alkali is therefore called *neutralisation* and the result of the reaction is the formation of a *salt*.

If a little sodium hydroxide solution, alkali, is put in a shallow dish and hydrochloric acid is added to it a little at a time until testing with litmus shows it is neutral and the solution is then evaporated, white crystals of common salt, sodium chloride, will remain.

$$\underset{HCl}{\text{Hydrochloric acid}} + \underset{NaOH}{\text{Sodium hydroxide}} \rightarrow \underset{NaCl}{\text{Sodium chloride}} + \underset{H_2O}{\text{Water}}$$

Notice how in forming the salt, the hydrogen of the acid is replaced by the metal (sodium). An acid is defined as a substance with replaceable hydrogen.

Many different salts are used as cosmetic and toiletry ingredients. Some are soluble and are chemically active materials. Sodium carbonate, sodium sesquicarbonate and a variety of sodium phosphates are used as water-softeners. Calcium sulphide is an active material in hair-removing creams or depilatories. Other salts are insoluble and not very chemically active. They are used for their physical properties as powders. Calcium carbonate is chalk. Hydrated magnesium silicate is talc. Both are used in talcum powders.

Acidity, alkalinity and indicators

To find out whether a substance is acidic or alkaline an *indicator* may be used. The most well known of these is *litmus*. Litmus is a dye and, like many dyes, its colour will change depending on whether it is in acidic or alkaline conditions. For different dyes the colour change takes place at different levels of acidity or alkalinity. The value of litmus is that it changes sharply at the neutral state.

Litmus

Although this is available as a solution to add to the substance being tested, it is most useful in the form of litmus paper. Red litmus paper and blue litmus paper are available. To do a test, a piece of each colour is dipped into the solution being tested.

If the *red* litmus paper turns *blue*, an *alkali* is present.
If the *blue* litmus paper turns *red*, an *acid* is present.
If neither changes, conditions are *neutral*.

Universal Indicator

Litmus can only show if a substance is acidic or alkaline. It cannot show *how strong* the acidity or alkalinity is. To do this a *universal indicator* may be used. This is a mixture of dyes which produces a full spectrum of colour change from red, for the strongest acid, to purple for the strongest alkali. What each colour indicates in terms of acidity or alkalinity is shown on a colour chart which is supplied with the indicator. Universal indicators are available in both liquid and test strip form.

A useful variation of universal indicator is the test strip impregnated with separate segments of the four different indicator dyes. It is much easier to use but more expensive.

pH – the measure of acidity and alkalinity

The pH scale is a number scale used as a measure of acidity and alkalinity. The scale ranges from 0 to 14. pH 7 is neutral. pH values below 7 are acidic; the lower the number the stronger the acid. pH values above 7 are alkaline; the higher the number the stronger the alkali. It is a logarithmic scale so each number is ten times the acidity or alkalinity of the previous one: pH 5 is ten times stronger acid than pH 6 (see figure 2.6).

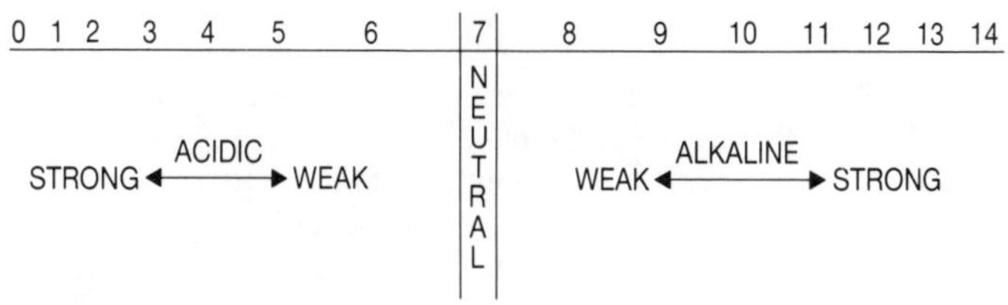

Figure 2.6 The pH scale

pH Meter

The pH meter is an electronic instrument to measure pH values accurately. A special glass probe is inserted into the liquid to be tested and the pH is read from the meter scale (see figure 2.7).

With most pH meters, before taking readings, it is necessary to set the instrument against either an internal reference or by dipping the probe in a solution of known constant pH, a *buffer* solution.

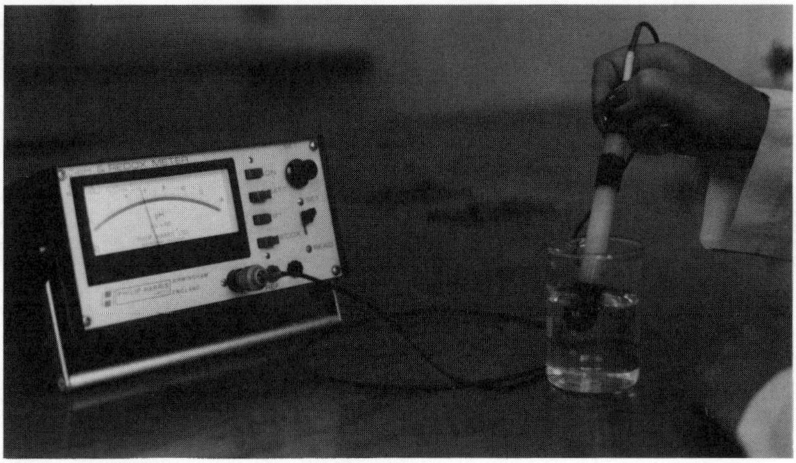

Figure 2.7 Using an electronic pH meter

pH of the skin

If a small drop of *universal indicator* is spread on the skin of, say, the wrist, it will show a colour change which compared with the colour chart should indicate a pH of between 4.5 and 6. The indicator should be washed off at once to avoid staining the skin.

The area of skin should now be washed really well with soap and water. Soap has a moderately alkaline pH of 9 or 10. The skin pH should be tested again. One might expect it now to indicate a much more alkaline pH. However, this is not so; the pH will have changed *very little* from its original value. Not only does skin have a natural *acidity*, it also has the means of resisting any change to its acidity. It is *buffered*.

Only by repeated washing of the skin with soap and water can its pH be made to deviate greatly. The washing removes the *sebum*, the natural grease from the skin. The acidity is derived from a combination of *lactic acid* and one of its salts, a *lactate*, which are part of the sebum.

A combination of an acid and one of its salts sets a constant pH. It is a *buffer*.

The 'acid mantle' of the skin

To appreciate the significance of the acidity of the skin, we must consider its *functions*.

One function of skin is to act as a *barrier* to prevent loss of materials from the body and the ingress of materials from the outside. You may have noticed that if your hands stay in soapy water for a long time, the skin swells and wrinkles. The alkaline soap has removed the sebum then penetrated the *keratin* protein of the outer layer of the skin causing it to swell. If soapy water can penetrate the skin so now can other materials. The skin has lost its barrier function.

Another important function of the skin is to protect the body from infection. Even a 'clean' skin is host to a wide variety of bacteria. The acid conditions of a normal skin keep the bacteria in check by making them less active. Should the acidity be lost, bacteria can become more active and could gain entry through a skin that has lost its barrier function.

Measuring skin pH with a pH meter

A more accurate measure of skin pH can be obtained using a pH meter, but it requires considerable care if the delicate probe is not to be damaged. If possible use an 'older' probe.

So that the glass membrane bulb of the probe may be placed in contact, the protective cover must be removed. The probe is then wetted with distilled water and rubbed very gently but firmly on the skin until a steady reading is obtained.

After repeated use for this purpose the glass bulb membrane may be affected by protein deposits picked up from the skin. To remove them, it should be soaked for 24 hours in a solution of a protein-digesting enzyme such as the protease used in biological washing powders.

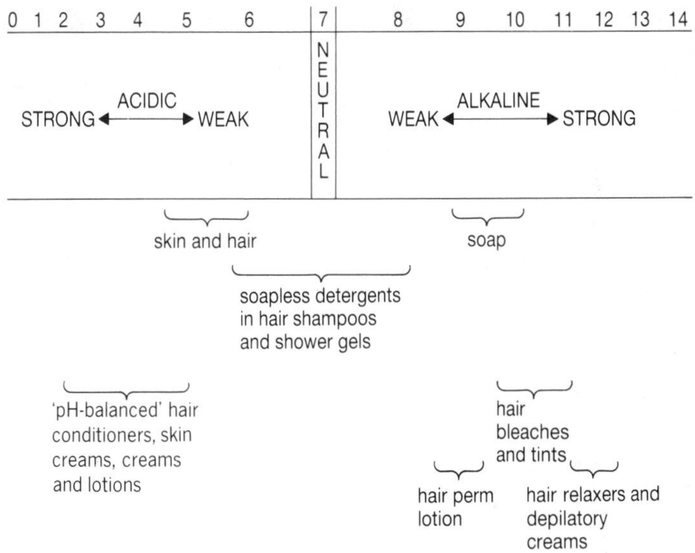

Figure 2.8 pH values of some skin and hair care products

Things to do

1 Try to identify substances around you as elements, compounds or mixtures.

2 Demonstrate to yourself the cooling effect of evaporation. Moisten a little cotton wool with alcohol and dab it on your wrist. You will feel the cooling.

3 Try the chemical reactions described in the chapter:
   a the magnesium ribbon experiment;
   b the burning of sulphur experiment;
   c the neutralising of sodium hydroxide with hydrochloric acid to make sodium chloride.

4 Use a set of molecular models (a) to show valency and (b) to illustrate chemical reactions.

5 Use universal indicator or a pH meter to test the pH of your skin before and after thorough washing with soap.

6 Test the pH, using a meter or universal indicator of a selection of skin and hair care products.

Self-assessment questions

1 What is (a) an atom, (b) a molecule?

2 Define (a) a solid, (b) a liquid, (c) a gas.

3 Explain briefly why a substance expands when heated.

4 What is meant by the terms (a) viscous, (b) thixotropic?

5 Explain why evaporation has a cooling effect.

6 Distinguish between (a) an element and (b) a compound.

7 What is the pH range of a normal skin? What is meant by the term 'buffering'? Explain the significance of the pH of the skin in terms of its role in protecting the body from the environment.

3 Atoms, molecules & ions

The structure of atoms; atoms in molecules; molecule models; chemical bonds; ions and ionisation

The structure of the atom

In many facets of beauty therapy an appreciation of the basic structure of atoms and molecules will contribute greatly to a much better understanding:

Anionic, cationic and *non-ionic* materials in cosmetic products.
The passage of electric currents through the body in electrotherapy – in particular the chemical effects of *galvanic electrotherapy*.
The effects of *ionising radiations* such as ultra violet.

It has been known for a long time that atoms are not the smallest particles of matter. Atoms are composed of smaller particles.

Research into *atomic structure* is still going on and from time to time 'new', hitherto unknown atomic particles are discovered. However for our purposes, we can assume that an atom is made of *three* types of particles:

Protons – Each proton carries a *positive* electric charge
Neutrons – A neutron has *no* electric charge
Electrons – Each electron has a *negative* electric charge

The protons and neutrons are clustered at the centre of the atom and constitute its *nucleus*. They account for most of the mass of an atom.

The electrons are in layered orbits or *shells* in the space around the nucleus. They occupy a large space but have very little mass (see figure 3.1).

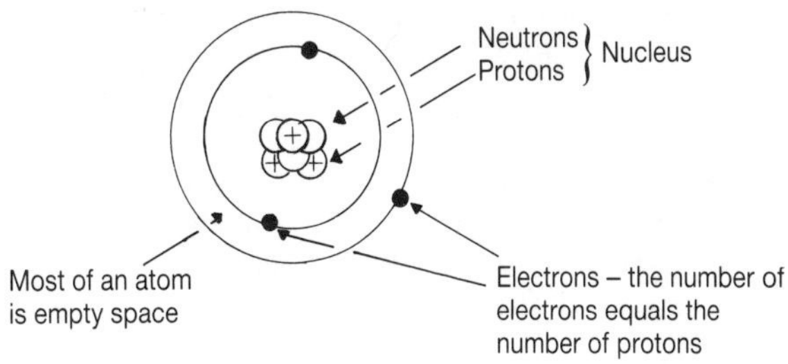

Figure 3.1 The structure of an atom

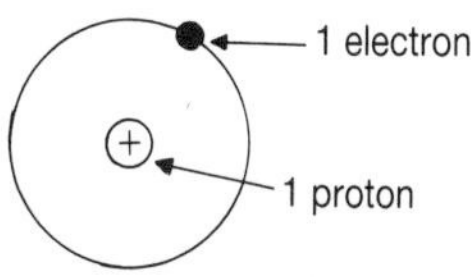

Figure 3.2 Element number 1 – hydrogen

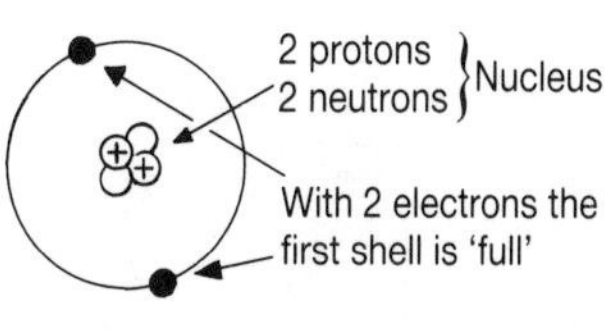

Figure 3.3 Element number 2 – helium

The numbers of protons and electrons in an atom are *equal* so the atom has *no* nett electric charge.

The atoms of the different elements differ from each other in the numbers of protons, neutrons and electrons of which they are made. The 'simplest' element is hydrogen. A hydrogen atom consists of just one proton and one electron (figure 3.2).

Element number 2 is helium. Its atoms have two protons and two neutrons in the nucleus surrounded by two electrons in a single shell (figure 3.3).

Lithium is element number 3. It has three protons and four neutrons in its nucleus and three electrons. The third electron has to be in the second shell. By element number 10, neon, the second shell has its full complement of eight electrons. Notice how they form four *pairs*. The significance of the pairing of electrons will be seen later in the chapter (see figure 3.4).

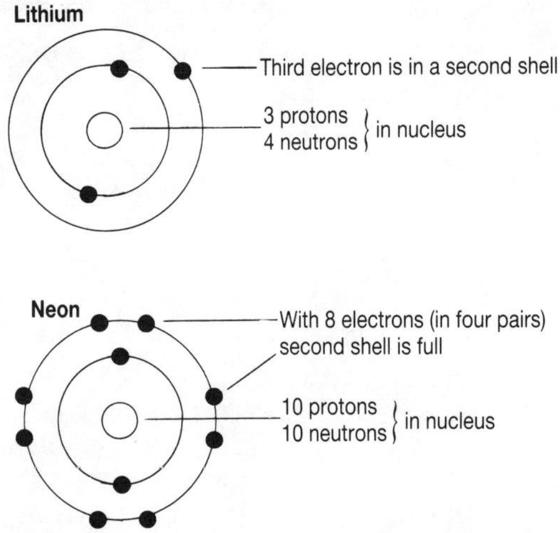

Figure 3.4 Element number 3 – lithium, and element number 10 – neon

Two elements which are important in beauty therapy are number 11 sodium and number 17 chlorine. These are the elements of sodium chloride, common salt (see figure 3.5).

Any element whose atoms do not have a full outer electron shell is potentially unstable. It could reach a more stable state if the outer shell could gain or lose electrons to leave an outer full shell.

If the chlorine atom (see figure 3.5) could gain an electron it could have a full outer shell. Chlorine is a non-metal element. Non-metals have between four and seven electrons in the outer shell. They can best reach the stable eight by gaining electrons.

The sodium atom (see figure 3.5) could best reach the stable state by losing the odd electron in its outer shell. Sodium is a metal. Metal atoms have one, two or three electrons in the outer shell and can best reach stability by giving them away.

In a piece of metal the atoms are closely packed together and the 'odd' electrons of the outer shells are able to 'wander' from atom to atom. They are '*free electrons*'.

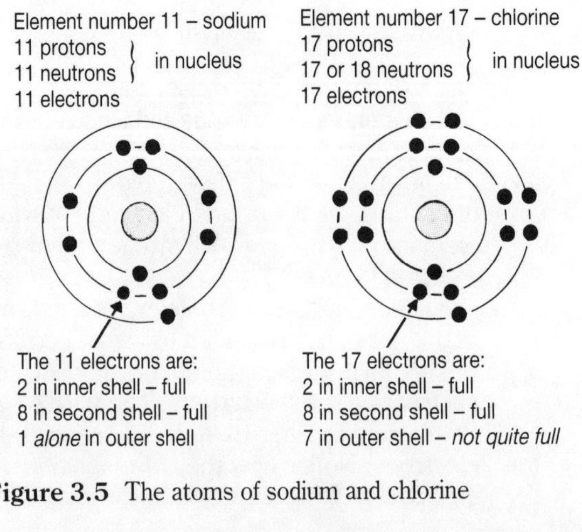

Figure 3.5 The atoms of sodium and chlorine

Metals as conductors of electricity

The ability of a metal wire to carry an electric current makes use of these 'free electrons'. Figure 3.6 shows what happens in a wire when an electric current is flowing. Note how the flow of electrons is *from negative to positive*. One usually imagines that electricity flows from positive to negative.

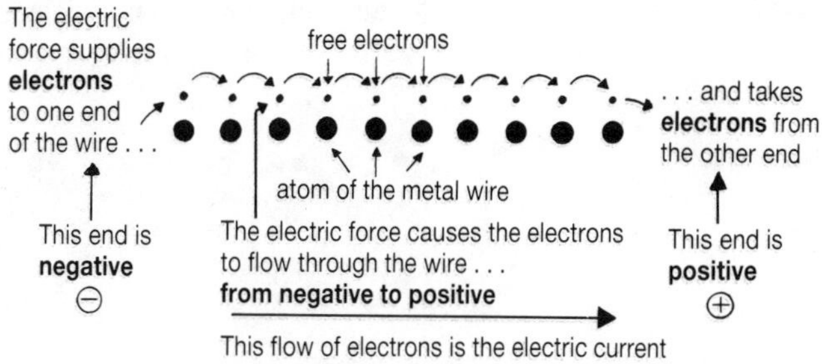

Figure 3.6 The passage of an electric current through a wire

Non-metals as insulators

In a non-metal, the many electrons in the outer shell are more strongly held by the atoms and cannot 'wander' like those of a metal. Because of this, non-metals do not allow the passage of an electric current. They are insulators.

There are, however, some notable exceptions such as *carbon* and *silicon*. The four unpaired electrons in the outer shell of carbon atoms can wander. Carbon is a conductor.

Silicon has rather special powers to conduct electricity in a very controlled way. It is a *semi-conductor*. Silicon is the basis of the *transistors*, *diodes* and '*chips*' in modern electronic equipment. Modern electrotherapy equipment is full of these electronic devices.

The atoms in molecules

When atoms link together to form molecules, the *bonds* between them are formed by the electrons of the outer shell.

As previously mentioned, the electrons prefer to be in *pairs*. In an uncombined atom, some of the electrons are unpaired. They can however become paired with the unpaired electrons of a nearby atom. In doing so a *bond* is formed. Figure 3.7 shows how atoms of hydrogen join to form a hydrogen molecule.

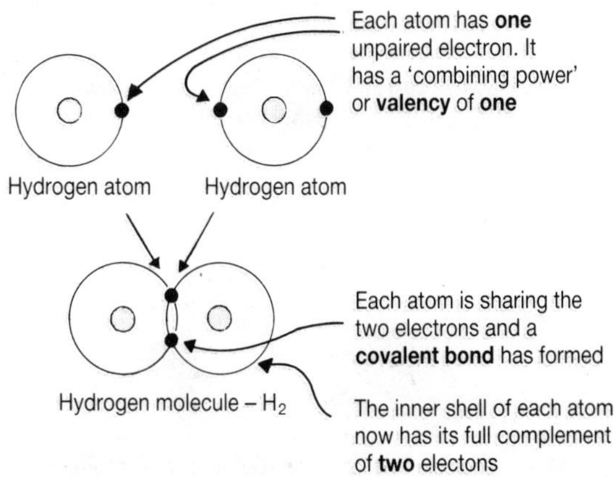

Figure 3.7 Two hydrogen atoms join to become a molecule of hydrogen

Molecule models

Models of molecules are frequently made from coloured balls to represent the atoms joined by flexible sticks – the bonds. Hydrogen atoms are represented by white balls, with a single hole for a stick. Two white balls joined by a single stick model a hydrogen molecule (see figure 3.8).

Figure 3.8 Model of a hydrogen molecule

Now let us see how an oxygen molecule is formed from oxygen atoms. Oxygen, element number 16, has six electrons in the outer shell, two of them unpaired (figure 3.9).

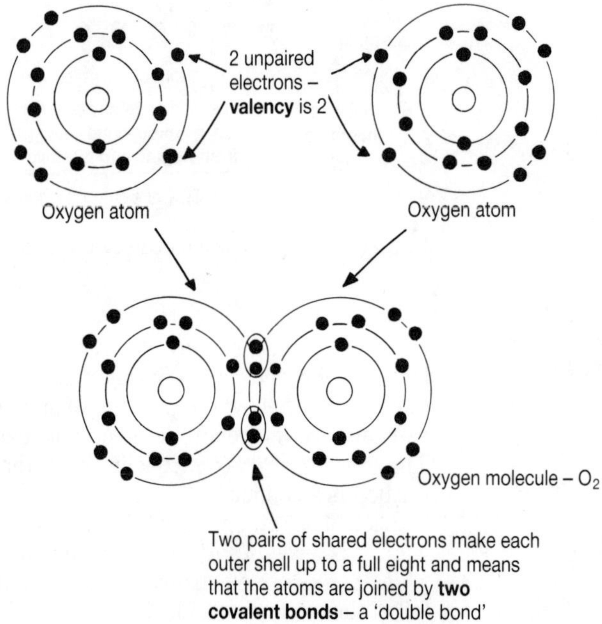

Figure 3.9 Two oxygen atoms join to form an oxygen molecule

Figure 3.10 Model of an oxygen molecule

In model form an oxygen atom is represented by a *red ball* with two holes. In the *oxygen molecule* model two plastic sticks form the double bond (see figure 3.10).

Carbon atoms have four unpaired electrons in the outer shell. *Carbon* – element no. 6 – can make *four covalent bonds* to other atoms; for example, the carbon and hydrogen atoms of ethane, formula C_2H_6 (see figure 3.11).

A molecule is actually three-dimensional and the four bonds of carbon are at the corners of a tetrahedron or triangular pyramid. The model shows this well (figures 3.12 and 3.13). A black ball with four holes represents a carbon atom.

Note how carbon atoms can join to each other and to other atoms at the same time. This means that *carbon* with the help of hydrogen can be the basis of literally thousands of different compounds, the *organic compounds*. These are the subject of the next chapter, chapter 4.

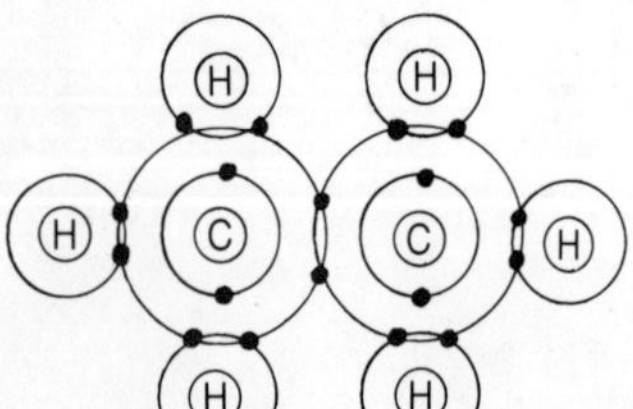

Figure 3.11 The atoms of an ethane molecule – C_2H_6

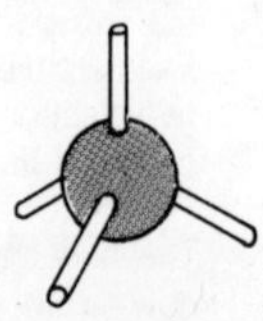

Figure 3.12 Model of a carbon atom

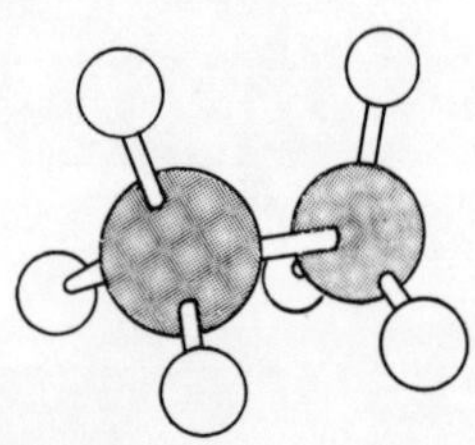

Figure 3.13 Model of an ethane molecule

Electrovalent bonds

When a *salt* molecule is formed from its *metallic* (alkaline) and *non-metallic* (acidic) parts, a different kind of bond is formed. For instance, a *sodium* atom and a *chlorine* atom combine to form *sodium chloride*, common salt. The bond formed is an *electrovalent bond* sometimes referred to as a 'salt-linkage' (see figure 3.14).

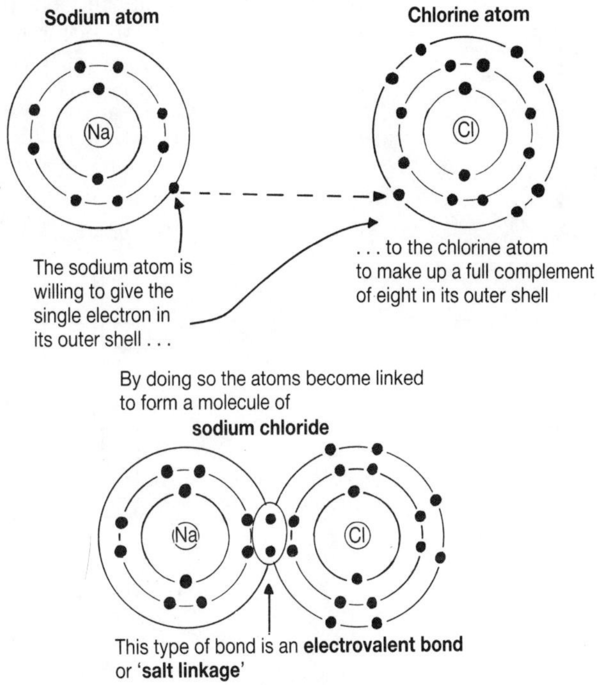

Figure 3.14 The electrovalent bond in a salt molecule

Ionisation

Many compounds will dissolve in water. If, like salt, the molecule contains *electrovalent bonds*, it will split up, not into atoms but into electrically charged particles called *ions*. The process is called *ionisation*. Figure 3.15 shows what happens.

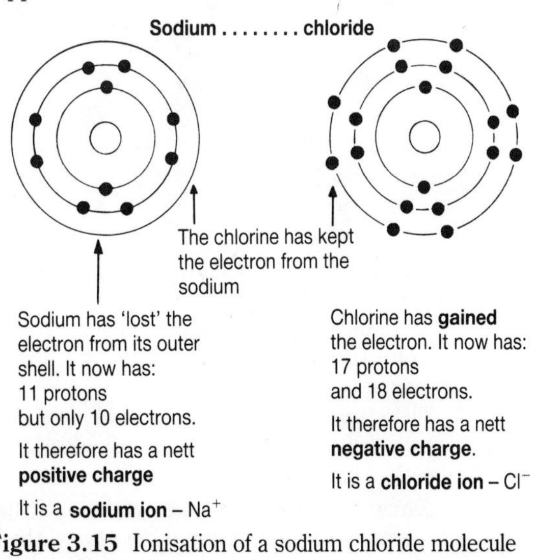

Figure 3.15 Ionisation of a sodium chloride molecule

The passage of electricity through solutions

If ionisation has occurred in a solution, it will be a *conductor* of electricity. A solution which will conduct electricity is called an *electrolyte*.

Figure 3.16 illustrates how an electric current may be passed through a solution of sodium chloride. You will notice that the electric current causes the *ions* to move through the solution. The flow of ions is the electric current.

When the ions arrive at the electrodes, the electrical connections, they cause chemical reactions to occur between the ions and the electrodes. These chemical reactions are called *electrolysis*.

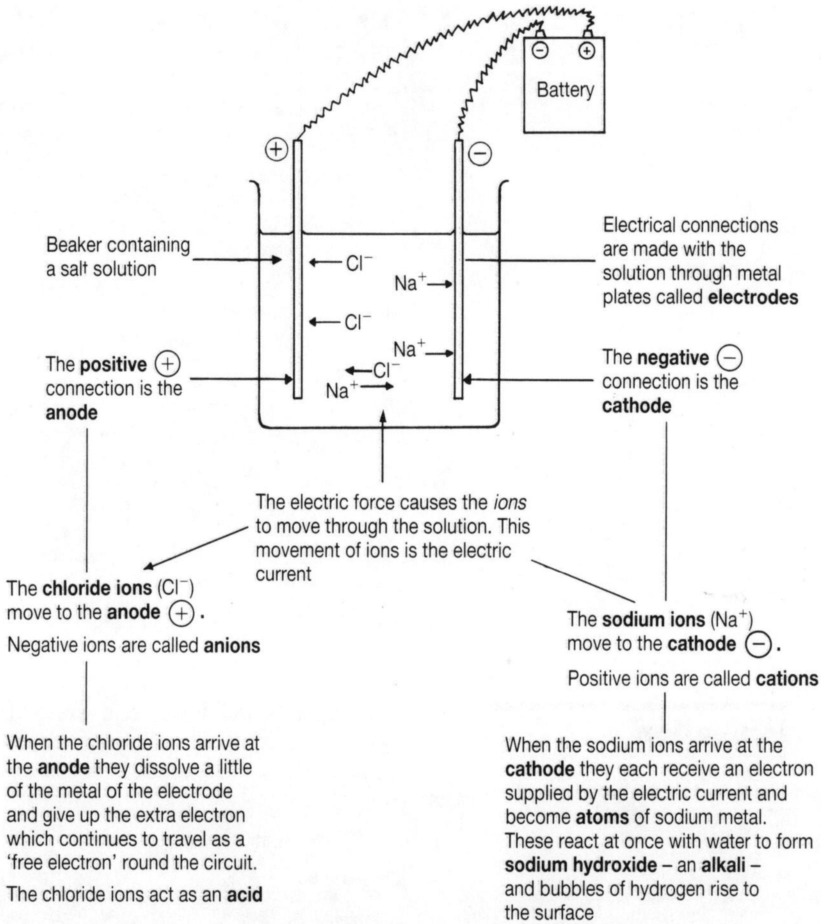

Figure 3.16 The passage of electricity through a salt solution

Importance of the electrical conductivity of solutions

The main significance is the passage of electricity through the body either by accident, causing *electric shock*, or by design in *electrotherapy*.

The human body is composed largely of water with a host of materials dissolved in it. Because many of these materials are *ionised*, the body is a *conductor* of electricity.

The *stratum corneum* of the skin has a low water content and is coated with greasy sebum so it is difficult to pass electricity through it into the body, but once in, the current travels quite easily.

A number of effects of electric currents are used in *electrotherapy*. The movement of ions brought about by the electric current is employed in *'through-body' galvanism* and *'iontophoresis'*. In 'through-body' galvanism the movement of ions stimulates the metabolism in the tissues being treated. In 'iontophoresis' the active ions of special cosmetics are forced into the skin by the electric current.

The chemical effects of electrolysis, particularly the alkaline effects around the *cathode* are used in:

'Disincrustation – to remove excess sebum from a greasy skin.
'Skin-peeling' – to remove excessive thickness from the *stratum corneum*.
'Galvanic epilation' – to remove unwanted hairs permanently.

Pulsed electric currents are used to stimulate muscles to contract in *'faradic treatment'*.

Rapidly alternating high voltage electric currents are used to warm and stimulate the tissues in *'high frequency'* and *'diathermy'* treatments.

All these electrotherapy treatments are described in full detail in Volume 2.

Things to do

1 To find out more about the structure of the atom, ions and ionisation, and the passage of electricity through substances, refer to textbooks on Chemistry at GCSE and 'A' level.

2 Use an electrician's test meter to find if substances are conductors or insulators of electricity. Set the meter to 'resistance' and touch the two probes against the substance.

3 To show the chemical effects of an electric current, try the experiment in figure 3.16.

Self-assessment questions

1 What electric charge is carried by (a) a proton, (b) a neutron, (c) an electron?

2 Why is a metal able to conduct electricity?

3 Which non-metal is a conductor of electricity?

4 What is ionisation?

5 Distinguish between a cation and an anion.

6 What is an electrolyte?

7 Distinguish between a cathode and an anode.

8 Why is the human body a conductor of electricity?

4 Organic compounds in cosmetics

The special properties of carbon; hydrocarbons; alcohols; organic or fatty acids; soaps; esters; waxes; fats and oils; amines; aldehydes and ketones; ethers

Properties of carbon

The majority of raw materials used in the manufacture of cosmetics and toiletries are *organic compounds*. They are some of the thousands of compounds based on the element *carbon*. The carbon atom has a valency of *four*. Figure 4.1 shows how it is represented in model form and on paper.

A carbon atom is able to form four covalent bonds with other atoms including other carbon atoms. In the molecules of organic chemicals, carbon atoms link together to form the main framework of the molecule. Figure 4.2 shows how they can link in straight or branched chains or in rings. The 'spare' valencies are then able to link with atoms of other elements notably *hydrogen*. Organic molecules can be of any size from just a few atoms to literally millions of atoms in each.

In model form the carbon atom is represented by a black ball with four holes for the plastic stick bonds

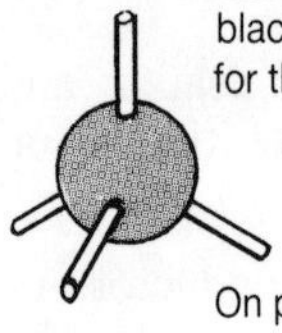

On paper it is shown as

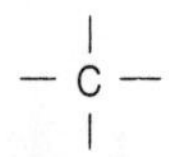

Figure 4.1 The carbon atom in model form and in writing

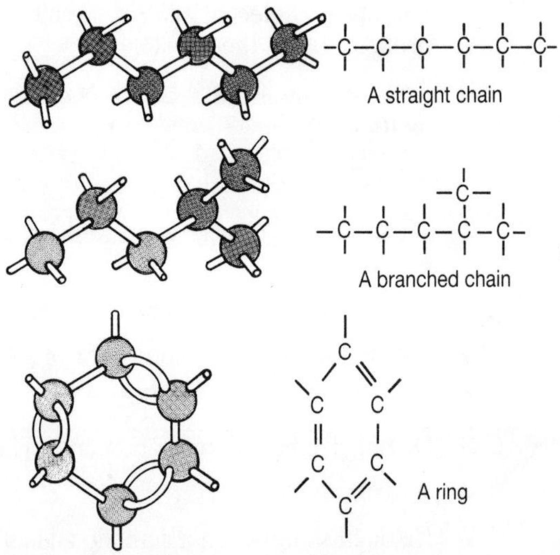

Figure 4.2 Carbon atoms link together to form organic molecules

Hydrocarbons

The simplest organic chemicals composed of carbon and hydrogen only are the hydrocarbons. Note how the compounds form a series with the molecule being one carbon atom longer in each case (see figures 4.3 and 4.4).

The four hydrocarbons shown in figures 4.3 and 4.4 with one, two, three

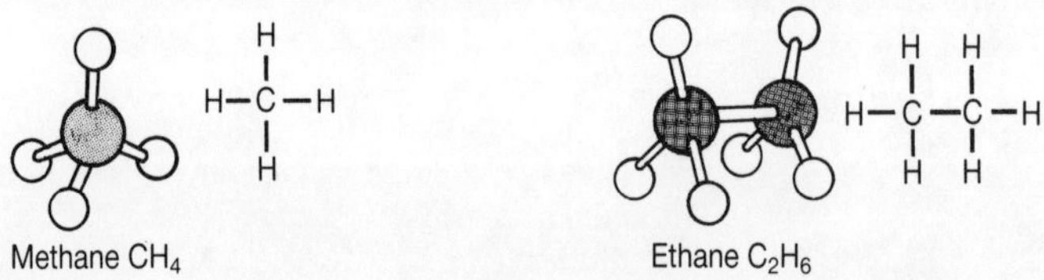

Figure 4.3 The molecules of methane and ethane

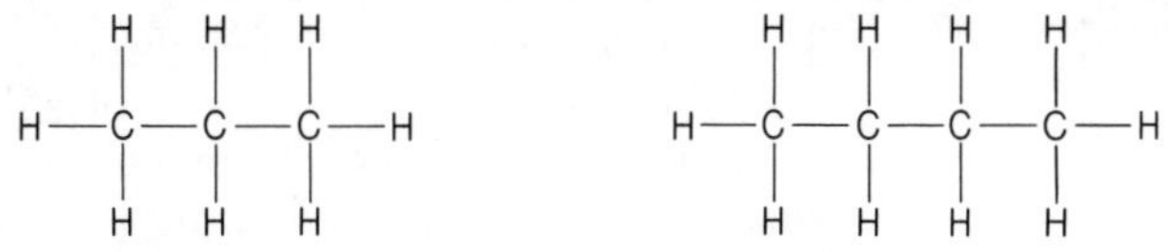

Propane, C_3H_8 *Butane*, C_4H_{10}

Figure 4.4 The molecules of propane and butane

and four carbon atoms in their molecules are all *gases*. Methane is 'natural gas' and propane and butane are the 'bottled' gases such as 'Calor' and 'Camping Gaz'.

Hydrocarbons with six to seventeen carbon atoms are *liquids*. C_6 to C_8 are petroleum spirit – petrol. C_9 to C_{17} are the oils. In cosmetic products much use is made of *mineral oil* or liquid paraffin.

Hydrocarbons with over eighteen carbon atoms in their molecules are *solids*. With around twenty carbon atoms are the *soft paraffins* or petroleum jelly. With thirty or more are the *hard paraffins* or *paraffin waxes*.

All hydrocarbons are *flammable* – they are *fuels*. They come from natural oil and gas. They will *not* mix with water: indeed they *repel* water. They are *hydrophobic*.

Oils, waxes and natural gases will all mix with each other. They are *lipophilic* – which means they are attracted to oil.

Alcohols

An alcohol molecule includes one or more atoms of *oxygen* in addition to the carbon and hydrogen. Methanol and ethanol are the simplest two alcohols (see figure 4.5). Note the position of the oxygen atom. It forms a group —OH which is known as a *hydroxyl* group. This is the distinguishing feature of an alcohol molecule.

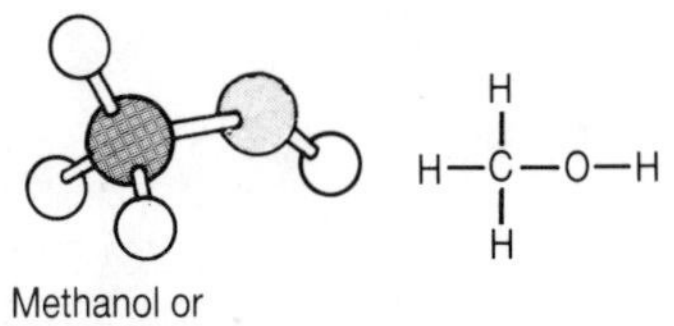

Methanol or
Methyl alcohol CH_3OH

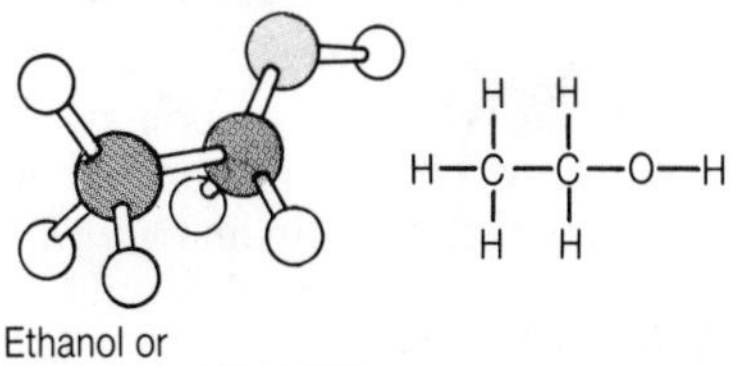

Ethanol or
Ethyl alcohol C_2H_5OH

Figure 4.5 The molecules of methanol and ethanol

Ethanol is the alcohol of alcoholic drinks. It is also a very useful solvent in cosmetic products, for example in perfumes, after-shaves and hairsprays. However, drinkable alcoholic products attract a very high Customs and Excise Duty which would make the cost of using alcohol in cosmetic products exorbitant.

To overcome this, a blend of 95% *ethanol* and 5% *methanol* is available.

This is *methylated spirit*. The methanol in it is *poisonous*, thus making methylated spirit undrinkable so it is available *duty-free*. Because the cosmetic and industrial grades cannot contain the blue dye and the foul flavour of pyridine which identifies commercial '*meths*', they are obtainable only with a Customs and Excise permit.

Methanol and ethanol are both able to mix with *water*. A look at the structure of the molecule in figure 4.6 will explain why. The hydroxyl group, —OH, is 'almost water'. It confers on the alcohol molecule a 'liking' for water: it makes it *hydrophilic*. The rest of the molecule remains *lipophilic* allowing alcohols to mix with waxes, fats and oils.

A molecule with this dual affinity for both oily substances and water is said to be *amphiphilic*. It gives ethanol the ability to dissolve both water-soluble and oil-soluble substances even at the same time. This makes ethanol such a useful solvent in cosmetic products.

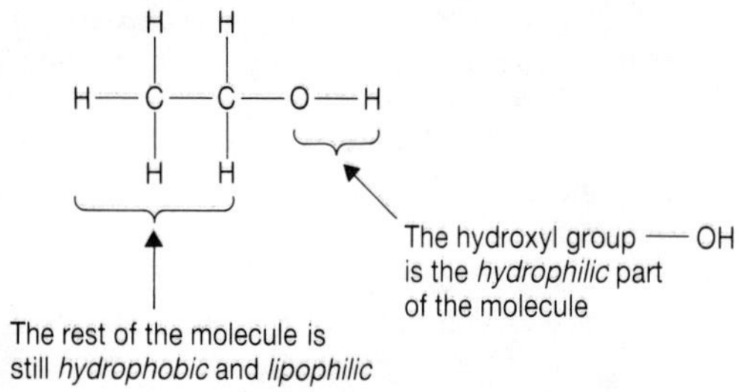

Figure 4.6 The amphiphilic nature of the ethanol molecule

In an alcohol with small molecules, such as methanol or ethanol, the hydrophilic part is 'strong' enough to allow these alcohols to mix completely with water. Alcohols with larger molecules, the *higher alcohols*, are wax-like solids. They are much less water-soluble because the larger hydrophobic part of the molecule predominates. An example is *lauryl alcohol* or *dodecanol* (see figure 4.7).

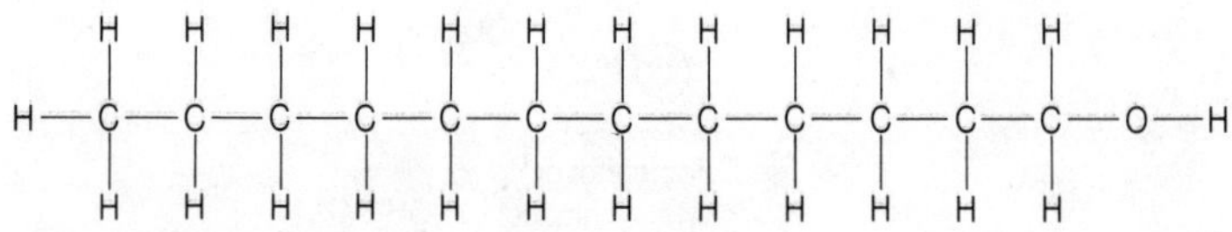

Figure 4.7 Lauryl alcohol or dodecanol

The molecule is twelve-carbon-atoms long. This alcohol is *not* able to dissolve in water, but if it is included in a mixture of oils and water, it will stabilise the mixture to form an *emulsion*. It is an *emulsifier*.

Polyhydric alcohols

These are alcohols whose molecules have more than one *hydroxyl* group. This greatly increases the *hydrophilic* property to the extent that polyhydric alcohols are able to *attract* and *hold* water. They are *humectants*. The main examples used in cosmetics are

propandiol or *propylene glycol* *glycerol, glycerin* or *propantriol* *sorbitol*

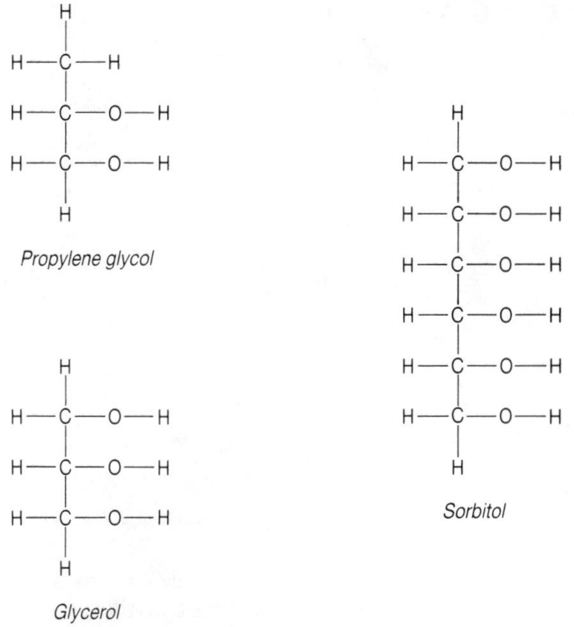

Figure 4.8 The polyhydric alcohols

The molecules of these alcohols are shown in figure 4.8.

The *humectant* property of polyhydric alcohols is used in skin creams and lotions to enable them to hold *moisture* in contact with the skin. They are *moisturisers*.

Organic or 'fatty' acids

In cosmetic products, much use is made of *organic* or *fatty acids*. Like the mineral acids – sulphuric, hydrochloric and nitric – they turn litmus red and form salts with metals but they are usually much less acidic in character and are not so *corrosive* in their action.

The distinguishing feature of the molecule of an organic acid is the arrangement of oxygen and hydrogen atoms on one of the carbon atoms, usually the end one of the chain. This is called the *carboxyl* group. Like the hydroxyl group it is hydrophilic and the simpler fatty acids such as *ethanoic* or *acetic acid* are soluble in water (see figures 4.9 and 4.10).

Figure 4.9 The carboxyl group

Acetic acid is the acid of vinegar. Because of its electrovalent bond, when acetic acid dissolves in water, many of its molecules ionise. The hydrogen atom of the carboxyl group separates as a positive cation, the hydrogen ion.

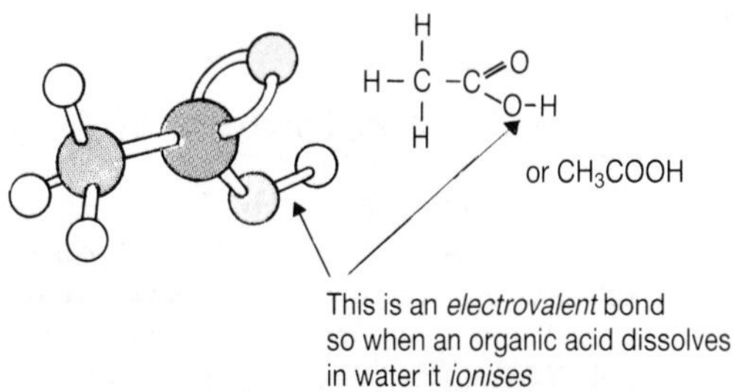

Figure 4.10 Acetic acid or ethanoic acid

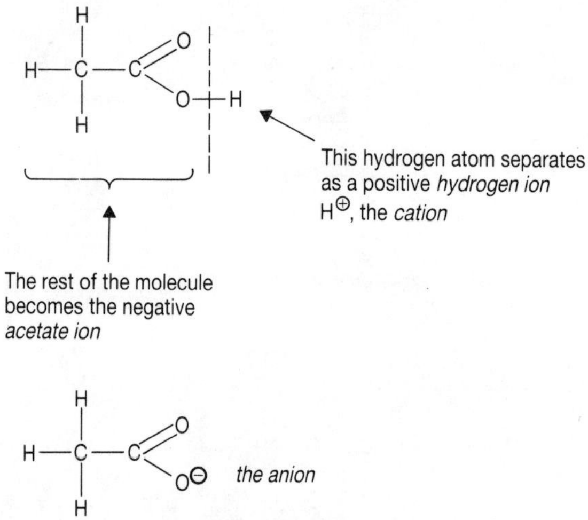

Figure 4.11 The ionisation of acetic acid

The rest of the molecule becomes the negative anion (see figure 4.11). Because the major part of the molecule constitutes the anion, this is an *anionic* substance.

The larger-molecule organic acids are to be found as constituents of *natural fats* and *oils*. They are either oily liquids or waxy solids. Two examples are *palmitic acid* and *stearic acid* (see figure 4.12). Both these are waxy solids and are frequently employed as a waxy component in cosmetic creams.

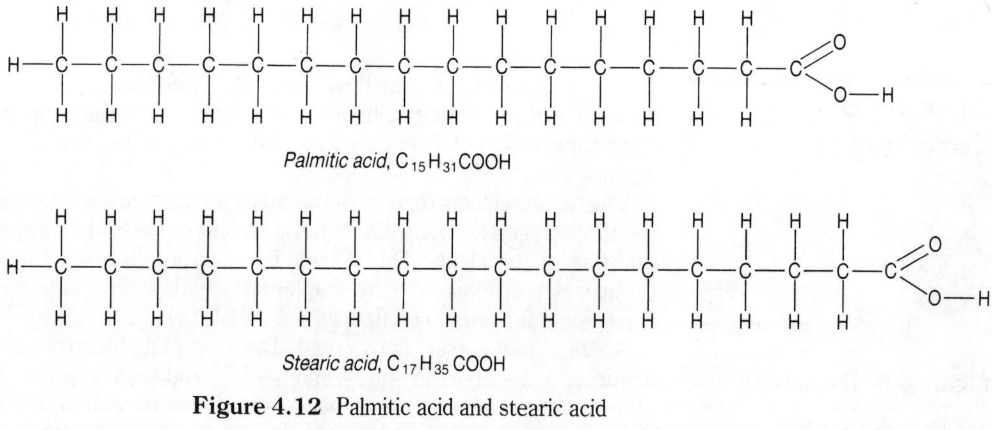

Figure 4.12 Palmitic acid and stearic acid

Saturated and unsaturated fatty acids

Palmitic and stearic acids are *saturated* fatty acids. Let us now look at the structure of a molecule of *oleic acid* (figure 4.13). Look carefully for the difference! Note that two hydrogen atoms are 'missing' and that the two carbon atoms involved are joined by a *double-bond*. This is an *'unsaturated'* link. The most obvious difference this confers upon the substance is that *oleic acid is an oily liquid*.

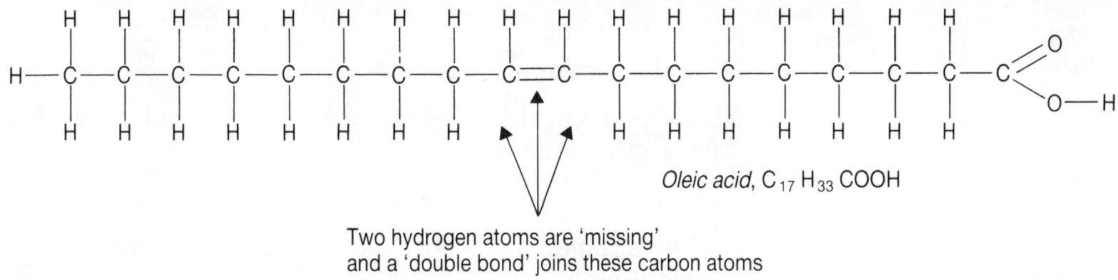

Figure 4.13 Oleic acid – an unsaturated fatty acid

Linoleic acid	$C_{17}H_{31}COOH$	has two unsaturated links
Linolenic acid	$C_{17}H_{29}COOH$	has three unsaturated links
Arachidonic acid	$C_{19}H_{31}COOH$	has four unsaturated links

These are the *poly-unsaturated fatty acids* which dietary experts insist are so good for us.

Soaps

Because the *hydrophobic* part of these fatty acid molecules is large, they will not dissolve in water, but like any acid they will react with an *alkali* such as sodium hydroxide. When they do so, the strength of the *hydrophilic* end of the molecule is given a boost and water-soluble salts called *soaps* are formed:

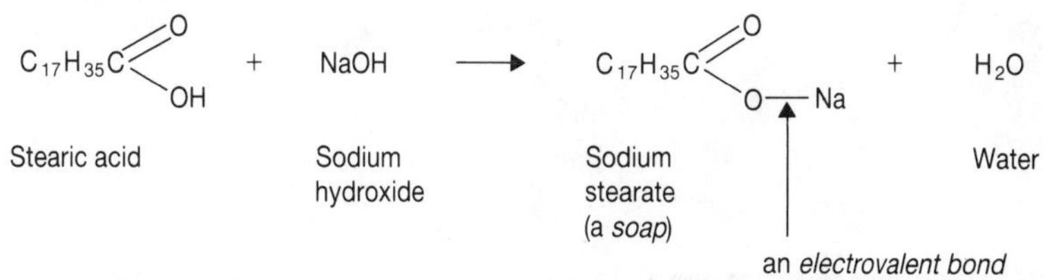

When an acid reacts with an alkali to form a salt, the bond between the acid and alkaline parts of the salt molecule is an *electrovalent bond*; so when a salt such as *soap* is dissolved in water, many of its molecules *ionise* dividing at the electrovalent bond:

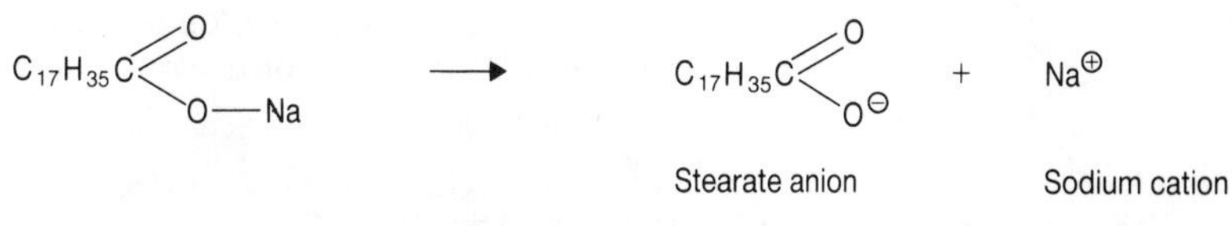

The balance of the strong hydrophobic and strong hydrophilic parts of a soap *anion* makes *soap* important as a *detergent cleanser* and as an *emulsifier* in making creams and lotions.

Esters

If an acid reacts with an *alcohol* rather than an alkali, the bond which forms between the acid and alcohol components is *covalent* and so cannot ionise. The result of the combination is an *ester*, not a salt. An example is the reaction of *acetic acid* with *ethanol* to form the ester *ethyl acetate*:

$CH_3COOH + C_2H_5OH \rightarrow CH_3COOC_2H_5 + H_2O$

Acetic acid Ethanol Ethyl acetate Water

In general terms:

Acid + Alcohol ⟶ Ester + Water

Simple esters tend to have strong fruity smells and are used as perfume and flavour raw materials:

Amyl acetate – pear, banana
Benzyl propionate – pineapple
Bornyl acetate – pine

They are also good solvents, particularly for plastics and resins, and are important in nail varnishes and enamels.

Waxes

A true wax is in theory the *ester* of a large-molecule alcohol and a large-molecule fatty acid. In practice the composition of a wax is far less well defined. It will contain esters of a variety of different alcohols and acids plus some uncombined fatty acids and alcohols too. This will give a natural wax a rather variable composition and therefore somewhat variable properties. Typical true waxes include:

Beeswax – from honeycomb
Lanolin – from sheep's wool
Sebum – the grease of human skin
Carnauba wax – a very hard wax from the leaves of the Carnauba palm.

Paraffin wax is *not* an ester and so is not a true wax.

Fats and oils

Natural fats and oils are *esters of fatty acids and glycerol*. Figure 4.14 shows the layout of a typical fat molecule.

The three fatty acid units in a fat molecule are frequently *different*. It is the mix of fatty acids in a fat or oil which gives it its identifiable character.

A *fat* is solid at ordinary temperatures. It contains a high proportion of *saturated* fatty acids such as palmitic and stearic acids.

An *oil* is liquid at ordinary temperatures. It contains a high proportion of *unsaturated fatty acids* – for example, oleic acid.

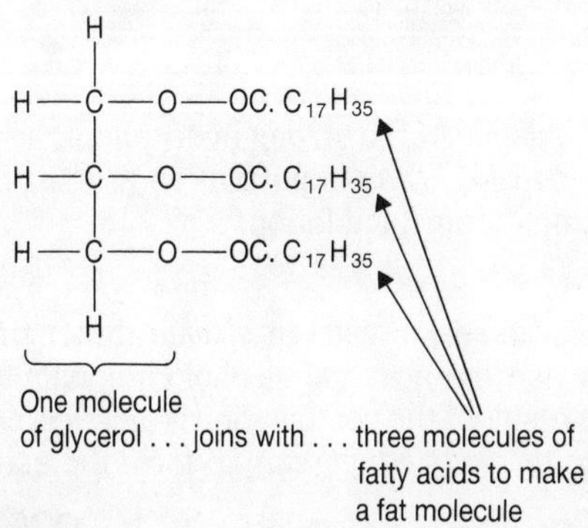

Figure 4.14 The molecule of a fat – glycerol tristearate

Fats are mostly of animal origin. Little direct use is made of them in cosmetics but they are used extensively for the *manufacture of soap* and for *the extraction of fatty acids*.

Oils too are much used in soap manufacture. They are mostly of plant origin. Many are used as such in cosmetics and in beauty treatments:

Olive oil – from olives
Almond oil – from almond kernels
Arachis oil – from groundnuts
Jojoba oil – from jojoba plants

The iso-propyl esters

These *light oils* are esters manufactured from fatty acids and an alcohol – *isopropanol* or *propan-2-ol* (figure 4.15). *Isopropyl myristate* and *isopropyl palmitate* are two very useful light oils for use in cosmetics. They are much less viscous and 'sticky' than mineral oil.

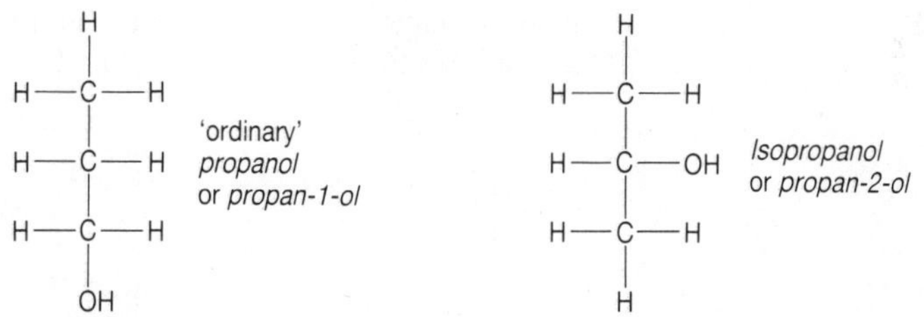

Figure 4.15 The molecules of propan-1-ol and propan-2-ol

Amines

These are organic chemicals which are *basic* or *alkaline* in character. This is due to the presence of a group of atoms —NH_2, the *amine group*. A simple example is *ethylamine* (figure 4.16).

Figure 4.16 Ethylamine

The amine group is very similar to *ammonia* (NH_3). Ammonia dissolves in water to form *ammonium hydroxide* (NH_4OH). This is an *alkali* just like the metal hydroxides, sodium hydroxide and potassium hydroxide.

Amines too can behave as alkalis, but they are usually much milder – much less *caustic*. Examples in cosmetics include:

Ethanolamine and **triethanolamine** –
These combine with fatty acids to make soaps and detergents

Phenyl amines –
A variety of these are the colorants in permanent and semi-permanent hair dyes

Amino acids

These are the 'building units' of the *proteins* which are an important part of the structure of our bodies. Some twenty three different amino acids are found in our bodies, but they all have in common the 'hybrid' combination of an amine and an organic acid. A simple example is *glycine* (figure 4.17).

More about amino acids and how they behave to form proteins may be found in chapter 17, 'Hair'.

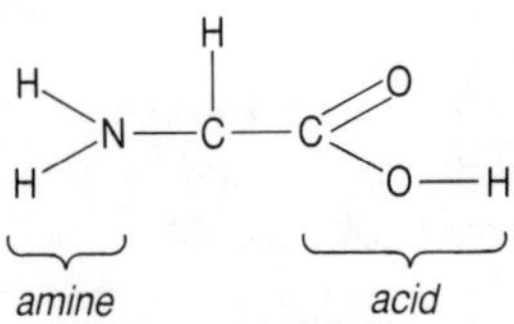

Figure 4.17 Glycine – an amino acid

Aldehydes and ketones

These organic chemicals contain a group of atoms >C=O. Aldehydes have it on an 'end' carbon atom. The example shown in figure 4.18 is acetaldehyde.

Ketones have the >C=O group on a carbon atom, *not* at the end of the molecule. Acetone is shown in figure 4.18.

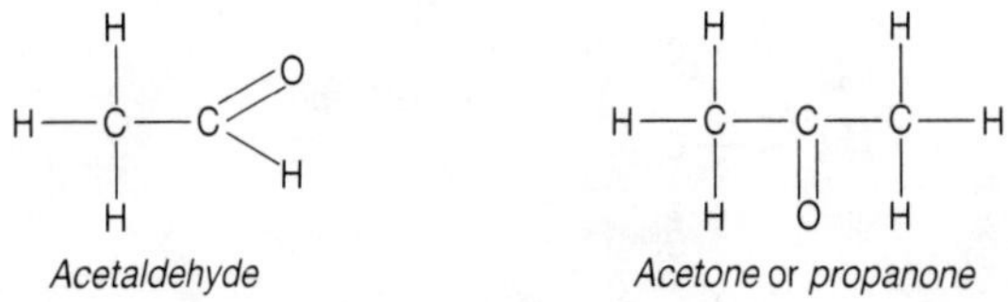

Figure 4.18 Acetaldehyde and acetone

In perfumery, large-molecule aldehydes and ketones have very useful floral odours. An example is *ionone* which smells of violets.

Acetone is a powerful solvent, frequently used as the basis of nail lacquer remover. *Formaldehyde* has an effective bactericidal action. It is sometimes used as a preservative in cosmetics. A solution of it in water is *formalin*. It was formerly used in fumigant sterilising cabinets to sterilise equipment.

Ethers

In the molecule of an *ether*, two chains of carbon atoms are linked by a single atom of oxygen. The most famous example is *ether* the anaesthetic. This is *diethyl ether* (figure 4.19).

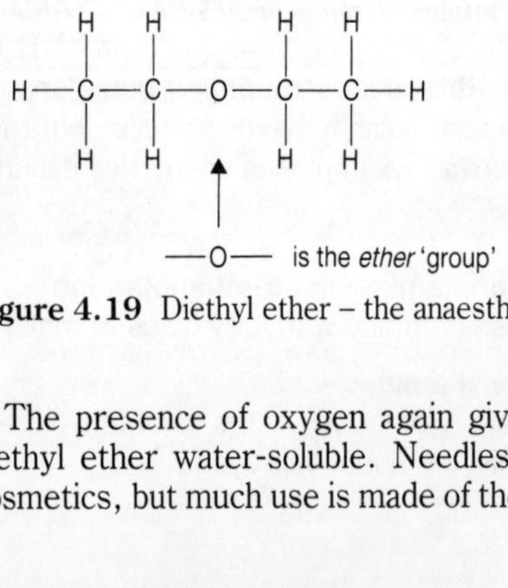

Figure 4.19 Diethyl ether – the anaesthetic ether

The presence of oxygen again gives a *hydrophilic* property and makes diethyl ether water-soluble. Needless to say this ether is not for use in cosmetics, but much use is made of the hydrophilic tendency in the *ether type detergents and emulsifiers*, or *ethoxylates* as they are known. These are described in chapter 8, where it will be seen that use of different numbers of ether linkages in the surfactant molecule makes it possible to 'tailor-make' the best surfactant for any required purpose.

Things to do

1. If you have access to a stock of cosmetic raw materials, identify those which are organic and those which are inorganic.
2. Having decided which are organic, next identify which are hydrocarbons, alcohols, fatty acids and so on.
3. Use a set of molecular models to construct models of the molecules of some of the organic raw materials described in this chapter.

Self-assessment questions

1. Which chemical element is the basis of organic chemicals?
2. What property of hydrocarbons could make them a safety hazard?
3. What is meant by the terms (a) hydrophilic and (b) hydrophobic?
4. What is an amphiphilic substance?
5. Why are amphiphilic substances useful in the making of cosmetic creams?
6. Distinguish chemically between a vegetable oil and a mineral oil.
7. Distinguish chemically between a paraffin wax and a true wax such as beeswax.
8. What is the chemical difference between a saturated and an unsaturated fatty acid?
9. What in chemical terms is a soap?
10. What is an amino acid?

5 Water

Water supplies: distilled and deionised water; microbiologically pure water; hard and soft water; water softening

Water is a substance which we all take very much for granted, yet we demand it in far greater quantities than any other raw material. At the same time we expect our water supply to be clean, 'pure' and free from infection and pollution. Water is a major ingredient of most cosmetics and toiletries. For this purpose the quality of the water is particularly important.

Water as a chemical substance

Water is a colourless, odourless and tasteless liquid which, when pure, freezes at 0°C and boils at 100°C. Chemically it is hydrogen oxide, H_2O. Figure 5.1 shows a water molecule in model form.

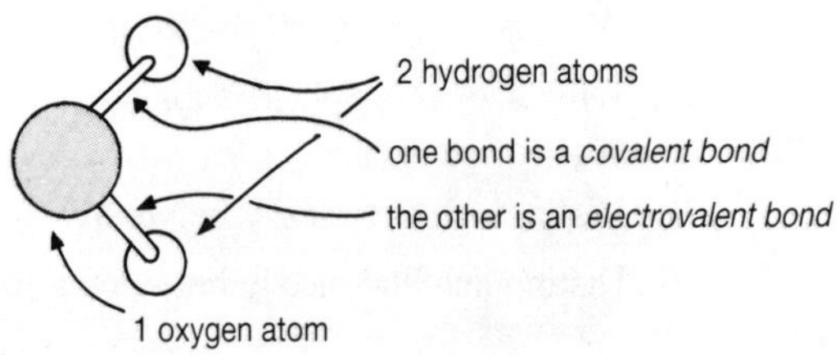

Figure 5.1 The water molecule

A few of the molecules in water are *ionised*, dividing at the electrovalent bond:

H_2O	$\rightarrow$	H^+	+	OH^-
Water molecule		Hydrogen ion		Hydroxide ion

Ionising to produce hydrogen ions is the feature of an *acid*. Ionising to produce hydroxide ions is an *alkaline* property. Water ionises to produce both in *equal quantities*, so it is equally acidic and alkaline; it is *neutral*. It has pH 7.

Water for supplies

By far the largest accumulation of water on earth is in the oceans – "water, water everywhere but not a drop to drink"! Because of its very high content of dissolved salts it is not feasible to process seawater for supplies on a large scale unless no other source is available as is the case in many of the Arabic countries.

The usual source of water for supplies is *rainwater*. Water which falls as rain has evaporated mostly from the oceans but in doing so has left behind all its dissolved salts. Rainwater is therefore relatively pure: it has been naturally *distilled*. It will however collect some impurities from the atmosphere. Notably, it will dissolve *carbon dioxide* and *sulphur dioxide*. Both are acidic oxides and will make rainwater slightly *acidic*. The significance of this will be considered later. It will also bring down dust and microorganisms floating in the air.

Collection of water for supplies

There are three main sources of water for water supplies:

1 Reservoirs
2 Wells and bore-holes
3 Large rivers

In high-rainfall mountain areas, large quantities of relatively pure rainwater can be collected by building dams to hold back mountain rivers and streams to form reservoirs (see figure 5.2).

Where the underlying rock is porous, much of the rainfall soaks into the ground and accumulates in the rocks. By drilling bore-holes or wells, this water may be pumped out. Figure 5.3 shows a typical pumping station. Such water is very clean, having been filtered by the rocks, but frequently, the acidity of the rainwater enables it to dissolve *lime* minerals from the rocks and make it *hard* (see later in the chapter).

In recent times, mountain areas and bore-holes have become inadequate to supply the vast need for water. To supplement supplies, water is drawn from large rivers. Figure 5.4 shows a river bank pumping station for this purpose. This water is quite likely to be very dirty and highly populated by microorganisms which could make it hazardous to health.

Figure 5.2 Water for water supplies collected in a reservoir

Figure 5.3 A pumping station pumps water from a borehole

Figure 5.4 Pumping water from the River Severn in Shropshire

Treatment of water for supplies

All the water supplied via the mains to our homes, factories and salons must be *'clean and wholesome'*. At a *water works* it must be *filtered* to remove solid impurities. This is done by letting it soak through *filter beds* containing fine sand (see figure 5.5). It must then be *sterilised* to kill microorganisms, particularly those which could cause such diseases as *typhoid*, *cholera* and *dysentery*. This is done by metering into the water one part of *chlorine* per million parts of water. Figure 5.6 shows a chlorination plant. Filtering and chlorination *must* be done to all water intended for water supplies.

Two other treatments *may* be performed at the water works. One of the problems with *hard* water is that it tends to deposit a scale of lime inside the pipes through which it flows. In very hard water areas it may be necessary to partially *soften* the water so it does not eventually block the water mains.

To soften the water, a large *settling tank* is filled with water. A measured amount of *milk of lime*, a suspension of calcium hydroxide, is stirred in. This

(a) **(b)**

Figure 5.5 Filter beds. (a) In the flocculator, added alum settles out most of the sediment. (b) Sand filter beds filter out the remainder (courtesy of the South Staffordshire Water Company)

(a) **(b)**

Figure 5.6 Chlorination plant. (a) The evaporator vaporises the liquid chlorine for use. (b) The chlorinators meter its addition to the water (courtesy of the South Staffordshire Water Company)

causes some of the *lime minerals* to settle out as a sediment. The softened water is then drawn off. The tank is cleaned out and the process is repeated with the next batch of water.

The other 'optional' treatment is *fluoridation*. This is a 'mass-medication' process in which a few parts per million of a *fluoride* added to the water checks *tooth decay*. The decision to include fluoride in the water rests with each Local Authority.

Distilled and deionised water

Although the water from the mains supply may be fit and safe to drink, it is *not pure* in the chemical sense. It still contains impurities, mostly dissolved salts, which may affect its use for scientific and industrial purposes.

Distilled water is chemically pure water. Water is boiled in a *still*. The steam is collected and condensed back to liquid water. When impure water boils it leaves behind any dissolved impurities in the boiler of the still. The purest water will have been *double-distilled*, that is, distilled *twice*. Producing distilled water is expensive particularly if large quantities are required. Figure 5.7 shows a typical still.

For most purposes, *deionised* water is an acceptable alternative. Most of the chemical impurities in water are dissolved salts. If the water is passed through a *deioniser*, its special resin granules are able to attract and hold the ionised molecules of the impurities and virtually pure water emerges. A deioniser does not boil the water so it operates at a fraction of the cost of a still. Figure 5.8 shows a deioniser suitable for use in a laboratory.

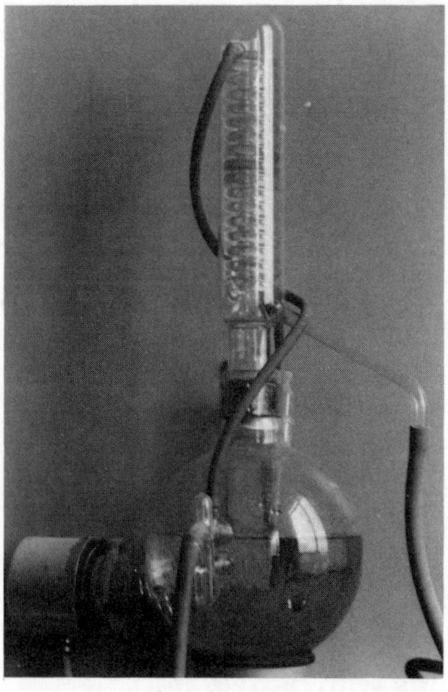

Figure 5.7 A still for preparing distilled water

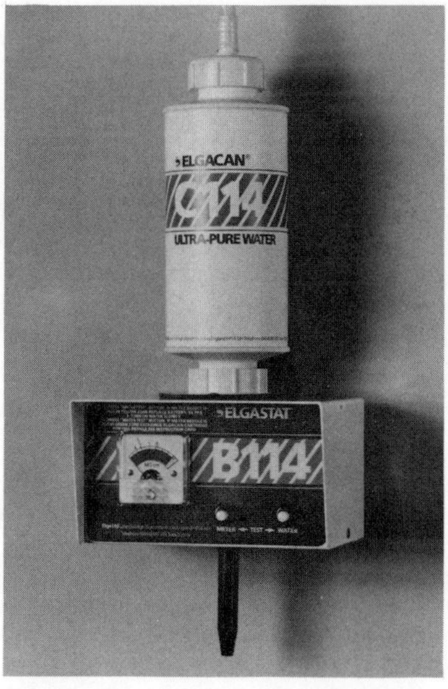

Figure 5.8 A deioniser (courtesy of Elga Ltd)

Microbiologically pure water

In the manufacture of cosmetics and toiletries the golden rule and indeed the first requirement of the *EEC Cosmetics Directive* is that cosmetics and toiletries shall not harm the user.

A major consideration is that no infection shall be passed via a cosmetic or toiletry product to its user. Although *preservatives* are included in products to prevent the build up of bacteria and moulds during storage and use, it is not desirable to use them at the high levels required to sterilise a highly contaminated product. The raw materials, production equipment and packaging must therefore be as free from infection as possible and this includes the *water*. A product is required by the *Directive* to contain less than ten viable bacteria in each cm^3.

When water has been chlorinated at the water works it contains very few bacteria, but then it is stored in a closed reservoir to allow much of the chlorine to escape so it is drinkable! It can however become reinfected and, if the water is stored for any length of time, the bacterial population can build up. Bacteria can even build up in stocks of stored distilled water. Only *freshly* distilled water should be used in products.

Deionised water is *not* sterilised by the process, but it can be made bacteriologically acceptable by passing it through a microbiological filter connected to the output of the deioniser. Again water should be treated for *immediate use*. Figure 5.9 shows a suitable microbiological filter for a laboratory water supply.

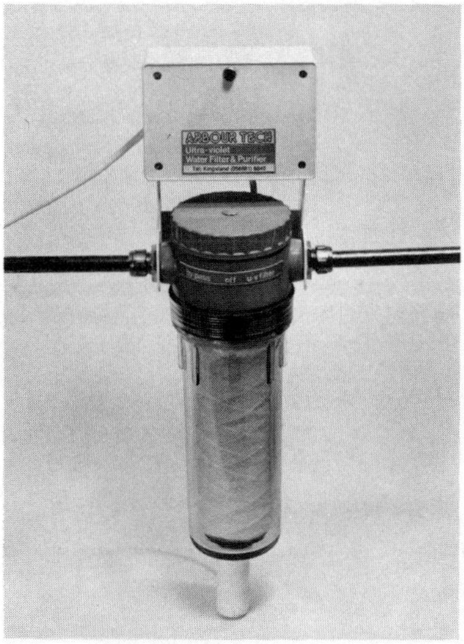

Figure 5.9 A microbiological filter employing the bactericidal effect of ultraviolet light (courtesy of Arbour-Tech Ltd)

Hard and soft water

In some areas, particularly where water is drawn from wells and bore-holes, it is difficult to obtain a lather with soap. This is because the water is *hard*.

Hard water lathers with difficulty with soap and leaves a sticky *scum*
Soft water lathers easily with soap and leaves *no scum*.

Problems with hard water

The difficulty in producing a lather with soap wastes soap. Until enough soap is used to form a lather it has no 'cleansing power'.

The sticky scum left after using soap in hard water is difficult to remove from baths and basins. It is even more difficult to rinse from the skin and hair and from clothing.

An average bath of hard water contains around 25 g of lime and will need 125 g of soap before the water will lather. This is more than a whole bar of soap! Not only that, it will produce 125 g of soap scum!

Figure 5.10 A lime-encrusted immersion heater

When hard water is heated to over 70°C much of the hardness settles out to coat the inside of boilers, kettles and hot water pipes. The most common cause of failure of electric kettle elements and immersion heaters is overheating due to being encrusted with 'lime scale' or 'fur'. The instant water heaters of shower units are particularly susceptible. Look at the heavily encrusted immersion heater in figure 5.10 and the section of scale-blocked water pipe in figure 5.11.

Hard water does however have some advantages – as *drinking water*. It contains *calcium* which it contributes to the diet – and it *tastes better*!

Figure 5.11 Water pipe almost blocked by lime scale

How water becomes hard

Water falling as *rain* dissolves carbon dioxide and sulphur dioxide from the air and as a result becomes slightly *acidic*. If this rainwater soaks through *limestone rocks* or through soils containing lime, it will dissolve limestone minerals.

Limestone is *calcium carbonate* and *magnesium carbonate*. Both are insoluble in water but can be reacted upon by the carbon dioxide and sulphur dioxide in rainwater to form the soluble salts which dissolve in the water to make it *hard*.

Calcium carbonate	+	Carbon dioxide	+	Water	→	Calcium bicarbonate
Magnesium carbonate	+	Carbon dioxide	+	Water	→	Magnesium bicarbonate
Calcium carbonate	+	Sulphur dioxide	+	Water	→	Calcium sulphate
Magnesium carbonate	+	Sulphur dioxide	+	Water	→	Magnesium sulphate
↑ Limestone						↑ Water hardness

The calcium and magnesium bicarbonates and sulphates dissolve in water to make it *hard*. It is these substances which react with *soap* to form *scum*:

Calcium bicarbonate (Water hardness)	+	Sodium stearate (soap)	=	Sodium bicarbonate	+	Calcium stearate (soap scum)

All the hardness substances and all soaps react in a similar fashion.

Only the *bicarbonates* are affected by heating the water. At around 70°C the bicarbonates revert to insoluble carbonates which coat the walls of kettles, pipes and boilers as *'fur'* or *'scale'*.

Temporary and permanent hardness

That part of the hardness removed by heating the water over 70°C is *temporary hardness*. It is caused by the calcium and magnesium *bicarbonates* in the water. If water is partially softened at a water works, it is the temporary hardness that is removed by the *milk of lime*.

The hardness caused by the calcium and magnesium *sulphates* is *not* removed by heating. It is termed *permanent hardness*.

Estimating the hardness of water

A very simple indication of how hard water is can be found by using *soapflakes*. Whole flakes selected from a packet of 'Lux' flakes are used in this test.

Half fill a test-tube with the water to be tested. Add *one* flake and shake the tube vigorously until the flake has dissolved. Add another and shake again. Continue until a lather forms which will last at least one minute.

If the water is *soft* or *distilled*, one flake will be sufficient. In hard water, a number of flakes will be required: the harder the water, the more flakes will be needed. Note how soft water remains clear while hard water becomes clouded with scum.

If a sample of hard water is boiled for two minutes, then cooled before testing, the number of flakes required will be less. The difference represents the temporary hardness.

Should soapflakes not be available, a *soap solution* may be used. Measure 10 cm^3 of a water sample into a small conical flask. Add the soap solution to it 1 cm^3 at a time from a *burette* and shake well. Note how many cm^3 of soap solution are needed to produce a persistent lather. The more soap required, the harder is the water.

Water softening

So that the action of soap is not impaired by hard water, it is desirable to remove *all* the hardness, both temporary and permanent. Both types interfere with the action of soap. There are two methods of softening water:

1 by the addition of an alkaline sodium salt to the water;
2 by passing the water through a water softening machine.

Water softening additives

There are several crystalline or powder water softening additives. Here are some examples.

Sodium carbonate
This is washing soda or soda crystals. Coloured and perfumed it becomes bath crystals. If the crystals become damp in storage, they may set into a hard mass.

Sodium sesquicarbonate
This hybrid compound of sodium carbonate and bicarbonate is a free-flowing powder. It is used as a laundry water softener and in bath salts and bath cubes.

Sodium hexametaphosphate
This is marketed as 'Calgon'. It is one of a number of phosphates used in washing powders and bath salts.

These substances all work by exchanging their sodium for the calcium and magnesium of the hardness which then settles out as a *non-sticky* sediment. The powdery sediment in the bottom of the bath after using a bath cube is not undissolved bath cube, it is the hardness from the water.

Calcium bicarbonate (Hardness)	+	Sodium carbonate (Softener)	→	Sodium bicarbonate (Remains in water)	+	Calcium carbonate (Sediment)

Water softening machine

This very simple device is a cylinder filled with granules of an *ion-exchange resin*. The resin possesses *sodium ions* (Na^+). As hard water passes through the resin it gives up its calcium and magnesium in exchange for the sodium ions. This is an *ion-exchange* process. The hardness is retained in the softener so there is no sediment in the water. Figure 5.12 shows an example of a water softening machine.

After a period of use all the sodium ions in the resin will have been exchanged for calcium and magnesium. It will then need *recharging* by putting *salt*, sodium chloride, on top of the resin in the cylinder and flushing it through with water. This flushes out the calcium and magnesium, replacing them with sodium once more.

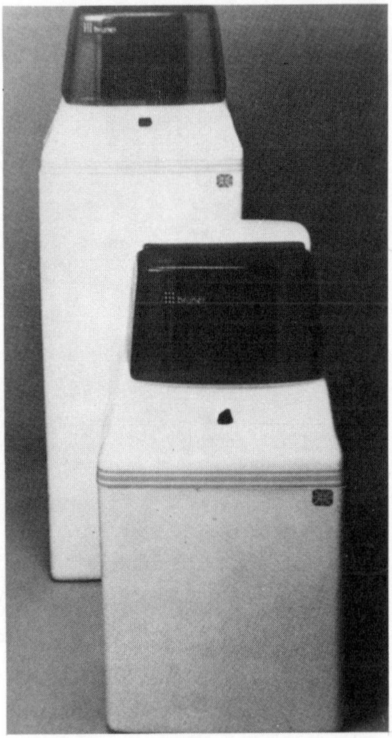

Figure 5.12 Water-softening machines (courtesy of Plaseuropa Ltd)

Things to do

1 Look around your neighbourhood for water treatment works, pumping stations and reservoirs. Arrange to visit your local water treatment works. Find out the daily consumption of water in your area.

2 Find out if your local water supply is hard or soft.

3 Collect information on water softening and purification equipment available for use in the home or salon.

4 Make your own bath crystals and bath salts. The formulations are in chapter 11.

Self-assessment questions

1 Why is seawater unsuitable for water supplies?

2 What two treatments *must* be done to all water for supplies?

3 Why is a fluoride sometimes added to water supplies?

4 How does water become hard?

5 Distinguish between temporary and permanent water hardness.

6 What is distilled water?

7 Why should only *freshly* distilled or *freshly* drawn deionised water be used to make cosmetic products?

8 How does the hardness of water affect the action of soap?

9 What is the main active ingredient of (a) bath crystals (b) bath salts?

10 A water softening machine works by ion-exchange. Explain briefly what this means.

6 Cosmetics & toiletries as mixtures

Mixtures of liquids and solids; powder mixtures in cosmetics; solutions and solubility; suspensions and dispersions; emulsions; making creams and lotions in the laboratory; use of preservatives in cosmetics; industrial manufacture of creams and lotions

Mixtures

Cosmetics and toiletries are *mixtures*. Although a product may appear to be a single substance, it will be formulated from a number of different raw materials which in the main will *not* be chemically combined with each other. Each raw material will, though, be in the form of tiny particles or droplets, even individual molecules. These should be so *thoroughly intermixed* that the product looks and behaves as a single entity and the presence of the individual components is not immediately obvious. No-one wants make-up which streaks on the skin or talcum powder with lumps or skin creams that curdle and separate. Much of the expertise and skill in the manufacture of cosmetics and toiletries is in the production of mixtures.

Solid mixtures

These are the *powder products* such as talcum powders and powder make-up. They will be made almost entirely from raw materials which are themselves powders. Minute amounts of liquids such as perfumes can be incorporated into powder products without loss of their free-flowing character.

Liquid mixtures

These are the *creams* and *lotions*. Although they will contain a high proportion of liquid raw materials such as water, alcohol or oils, they will most likely also include substantial amounts of solid raw materials too, such as fats and waxes, powders or gums and resins. Liquid mixtures include:

Solutions	– perfumes and shampoos are solutions
Suspensions and **dispersions**	– liquid make-up is a suspension
Emulsions	– creams and milky lotions are emulsions

Mixtures of powders

At first sight, making a powder product seems easy: weigh out the materials, put them together, a quick shake-up and there is your mixture! In practice the quick shake-up is going to produce a very poor mixture: the particles of the ingredients will not be well dispersed among each other. This will be particularly obvious in a powder colour cosmetic. It may appear to be well mixed, but just try smoothing a little on the skin and watch the streaks appear.

Figure 6.1 An industrial mixer-blender for powder products (courtesy of Apex Construction Limited)

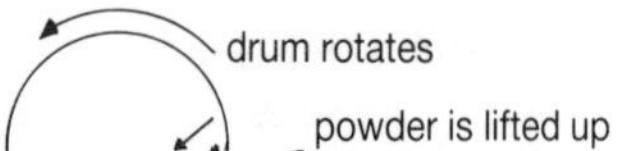

Figure 6.2 The action of a tumbler mixer

Then try to wash it off! The streaks of pigment will be difficult to remove.

In the cosmetic industry, talcum powders and powder cosmetic bases are usually mixed in some kind of tumbler-mixer. This may be a rotating cylindrical drum. As it rotates slowly, the powder is lifted up the side then flows back to the bottom. Each batch of powder may be tumbled for many hours before it is satisfactorily mixed (see figures 6.1 and 6.2).

Hard steel or ceramic balls can be added to the product in the drum making a *ball-mill*. As the balls tumble with the powder, they will break up any lumps and assist the mixing.

Another type of tumbler-mixer rotates the drum end over end. A particularly effective version of this type of mixer has a Y-shaped drum. As the Y inverts the contents fall into the fork of the Y and are split into two portions. As it returns to upright the two portions are brought together again as they fall into the stalk of the Y (see figure 6.3).

Figure 6.3 A Y-cone tumbler mixer-blender (courtesy of Apex Construction Limited)

Figure 6.4 A tumbler mixer mixing powders in the laboratory

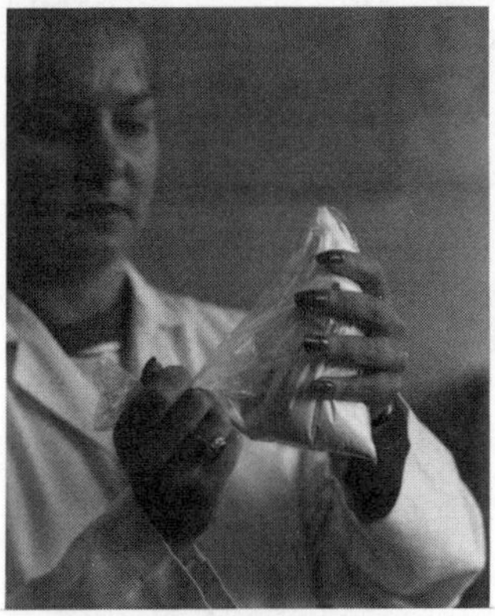

Figure 6.5 Mixing a powder sample in a polythene bag

In the laboratory a roller-driven tumbler mixer of the type used to polish gem-stones is very useful. Small batches of powders may be put into glass jars which can then be rotated in the mixer, preferably for at least an hour (see figure 6.4).

If no mixer is available then the mixture may be tumbled by hand in a strong polythene bag. The bag must be less than half full. The bag is held tightly closed with one hand and the contents are 'fluffed-up' with the other. Do not forget to allow dust to settle before opening the bag! (see figure 6.5.)

Making colour cosmetic powders

When making powder colour cosmetics such as face powder, eye-shadow or blusher, thorough mixing is particularly important when incorporating the colour pigment into the white base powder, unless one wants that streaky effect on the skin which is so difficult to wash off!

The pigments are much finer-grained powders than the base ingredients. When thoroughly mixed the particles of base will attract and hold a coating of pigment particles. The pigment colours the powder, not your skin! (see figure 6.6.)

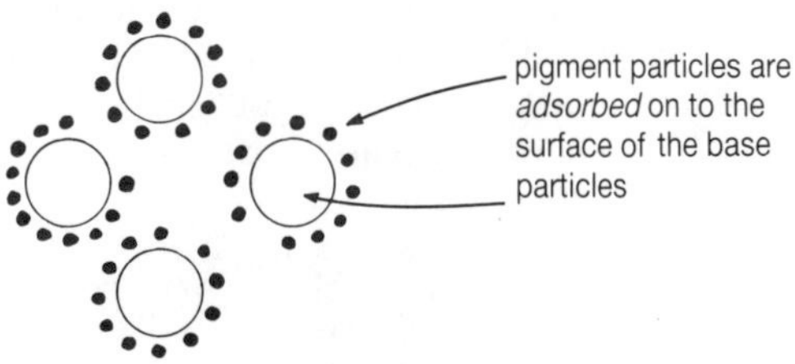

Figure 6.6 The incorporation of the pigment into a powder base

In industrial manufacture, the pigments and powder base will usually be tumbled together for perhaps 24 hours to disperse the pigments thoroughly. Then the mixing is completed by putting the mixture through a *roller mill* or a *hammer mill*.

The roller mill consists of a pair of rollers which press together like a wringer but rotate at different speeds. As the powder is fed through, the smearing action of the rollers breaks up any small lumps and thoroughly mixes the particles (see figure 6.7).

Figure 6.7 A roller mill for thoroughly dispersing the components of cosmetic products (courtesy of Marchant Bros Limited)

The hammer mill has rotating metal flails or hammers which literally smash the mixture through fine holes in a curved metal screen (see figure 6.8).

In the laboratory, small experimental samples of powder make-up can be made either with a pestle and mortar or by using a test tube and glass rod. If a pestle and mortar are used they should be of glass rather than earthenware which tends to be stained by the pigments.

The test tube and glass rod can be used as a miniature roller mill. A thick-walled test tube is one-third filled with the powder sample. The tube is held almost horizontally in one hand so the powder spreads along the tube. The rod

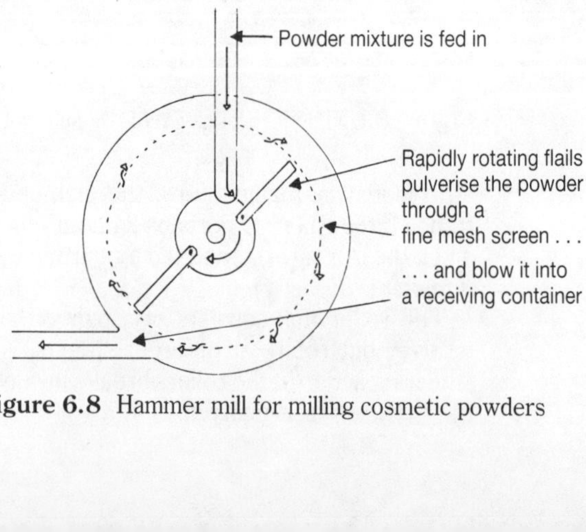

Figure 6.8 Hammer mill for milling cosmetic powders

Figure 6.9 'Test tube and rod' method for mixing a face powder

is held in the other hand, inserted in the tube, and rotated and pressed against the side of the tube, producing a smearing and mixing action like the roller mill. After a few minutes the sample will cease to look streaky; it will be thoroughly mixed (see figure 6.9).

Solutions

If salt is added to water and stirred, the salt disappears. It *dissolves* to make a *solution*. A solution consists of two parts, the *solvent* and the *solute*.

The *solvent* is a liquid in which a substance dissolves. Water is the commonest solvent. Alcohol, acetone and amyl acetate are also solvents.

The *solute* is the substance which dissolves in the solvent.

Solubility

This is the ability of a solute to dissolve in a solvent. If a substance dissolves easily it is *soluble*. Salt is soluble in water. Some substances may dissolve only in small quantities in a solvent. Such substances are *sparingly soluble*. Other substances may not dissolve at all. They are *insoluble*.

A substance insoluble in one solvent may dissolve in another. Nail varnish plastic is insoluble in water – it will not wash off the nails – but it dissolves easily in acetone, so acetone may be used as nail varnish remover.

Solubility of solids

Solubility is affected by the *temperature* of the solvent. *Solid* solutes dissolve more easily and to a greater extent in *warm* solvent than in cold.

The solubility of solids *increases* with temperature.

When, at a particular temperature, a solvent has dissolved the *maximum* amount of solute it can hold and will dissolve no more, the solution is *saturated*. If a warm saturated solution is cooled, some solute will be expelled. It will settle out as a solid *precipitate*. Also, if some of the solvent evaporates from a strong or saturated solution, precipitate will settle out. This is what is happening in the experiment in chapter 2, when the salt crystals appear.

Solubility of gases

Solutions of *gases* behave very differently. If a liquid containing a dissolved gas is warmed, gas is *driven off*. Water freshly drawn from the tap contains dissolved air. If it is warmed, small bubbles of air rise from it.

Special care is necessary in the storage and use of solutions of gases. They must be kept well stoppered to prevent loss of gas. They must be kept *cool* otherwise pressure will build up, possibly sufficient to burst the bottle. When the bottle is opened there will be a release of pressure so it must be opened carefully.

Many bottled drinks, beers and 'pop' are 'carbonated'. They contain carbon dioxide dissolved under pressure. Opening the bottle releases the pressure and the gas escapes as 'fizz'.

Although not truly a solution of a gas, *hydrogen peroxide solution* behaves rather like one. Keep it *cool* and *tightly stoppered*. Additionally keep it *dark*. Light decomposes hydrogen peroxide, releases its oxygen and builds up pressure, perhaps sufficient to burst the bottle.

Miscibility of liquids

In almost all cases, dissolving one liquid in another is a case of either it will or it will not! They either mix with each other in *all proportions* or they do not mix at all. If they do mix they are said to be *miscible*. The term 'soluble' is not used because it is often difficult to say which liquid is dissolving in which! If they do not mix, they are *immiscible*.

Alcohol and water are miscible. Perfume colognes and after-shaves are mainly alcohol and water.

Oil and water are immiscible. Try to mix them together and the oil will separate and float as a layer on top.

Oils will mix with each other and will also mix with alcohol. Perfumes are mixtures of oily materials dissolved in alcohol.

Crystalloids and colloids

In a true solution the solute dissolves in the solvent to produce a mixture which is clear and transparent, though it may be coloured. In such a solution the molecules of the solute will have parted company with each other and become thoroughly dispersed among the molecules of the solvent. Such a solution is a *crystalloid*.

Often the molecules of solute will split up further into *positive* and *negative* charged *ions*. Such a solution will conduct electricity and is called an *electrolyte* (see chapter 3). If the molecules do not split into ions, the solution will not conduct electricity and is a *non-electrolyte*.

If the solute molecules remain in large groups, or if the molecules are very large, the solution will have different properties. It is called a *colloid*.

In a colloid, the solute particles may be large enough to 'catch' or scatter the light so, instead of being clearly transparent, the solution may be cloudy or pearlescent. Not all colloids are cloudy.

If a colloid is concentrated, that is, if it contains a lot of solute, it may be quite viscous. The particles or molecules of solute tend to bond lightly to each other and so the solution cannot flow freely. If the colloid is very concentrated it may be unable to flow at all. It will be a *gel*.

Many cosmetic products are either viscous liquids or gels. For instance shampoos, toothpastes and skin lotions all contain colloidal materials which impart the viscosity. In shampoos it is the large detergent molecules which give the viscosity. Toothpastes and skin lotions may have special thickening materials such as methyl celluloses added to them.

Suspensions and dispersions

If an insoluble powder substance is shaken with a liquid it will disperse to form a *suspension*. The powder particles give the mixture a milky appearance. If left to stand the particles will sooner or later settle to the bottom.

Calamine lotion is a suspension of pink coloured – to match your sunburn! – zinc carbonate in water. Before each use, you must shake the bottle to redistribute the zinc carbonate. Soon after use it will settle out again. Liquid mascara and liquid make-up are also suspensions.

The settling out of a suspension can be slowed or even prevented by adding a *thickening agent* to make the product more viscous. For instance, a toothpaste might be a suspension of a polishing powder such as calcium carbonate suspended in a detergent solution thickened with carboxy methyl cellulose.

If a relatively large proportion of powder is mixed with a small amount of liquid, a paste or *dispersion* will result. Such a large proportion of powder particles will be unable to settle, so the mixture will be stable.

Earth-based face packs are dispersions, consisting of clay materials such as kaolin or fuller's earth or chalk materials such as calcium or magnesium carbonates mixed in water or an oil.

The particles of kaolin and bentonite – a volcanic ash – are so fine that they are *colloidal*. Quite small amounts of them mixed in water can produce gels which are very acceptable as face packs.

Emulsions

Cosmetic products which are *creams* or *milky lotions* will most likely be *emulsions*. An emulsion is a mixture of oils, fats and waxes and *water* which has been made *stable*.

Normally, oily substances and water are *immiscible*. If a little oil is added to water and shaken vigorously, the oil breaks up into small droplets which become dispersed in the water. However, on being allowed to stand for a short time, the oil droplets will be seen to join with each other and rise to form a separate layer on the surface of the water.

If some detergent is added and the mixture is shaken again, it will disperse once more and this time will not separate on standing. The detergent is acting as an *emulsifying agent* or *emulsifier*. It serves to *stabilise* the emulsion.

A wide variety of emulsifiers is available. What an emulsifier is and how it works is described in chapter 7.

Oil-in-water and water-in-oil emulsions

There are two possible ways in which oils and water can mix to form an emulsion. If the oil is dispersed as droplets in the water it is an '*oil-in-water*' emulsion – often indicated as O/W (figure 6.10a).

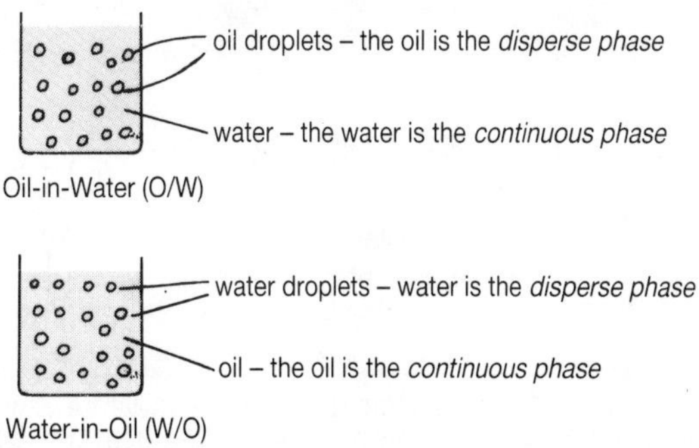

Figure 6.10 Oil-in-water and water-in-oil emulsions

If the water is dispersed as droplets in the oil then it is a *'water-in-oil'* emulsion – indicated as W/O (figure 6.10b).

Which type of emulsion is formed depends only in part on the relative proportions of oils and water in the formulation. If oils form the lesser proportion, the tendency will be to form an 'oil-in-water' emulsion. If the oils form the greater proportion a 'water-in-oil' emulsion is more likely.

The other deciding factor as to which type forms is the choice of emulsifier. Some emulsifiers will tend to produce 'oil-in-water' emulsions and others 'water-in-oil'.

In cosmetics, the lighter creams and milky lotions will be 'oil-in-water' emulsions while heavier creams are often 'water-in-oil'.

Making cosmetic emulsions in the laboratory

When making a sample of an emulsified product in the laboratory, you must first study the formulation to separate the oils, fats and waxes of the *oil phase* from the water and water-soluble materials which constitute the *water phase*. In a published formulation it is usual to print the oil phase materials first.

You also need to establish whether the product is likely to be an 'oil-in-water' or 'water-in-oil' emulsion, as this will decide the method of mixing. This is done by comparing the proportions of oil phase and water phase materials and seeing what is being used as the emulsifier.

Look at these two formulations for *general purpose skin creams* as they might appear in a textbook or in a technical brochure. Often little or no instructions are provided as to how to make up the formulation.

General purpose skin cream 1

Mineral oil	– 38	These will be the *oil phase*. It forms 56% of the formulation
White beeswax	– 3	
Spermaceti wax	– 3	
Glycerol monostearate (self-emulsifying grade)	– 12	
Glycerol	– 4	These will be the *water phase*. It forms 44% of the formulation.
Water	– 40	

The glycerol monostearate is the emulsifier. It is a 'water-in-oil' type so this cream will be a 'water-in-oil' emulsion.

General purpose skin cream 2

Mineral oil	– 30	The oil phase – 45%
Lanolin, anhydrous	– 3	
Stearic acid	– 12	
Triethanolamine	– 1.5	The water phase – 55%
Carboxymethyl cellulose	– 5	
Water	– 48.5	

The stearic acid and triethanolamine will combine chemically to form a soap which is an 'oil-in-water' emulsifier.

This formulation will produce an 'oil-in-water' emulsion.

A general method for making samples of cosmetic creams

This method may be used to make up any of the formulations for creams described in this book. Any variations from this general method will be indicated by the formulation. The following apparatus will be required:

Porcelain, glass or stainless steel basin as a *mixing vessel*. A 150 mm diameter evaporating basin, preferably round bottomed, will easily accommodate a 100 g sample formulation.

Large, thick walled test tube or boiling tube to use as a *stirrer*. As will be explained later, this gives more effective stirring than a slim stirring rod.

Waterbath over which to heat the basin. This should be either an electrically heated type or one which can be heated on an electric hotplate. Heating the basin on a water bath standing on a tripod over a bunsen burner presents a very unstable and potentially dangerous situation.

Balance to weigh out materials (see chapter 1).

Beaker of 100–150 ml capacity in which to mix the water phase materials.

Measuring cylinder – to measure the water.

Thermometer, −10 to 110°C stirring type, to monitor temperatures during the process.

Procedure

Set up the water bath so it may come to the boil to be ready when needed.

Weigh out the oils and waxes directly into the mixing basin. First weigh the basin or set the *tare* facility on the balance to account for it. Then weigh the oil phase materials one at a time into the basin on top of each other. Weigh the hard waxes first, then any flake or powder materials, then greasy materials and finally the oily liquids. Take care not to add too much of any ingredient, you cannot take it out again! (See figure 6.11.)

Figure 6.11 Weighing out the oil-phase materials

Figure 6.12 Heating the oil phase on a water-bath

Place the mixing basin on the water bath and leave for the oil phase to melt. Heating the oil phase over boiling water on a water bath means that it cannot overheat. The maximum temperature in the basin is unlikely to reach more than 75–80°C. Usually all will be molten at 65–70°C (see figure 6.12). Oil phase materials have very high boiling points. If they are heated by direct heat they can easily go way above 100°C. Indeed, like an unattended 'chip' pan

Figure 6.13 Heating the water phase

they can quickly reach 'smoke point' and possibly burst into flames. In any case if the water phase is added to oils at over 100°C, it will 'flash boil' causing rapid foaming and boiling over.

Measure out the water and weigh out the water-soluble materials. Mix them in the beaker. It is best to weigh viscous liquids like glycerol directly into the beaker. Heat the water phase to the same temperature as the oil phase, 65–70°C. Direct heat will be all right for this (see figure 6.13).

Slowly add the water phase to the oil phase while the basin is still on the heat. Stir continuously during the addition (see figure 6.14).

Remove the basin from the heat and stir continuously until cool.

Water-in-oil emulsions should be stirred *slowly* but steadily to avoid including air bubbles which will adversely affect the stability of the emulsion.

Oil-in-water emulsions should be stirred more vigorously. An electric stirrer is useful here.

When stirring with the large test tube let it run along the bottom of the basin. This will trap and smear droplets of disperse phase, breaking them up to produce a smoother emulsion. This is *homogenisation*.

When the emulsion has cooled to 40°C (hand-hot) the perfume may be added. Six to eight drops of a suitable perfume concentrate per 100 g of product is all that is required (see figure 6.15). When making cosmetics, the atmosphere in the laboratory soon becomes very laden with perfume. This dulls the sense of smell and makes it very easy to over-perfume products.

When cool, the cream may be packed in a clean pot. A label must be affixed showing the name of the product, a reference to its formulation, the date and the name of the maker.

Figure 6.14 Adding the water phase to the oil phase

Figure 6.15 Adding the perfume

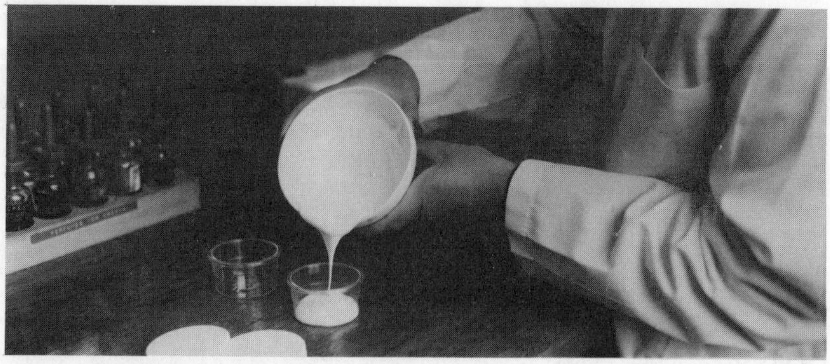

Figure 6.16 Potting the finished cream

The use of preservatives

Even though every care may be taken during manufacture to ensure products are free from microbial contamination which will affect their keeping quality, when a product is in use it can easily become contaminated. For this reason it is desirable to include a preservative.

A suitable preservative for these laboratory samples might be *methyl-4-hydroxybenzoate* (methyl paraben); 0.1–0.2% is included in the water phase before mixing. If desired a similar amount of propyl-4-hydroxybenzoate (propyl paraben) may be added to the oil phase.

If no preservative is used, the product must be kept in a refrigerator and used within one month of making.

pH check on soap-emulsified creams

When creams are emulsified by a *soap*, it is usual to make the soap *in situ* from a fatty acid in the oil phase and an alkali in the water phase. This is the case in the second formulation on page 52. Always check the pH of the finished cream to see if all the alkali has been used. Check with pH paper or meter. A high pH of over pH 9 will indicate that not all the alkali has reacted.

Industrial manufacture of creams and lotions

Most creams are manufactured by a scaled-up version of the laboratory process. The mixing vessel is usually a large round bottomed vessel surrounded by a water jacket by which it can be heated. The stirring mechanism is mounted on the lid. A complex stirring mechanism, often including blades to scrape the sides of the vessel, ensures mixing is thorough. The lid can be sealed and air pumped from the vessel to prevent air being stirred into the product. A typical mixer is shown in figures 6.17 and 6.18.

Figure 6.17 An industrial mixing vessel for creams and similar products (courtesy of Staffs Aerosols and Packaging Ltd)

Figure 6.18 The industrial mixer showing the mixing blades (courtesy of Staffs Aerosols and Packaging Ltd)

The oil phase materials are weighed into the mixer and heated to mixing temperature. The stirring mechanism is turned on to mix the oil phase. The water phase is then run in and mixed in thoroughly. The temperature is then allowed to fall while mixing continues. The finished product may be drawn off through a valve at the bottom of the vessel or the vessel may be tipped to empty the contents.

Things to do

In this chapter are described the methods for making cosmetic powders and creams in the laboratory. Use these methods to make samples of the formulations described in later chapters.

Self-assessment questions

1 Why is it important that cosmetics are thoroughly mixed during their manufacture?

2 What is (a) a solvent (b) a solute?

3 Why is it important that solutions of gases such as ammonia are kept cool during storage?

4 What is the difference between a suspension and a dispersion?

5 What is meant by the term 'immiscible'?

6 What is a colloid?

7 What is the purpose of an emulsifier or emulsifying agent?

8 What method should be used to heat up waxes so there is no danger of seriously overheating?

9 What is meant by homogenisation?

10 Describe briefly how a sample of a cosmetic cream might be made in the laboratory.

7 Surface Activity, Emulsions & Detergency

Cosmetic creams and lotions as emulsions; detergent cleansers; surface tension; reducing surface tension with surfactants; solubilisation; forming an emulsion; oil-in-water and water-in-oil emulsions; choosing a surfactant; cleansing action of detergents; lathers and foams

Importance of surface activity

Forming an *emulsion* is the fundamental process in both the production of *cosmetic creams* and *lotions* and in the action of *detergents* as cleansers. Surface activity is also involved in the passage of substances into the skin in *percutaneous absorption*.

Cosmetic emulsions

Cosmetic creams and lotions are mixtures of 'oil phase' and 'water phase' materials which will not remain mixed without the action of an *emulsifying agent* (see chapter 6).

When oil and water are mixed together, one liquid forms droplets within the other. If no emulsifying agent is used the mixture soon separates into two layers – oil on top and water beneath.

While the liquids are mixed, the oil and water are forced to meet each other surface to surface, even though they virtually repel each other. This is shown in figure 7.1.

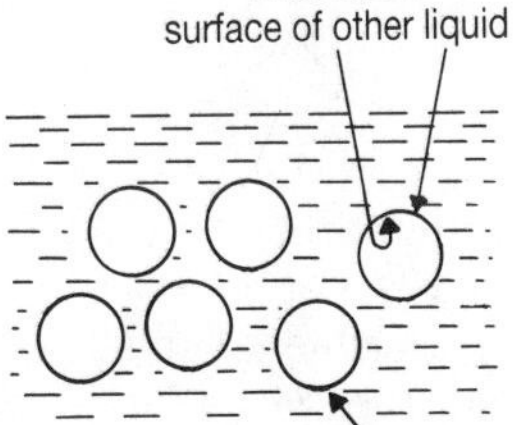

Figure 7.1 The droplets in an oil and water mixture

Soon, as the droplets come into contact with each other, they will join with each other and eventually the mixture separates into its two layers.

The presence of the *emulsifying agent* stabilises the emulsion so that it does not separate. It makes the oil and water not repel each other any more and prevents the droplets joining with each other. To do this it must act at the surface of the droplets where the oil and water meet. The emulsifying agent is a *surface active agent* or *surfactant*.

Detergents as cleansers

Without a detergent, water is not effective as a cleanser for greasy surfaces. If water is put on the greasy surface, it is *repelled* by the surface and either runs off or forms into spherical droplets. The surface does not even become properly *wet*.

With a detergent, the water will spread over the greasy surface and *wet* it. The detergent is acting as a *wetting agent*. To do this it is again working on the *surface* of the water. The detergent, too, is a *surface active agent* or *surfactant*.

The water with detergent will then go on to form an *emulsion* with the grease and so remove it from the surface.

Surface tension

The tendency for liquids to form into droplets and for the droplets to join with each other is the outcome of a phenomenon called *surface tension*.

Although it is called *surface tension*, it is the result of those attractive or

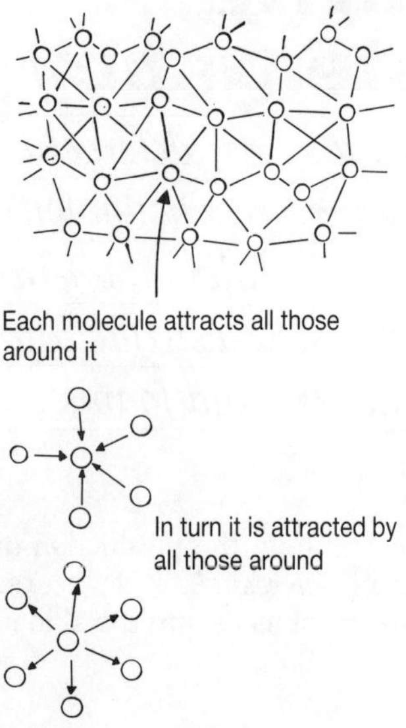

Figure 7.2 The attractive forces between the molecules of a liquid

cohesive forces described in chapter 2 which hold the molecules of a liquid together. These forces are present right through the liquid. In figure 7.2 the spots represent the molecules and the lines the forces between them.

A molecule deep within the liquid is pulled equally in all directions by those around it so there is *no nett pull* in any particular direction. It is free to move in any direction through the liquid. But if a molecule is on the surface of the liquid the attractions are *not* equal in all directions. It will be attracted by those each side and below, but there are no molecules above (see figure 7.3).

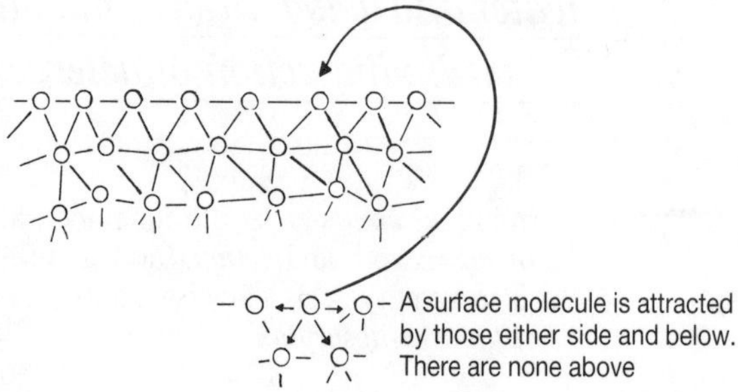

Figure 7.3 The attractive forces on a molecule at a liquid surface

The nett effect is that a surface molecule is held down on the surface so it cannot easily escape. In attracting those around it, the effect of the forces on the neighbouring surface molecules is to pull them together and try to make the surface of the liquid *as small as possible*. This is *surface tension*.

Surface tension explains why a liquid droplet always tries to be spherical. Surface tension tries to make the surface area of the droplet as small as possible and a sphere is the shape which has the smallest surface area for a given volume. For instance, a spherical droplet with a volume of 1 mm^3 has an area of 4.84 mm^2. A cube of the same volume has a surface area of 6 mm^2. For those proficient at maths, figure 7.4 shows how this can be calculated.

Surface tension also explains why if two droplets come into contact they will join to form one larger droplet. The area of the double-sized droplet is less than the area of the two single droplets. This can be worked out by the same method as above.

Two droplets of volume 1 mm^3 each have a surface area of 4.84 mm^2, a total of 9.68 mm^2.
When the two droplets join they produce a single droplet of volume 2 mm^3. Its surface area is a mere 7.68 mm^2.

To find the surface area of a spherical droplet of 1 mm^3 volume.
This must be done in two stages.

1. Use the 'volume of a sphere' formula:

$$V = \frac{4}{3}\pi r^3$$

Rearrange it to find the radius (r) of the droplet:

$$r = \sqrt[3]{\left(\frac{V}{\frac{4}{3}\pi}\right)}$$

Working this out for a 1 mm^3 sphere gives a radius of 0.62 mm.

2. Use the 'area of a sphere' formula:

$$a = 4\pi r^2$$

Working this out for a radius of 0.62 mm gives an area of 4.84 mm^2.

Figure 7.4 Finding the surface area of a spherical droplet

The need to reduce surface tension

Before water can cleanse a greasy surface, it must be able to spread over the surface and actually wet it.

Before an emulsion can be stable, the droplets of the disperse phase must lose their desire to join together when they come into contact with each other.

In both instances the *surface tension must be reduced.*

Reducing surface tension

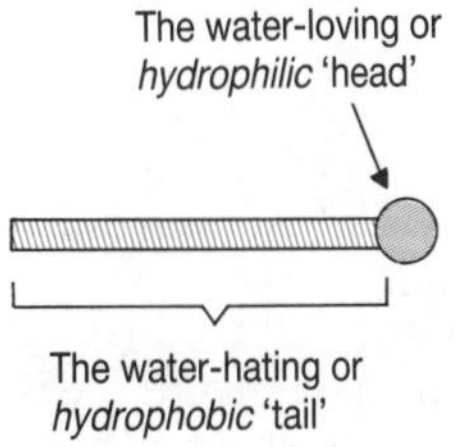

Figure 7.5 An amphiphilic molecule

Obviously if the surface tension of a liquid such as water is to be reduced, something must be added to it; but what? To have any effect on surface tension it must be something which will act on the *surface*.

If something is added which dissolves fully in the water, it goes right into the liquid and does not concentrate itself at the surface. Indeed if something like *salt* is added to water it actually *increases* the surface tension – not quite what is required! Have you noticed the beads of perspiration on someone's skin or the way seawater forms droplets on the skin after bathing in the sea?

An insoluble substance can of course have *no* effect on surface tension.

What is required is a substance whose molecules are partly attracted to water and partly repelled by it: that is partly hydrophilic and partly hydrophobic. Such a molecule is shown in figure 7.5 (see also chapter 4).

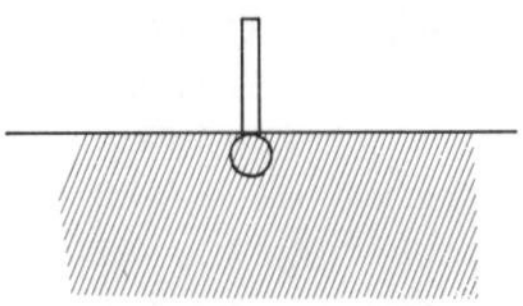

Figure 7.6 An amphiphilic molecule on a water surface

When added to water, the hydrophilic part of such molecules tries to dissolve. The hydrophobic part wants to stay out of the water, so the molecule stays at the surface (see figure 7.6).

All the molecules will try to find places at the surface and in order to make room, they will try to make the surface *larger* (see figure 7.7).

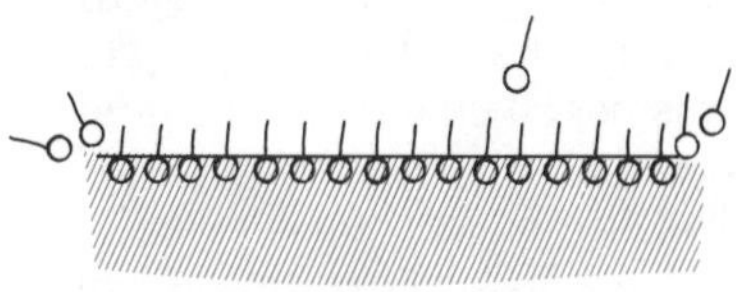

Figure 7.7 Amphiphilic molecules find places on a water surface

Surface tension tries to make the surface smaller. The substance tries to make it larger. The nett effect is that *surface tension is reduced.*

A substance which works at the *surface* of a liquid in this way is a *surface active agent* or *surfactant.*

The wetting action of a surfactant

If a surfactant is added to water, it more easily spreads over a greasy surface and *wets* it. Two factors bring this about. Firstly, the reduced surface tension reduces the tendency for water to form droplets: it spreads out instead.

Secondly, if the water surface is covered with surfactant, molecules with their *water hating–oil loving ends* sticking *out*, the surface is in effect no longer oil-hating water, but oil-loving surfactant which is *attracted* to the greasy surface.

Micelles

In even the smallest amount of surfactant added to the water it is quite likely that far more molecules will be added than can find places on the surface. The rest will fall through to be completely immersed in the water and get their hydrophobic 'tails' wet! Or will they? To keep their 'tails' dry, the submerged

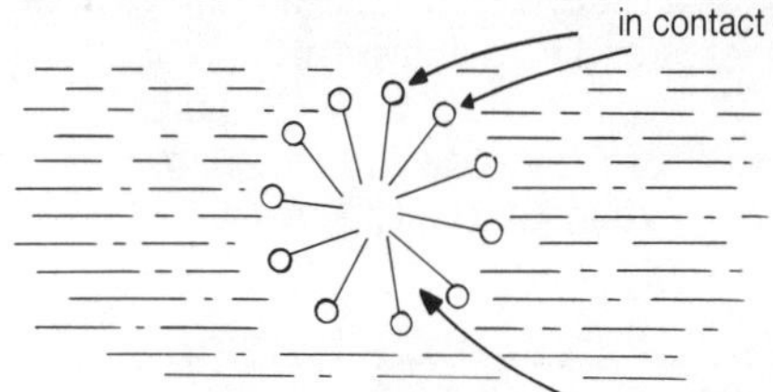

Figure 7.8 A micelle

surfactant molecules will cluster together in such a way that the hydrophobic parts can be 'out of water'. Such a cluster is a *micelle* (see figure 7.8).

In the form of micelles a surfactant can dissolve quite well in water, making a solution which is quite stable and transparent.

In dilute surfactant solutions, the micelles are usually spherical. However in very concentrated solutions the molecules might have to become arranged in a more regular almost crystal-like fashion, possibly forming alternate layers of surfactant and water. These arrangements give surfactant concentrates a high viscosity and might make it difficult to dilute them with more water.

Solubilisation

The centre of each micelle is a minute water-free space within the surfactant solution. Into the spaces can be introduced tiny amounts of oil to produce what is in effect a 'solution' of oil in water. The result is still a transparent liquid; it is not an emulsion. The process is called *solubilisation*.

This method is commonly used to incorporate small quantities of oils into water-based products; for instance, to include perfume oils into products such as shampoos, hair setting lotions and bath essences.

A synthetic *rose water* may be easily produced by solubilising a rose essence into water using a suitable surfactant.

A rose-water formulation

Rose perfume concentrate	– 1
Tween 20 (solubiliser)	– 6
Water	– 93

To make this formulation, the perfume concentrate is mixed thoroughly with the solubiliser. The water is added gradually with constant stirring.

Forming an emulsion

If a greater proportion of oil is mixed with a surfactant solution, the surfactant molecules will desert the micelles to surround the oil droplets to form an *emulsion* (see figure 7.9).

The surfactant therefore *stabilises* the emulsion. It is acting as an *emulsifying agent*.

Because of the size and number of oil droplets in the emulsion, unlike a solubilised oil 'solution', it is *not* transparent. Unless coloured otherwise, an emulsion is usually white or cream.

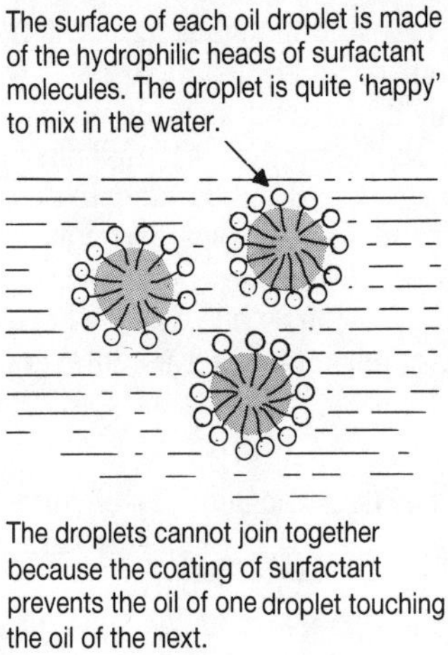

Figure 7.9 The formation of an oil-in-water emulsion

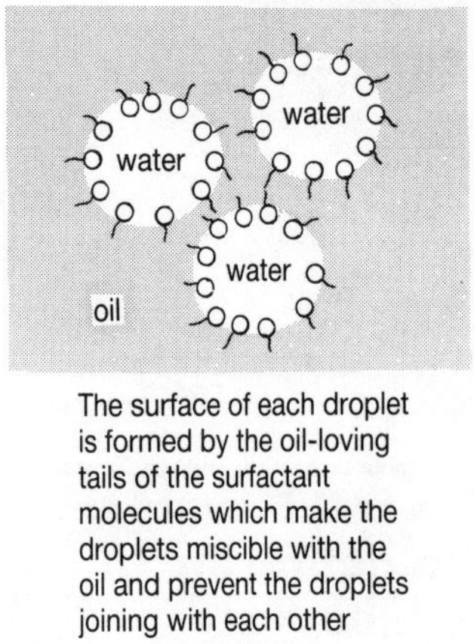

Figure 7.10 The formation of a water-in-oil emulsion

Oil-in-water and water-in-oil emulsions

Figure 7.9 shows an oil-in-water emulsion where the oil is in the form of droplets as the disperse phase and the water forms the continuous phase. In a water-in-oil emulsion the situation is reversed. The water is in the form of droplets in a continuous phase of oil (see figure 7.10).

As stated in chapter 6, whether an oil-in-water or water-in-oil emulsion forms depends greatly on the choice of emulsifying agent or surfactant and not just on the relative proportions of oil and water.

Surfactant molecules

If a surfactant is to work at all, the hydrophilic and hydrophobic parts of the molecules must be of comparable 'strength'. If the strength of either part overwhelms the other, the substance will have little or no surfactant property. For example, the molecule of ethanol is so strongly hydrophilic that it is completely water soluble, whereas the stearic acid molecule is too hydrophobic which makes it insoluble in water. Neither is of real use as a surfactant (see figure 7.11).

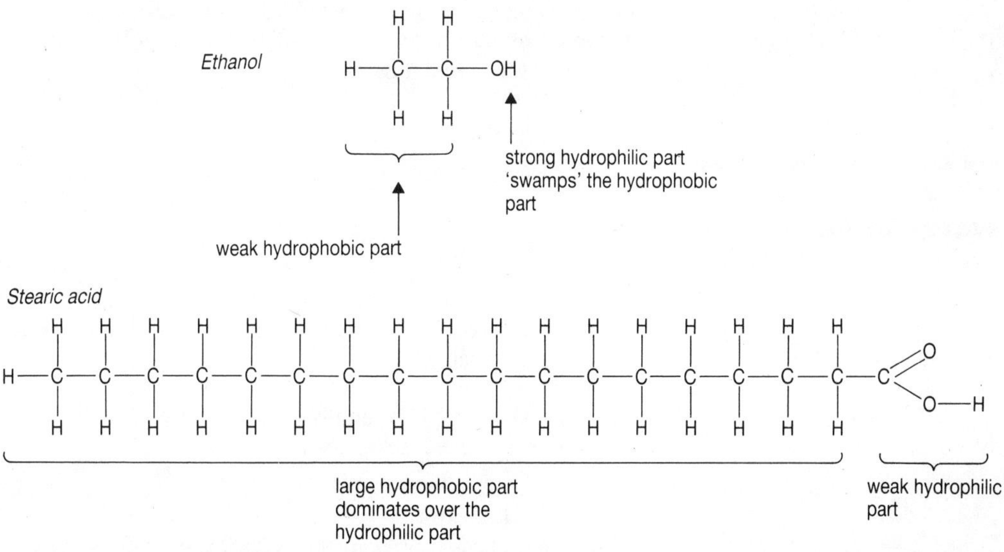

Figure 7.11 Comparison of the surfactant properties of ethanol and stearic acid

Choosing a surfactant

The choice of a suitable surfactant will have a great influence on the texture and behaviour of an emulsion. Indeed with an inappropriate surfactant, the emulsion might be quite unstable or may fail to form at all. Among the many surfactants which can act as emulsifiers, there is a wide range of relative strengths of the hydrophilic and hydrophobic/lipophilic parts. This makes each surfactant suitable for a particular purpose.

Those in which the hydrophobic/lipophilic part is dominant tend to form water-in-oil emulsions while those where the hydrophilic part dominates form oil-in-water emulsions or act as detergent cleansers or as solubilisers.

The HLB system for selecting an emulsifier

One of the leading manufacturers of surfactants, the Atlas Chemical Company, devised a system of HLB values for surfactants to help users choose the most appropriate for a particular purpose.

HLB means *hydrophile-lipophile balance*. That is, the balance of hydrophilic and hydrophobic parts of the surfactant molecule. The value is calculated from the chemical structure. The hydrophilic part adds to the value, the number of carbon atoms in the hydrophobic part subtracts from it.

Surfactants with low	HLB values	3 to 6 are water-in-oil emulsifiers
Surfactants with high	HLB values	8 to 18 are oil-in-water emulsifiers
Surfactants with	HLB values	13 to 15 are detergent cleansers
Surfactants with	HLB values	15 to 18 are solubilisers

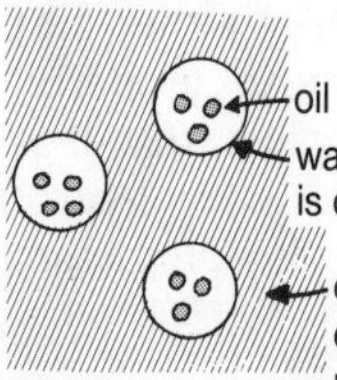

Figure 7.12 A complex emulsion

As an example of the system in action, let us imagine we are to make a cream from mineral oil and water. If we choose soap, sodium stearate, HLB 18, it will form an *oil-in-water* cream. If we use glycerol monostearate, HLB 3.8, as an emulsifier it will form a *water-in-oil* cream.

Frequently a formulation will use a blend of two or more emulsifiers of different HLB values, and frequently the resulting emulsion is more complex than just water-in-oil or oil-in-water. For instance, it is quite possible that a water-in-oil emulsion could have minute oil droplets emulsified *inside* its water droplets! (See figure 7.12.)

Oil-in-water or water-in-oil

Two tests will show whether an emulsion is an oil-in-water type or water-in-oil:

1 Dilution

An emulsion can be diluted only with more of its continuous phase.

Try adding *water* to the emulsion and mixing it in:
If it *will* mix without breaking the emulsion it is *oil-in-water*.
If it will *not* mix properly and possibly breaks or 'cracks' the emulsion it is *water-in-oil*.
Try adding oil to the emulsion and mixing it in:
If it mixes, the emulsion is *water-in-oil*.
If it does not mix properly it is *oil-in-water*.

2 Electrical conductivity

The water phase of an emulsion will allow electricity to pass, the oil phase will not.

Use an electrician's test meter. Switch it to 'resistance' or 'continuity'. Dip the two probes into the emulsion.

If the meter shows a reading of low resistance the water is the continuous phase: the emulsion is *oil-in-water*.

If it shows no reading, the oil is the continuous phase; the emulsion is *water-in-oil*.

Problems with emulsions

Even when stabilised with an emulsifying agent, an emulsion is still potentially unstable. A number of things can go wrong with it, both during manufacture and storage. Some can be attributed to poor design of the formulation, some to human error and sometimes an emulsion goes wrong for no apparent reason. You will find if you make up some of the formulations in this book that even quite small variations in the method from one batch to the next can produce quite different results.

Creaming

Milk is an emulsion. It is one which has a low oil content – around 3.5%. If a bottle of milk is left to stand, the droplets of the small proportion of oil rise to collect near the surface as *cream*. The process is called *creaming*.

The emulsion has not broken up, the oil phase is still in droplets which can easily be redispersed by gently shaking the bottle. While we will accept creaming in a bottle of milk, we are less keen to do so with a cosmetic such as a hand, face or body lotion. We think something is wrong with it.

Prevention of creaming

Two things can be done to prevent creaming:

1 Make the lotion more viscous by adding a thickener such as a gum or methyl cellulose to the water phase. The oil droplets cannot then rise so quickly.
2 Break up the droplets of the oil phase so they are *very* small. This is *homogenisation*. Most commercially made creams are *homogenised*. This can be done in two ways:
   a by pumping the product through very fine jets;
   b by squashing the droplets between the rollers of a roller mill.

The latter effect is simulated in the laboratory method of making creams by stirring with the large test-tube against the bottom of the mixing bowl.

Inversion

Although milk is an oil-in-water emulsion, cows for some reason, choose to emulsify it with the *calcium* salts of fatty acids. These have a low HLB value and are more appropriate for a water-in-oil emulsion.

If the cream separated from milk is stirred gently and continuously, the oil droplets will join to each other so that oil becomes the continuous phase and the water becomes the droplets. The oil-in-water cream has turned to water-in-oil – *butter*! This is *inversion*.

Inversion often occurs in the mixing of water-in-oil emulsions during the continuous stirring process as the emulsion cools. If you are not aware of it, there can be some anxious moments as at times it might appear that the emulsion is going to fail to form.

Cracking or break-up of an emulsion

If a completely unsuitable emulsifier is chosen for a particular purpose, the emulsion may separate out into oil and water layers. It will *crack* or *break up*.

Sometimes one of the other ingredients in a formulation may so badly affect the emulsifier that it cannot work. For instance an alkali-preferring soap emulsifier might be affected by including acids in the formulation.

The cleansing action of a detergent

When water with detergent added to it is used to cleanse a greasy surface, there are *three* stages to the cleansing process:

1 **Wetting**. The detergent reduces the surface tension of water so it is able to spread over and actually *wet* the greasy surface.

2 **Emulsification**. The detergent molecules embed their hydrophobic/lipophilic 'tails' in the grease and gradually – layer-by-layer – prise it off the surface. Figure 7.13 illustrates this process.

The emulsification of the grease is helped by:

a the water being *warm* to melt the grease and help it form into droplets, and

b a certain amount of *agitation* to move away the droplets of emulsified grease and bring fresh detergent to the surface to emulsify the next layer of grease.

3 **Rinsing**. When all the grease has been removed, any solid dirt which was held to the surface is loose. Rinsing with clean water washes away the emulsified grease and loosened dirt to leave the surface *clean*

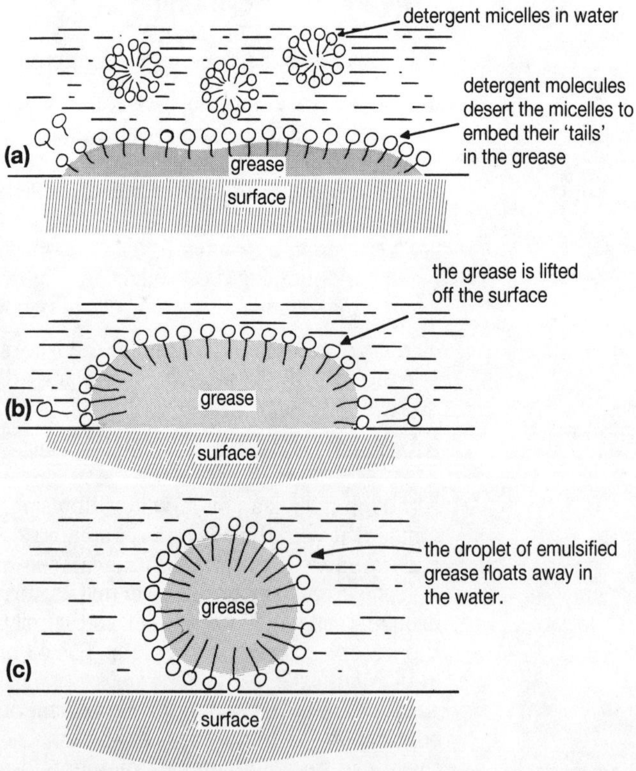

Figure 7.13 The cleansing action of a detergent

Lather and foam

You will probably have noticed that no mention has so far been made of *lather*. This is because it plays little or no part in the actual cleansing action of the detergent. Indeed in some applications lather can be a real nuisance:

1 In *floor washing*, rinsing with copious water is not practicable so the lather from a high-lathering detergent cannot be washed away. Special 'low-lather' products are available for floor washing.

2 In an *automatic washing machine*, the 'wash' stage of the programme uses a high concentration of detergent in a small amount of water. If a high-lathering detergent were used all the water would be incorporated in the foam, leaving none to do the actual washing. A 'low-lather' detergent specially designed for automatics must be used.

3 A *dishwasher* sprays high-pressure jets of water plus detergent at the crockery. Here a *non-foaming* formulation is essential.

Lather does however frequently serve a useful purpose:

1 As an *indicator* that detergent activity remains. When all the detergent has been used to emulsify grease, the lather disappears. This is because the detergent molecules will be drawn from the foam to emulsify grease.

2 A foam may *hold the cleanser on the surface*. For example, soap and water on the face or shampoo on the head.

3 A *psychological indicator of 'cleansing power'*
Consumers have been conditioned to believe that copious foam means lots of 'cleansing power'. Often the reverse is true. A shampoo is expected to produce a rich, creamy foam, yet it would be disastrous for the condition of the hair if it were a really powerful cleanser.

How a foam forms

When dissolved in water, a detergent will welcome any opportunity for its molecules to find places at a surface. It is ever ready to take advantage of any increase in the surface area of the water.

When you put bubble-bath in your bath and whisk it vigorously, the whisking takes bubbles of air into the water. Each bubble is in effect a water surface and immediately it will be lined with a layer of surfactant molecules (see figure 7.14).

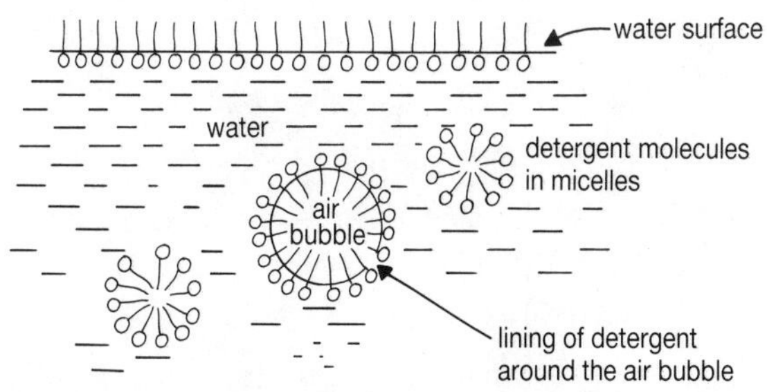

Figure 7.14 The formation of a detergent bubble

Being very light, the bubble will quickly rise and lift clear of the surface. The wall of a bubble is in effect a sandwich of two layers of detergent molecules with a thin layer of water between (see figure 7.15).
Gradually the water layer drains from the top of the bubble towards the bottom until none is left at the top to hold it together and the bubble bursts.

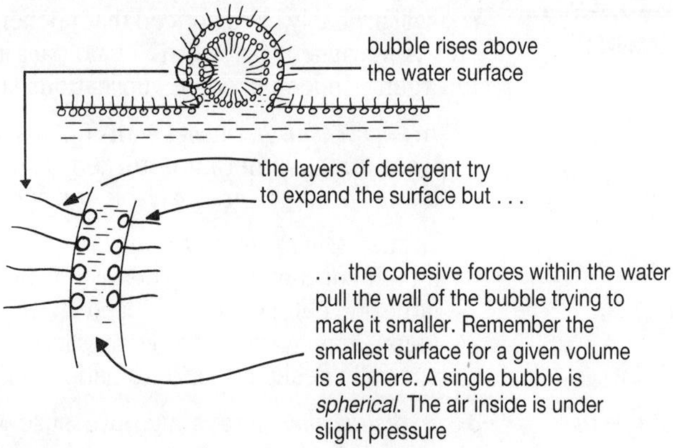

Figure 7.15 The structure of a detergent bubble

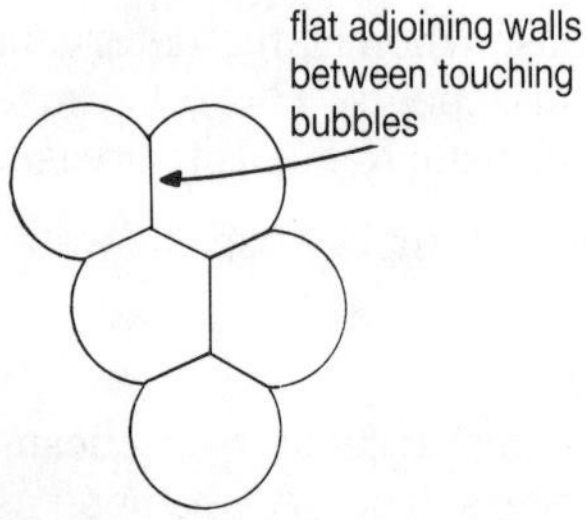

Figure 7.16 The bubbles of a foam

You can see the draining and bursting of a bubble with a pot of 'bubble mixture' – a solution of washing-up liquid will do – and a wire or plastic loop. Blow a single bubble and hold it on the loop – watch the water drain to the bottom until it bursts.

To show the pressure in the bubble, ask a smoker to draw on a cigarette, then blow some bubbles – they will be full of smoke. Then watch the puff of smoke as each bubble bursts.

Next try to blow two bubbles and hold them together on the loop. Notice that the joining wall of the two bubbles is *flat* because the pressure in each bubble is the same (see figure 7.16). In a lather or foam, all the walls between the bubbles are flat.

Self-assessment questions

1 Why does a liquid droplet try to be spherical?

2 When using water as a cleanser, give two reasons why its surface tension should be reduced.

3 Why is a surfactant so called?

4 What is the wetting action of a surfactant?

5 Show diagrammatically how the molecules of a surfactant can reduce the surface tension of water.

6 What is a micelle?

7 What is solubilisation?

8 Distinguish between an oil-in-water and a water-in-oil emulsion.

9 What is meant by HLB? How can it help in selecting an emulsifier for a particular purpose?

10 How can one test if an emulsion is oil-in-water or water-in-oil?

11 What is meant by 'creaming' of an emulsion? How can it be prevented?

12 What is the 'inversion' of an emulsion?

13 What is the 'cracking' of an emulsion?

14 Give two instances where it is undesirable for a detergent product to foam.

15 Briefly describe the action of a detergent in cleansing a greasy surface.

8 Detergents & Emulsifiers

Soaps and soapless detergents; classification of surfactants; anionic, cationic, amphoteric and non-ionic surfactants; manufacture of soaps and soapless detergents; pH of surfactants; thickening detergent products

The diverse range of surfactants

The hundreds of different surfactants available are of a wide variety of types, each being more suitable for a particular purpose. Some are good detergent cleansers. Others are good solubilisers. Some are oil-in-water emulsifiers; others are water-in-oil emulsifiers.

With such variety it is natural and necessary to want to classify them. Most basic science books classify detergents as either *soaps* or *soapless.* This is unsatisfactory because it separates one group of surfactants, the *soaps*, from *most* other surfactants which are 'lumped' together as *soapless.* Many other surfactants do not fit this classification at all.

Soaps and soapless detergents

The distinction between these two groups of surfactants is based on their behaviour in *hard water* (see chapter 5).

If a *soap* is added to *hard water*, it will fail to lather and will have *no* cleansing action until quite a large amount has been dissolved. The water becomes clouded with *soap scum* which settles to form a sticky deposit on surfaces and is difficult to rinse away.

A *soapless detergent* is not so affected by hard water. It will lather straight away and will not form scum. Its cleansing performance is not impaired.

In *soft water*, there is no difference in performance between soaps and soapless detergents. They both work well without forming a scum.

Classification of surfactants

A frequently used classification of surfactants is based on the following factors:

1 Whether the surfactant is water-soluble or oil-soluble.
2 If water-soluble, whether or not its molecules *ionise* in solution.
3 If it does ionise, whether the surfactant part of the molecule is the *anion* or the *cation* (see figure 8.1).

Anionic surfactants

Anionics are currently the most common group of surfactants. They include the *soaps* except those which are not water-soluble and many of the frequently used *soapless detergents* and *emulsifiers.*

Soaps are formed from a combination of an alkali and a fatty acid. An example is *sodium stearate.* Its molecule is shown in figure 8.2.

Most soaps have two disadvantages. Firstly, being salts of a *weak acid* (the fatty acid) and a *strong alkali*, they are not neutral but quite *alkaline* in character. Soapy water has pH 9–10. Prolonged contact with soapy water is not good for the skin or hair.

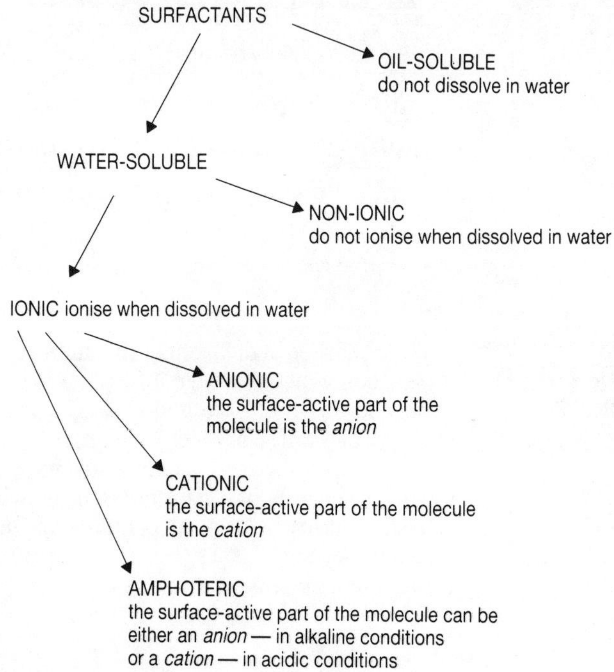

Figure 8.1 The classification of surfactants

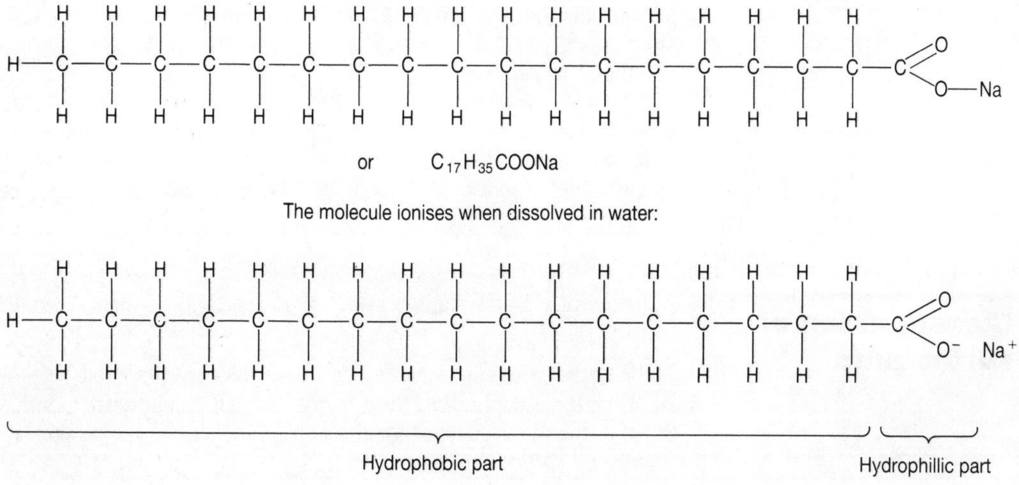

Figure 8.2 The ionisation of a soap molecule

Secondly, in hard water they form a *scum* of an *insoluble* soap when they react with the substances in the water which make it hard:

$CaSO_4$	$+ 2C_{17}H_{35}COONa \longrightarrow$	$(C_{17}H_{35}COO)_2Ca\ +$	Na_2SO_4
Calcium sulphate (Water hardness)	Sodium stearate (soap)	Calcium stearate (Scum)	Sodium sulphate

What happens is that the sodium of the soap actually prefers to pair with the sulphate of the water hardness, leaving the calcium to combine with the stearate. The resulting calcium stearate is still a 'soap' but it is *insoluble* in water and settles out as the sticky soap scum (see chapter 5).

Apart from their well known use as *cleansers*, soaps are frequently used as *emulsifiers* in cosmetic creams and lotions producing oil-in-water emulsions. In the latter use, the alkalinity of the soap could be a problem, making the cream too alkaline.

Triethanolamine soaps overcome the alkalinity problem. They are formed from the relatively weak alkali *triethanolamine* and a fatty acid so that the acid and alkali parts are now of equal strength, or weakness! An example is *triethanolamine stearate*. This is often the emulsifier in a cream or lotion. It does however have the disadvantage of being yellowish in colour, so emulsions formed using it tend to be cream-coloured rather than white.

Soapless anionic surfactants

In these the alkalinity is overcome not by using a weak alkali, but by boosting the strength of the fatty acid with a *strong acid* such as *sulphuric acid* or *sulphonic acid*.

These acids are intensely hydrophilic so the hydrophilic property of the surfactant is quite high – they have high HLB values and so are good cleansers but not of much use as emulsifiers for creams. A typical soapless anionic surfactant is *sodium lauryl sulphate:*

$$\underbrace{C_{12}H_{25}OSO_3^-}_{\text{Surfactant anion}} \quad Na^+$$

It is available as either a white powder or a paste concentrate. The latter is preferred in most cases because the powder creates an irritant dust. It is frequently used in shampoos for the hair and in some liquid skin cleansers, but it has limited solubility in water and clear products tend to become cloudy in cool conditions.

Sodium lauryl sulphate used to be used in combination with soap to produce the once popular cream paste shampoos.

Other frequently used soapless anionics include:

Triethanolamine lauryl sulphate Monoethanolamine lauryl sulphate Ammonium lauryl sulphate	liquids varying from pale yellow to deep amber
Sodium lauryl ether sulphate	– colourless liquid
Sodium alkyl benzene sulphate	– powder or paste

The first three and particularly the first two are frequently the main detergent in hair shampoos. With the assistance of a second detergent as a *foam booster*, they form the rich, stable foams one has been led to expect from a shampoo. Their major disadvantage is their colour. The ammonium or amine part tends to give them a yellow colour which can be anything from a pale straw colour to a deep amber. This does tend to limit the colour range available for the finished product.

Sodium lauryl ether sulphate is, however, colourless and crystal-clear. This obviously means that there is no limit to the colour choice for products containing it. Its ability to foam instantly and profusely when whisked in water means it is a valuable detergent for bubble baths and shower gels.

When any of the liquid lauryl sulphates is used in a product, it is possible to adjust the viscosity of the product to anything from a fairly runny liquid to quite a stiff gel by judicious use of the secondary foam-boosting detergents and *electrolytes* such as common *salt* – sodium chloride. In this way a hair shampoo formulation could be made as a freely running liquid to pack in a glass bottle, as a more viscous liquid to pack in individual sachets or as a gel to pack in a tube. More about the effect of salt on the viscosity of detergent products is given later in this chapter.

Sodium alkyl benzene sulphonate is rather harsh to use in personal products, but it is relatively cheap to produce and is used as the main detergent in most laundry washing powders and washing-up liquids.

Cationic surfactants

These are *'quaternary ammonium'* compounds. The term 'quaternary ammonium' needs explaining.

When an ammonia molecule (NH_3) forms compounds it gains a hydrogen ion (H^+) from the water in which it is dissolved to form an *ammonium ion* $(NH_4)^+$ (see figure 8.3).

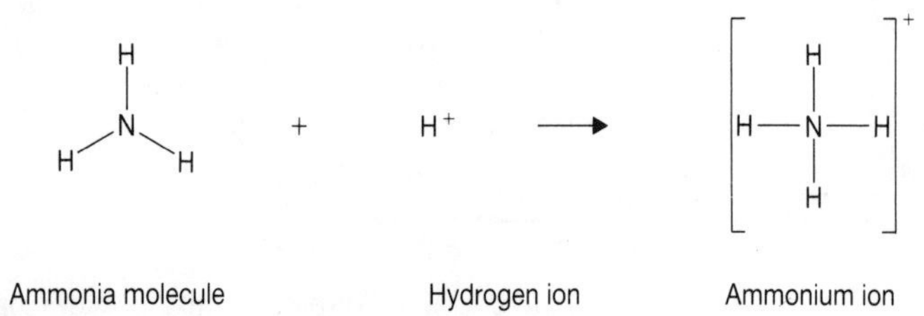

Figure 8.3 The formation of an ammonium ion

There will be in the water an equal number of hydroxide ions $-OH^-$ and so the solution of ammonia in water is ammonium hydroxide. It behaves like any other soluble hydroxide. Like sodium hydroxide or potassium hydroxide, it is an *alkali*.

It has however a useful additional property in that up to four organic molecules can attach themselves to the ammonium ion instead of the four hydrogen atoms. For example, combining one *cetyl* ($C_{16}H_{33}$–) and three *methyl* (CH_3–) with ammonium gives the *cetyl trimethyl ammonium* ion. Figure 8.4 shows the molecule of cetyl trimethyl ammonium bromide, *cetrimide* for short. The cetyl part of the molecule forms the hydrophobic 'tail'; the $-\overset{|}{\underset{|}{N}}-^{+}$ is the hydrophilic 'head'.

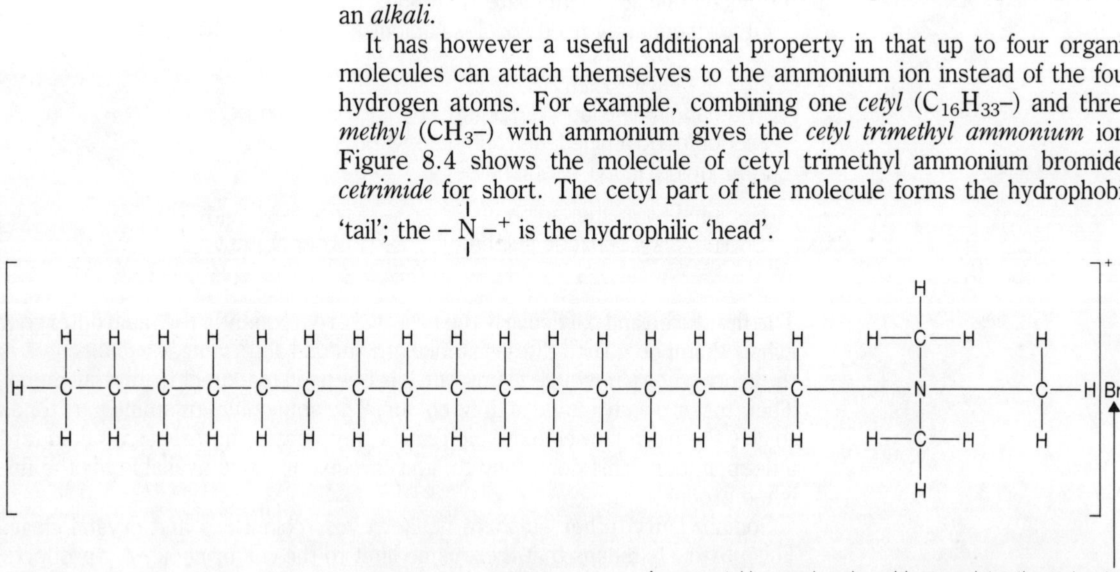

Figure 8.4 The molecule of cetyl trimethyl ammonium bromide

Cationic surfactants are not particularly good cleansers or emulsifiers and they do not foam well, but they are valuable materials in two respects:

1 As *conditioners* for hair and textile fibres. Hair stripped of its sebum and exposed to harsh alkaline treatments such as perms and bleaches will be in poor condition. The friction of combing causes a negative static charge to build up on the hairs so they repel each other, resulting in 'fly-away'. The positive ions of a cationic surfactant are attracted and held by the hair, covering it with what is in effect a coating of 'oil', and neutralising the static charge.

2 Cationics have a substantial *bactericidal* action. Cetrimide is used in antiseptic/disinfectant products such as Savlon or Cetavlon. Another cationic, domiphen bromide, is Bradosol – used in the well known brand of antiseptic throat lozenges.

Amphoteric surfactants

These were formerly called *ampholytic* surfactants. Depending on whether it is in acidic or alkaline conditions, the amphoteric molecule can ionise in two different ways. In acidic conditions it ionises to behave as a *cationic*; in alkaline conditions it is *anionic*. Figure 8.5 shows a typical example, N-alkyl betaine.

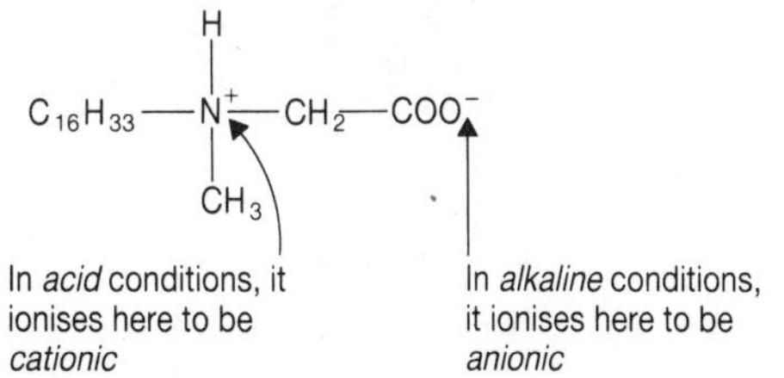

Figure 8.5 The amphoteric molecule of N-alkyl betaine

Compatibility of surfactants

You will have noticed already that it is common to use two or more surfactants together in a product. When this is done care has to be taken to ensure that they 'agree' with each other, otherwise the product could fail to emulsify.

An *anionic* and a *cationic* cannot be used in the same product; for instance, a cationic conditioner cannot be included in a shampoo formulation based on an anionic surfactant.

An *anionic* and an *amphoteric* cannot be used together in an *acidic* product – the amphoteric will act as a *cationic!* Similarly a *cationic* and an *amphoteric* cannot be used in the same product if it is *alkaline* – the amphoteric will act as an *anionic.*

Care also has to be taken in using *anionics* in *very acidic* products and *cationics* in *very alkaline* products. In such conditions the surfactant will not ionise and if this does not happen, it cannot perform its surfactant function.

Non-ionic surfactants

Until recent years, the *non-ionics* have been the 'Cinderellas' of the surfactant world, yet the fact that they *do not ionise* in solution means:

1 there is *no alkaline harshness* on the skin;
2 they are entirely *unaffected* by *hard water*;
3 there are *no incompatibility problems* with other ingredients.

Among the many non-ionics are:

1 good cleansing agents, though in general they do not foam well;
2 good solubilisers, particularly for perfumes;
3 good emulsifiers, for both oil-in-water and water-in-oil emulsions.

There are three main types of non-ionics:

1 Esters,
2 Ethers, and
3 Amides.

Surfactant esters

An ester is a combination of a fatty acid and an alcohol. The fatty acid provides the hydrophobic part of the molecule; the alcohol – usually *glycerol* or *sorbitol* – is the hydrophilic part.

Two examples are *glycerol monostearate* and *sorbitan monostearate.* Both these are used as emulsifiers for creams. Most esters are not truly soluble in water but mix with water by emulsifying themselves. Figure 8.6 shows the molecule of glycerol monostearate.

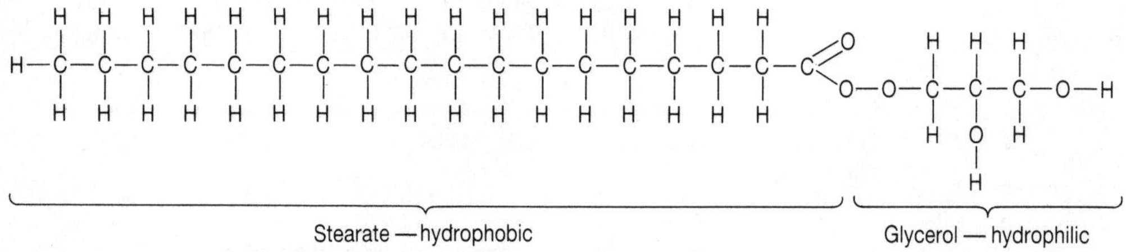

Figure 8.6 The molecule of glycerol monostearate

Surfactant ethers

These are variously called polyethylene-glycol surfactants, polyoxyethylene surfactants or *ethoxylates.* The hydrophilic end of the molecule is made of a number of *ethylene oxide* units. The ethylene oxide unit is:

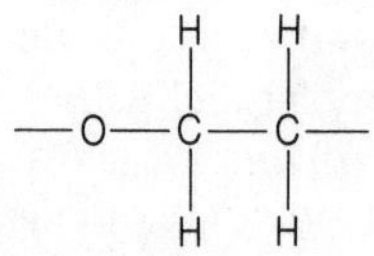

It is derived from ethylene glycol:

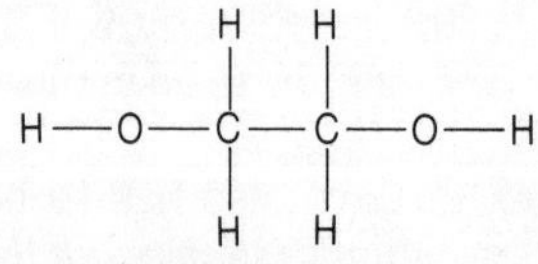

Up to fifty of these units can join end to end by ether linkages to form a hydrophilic 'tail' rather than a 'head' to the surfactant molecule. The greater the number of units, the more water-loving is the molecule and the higher its HLB value. The number of units can be controlled during manufacture to produce surfactants which are literally 'tailor-made' for their purpose. Figure 8.7 shows polyoxyethylene cetyl ether.

Other types of surfactants can be *ethoxylated.* For instance, the water-attracting capability of the *esters* can be increased by incorporating ethylene oxide units into their molecules, and the incorporation of two or three

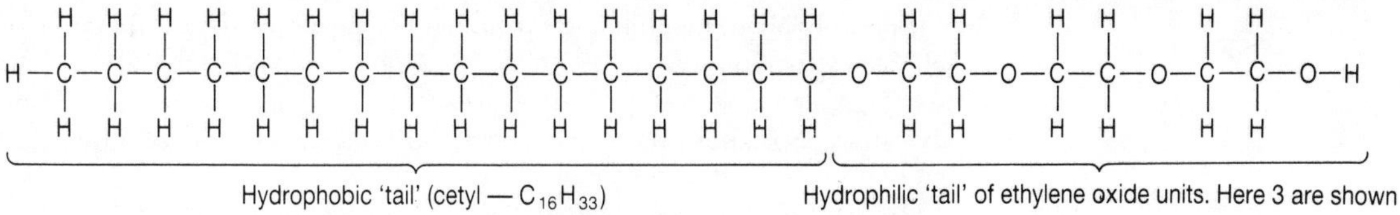

Figure 8.7 The molecule of polyoxyethylene (3) cetyl ether

ethylene oxide units in sodium lauryl sulphate vastly increases its water solubility thereby forming sodium lauryl ether sulphate.

Amide surfactants

Ethanol – ethyl alcohol – and ammonia can unite to form ethanolamine. This in turn can be combined with a fatty acid to form one of the *fatty acid ethanolamides*. Their main application is as *foam boosters* in detergent cleansing products. A commonly used example is coconut ethanolamide.

Oil-soluble surfactants

Quite an assortment of materials which are insoluble in water may be included in the oil phase of emulsified products, where their limited hydrophilic properties will help to stabilise the emulsion. Such substances include:

Cholesterol	Beeswax
Cetyl alcohol	Lanolin and lanolin products
Oleyl alcohol	Sorbitan oleate
Stearic acid	Calcium oleate

Manufacture of soap

Soap is made by reacting together animal and vegetable fats and oils with a caustic alkali; sodium hydroxide for hard soap or potassium hydroxide for soft soap. The type of fat or oil used usually depends on its availability and cost.

Soap is traditionally made by a batch process in large vats or '*kettles*', each holding fifty tonnes or more. Soap making is a process which works well on a large scale but not so well on the small, school laboratory scale.

The molten fat or oil is mixed with the caustic alkali solution as it is poured into the kettle. Heat from the injection of steam starts the process which is then sustained by producing its *own heat* until it is almost finished. It is an *exothermic* reaction. To complete the reaction, steam is again injected to maintain the temperature (see figure 8.8).

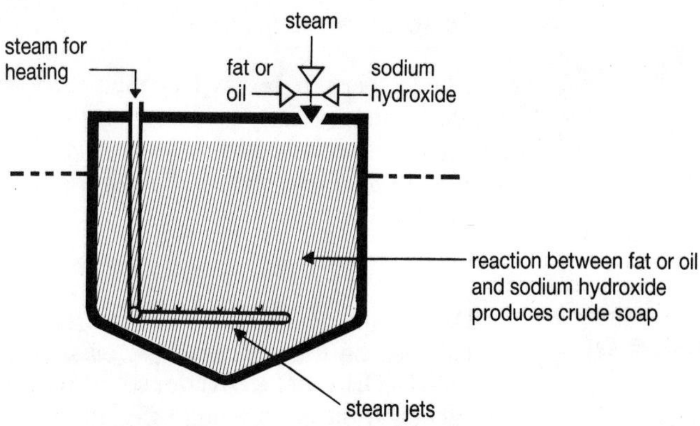

Figure 8.8 Making soap in a soap kettle

It is probably in maintaining a suitable temperature where the small-scale school preparations of soap run into difficulties. A small batch will not retain its own heat and one has to be very careful in boiling caustic alkalis in the laboratory. Splashes on the skin and in the eyes can burn. Protective clothing and eye protection *must* be worn.

The natural fats and oils are *esters* of the alcohol *glycerol* and a variety of fatty acids, notably *stearic acid* ($C_{17}H_{35}COOH$), *oleic acid* ($C_{17}H_{33}COOH$) and *palmitic acid* ($C_{15}H_{31}COOH$).

In the reaction, the fat or oil is acted upon by the alkali to produce a mixture of *soap and glycerol.* The reaction is called *saponification.*

$$\begin{array}{l} CH_2OOCC_{17}H_{35} \\ | \\ CHOOCC_{17}H_{35} \\ | \\ CH_2OOCC_{17}H_{35} \end{array} + NaOH \longrightarrow NaOOCC_{17}H_{35} + \begin{array}{l} CH_2OH \\ | \\ CHOH \\ | \\ CH_2OH \end{array}$$

Glycerol tristearate (Fat)	Sodium hydroxide (Alkali)	Sodium stearate (Soap)	Glycerol

In making *hard soap*, the next stage is *'salting out'*. Strong salt solution, *brine*, is pumped into the mixture in the kettle. The soap separates as a floating *curd*, leaving the glycerol and the salt in the water beneath. The water layer is drawn off and the very valuable glycerol is recovered from it.

Next the soap is washed with brine to remove any remaining traces of alkali. This process is *'fitting'*. The molten soap is then drawn from the kettle to be milled through *plodders* which are like large domestic mincing machines, to mix in colour and perfume before being moulded into tablets or formed into flakes or powder. These are variations of *hard* soap which was made with the alkali *sodium* hydroxide.

Soft soap and liquid soap

Before the days of soapless detergents, soft and liquid soaps were the usual basis of hair shampoos. In more recent times they are enjoying a comeback in pump-dispensers for hand and face washing.

These soaps are made with *potassium* hydroxide as the alkali. They are not salted out. The glycerol is left in.

Soap as an emulsifier

When a soap is to be used to emulsify a cosmetic cream, it is usual to form it *in situ.* A suitable fatty acid such as *stearic acid* is included in the *oil phase.* An alkali is dissolved in the *water phase.* When the two meet in the mixing process, the fatty acid and alkali combine to make a soap which goes on to emulsify the cream.

Manufacture of soapless detergents

Most of the non-soap surfactants require a *fatty alcohol* as a starting point. This can be from a vegetable oil source; coconut oil yields *lauryl alcohol* ($C_{12}H_{25}OH/C_{14}H_{29}OH$), or they may be synthesised from the *naphtha* fraction from the refining of crude oil. A stronger hydrophilic part is then added to the fatty alcohol molecule.

For instance, to make the *lauryl sulphates*, the fatty alcohol is *sulphated* by reacting it with very powerful sulphuric acid known as 'oleum'. This reaction is too dangerous to be recommended as a laboratory experiment. The *lauryl sulphate* is then further reacted with an alkali:

Lauryl sulphate + Sodium hydroxide → Sodium lauryl sulphate
Lauryl sulphate + Triethanolamine → Triethanolamine lauryl sulphate
Lauryl sulphate + Monoethanolamine → Monoethanolamine lauryl sulphate

Selecting surfactants for skin care products

When choosing a surfactant for a skin care product a number of factors must be taken into consideration.

For *personal washing*, the bar or tablet of soap has long been the clear favourite; but why does the bar have to be *soap?* Apart from its relative cheapness a major reason is oddly its *limited solubility in water!* Should you carelessly leave the soap in the bathwater it may soften a little on its outside, but it will not dissolve away.

There have been many attempts to popularise a *soapless* bar, usually with only limited success and short commercial life. The main reason is that they are *too soluble.* Left in the bath or even in a waterlogged soapdish, they soften to become a useless gelatinous mess.

In the hair shampoo market however, soap has almost entirely given way to the soapless surfactants for a number of reasons:

1 Alkalis are not good for either skin or hair. Although the skin is protected from its fleeting encounters with alkaline soap by the buffering action of the sebum, the hair is far less tolerant of the thorough massage in a soap shampoo and is left coarse and dull.
2 In hard water, *scum* is far more difficult to rinse from the hair than from the skin.
3 Soap cannot easily produce a transparent liquid shampoo.

Care must be taken, however, with the concentration of soapless surfactants. They tend to degrease the hair *too* thoroughly.

The current explosion in the popularity of taking a *shower* rather than a bath has led to the modification of the soapless hair shampoo to form the body shampoo or shower gel. This, in its plastic tube with a hook to hang from the shower head, is gaining popularity against the wayward habits of a tablet of soap. Where *do* you put your soap down in a shower?

Measuring the pH of surfactants

Make an approximately 5 per cent solution of each of a variety of surfactants (1g in 20 cm^3 of water), and test its pH with either a pH stick (Universal indicator) or with a pH meter. You will notice:

- the *alkalinity* of *soaps*
- the lesser alkalinity or even acidity of the *lauryl sulphates*
- the *acidity* of the *cationics*

The salt trick: thickening detergent products with salt

Although a hair shampoo is a relatively dilute detergent solution at between 8 and 25 per cent active surfactant, it must give the user the impression of being a rich and powerful product.

Here is the basic formulation for a *soapless liquid* shampoo for dry/normal hair:

Monoethanolamine lauryl sulphate } or Triethanolamine lauryl sulphate }	– 10.5
N-alkyl betaine – foam booster	– 1.5
Water	– to 100

First we must take account of the strength of the detergent solutions available.

Triethanolamine lauryl sulphate is 42 per cent active matter, and therefore needs:

$$10.5 \times \frac{100}{42} = 25 \text{ parts in formulation}$$

Monoethanolamine lauryl sulphate is either 33 per cent or 27 per cent active, and therefore needs:

$$10.5 \times \frac{100}{33} = 32 \text{ parts of 33 per cent}$$

or

$$10.5 \times \frac{100}{27} = 39 \text{ parts of 27 per cent}$$

N-alkyl betaine is 30 per cent active matter, and therefore needs:

$$1.5 \times \frac{100}{30} = 5 \text{ parts in formulation}$$

So we must now revise the formulation to take account of the strength of the surfactants:

1	Triethanolamine lauryl sulphate (42 per cent active)	25
	N-alkyl betaine (30 per cent active)	5
	Water	70
2	Monoethanolamine lauryl sulphate (33 per cent active)	32
	N-alkyl betaine (30 per cent active)	5
	Water	63
3	Monoethanolamine lauryl sulphate (27 per cent active)	39
	N-alkyl betaine (30 per cent active)	5
	Water	56

Very often a manufacturer of these surfactants will make the job of formulating a shampoo easier by including a suitable amount of salt and even the foam booster with the main detergent.

If the following experiment to show the effect of *salt* is to work, we must use detergent concentrates which are:

1 *'not-built'* – that is, no foam booster has been added;
2 *'sans-cerebos'* – that is, without salt.

This must be specified when ordering supplies of the detergents.

To show the effect of salt

Make up 300 g of one of the formulations. Add a preservative: methyl-4-hydroxybenzoate at 0.125 per cent (0.4 g). Divide the formulation into *six* portions of 50 g each.

To portion	
1	add no salt
2	add 1 per cent salt – (0.5 g)
3	add 2 per cent salt – (1.0 g)
4	add 3 per cent salt – (1.5 g)
5	add 4 per cent salt – (2.0 g)
6	add 5 per cent salt – (2.5 g)

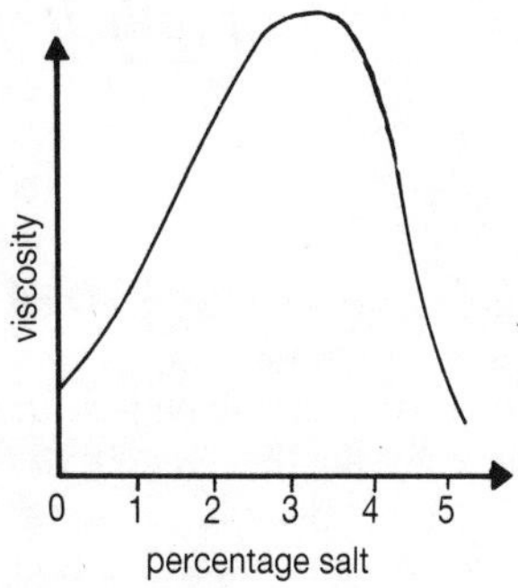

Figure 8.9 The effect of salt on the viscosity of a shampoo

Stir the salt well into each portion and note any change in the viscosity.

Leave the samples to stand for 24 hours until all bubbles have risen from them, and note again the viscosity of each.

Note how, up to a certain maximum, the viscosity is *increased* by the salt. Beyond that it decreases again (see figure 8.9).

After the experiment, any 'usable' samples may be coloured, perfumed and packed for trial use.

Self-assessment questions

1. List differences between soap and soapless detergents.
2. Describe briefly how soap behaves in hard water.
3. What is the difference between anionic, cationic, amphoteric and non-ionic surfactants?
4. Apart from their cleansing and emulsifying actions, give two other important properties of cationic surfactants which make them valuable ingredients in hair and skin care products.
5. Give three advantages of non-ionic surfactants over ionic ones.
6. What raw materials are used to manufacture soap?
7. Explain the chemical difference between hard and soft soap.
8. What is meant by 'salting out' in soap manufacture?
9. Why have not soapless detergents replaced 'old fashioned' soap for personal cleansing?
10. What is the reason for adding salt to shampoo formulations?

9 Skin

The body and the environment; the functions of the skin; the structure of the skin; the epidermis, its functions, structure and growth; the dermis, its structure and significance; the blood supply; the nerve supply; the sweat glands; the sebaceous glands; the hair follicles; skin colour

The body and the environment

It is not sufficient to consider the skin as being simply a wrapper for the body. It is a *very busy frontier* between the body and the environment.

Life is hard; particularly a life on land. It is an environment which is at the same time both a life-giver and a life-taker: friendly yet hostile.

The air provides life-giving oxygen but it would take away life-essential water. The sun provides life-giving warmth and light yet bombards the body with harmful radiations. Countless organisms share the environment, most too small to be seen with the unaided eye. Some are friends; others are deadly enemies.

Functions of the skin

The skin must:

1 Control the loss of valuable water from the body.
2 Protect the body from the harmful radiations of the sun.
3 Control the entry of foreign materials.
4 Prevent the entry of harmful microorganisms.
5 Cushion the body against the mechanical shock from bumps and knocks.
6 Regulate the loss of heat from the body.
7 Receive information from the environment and relay it to the brain.
8 By its colour, texture and odour, transmit social and sexual signals to others.

Additionally the skin must *last a lifetime*. It must not wear out; it must maintain itself against the ravages of wear and tear.

The skin must *always fit*. It must grow as its owner grows and be resilient and elastic enough to stretch and contract to allow the body freedom of movement.

For the *beautician* trying to improve the skin by decoration or the *beauty therapist* attempting to prevent or repair the ravages wrought by the environment, an understanding of the workings of the skin is essential.

The extent of the skin

At birth a baby might have some 2500 cm^2 of skin. By the time he or she has become an adult this will have grown to 18 000 cm^2 or more. The skin is one of the larger organs of the body, weighing over 3 kg in an 'average' woman and almost 5 kg for a man.

There are two types of skin. Much of the body is covered by a type of skin bearing hairs which grow from pores or follicles. The palms of the hands and the soles of the feet have a special skin devoid of hairs and hair follicles and marked by a complex pattern of tiny ridges and furrows unique to each person.

The structure of the skin

The two major layers of the skin are the *epidermis* and the *dermis*. An underlying layer of fatty tissue separates the skin from the muscle of the body wall beneath (see figures 9.1 and 9.2).

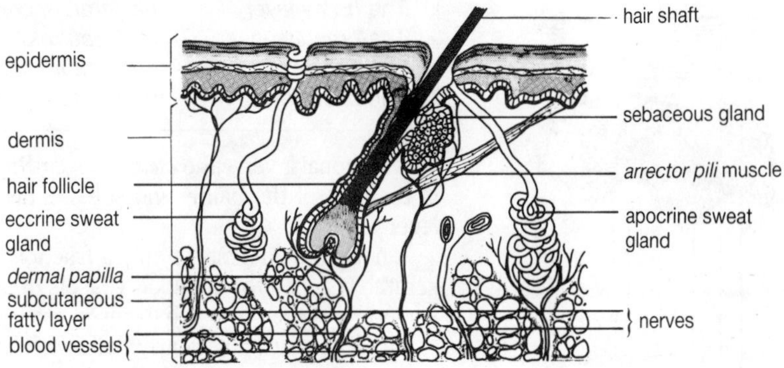

Figure 9.1 Diagrammatic representation of a vertical section through the skin

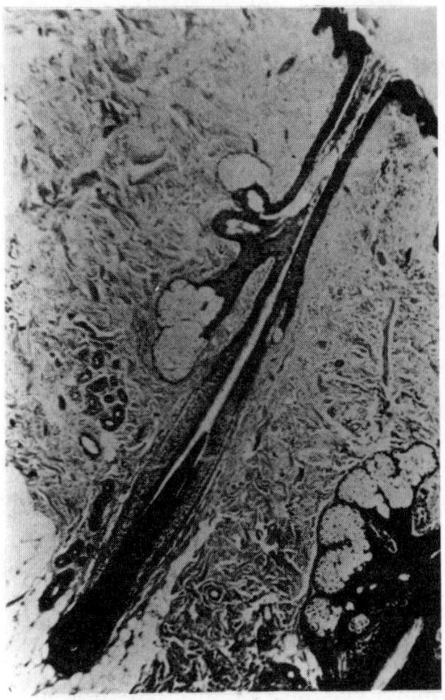

Figure 9.2 Micrograph of a vertical section through the skin (courtesy of Unilever)

The epidermis

The outer layers of the epidermis are the body's actual frontier to the outside world, protecting the living tissues within from the ravages of the environment:

The drying effect of the air The harmful rays of the sun Harmful organisms – particularly bacteria Chemical substances dangerous to living cells

The underlying layers are concerned with the replacement of the outer layers to counter wear and tear.

The layers of the epidermis

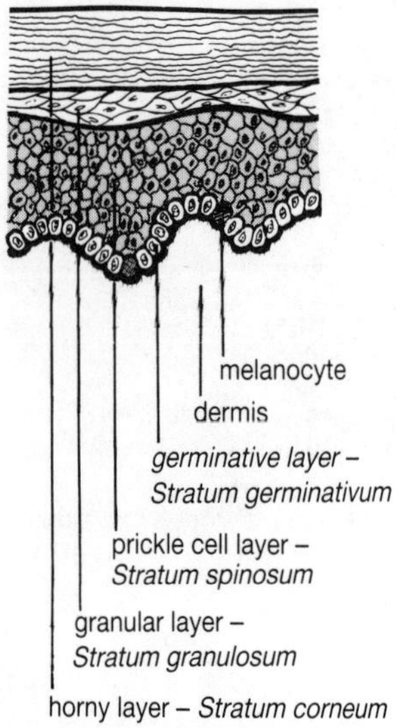

Figure 9.3 The layers of the epidermis

It is customary to recognise *four* layers of the epidermis (see figure 9.3). From the outside these are:

The *horny layer*	– the *Stratum corneum*
The *granular layer*	– the *Stratum granulosum*
The *prickle cell layer*	– the *Stratum spinosum*
The *basal layer*	– the *Stratum germinativum* or *basale*

An additional layer – the *clear layer* or *Stratum lucidum* – is recognisable only in the skin of the palms and soles. This is between the granular and horny layers.

A normal epidermis is only a fraction of a millimetre thick – even a slight scratch reaches to the blood vessels of the dermis and bleeding occurs. The epidermis of the soles and palms is much thicker, perhaps several millimetres.

The layers are not clearly defined. The outer layer, the *horny layer*, is the mature epidermis which performs the frontier-barrier role. The layers beneath represent stages in the development of new horny layer cells as they migrate from the basal layer where they were produced until they take their place as part of the horny layer.

The horny layer, the *stratum corneum*

To living cells air is lethal. It is *too dry*. A living cell is about 80 per cent water; air is at most 1 per cent water. In direct contact with the air a living cell would dry up and die.

The body therefore deliberately surrounds itself with layers of dead cells, the *horny layer*, to protect the living cells within.

The cells of the horny layer are little more than flat sheets of a hard, resistant protein called *keratin*. They act as a by no means perfect barrier to the loss of water from the body and the entry of harmful bacteria, chemicals and rays.

Where living cells *must* be very close to air such as those lining the nose, mouth, throat and lungs, they must at *all times* be kept *wet* with mucus. If this wetness fails, for instance as a result of infection, the cells lining these parts become distressed and irritate. The result is a sore throat.

Even the dead cells of the horny layer can become too dry if not protected by a layer of waterproofing *sebum*. This is a greasy mixture which oozes on to the skin surface from the sebaceous glands. Its effect is illustrated by figure 9.4.

Frequent washing of the skin, for instance of the hands, removes the sebum. The dead cells of the horny layer become hard and brittle. The skin roughens, chaps and cracks.

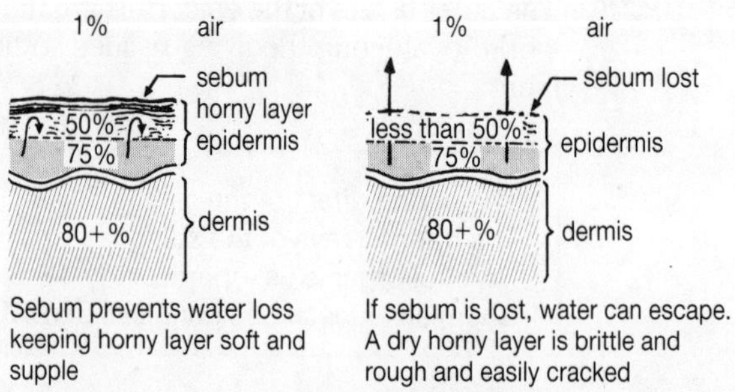

Figure 9.4 Sebum cuts down the loss of moisture from the skin

In winter's windy cold weather, the output of sebum to exposed skin of the hands and face is reduced. The skin becomes dry and flaky.

The *waterproofing action* of the skin is to prevent the body losing too much moisture – *not* to keep it dry in wet weather!

The epidermis as a guard against harmful rays

The horny layer is greatly involved in protecting the body against the ultra-violet rays of the sun which in excess are lethal to living cells.

The rays are partially reflected by each of the layers of the horny layer cells so that very little penetrates the full thickness of the epidermis. Also involved in screening against ultra-violet is the brown *melanin* pigment of the skin. This function is described in more detail in chapters 12 and 15.

The epidermis as a guard against the entry of chemicals

The sebum covering the skin is basically hydrophobic and tends to discourage not only water but also water-soluble chemicals from passing through it. The keratin of the horny layer is essentially hydrophilic and similarly tends to hinder the passage of oils and oil-soluble substances into the skin.

Between them they form a barrier to the entry of chemical substances through the skin. The barrier is however far from perfect and the skin is permeable to a wide variety of substances. Hence there is an *irritation* system which should respond when undesirable substances do enter.

Percutaneous absorption

Sebum is not fully effective as a barrier because it does contain a proportion of naturally surfactant substances such as fatty acids and fatty alcohols (see chapter 4) which can assist the passage of water and water-solubles through it. In any case, prolonged contact with surfactant products such as soaps and detergents will emulsify and remove the sebum from the skin.

While the keratin of the scales of the horny layer is hydrophilic and permeable to water and water-soluble substances, the scales are joined to each other by a surfactant fatty film (see figure 9.5). Although the film hinders the passage of water and water-solubles, they can pass with difficulty. If however the water contains a surfactant of a suitable HLB value (see chapter 7) it will pass easily from scale to scale through the film.

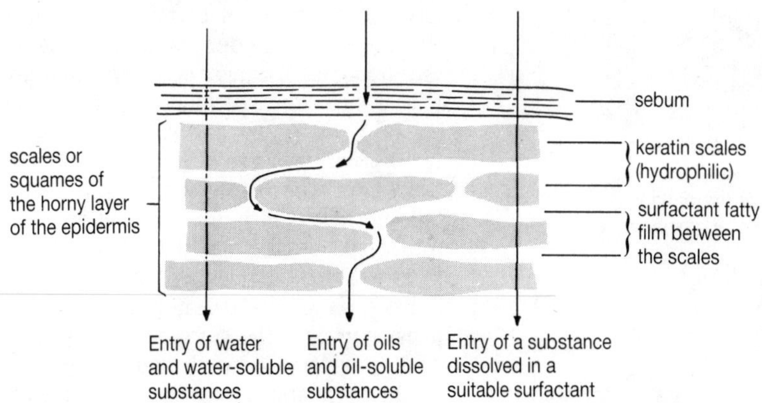

Figure 9.5 Percutaneous absorption

Oils and oil-soluble substances can enter the skin by zig-zagging between the scales through the fatty film.

Percutaneous absorption of substances is currently of great interest in several respects:

1 Finding out how irritants and allergens produce their irritant or allergic effects.
2 Substantiating the claims made for herbal extracts and aromatherapy oils applied to the skin.
3 Using the percutaneous route for administering medicinal drugs as an alternative to taking by mouth or giving injections.

The epidermis as a protection against bacteria

The horny layer acts as a physical barrier against entry of bacteria. There are however pores in the horny layer, notably the hair follicles, through which bacteria could gain entry. The sebum and the sebaceous glands are able to prevent their entry. The sebum on the skin is deliberately *acidic* and bacteria are inhibited by acids. The sebaceous glands are able to destroy any bacteria that might enter them through the hair follicles. How they do this is part of the action of the sebaceous glands explained later in this chapter.

The continuous growth of the epidermis

Although the skin as a whole must last a lifetime, obviously the same dead cells will not wear for very long. In fact the surface layer of the horny layer lasts only a few days. Probably some 500 000 000 horny layer cells or *squames* will be lost each day, being sloughed off by *desquamation*.

Lost horny layer cells actually contribute very largely to the *dust* in our homes against which housewives constantly do battle! Many of these skin scales provide food for tiny *mites*, shortlegged spider-like organisms, which devour them. They live in all our homes and particularly our beds.

As the horny layer scales are lost by desquamation, so they must be replaced. This is the function of the other layers of the epidermis.

Stratum germinativum – the germinative layer

Figure 9.6 The dermal *papillae* provide the blood supply for the germinative layer

This layer is also known as the *Stratum basale* or basal layer. It is the innermost layer of the epidermis adjoining the underlying dermis. It is not level but thrown into finger-like folds rather like an egg-tray. The epidermis has no direct blood supply of its own but is supplied by clusters of blood capillaries in the 'domes' of the dermis. These clusters of capillaries are *dermal papillae* (see figure 9.6). Similar *dermal papillae* are to be found at the base of each hair follicle, providing the blood supply for the growth of the hair.

The *Stratum germinativum* is a single layer of cells each of which is capable of *cell-division*. Each cell grows to double its depth, and then divides by the process of *mitosis* (see figure 9.7).

In normal skin the growth and division cycle takes from 5 to 12 days. Its rate is linked to the rate of desquamation – the loss of squames from the horny layer – so that the thickness of the horny layer remains more or less constant.

In *psoriasis*, an extremely unpleasant scaling disorder of the skin, the cell division cycle of the germinative layer may be as little as one and a half days. This results in only partly matured squames joining the horny layer and being sloughed off much sooner and in much greater numbers than those from normal skin.

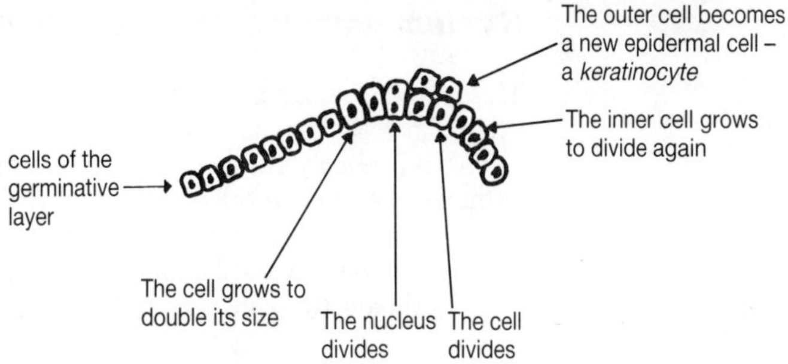

Figure 9.7 Cell division in the germinative layer

Stratum spinosum – the prickle cell layer

This and the germinative layer are the actively living layers of the epidermis and together are often referred to as the *Stratum Malpighi* or Malpighian layer.

The *Stratum spinosum* is composed of the newly formed epidermal cells. These are called *keratinocytes*. While the new keratinocytes are in this layer, they are joined to each other by spiny outgrowths. These give the individual cells the appearance of rather prickly gooseberries. Hence they are called '*prickle cells*'. The interconnecting outgrowths are called *desmosomes*. It was thought that because the epidermis has no direct blood supply the desmosomes were to allow rapid transfer of materials from cell to cell. More recent opinion is that this is not their function and that they serve merely to hold the cells together (see figure 9.8).

While in the prickle cell layer, the keratinocytes are probably in the early stages of producing what is to become *keratin* protein.

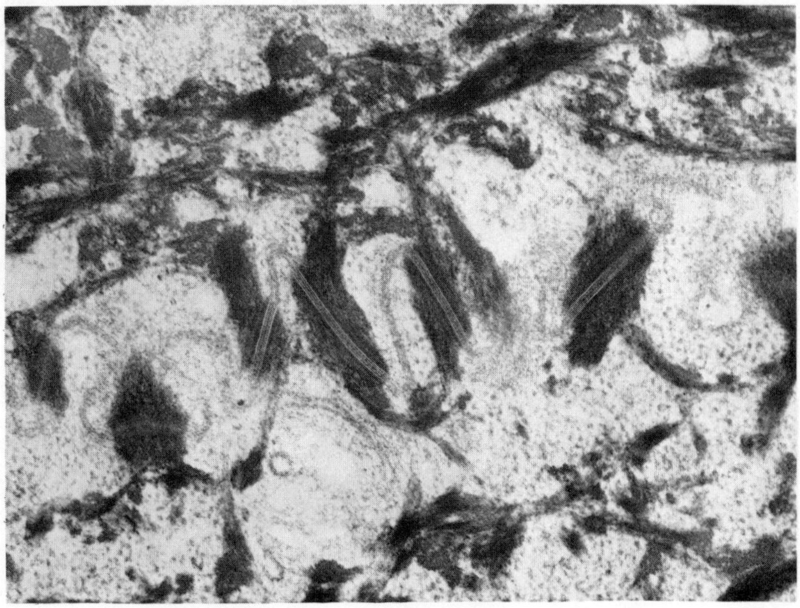

Figure 9.8 Electron micrograph of prickle cells of the *Stratum spinosum*

Stratum granulosum – the granular layer

This is so-called because when thin sections of skin have been stained with dyes to look at them under a microscope, this layer has a granular appearance.

This is probably because the keratin protein is being assembled to produce granules. Later each cell will become virtually filled with keratin. Its nucleus and other cell contents will disappear. It will become flattened into a sheet of keratin and will take its place as a mature *squame* as part of the new innermost layer of the horny layer.

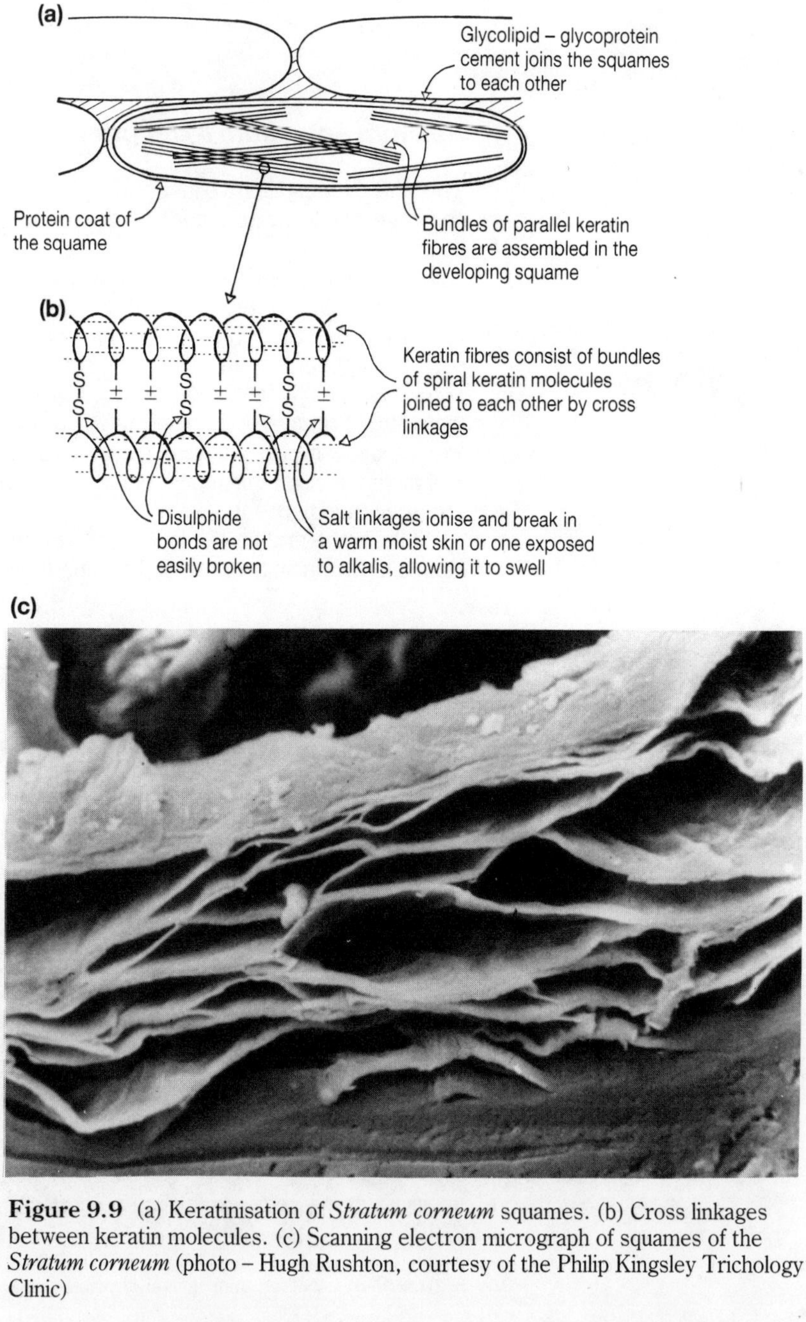

Figure 9.9 (a) Keratinisation of *Stratum corneum* squames. (b) Cross linkages between keratin molecules. (c) Scanning electron micrograph of squames of the *Stratum corneum* (photo – Hugh Rushton, courtesy of the Philip Kingsley Trichology Clinic)

Stratum corneum – the horny layer

The *Stratum corneum* comprises several layers of mature squames. The number of layers varies from one area to another, from one in the conjunctiva covering the eye to perhaps hundreds on the sole of the foot. Each squame is roughly disc shaped, about 0.03 mm in diameter and a thousandth of a mm thick. It has a tough protein wall and is packed with keratin. The adhesion of the squames to each other is augmented by the deposition of a cementing substance between them which consists of glycoprotein and glycolipid (see figure 9.9a).

Keratin of the stratum corneum

Keratin is a *protein.* Protein molecules are very long. They are made up from chains of smaller units called *amino acids* (see chapter 4). About 23 different amino acids make up the many different proteins of the human body. In forming a protein molecule the correct sequence of amino acids link together by *peptide bonds* to form a long chain called a *polypeptide* chain. The chain then automatically coils itself into a long spiral or helix. The chemical structure of some amino acids, the formation of peptide bonds and the formation of the spiral protein molecule are further detailed in chapter 17.

The molecules of the keratin protein in the squames of the *Stratum corneum* are aligned parallel to the surface of the skin and parallel to each other (see figure 9.9a).

Chemical cross linkages form between the molecules to bond them together to form a compact and relatively impermeable structure. There are two kinds of cross linkages – *disulphide bonds* and *salt linkages*. The disulphide bonds are fairly permanent but the salt linkages form only when the skin is slightly *acid* (at pH 4.5–6) and cool (see figure 9.9b). It is kept acidic by the 'acid mantle' of the *sebum.* If this is removed and the skin is allowed to become alkaline, the salt linkages ionise and break. This allows the keratin molecules to move further apart and the *Stratum corneum* to swell and lose its effectiveness as a barrier.

As successive generations of squames are produced, they gradually migrate towards the outer surface, eventually to be sloughed off. Desquamation, the loss of the outer squames, is the result of degradation of the glycoprotein–glycolipid cement between the squames. The life span of a keratinocyte from its formation from the germinative layer until its eventual loss by desquamation is about forty days.

The dermis

The dermis is the *tough elastic* layer of the skin: tough so that it can protect the body against *bumps* and *knocks*; elastic so that the skin will always *fit.*

It contains the nerve endings that perform the skin's *sensory* function. It contains the *blood supply* which nourishes both itself and the epidermis and helps to control body temperature.

Although they are of epidermal origin, it contains the glands of the skin: the *sweat glands*, the other part of the body's temperature control system, and the *sebaceous glands* which produce the *sebum* which waterproofs the epidermis. Also originating from the epidermis but extending deeply into the dermis are the *follicles* from which hairs grow.

Structure of the dermis

The main basic structure of the dermis is a dense network of criss-crossing *protein fibres* embedded in a mass of firm jelly (see figure 9.10).

The fibres are of *two* kinds:

1 *Collagen fibres* which amount to 75 per cent of the weight of the dermis are *tough* and *resilient*.

3 *Elastic fibres* account for only 4 per cent of the weight of the dermis and are, as their name implies, *elastic* – able to contract back after stretching to give the skin its snug fit.

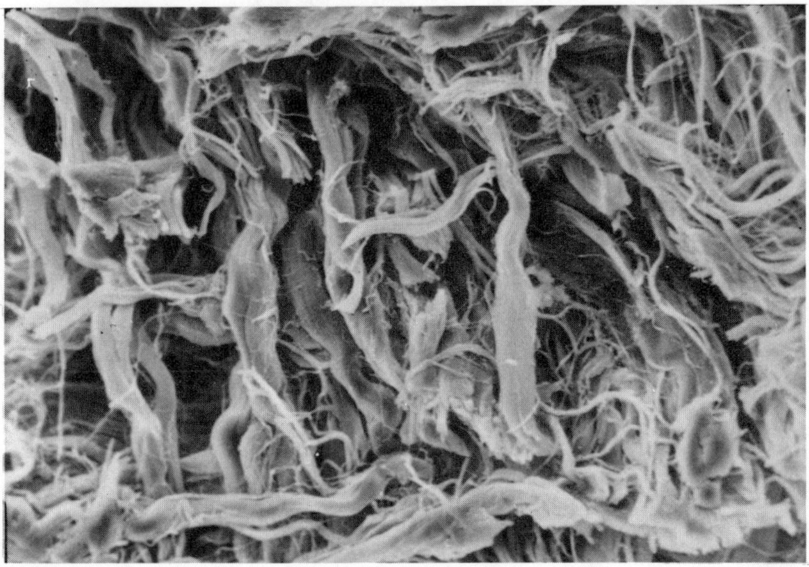

Figure 9.10 Scanning electron micrograph of the fibre network of the dermis (photo – Hugh Rushton, courtesy of the Philip Kingsley Trichology Clinic)

The jelly is a *colloidal gel* of assorted carbohydrate substances called *mucopolysaccharides* dissolved in *water*.

There are *very few cells* in the structure of the dermis. There are cells called *fibroblasts* which 'do the living' for the dermis and actually make the collagen and elastic fibres.

There are also *mast cells*. Their function is to *detect damage* to the skin. Should damage occur from whatever cause, these delicate and sensitive mast cells rupture and release *histamine* which causes *irritation* and *inflammation*. Irritation is a signal that something is wrong and inflammation is an indication that emergency repairs are under way. More about this is to be found in chapter 23.

The dermis is actually two layers. The outermost layer just beneath the epidermis is the *papillary layer*. It has in it the *dermal papillae* and the nerve endings. Beneath it and forming the bulk of the dermis is the *reticular layer* which has most of the protein fibres (see figure 9.11).

Beneath the dermis-proper, is the *subcutaneous layer*. This consists of *adipose* or *fatty tissue*. Its cells are packed with droplets of fat: the *energy store* of the body. The fatty layer is supposed to have an insulating function to keep in body heat but there is little evidence to show that fat people fare better in cold weather! Indeed the evidence tends the other way. Those whose bodies

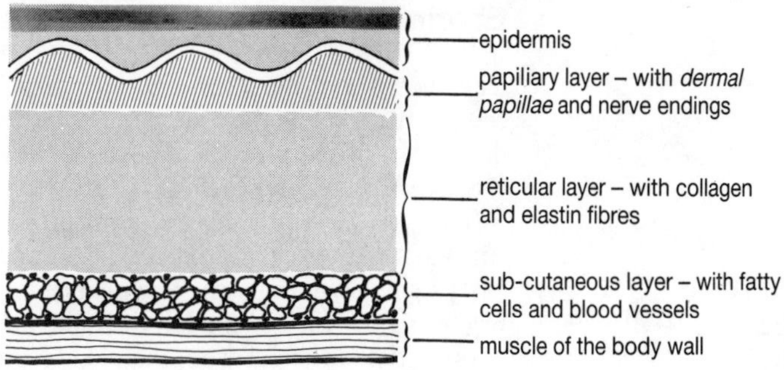

Figure 9.11 Vertical section of the dermis

'burn-up' excess energy to produce heat are better able to survive extreme cold than those whose bodies store the excess energy as fat.

Passing through the subcutaneous layer are the main blood vessels, nerves and lymph vessels which supply the skin. A main function of the *lymph vessels* in the skin is to *drain* away excess fluids – particularly fatty fluids – for disposal or use elsewhere in the body.

Blood supply to the skin

The main *arteries* and *veins* which supply the skin emerge through the muscular body wall. The network of blood vessels spreads through the *sub-cutaneous layer*. From there the supply loops through the dermis up to, but not into, the epidermis as shown in figure 9.12. Other loops and papillae supply the hair follicles and the glands of the skin.

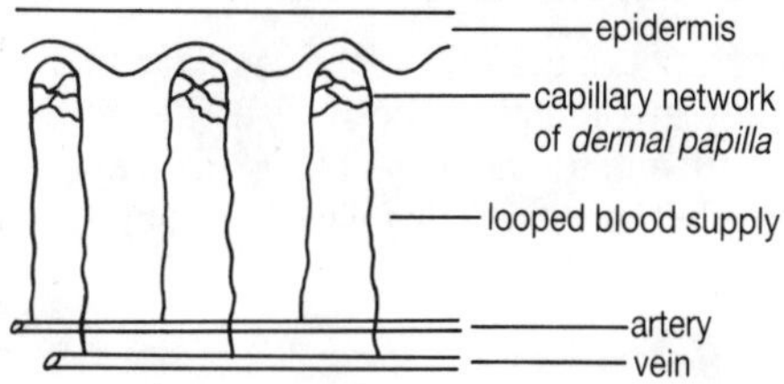

Figure 9.12 Blood supply to the skin

Nerve supply to the skin

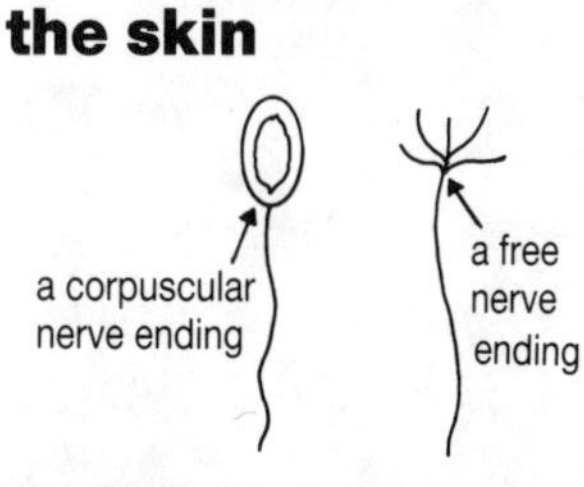

Figure 9.13 Sensory nerve endings found in the skin

Like the blood supply, the nerve supply too is confined entirely to the dermis. The skin is an important *sensory organ* so its nerve supply is almost entirely of *sensory nerves* with their *sensory nerve endings*.

Some of the nerves end in *corpuscles* while others have branched *free* endings (see figure 9.13). Both types are in the papillary layer of the dermis. The corpuscular nerve endings are of three types: the Pacinnian corpuscles are sensitive to *touch* and *pressure*, the organs of Raffini to *heat* and the Krause bulbs to *cold*. The free endings are sensitive to *pain*.

There is also a nerve supply to the hair follicles (hairs are very touch-sensitive), to the *arrector pili* muscles and to the sweat glands.

The glands of the skin

The skin has three types of glands – the *sebaceous* glands and two types of *sweat glands* called *eccrine* and *apocrine* glands.

Eccrine sweat glands and temperature control

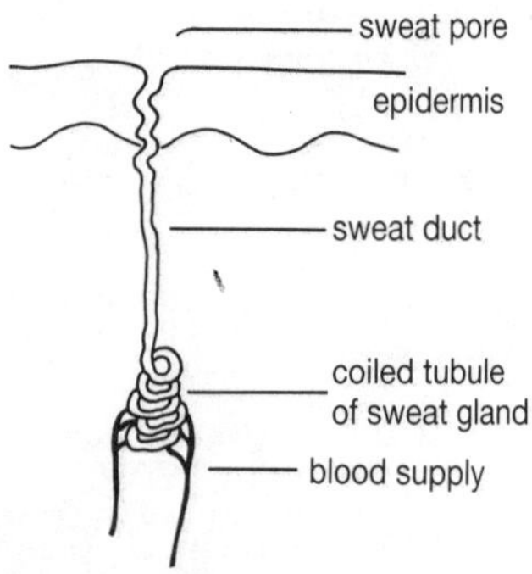

Figure 9.14 An eccrine sweat gland

The human body must maintain an internal temperature of 37°C, the optimum temperature for body chemistry or *metabolism*. Body chemistry does produce *heat*, deliberately so if necessary and excess heat must be brought by the *blood* to the *skin* to be dissipated to the environment.

The skin plays, therefore, a major part in controlling body temperature. The blood vessels in the skin *dilate*, or open up to allow a greater flow of heat-carrying blood to the skin. The heat is then dissipated in two ways. Some of it will be lost by *radiation* from the skin but most of it will be used to *evaporate* perspiration or sweat from the skin.

The *eccrine sweat glands* are supplied with water from the blood. The gland consists of a coiled tube lined with cells which pass the water through their cell membranes into the tube (see figure 9.14).

The water is secreted on to the surface of the skin to be evaporated by the heat of the body. An *eccrine* gland is a gland which secretes a watery fluid in this manner.

Eccrine sweat glands are found in *all* the skin. They are most numerous on the palms and soles where there are up to 500 per cm^2 of skin area (see figure 9.15). On the back there are 80 per cm^2.

Eccrine sweat is 99.5 per cent water plus 0.5 per cent salt and urea, which are probably there more by accident than design. There is a common tendency to call sweat gland activity '*excretion*'. Sweat is however secreted for a purpose – temperature control. *Secretion* is for a purpose; excretion is to eliminate waste.

Apocrine sweat glands

The apocrine sweat glands are far more localised than the eccrine glands. They are found in the axillae (the armpit), the groin and surrounding the mouth and the nipples. Their ducts open not directly on to the surface of the skin but into the hair follicles in these areas (see figure 9.1).

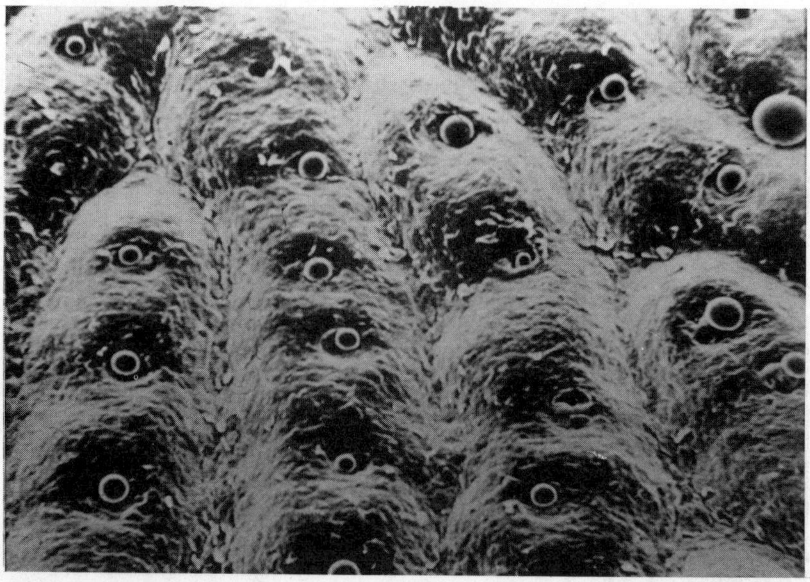

Figure 9.15 Scanning electron micrograph of sweat pores on the skin of the hand (courtesy of Unilever)

The apocrine glands only become active from the age of puberty. They secrete a milky sweat containing much organic matter. They do this by forming the sweat in vesicles or membrane-enclosed bubbles within the cells of the glands which then open to release the sweat into the tubule of the gland.

The output of apocrine sweat is not controlled by body temperature but by the body's hormonal activity. It seems that the sweat is probably a chemical *social signalling* substance: a *pheromone*.

What is definitely known is that apocrine sweat is prone to bacterial decay with the result that it *does* give chemical signals – unpleasant ones – the famous 'B.O.' if one does not look closely at one's personal hygiene!

Sebaceous glands

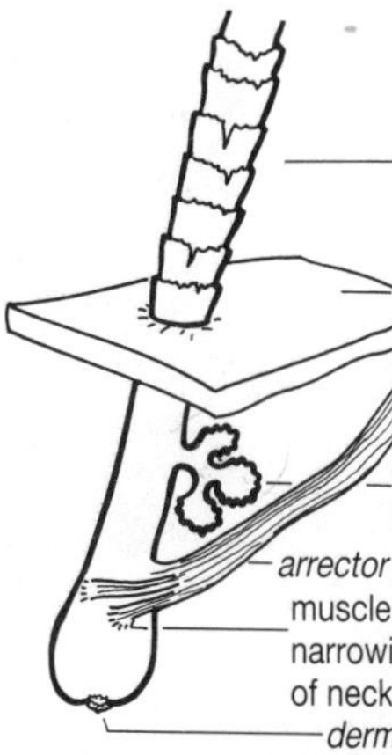

Figure 9.16 A hair in its follicle

Each hair follicle, whether or not it contains a hair, has associated with it a *sebaceous gland* (see figure 9.16). Its function is to secrete *sebum*, the waxy, oily mixture which spreads along the hair to give it gloss and spreads over the horny layer of the epidermis to act as an *emollient* to keep it feeling soft. It waterproofs the skin to help it retain its moisture.

The *sebum* is a mixture of fatty acids, fatty alcohols and esters or waxes, plus *lactic acid* and *lactate salts* which are responsible for maintaining the acid pH of the skin – pH 4.5 to 6. This is the '*acid-mantle*' of the skin. In these acid conditions the *keratin* protein of the horny layer is at its most compact and at its most effective as a *barrier*. Also in these acid conditions *bacteria* are at their least active and thus unlikely to cause trouble.

The cells of the sebaceous glands form the sebum within themselves. To release it, the cell must destroy itself. A gland which works in this way is a *holocrine gland*.

While the cells of the sebaceous glands are destroying themselves, they can also be destroying any other cells that happen to get into the glands, such as any bacteria which might enter the follicle or the cells of the root sheath which covers the root of the hair, which then falls away as it grows from the follicle.

The hair follicles

Hair follicles are found all over the body except on the palms and soles, but they do not always contain hairs. Empty follicles are common on the forehead and nose – despite being empty these follicles contain often *very* active sebaceous glands resulting in an oily centre panel to the face. Figure 9.16 shows a hair follicle containing a hair. It shows also the sebaceous gland and the *arrector pili* muscle, an involuntary muscle which contracts to make the hair stand more erect in response to cold or fright, producing a 'goose pimple' in the process.

A detailed account of the structure and working of the hair follicle and the growth and structure of the hair is the subject of chapter 17.

Skin colour

The novice artist who has tried and failed to mix an acceptable 'skin tone' from his or her paint box should consider carefully what contributes to the colour of the skin.

The skin is quite translucent and through it can be seen the red of the blood in the dermal blood vessels and the yellow of the subcutaneous fat. The main component of skin colour is the varying degree of brown contributed by *melanin*.

Melanin is produced by the *melanocytes* which are interspersed among the germinative cells of the *Stratum germinativum*. These amoeba-like cells put out projections called *pseudopodia* through which they inject granules of melanin into the newly produced cells of the epidermis. In dark races the melanocytes are continuously active, producing strongly coloured melanin granules. In white races the melanocytes may be producing uncoloured or partly coloured granules which only colour fully when exposed to ultra-violet rays. On the normally covered parts of the skin they might not be active at all.

Bearing in mind the brown, pink and yellow components of skin colour will make it much easier to mix paints and the pigments for face powders and camouflage make-up.

Self-assessment questions

1 List the eight functions of the skin.

2 Despite the changes in size and shape of the body due to movement, growth and slimming, why does the skin always 'fit'?

3 Name the four layers of the epidermis.

4 What is the additional layer of the epidermis of the palms and soles?

5 How does the epidermis guard against harmful radiation?

6 What is percutaneous absorption?

7 Give one advantage and one disadvantage of percutaneous absorption.

8 State two functions of the sebum.

9 What are prickle cells? Why are they so called?

10 Briefly describe the changes that occur to an epidermal cell from the time it is formed to the time of its eventual loss.

11 What is a *dermal papilla*?

12 State two functions of the subcutaneous fatty layer.

13 Distinguish between eccrine and apocrine sweat glands and between the sweat each type produces.

14 What is an *arrector pili* muscle?

15 Name the three main components of the colour of the skin.

10 A Clean Face

The nature of dirt on the skin; removing greasy dirt; formulation of cleansing creams; cold creams and cleansing lotions; astringents and skin tonics

Dirt on the skin

The skin becomes soiled with an assortment of solid particles which are stuck to it by the coating of greasy sebum. The solids include:

1 *Skin scales* which have become loosened but not fallen away.
2 *Dust* which is fine clay particles which settle out of the air or are picked up by contact.
3 *Soot* – fine particles of carbon from smoke.
4 *Salt* and *urea* left on the skin after the evaporation of sweat.
5 *Bacteria*, some of which are regular inhabitants of the skin. Others are picked up from the environment.

If make-up has been used, the skin will also be coated with the pigmented powders which have been made to adhere by the greases, waxes and oils of the make-up base.

Before the solid dirt will clean away, it must first be loosened by removing much of the sebum or other grease which binds it to the skin.

Removal of grease from the skin

There are three ways of removing grease from the skin:

1 *Emulsify it* with a detergent. Soaps, shower gels, bubble baths and cleansing lotions are all detergent products which remove grease by emulsifying it. The action of detergent cleansers is described in chapter 7.

2 *Dissolve it* with more oil. Cleansing creams, cold creams and body oils remove grease by dissolving it in oil.

3 *Absorb it* with an absorbent powder. A cleansing face pack is made from grease-absorbent powders such as kaolin, Fuller's earth or magnesium carbonate mixed to a paste in water. When applied, the water evaporates leaving the powders in close contact with the skin so they may absorb the grease by *capillary action*. The grease is drawn by surface tension into the narrow spaces between the particles.

When most of the grease has been removed, the dirt is loose and can be rinsed or wiped away.

Some dirt does become more deeply ingrained, particularly in the pores of the follicles and sweat glands. *Warming* the skin will *increase* the secretion of the sweat glands and sebaceous glands and so flush out the pores and 'deep cleanse' the skin. The warmth may come from hot water, a hot face pack, a steam bath, a sauna or a heat lamp. Followed by an astringent or skin tonic to close the pores this gives a marvellous, refreshing feeling of 'cleanliness'.

Cleansing creams and cold creams

Although most cosmetic formularies give separately formulations for *cold creams* and *cleansing creams*, they are essentially the same kind of product.

They are usually creams with a *high oil content* often as 'water-in-oil' emulsions. The emulsion, by design, is not particularly stable so that when applied the water content quickly *evaporates* causing a *cooling effect*; hence 'cold cream'.

This leaves the oil-phase to mix with, and dissolve, the grease on the skin so that it is removed when the cream is wiped away.

Formulations for cleansing creams and cold creams

Each of these formulations can be made by the method detailed in chapter 6. For convenience, the oil-phase and water-phase ingredients are grouped and the mixing temperature is indicated.

The first group of formulations are for *beeswax–borax creams*. Beeswax creams are among the oldest skin creams known. In the second century the Greek physician Galen made a crude cream by mixing water into a blend of molten *beeswax* and olive oil. By the late nineteenth century, *borax* was used to stabilise it.

The sodium of the borax – sodium tetraborate – combines with cerotic acid from the beeswax to form *sodium cerotate*, a kind of 'soap' which acts as the emulsifier and in effect turns beeswax into a self-emulsifying wax. Here is the basic formulation:

White beeswax	– 18	oil phase	mix at 70°C
Almond oil	– 61		
Borax	– 1	water phase	
Rose water	– 20		
Rose oil or essence	– q.s.		
Preservative	– q.s.		

The formulations which follow show how a product such as this has developed over the years. The vegetable oil creams tend to be very 'heavy'. In modern creams, *mineral oil* forms the bulk of the oil phase. This results in a much lighter product. Here are two formulations based on mineral oil:

White beeswax	– 16	oil phase	mix at 70°C
Mineral oil	– 50		
Borax	– 0.8	water phase	
Water	– 33.2		
Perfume	– q.s.		
Preservative	– q.s.		

White beeswax	– 9	oil phase	mix at 70°C
Mineral oil	– 45		
Paraffin wax	– 10		
Cetyl alcohol	– 1		
Borax	– 0.5	water phase	
Water	– 34.5		
Perfume	– q.s.		
Preservative	– q.s.		

In the latter formulation other waxes – *paraffin wax* and *cetyl alcohol* – replace part of the beeswax.

Note the use of *rose* perfume. Beeswax has a very distinctive odour. This is complemented well by rose perfumes. Hence rose has become virtually the 'signature' of skin creams.

In the next formulation the beeswax has given up its emulsifying role to a *non-ionic self-emulsifying wax*, Lanbritol wax N21:

Lanbritol wax N21	– 10	oil phase	mix at 70°C
Paraffin wax (55°C melting point)	– 5		
White beeswax	– 5		
Mineral oil	– 20		
Water	– 60	– water phase	
Perfume, preservative	– q.s.		

In the next two examples, beeswax has been replaced by *microcrystalline wax*, a paraffin wax which has a similar 'fudge-like' consistency.

Ingredient	Amount	Phase	
Lanbritol wax N21	6	oil phase	mix at 70°C
Microcrystalline wax	3		
Mineral oil	40		
Cetyl alcohol	2		
Water	49	water phase	
Perfume, preservative	q.s.		

The self-emulsifying wax in this example is an *anionic* one, Lanette wax SX. Anionic emulsifying wax BP is similar.

Ingredient	Amount	Phase	
Lanette wax SX	16	oil phase	mix at 70°C
Mineral oil	20		
Microcrystalline wax	3		
Glycerol	5	water phase	
Water	56		
Perfume, preservative	q.s.		

The glycerol in this cream gives it a 'moisturising' function. Soap is frequently used as an emulsifier in creams. The next formulation uses a soap – *triethanolamine stearate*. This is a light cream. Methyl cellulose is used to thicken it.

Ingredient	Amount	Phase	
Mineral oil	30	oil phase	mix at 70°C
Stearic acid	10		
Triethanolamine	2	water phase	
Methyl cellulose	0.5		
Water	57.5		
Perfume, preservative	q.s.		

Non-aqueous cleansing creams

As it is the oil phase of a cleansing cream which does the cleansing, there is no reason why the cleanser should not consist of just an oil phase and have no water phase at all.

Soft paraffin ('Vaseline') or mineral oil ('Liquid paraffin') can be used as cleansers just as they are. *Baby oil* is little more than a perfumed mineral oil. However neither product is easy to use. Soft paraffin tends to 'drag' and is difficult to wipe cleanly away. Mineral oil is a mobile liquid and is difficult to control when applying it to the face.

A mixture of carefully selected waxes, soft paraffin and oils can produce a *liquefying cleansing cream*:

Ingredient	Amount	Method
Isopropyl myristate	25	Melt together at 65°C, perfume and pour into jar
Mineral oil	25	
White soft paraffin	30	
Paraffin wax (55°C)	20	
Perfume	q.s.	

Isopropyl myristate and *isopropyl palmitate* are two similar esters which in appearance are much 'lighter' oils than mineral oil.

In the jar this is quite a firm, solid product, but as soon as it is disturbed by taking some from the jar and spreading it on the skin, it becomes quite mobile and spreads easily. The product is *thixotropic*. It has variable viscosity.

Cleansing milks

The main problem with oil-based cleansers is removing them from the skin afterwards! A cleanser based on water is much easier to wipe away or even to rinse away with clean water. Cleansing milks and lotions are water-based.

Cleansing milks are similar in formulation to cleansing creams but contain much more water plus sufficient 'spare' emulsifier to cleanse by *detergent* action. They *emulsify* the grease on the skin.

The first of the two formulations is emulsified with a soap – triethanolamine stearate. The second contains two emulsifiers, the non-ionic glycerol monostearate and the anionic sodium lauryl sulphate, the latter acting as a detergent cleanser.

Mineral oil	– 10	oil phase	mix at 70°C
Cetyl alcohol	– 0.5		
Stearic acid	– 3		
Triethanolamine	– 1.8	water phase	
Water	– 84.7		
Perfume, preservative	– q.s.		
Mineral oil	– 30	oil phase	mix at 70°C
Cetyl alcohol	– 1.5		
Glycerol monostearate SE	– 0.5		
Sodium lauryl sulphate	– 1.0	water phase	
Water	– 67		
Perfume, preservative	– q.s.		

This formulation forms quite a *viscous* lotion, perhaps more a light cream, and should be packed in a plastic 'squeeze' bottle or plastic collapsible tube rather than a rigid glass bottle.

Cleansing lotions

These are solutions of *detergents* in water. Usually there are no 'oil phase' materials so they are particularly useful on greasy skins where the additional greasiness of a cleansing cream or milk might aggravate the problem. A typical formulation is shown here. Any of the 'shampoo' detergents could be used but the proportion used should be adjusted to take account of its 'active matter' content (see chapter 8).

Triethanolamine lauryl sulphate (40 per cent)	– 5	stir together
Water	– 95	
Perfume, colour, preservative	– q.s.	

Fresh-up pads and tissues

A major 'plus' for cleansing creams and lotions is the ability to use them away from the bathroom situation. The ultimate portability is provided by *fresh-up pads* or *tissues*. These are discs of lint or squares of tissue impregnated with a detergent solution:

Triethanolamine lauryl sulphate (40 per cent)	– 1	stir together
Glycerin	– 2	
Water	– 97	
Perfume, preservative	– q.s.	

The lint circles or tissue squares are dipped in this lotion and stored in airtight tins or tubs.

Perfumes for water-based lotions

When selecting perfumes for products with a *high water content*, choose ones which are made specifically for such products. These will contain a *solubiliser* (see chapter 7) so they will 'dissolve' in the water-based product.

A product evaluation exercise

This chapter has described a wide selection of products all for the same purpose, to cleanse the skin of the face of greasy dirt and make-up.

If you have made up samples of each of the formulations, their effectiveness can be compared in a product evaluation test such as a manufacturer might use (see also chapter 23).

Make-up an area of skin such as the back of the hand or inside the forearm with a selection of make-up products. Put on bands of tinted foundation, eye make-up, lipstick, mascara.

Now use each of the cleansers in turn to remove some of each make-up product. For each product note the following properties:

1 Ease of application.
2 Any tendency to 'drag' on skin when applied.
3 Ease of mixing with the make-up.
4 Ease of removal from skin.
5 Its effectiveness at removing all trace of make-up.
6 The condition of the skin afterwards. Is it left dry, greasy, normal?

Tabulate the results, then pick a 'winning product' for your skin or your preference.

Astringents and skin tonics

Astringent lotions and skin tonics are not strictly cleansing products but their cooling and refreshing action provides the ideal finishing touch to the cleansing process.

Strictly speaking, an *astringent* is something which will close the pores of the skin, thereby reducing the secretion of perspiration and sebum. However, as this is the *natural* response of the skin to being *cooled*, products which cool and refresh the skin will be astringent too.

Astringent materials

Considering that the skin has no muscles of its own, it is difficult to imagine how the *Stratum corneum* can tighten and the pores can close as a result of using an astringent.

It can only happen as a result of reforming the salt-type cross linkages between the molecules of keratin (see chapter 9). This will happen either if the skin is *cooled* or if it is restored to its slightly acidic pH of 4.5 to 6.

Water and alcohol are astringent by virtue of the *cooling* effect on the skin resulting from their *evaporation*.

When a liquid evaporates, it changes to a gas or vapour. To bring about the actual change requires the input of a certain amount of *heat* energy. This is called the latent heat of vaporisation (see chapter 2). For a liquid evaporating from the skin, the latent heat is taken from the skin, hence the cooling effect.

Certain *aromatic* materials are astringent through an *irritant* effect. They trigger the cold sensing nerve endings in the skin producing a *cool sensation*. The skin then behaves as if it *were* cold. The superficial blood vessels contract, cutting the supply of warming blood. The skin cools. It tightens and the pores close. Such aromatics include menthol, sage and camphor.

Some multivalent *metal cations* such as *aluminium* (Al^{3+}) and *zinc* (Zn^{2+}) have an overall astringent effect as well as their direct *antiperspirant* action (see chapter 11). These ions are able to coagulate liquid proteins by causing cross linkages to form both within and between their molecules. They are able therefore to reform the cross linkages in keratin.

Alum (aluminium potassium sulphate) and *calamine* (basic zinc carbonate) are old favourites in astringent lotions. Zinc sulphate is an extremely mild astringent commonly used in eye lotions.

Formulations for astringent lotions

These are two formulations for *alum-based* astringent lotions – one is mild, the other much stronger:

	Mild	*Strong*
Aluminium potassium sulphate	1.0	4.0
Zinc sulphate	0.3	—
Glycerol	5.0	6.0
Rose water	50.0	35.0
Orange-flower water	—	35.0
Water	43.7	20.0
Colour	q.s.	q.s.

Dissolve the alum, glycerol and zinc sulphate in the water with gentle heat. Cool. Add the flower waters. Filter if necessary.

Note that some flower waters are produced using an *anionic* surfactant as a solubiliser. The alum is quite acidic and may be incompatible with these, causing the product to fail. Make sure that the flower waters used are solubilised with *non-ionic* surfactants. The flower waters described in chapters 7 and 22 will work.

Next is shown the formulation for a traditional *skin tonic* lotion:

Borax	– 2
Alcohol	– 10
Rose water	– 40
Water	– 48
Colour	– q.s.

Dissolve the borax in the water with heat. Cool. Add the water and rose-water. A trace of menthol may be included if desired.

Alcohol is the major astringent in modern perfume-colognes and after-shave lotions. For formulations, see chapter 22.

Things to do

1 Any of the formulations described in the chapter may be made and used.

2 If you have made a selection of the cleansers, use them as the basis of the Product Evaluation Exercise described in the chapter. See also chapter 23.

Self-assessment questions

1 Describe briefly the composition of dirt on the skin.

2 State three ways of removing grease-bound dirt from the skin.

3 Why is a cold cream so called?

4 How is the combination of beeswax and borax able to act as an emulsifier for creams and lotions?

5 What is meant by the term 'astringent'?

6 Give three examples of astringent raw materials?

7 What is the chemical name for alum?

8 Why is a lotion containing water or alcohol able to cool the skin?

11 Products for the Bath & Shower

Use of soaps and detergents for bathing; bubble baths and shower gels; softening the bath water; bath salts, bath crystals, bath cubes; bath oils and bath essences; talcs and dusting powders; antiperspirants and deodorants

Bathing with soap

Until comparatively recently, cleansing the body meant sitting in a bath of water and washing with *soap*. For a growing number of people, two developments have changed that. One was the development of soapless detergents and the *bubble bath*. The other is the fast growing trend towards the *shower*.

For many though, the preference is the ritual of a long soak in a hot bath. Very beneficial it is too, so long as you do *not* sit and soak in *soapy* water.

The brief encounter with *alkaline* soap when washing one's hands and face is not usually likely to be a problem. But *prolonged* contact with soapy water will first thoroughly degrease the skin. Then having removed the pH balancing *sebum*, the soap will cause the pH of the skin to rise. In *alkaline* conditions the cells of the horny layer of the skin *swell* and start to separate, leaving the skin '*open*' to possible entry of bacteria or harmful chemicals.

'Bath soakers' should either wash quickly then refill the bath with clean water for the soak, or soak first in the clean water and leave washing with soap until just before getting out.

Bubble baths or foam baths

Many 'bath-soakers' like the luxury of soaking in a bath amid the copious foam of a *bubble bath*, surrounded by the 'clean' smell of its *perfume*. But the owners of *dry skins* should *beware*.

Bubble bath detergents, like soaps, can excessively degrease the skin during a long soak. Those with dry skins should perhaps use a *bath oil* instead.

The initial impact of a bubble bath is its ability to produce a '*flash foam*', that is, to foam profusely with little agitation of the water. The best detergent for this is *sodium lauryl ether sulphate*. The foam is stabilised by either an amphoteric detergent such as a *betaine*, or a non-ionic coconut ethanolamide. Table 11.1 shows some formulations for *liquid bubble baths*. To make them, mix the surfactants and water together, warming gently if necessary. Then add the other ingredients.

Table 11.1 Formulations for Liquid Bubble Baths

	(1)	*(2)*	*(3)*
Sodium lauryl ether sulphate (25 per cent)	60	40	70
N-alkyl betaine	5	—	—
Coconut diethanolamide	—	5	10
Water	35	55	20
Preservative	q.s.	q.s.	q.s.
Suitable perfume	q.s.	q.s.	q.s.
Water-soluble colour	q.s.	q.s.	q.s.

Not so popular commercially, but an interesting novelty, are *powder bubble baths* or *foaming bath salts*. Here is an example:

Sodium lauryl sulphate (powder)	– 40
Sodium tripolyphosphate	– 5
Sodium sesquicarbonate	– 55
Perfume, colour	– q.s.

The dry ingredients are mixed in a tumble mixer (see chapter 6). In the laboratory a polythene bag can be used. Take care with sodium lauryl sulphate powder. Its dust flies and, if inhaled, may irritate the lungs. You will sneeze bubbles! In manufacture, perfume and colour are sprayed into the mixer. In the lab, mix these liquids first with a little *light magnesium carbonate* with a spatula on a watch glass. Then add to the main mix.

Shower gels and body shampoos

Showers have become a popular installation in our bathrooms and indeed are an effective way of cleansing the body. You wash with soap or a shower gel, then rinse in *clean* running water.

Soap is a problem in a shower, particularly as most shower cubicles have no soap dish. A 'soap-on-a-rope' is one solution; the other is a *shower gel* in a plastic collapsible tube with a hook to hang it from the shower head.

A shower gel has to be suitable to cleanse both body and hair. Some people, particularly men, like to shampoo their hair while taking a shower. The product needs to be viscous so it does not rinse away too quickly. Here are two typical formulations:

Monoethanolamine lauryl sulphate (33 per cent)	– 40
N-alkyl betaine	– 10
Water	– 50
Perfume, colour, preservative	– q.s.
Sodium lauryl ether sulphate (25 per cent)	– 80
Coconut diethanolamide	– 3
Sodium chloride	– q.s.
Water	– 17
Perfume, colour, preservative	– q.s.

Both formulations are made by mixing the surfactant and water together, warming if necessary. Salt is added to the second formulation, in sufficient quantity to adjust the viscosity.

If desired, the pH of both formulations may be adjusted to pH 6.5 by adding a little citric acid. It will not then irritate if it gets in the eyes.

Bath salts, bath crystals, bath cubes

In chapter 5, we saw the problems of *hard water*, particularly when used with soap: the formation of that *scum* which is so difficult to rinse from the bath after use.

We also saw that various alkaline sodium salts could be added to water to remove the hardness. Bath salts, crystals and cubes are attractive ways of adding water softeners and at the same time a pleasant perfume.

Bath crystals

Bath crystals are basically washing soda, *sodium carbonate* decahydrate ($Na_2CO_3.10H_2O$) to which colour and perfume have been added. Commercial washing soda consists of crystals of a wide variety of sizes. For bath crystals choose a graded type called, for obvious reasons, 'pea-crystals'.

The crystals are coloured with a dilute solution of suitable dye and perfumed with a few drops of liquid perfume. These are added to the crystals in a tumbler mixer or polythene bag and are mixed in gently. The crystals will take up quite an amount of liquid without getting physically wet. But *do not* overdo it.

Bath crystals have disadvantages. They dissolve slowly. If you get in the bath too soon you may sit uncomfortably! If they get too warm, over 35°C, they melt and then will set to a solid mass in the jar. If left open in a dry place, they *effloresce*: they lose water and collapse to a white powder.

Bath salts

These consist of a hybrid substance, *sodium sesquicarbonate*. This free-flowing crystalline powder is a combination of sodium carbonate and bicarbonate. It is readily available as a domestic laundry water softener from a well known chain of chemists. It is easily coloured and perfumed to make bath salts.

Put a batch of sodium sesquicarbonate in a tumble mixer or polythene bag. To colour it use a pigment powder suitable for cosmetics. Soluble powder colours are available for this purpose. The perfume may either be sprayed in or first be absorbed on to a little light magnesium carbonate which is then added to the powder in the mixer.

This formulation is for *effervescent bath salts* which will 'fizz' when added to the water. Carbon dioxide bubbles are produced when a mixture of a carbonate and an acid gets wet:

Sodium sesquicarbonate	– 25
Sodium bicarbonate	– 55
Tartaric acid	– 20
Perfume, colour	– q.s.

If a suitable press is available, this mixture can be sprayed with gum and pressed to form *bath cubes*. Here the effervescence is useful to break up the cube when it is added to the bathwater.

Not always does one want bath salts to soften the water. This formulation is just to perfume the bathwater:

Sodium chloride	– 95 to 99
Perfume	– 1 to 5
Colour	– q.s.

Bath oils and essences

These may be added to the bathwater for two purposes. First to leave a *lubricating film* of oil on the skin and second to *perfume* the bathroom.

The film of oil left on the skin as one leaves the bath is of particular value to dry skins which might have been aggravated by a soap and water bath.

The products are of two types:

Floating–spreading bath oils which remain on the surface of the bathwater
Dispersible bath oils and *essences* which mix with the bathwater

Floating–spreading bath oils

A basic bath oil might be:

Mineral oil	– 95
Perfume	– 5
Oil-soluble colour	– q.s.

Other oils might be used instead of the mineral oil, for instance, vegetable oils such as olive oil, groundnut oil, sunflower oil or castor oil. The oily film left by both vegetable and mineral oils does however tend to be rather greasy on the skin.

The fatty acid esters *isopropyl myristate* and *isopropyl palmitate* are much lighter oils and rub in well so they do not leave the skin greasy. Here is a formulation using them:

Isopropyl myristate or palmitate	– 95
Perfume	– 5
Oil-soluble colour	– q.s.

When added to the bath, these products will tend to form 'blobs' of oil on the water rather than spreading evenly. If a little of a suitable emulsifier is added, it will help the oil spread to form an even film on the water. A suitable emulsifier is a polyoxyethylene polyol fatty acid ester such as Arlatone T by Atlas Chemicals. It is included in this formulation:

Light mineral oil	– 46
Isopropyl myristate	– 48
Perfume	– 5
Arlatone T	– 1

A snag with floating bath oils is the oily ring left on the bath after it has been emptied. This is even more a problem if the water is hard and soap has been used for washing. The 'tidemark' then is oil plus soap scum.

Dispersible bath oils

If a suitable emulsifier is added to the bath oil formulation in a larger quantity, the product will then *disperse* into the water as a milky cloud. Brij 93 by Atlas (polyoxyethylene (2) oleyl ether) is such an emulsifier. Other emulsifiers of HLB value around 5 will probably do. This formulation includes Brij 93:

Mineral oil	– 65
Isopropyl myristate	– 20
Brij 93	– 10
Perfume	– 5

This formulation is known as 'Instant Bloom'. Some experimentation with different amounts of emulsifier may be needed to obtain the proper cloud effect as it is poured into the water.

Foaming bath oils

These are not truly bath oils as they contain no oil as such to form a film on the skin. They are just bubble baths with a high level of perfume. A solubiliser such as polyoxyethylene sorbitan monolaurate (Tween 20 by Atlas) is necessary to solubilise the perfume in the bathwater. Here is a formulation:

Perfume	– 5	Mix together	Mix together
Tween 20	– 20		
Sodium lauryl ether sulphate	– 40	Warm and mix together	
Coconut diethanolamide	– 2		
Water	– 33		
Preservative	– q.s.		

Bath essences

Bath essences are used for perfuming only. The perfume is solubilised into water with Tween 20. Here is a basic formulation:

Perfume	– 5
Tween 20	– 5 to 25
Water	– to make 100
Preservative	– q.s.

Mix the perfume and Tween 20, and then add water to the mixture. The amount of Tween 20 depends on the perfume and must be found by experiment: too little and the perfume will not fully mix, too much and the product will foam.

'*Perfume oils*' for the bath can be made by mixing the perfume with a suitable amount of Tween 20. No water is included.

Perfume concentrate – 15
Tween 20 – 85

The solubilisation will then occur when the product is added to the bathwater.

Talcs and dusting powders

A talc is applied to the body for two reasons. First it acts as a dry lubricant to impart a smooth feel to the skin. Second it dries perspiration and residual moisture left on the skin after a bath or shower.

Strictly speaking to be called *talcum powder* it must contain over 50 per cent of the mineral *talc*. If it does not, it is a dusting powder.

Raw materials for talcum powders

Talc is a mineral which occurs widely throughout the world. Chemically it is basically *hydrated magnesium silicate*. It is a very variable substance, different grades being found even in the same lump.

The best talc comes in the form of flat, plate-like particles which are able to slide over each other giving it a *lubricant* action. Talc itself is *hydrophobic*: it repels water. The '*drying*' effect of talc is because it remains dry, even on a moist skin.

To absorb moisture the talcum powder must actually contain water absorbents such as *magnesium carbonate, calcium carbonate, starch* or *kaolin.*

To assist adhesion of the powder to the skin, talcum powders often contain insoluble soaps such as *zinc, magnesium* or *aluminium stearates.*

Talcum powder formulations

The variations on the talcum powder theme are endless. Table 11.2 shows just five of the thousands of possible formulations.

Figure 11.1 Absorbing the perfume for a talcum powder on to light magnesium carbonate

Table 11.2 Talcum Powder Formulations

	(1)	*(2)*	*(3)*	*(4)*	*(5)*
Talc	95	85	70	70	75
Magnesium carbonate – light	5	—	—	—	5
Starch	—	10	—	10	—
Zinc oxide – a white pigment	—	5	—	—	—
Calcium carbonate – precipitated	—	—	25	—	—
Zinc stearate	—	—	5	—	5
Magnesium stearate	—	—	—	5	—
Kaolin	—	—	—	15	10
Colloidal silica – a very fine sand	—	—	—	—	5

In industry a talc is mixed in a tumbler mixer. The perfume is sprayed in. In the laboratory, samples may be mixed in a tumbler mixer or in a polythene bag. To perfume them, absorb the perfume on to a little light magnesium carbonate, then add this 'powder perfume' to the main mix (see figure 11.1).

Potential hazards of talc

In recent years there have been a number of 'scares' regarding the use of talc and other minerals in cosmetics and toiletries.

1 **Dust**. The finest particles of talc are able to remain floating in the air and if breathed in could cause respiratory problems. British Standards specifications demand that these fine particles are removed from cosmetic grades.

2 **Asbestos**. Some kinds of talc have a high content of Tremolite, a form of asbestos. These grades are not used for personal products because of possible cancer risk.

3 **Tetanus**. Talc, the mineral, is sterile but, like any mineral, it can become contaminated with tetanus spores from the soil during quarrying. Talcs for personal use have been sterilised. If, however, you wish to make sure, you can 'stove' any mineral raw material by spreading it on shallow trays and heating in an oven at 200°C for at least one hour.

Antiperspirants and deodorants

Following a bath or shower an antiperspirant or deodorant may be used to *preserve* one's personal freshness. People are often confused by there being *antiperspirants, deodorants* and even '*antiperspirant deodorants*'. What is the difference between them? Indeed is there any difference? They are after all for use on the same area, the underarms.

A *deodorant*, as its name implies, is to eliminate unpleasant body odour.

An *antiperspirant* is to reduce the level of perspiration and eliminate that unsightly wetness in the underarm area. In doing so the antiperspirant also eliminates the odour – hence 'antiperspirant deodorant'.

To understand the working of antiperspirants and deodorants, we must first remind ourselves of the special problems of maintaining freshness in the underarm area. Almost all the skin has *eccrine sweat glands* producing watery sweat in response to the need to cool the body. The problem in the underarms is that with two layers of skin facing each other the sweat cannot evaporate – hence the wetness. The underarms also have *apocrine sweat glands* producing their milky sweat which in the warm, enclosed conditions is acted upon by bacteria resulting in the unpleasant odour, 'B.O.'.

Deodorants

To eliminate 'B.O.' most deodorants attack its cause, the bacteria. They contain a variety of skin bactericides.

Permitted bactericides under the *EEC Cosmetics Directive* include:

Bradosol	Chloroxylenol	Hexachlorophene
Bronopol	Dichlorophen	Thimersol
Cetrimide	Dichloroxylenol	Triclosan

The bactericide at its recommended level is incorporated into an alcohol and water lotion, probably to be used as a spray, or it may be included in a talcum powder.

Remember that soap and water are quite good at removing bacteria from the skin. A good wash under the arms is a good start to personal freshness. The deodorant then serves to *preserve* the freshness.

Antiperspirants

Antiperspirants tackle the personal freshness problem at its root-cause. By strong *astringent* action they close the pores and drastically reduce the output of both kinds of sweat.

They work by the action of certain multivalent metal cations, notably aluminium (Al^{3+}) and zirconium (Zr^{3+}). How they work though is not really known.

The aluminium and zirconium compounds used are rather *acidic* in character. In acid conditions the level of bacterial action is reduced which helps to prevent 'B.O.'.

The aluminium chloride or sulphate used in early antiperspirants proved rather *too* acidic at pH 2 with the result that they tended to irritate the skin and rot one's clothing.

Nowadays the commonly used antiperspirant materials are:

Aluminium chlorohydrate (or hydroxychloride) and
Zirconium aluminium chlorohydrate

A chlorohydrate is a hybrid chloride–hydroxide compound. Aluminium chlorohydrate is used in spray, 'roll-on' and 'stick' antiperspirants. The zirconium complex is probably more effective, but because it is more irritant to the respiratory system if breathed in, it cannot be used in spray products.

Formulations for antiperspirants

This is a basic formulation for a liquid spray antiperspirant that may be packed in a plastic squeeze bottle or as a 'wet-spray' aerosol.

Aluminium chlorohydrate	– 20
Propandiol	– 5
Alcohol	– 10
Deodorant bactericide	– 0.2
Water	– 64.8
Perfume	– q.s.

For a 'roll-on', the product may be thickened in two ways:

1 Disperse methyl cellulose (q.s.) in part of the water. Let it stand overnight, then add to the main formulation.

2 Add sufficient sodium citrate or sodium tartrate to the lotion to give the required viscosity. It thickens by reacting with the chlorohydrate.

The problem with both wet spray and roll-on antiperspirants is that they take quite a time to dry before you can dress.

Aerosol antiperspirants nowadays are almost all '*dry*' products. The aluminium chlorohydrate is mixed with a fine talc plus a silicone to stop it clogging the aerosol valve. The aerosol is pressurised with a propellant such as propellant-12 which emerges from the valve as a gas so there is no wetness on the skin when the product is used. Aerosols are described in chapter 24.

Although aerosol dry antiperspirants are easy to apply, they can leave a lot of powder drifting in the air which many people find irritant if inhaled. An alternative dry product is the *stick antiperspirant*. Here the antiperspirant ingredient diluted with talc is incorporated into a wax base and cast into sticks in the same way as the stick make-up described in chapter 14. Here is a possible formulation:

Mineral oil	– 47.5	Wax base
Paraffin wax 55°C	– 3.5	Wax base
Beeswax	– 1.5	Wax base
Carnauba wax	– 4.0	Wax base
Aluminium chlorohydrate	– 20.0	
Talc	– 23.5	

Melt together the ingredients for the wax base. Mix together the aluminium chlorohydrate and talc then thoroughly mix this in the molten wax base. Add a suitable perfume, then cast into sticks directly into clean stick containers.

Things to do

Any of the formulations described in the chapter may be made and used. Should there be any difficulty in obtaining certain raw materials, the names and addresses of suppliers may be found in advertisements in the 'trade' journals such as *Soap, Perfumery and Cosmetics* and *The Manufacturing Chemist*.

Self-assessment questions

1 Why is it inadvisable to soak oneself for long periods in soapy water?

2 What is the water-softening ingredient in (a) bath salts and (b) bath crystals?

3 What gas is given off when a mixture of a carbonate and a crystalline acid is added to water?

4 What is the chemical name for talc?

5 How does talc perform its 'drying' function?

6 What illnesses could result from using talc contaminated (a) with Tremolite asbestos and (b) with bacterial spores?

7 Distinguish between an antiperspirant and a deodorant.

8 Name one active material used in an antiperspirant.

12 Skin Care – the Problems

Problems of the younger skin; dry skin; emollients; moisturisers; acids in skin care; greasy skin; acne; caring for greasy skin; the aging skin; the natural aging process; premature aging; the effects of ultra-violet rays

Caring for the skin

Keeping the skin in good order it would seem, is a constant and life long battle. There are skin care problems both for the young and for those showing the signs of being not so young any more.

This chapter discusses the skin care problems and the products available to overcome them. The formulation of skin care cosmetics is the subject of the next chapter, chapter 13.

Problems of the young skin

The owner of the young face is quite likely to be very preoccupied with whether or not her skin is *greasy*, *dry* or '*normal*'.

A *normal* skin is one which has just sufficient sebum to prevent it showing the symptoms of dryness, yet not so much as to give it a greasy shine. In addition, within the squames of the horny layer there is sufficient of a *Natural Moisturising Factor* or NMF, to hold in the moisture necessary to keep the skin soft and supple.

The presence of this natural moisturising factor has been demonstrated experimentally but is chemical nature is far from certain. It has been variously described as *aminolipid*, *mucoprotein* or *lipomucopolysaccharide* which means it could be a complex of protein and fatty substances, carbohydrate and protein, or fat and carbohydrate!

It is rare to find a face which has 'normal' skin all over. Because of the greater number of sebaceous glands on the forehead, on and around the nose, above the upper lip and on the chin, the so-called *centre panel* often tends to be greasy. In contrast, the cheeks with their sparcer population of sebaceous glands tend to be dry. This is the very common '*Combination skin*'.

Dry skin

A dry skin is defined as a skin which 'looks dry' and which is improved by the application of emollients or moisturisers. Research has shown that the moisture content of a dry skin is no less than that of a normal skin. However, for it to look normal, a dry skin needs to have a *higher* than normal moisture content and sebum cover. If it has not the extra sebum and 'natural moisturising factor', it will be unable to hold the extra moisture.

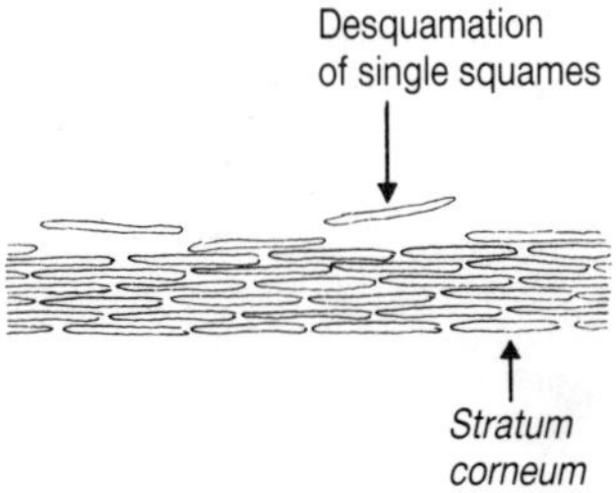

Figure 12.1 Normal desquamation

The fault with a dry skin lies in the mechanism of *desquamation* (see chapter 9). In a normal skin the glycoprotein–lipoprotein 'cement' which holds the surface layer of squames degenerates completely so they fall away individually and invisibly (see figure 12.1).

In a dry skin, the cement does not degenerate completely and the surface squames tend to 'hang on'. Moisture loss causes them to curl up at the edges rather like slices of stale bread. This makes the skin *rough* to the touch and matt or dull in appearance (see figure 12.2). It is often itchy too.

When the squames do break away they come away in groups or aggregates as visible scales like dandruff. This is *scaling* (see figure 12.3).

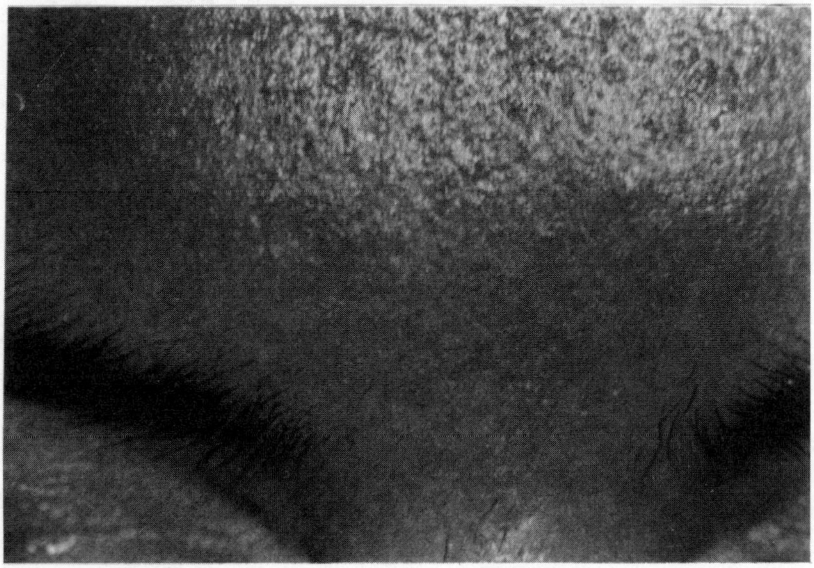

Figure 12.2 Dry skin on the forehead

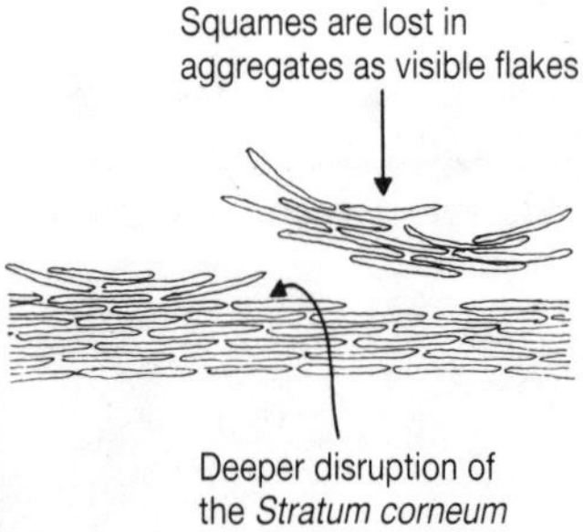

Figure 12.3 Scaling desquamation of a visibly dry skin

Chapped and cracked skins

Exposure to *wind* and *cold* reduces the sebum production of the sebaceous glands and allows the skin to lose more moisture than usual. This can induce the symptoms of dryness in an otherwise normal skin as well as further aggravating the problem of a dry skin. Excessive use of detergents and grease solvents on the skin can also have this effect.

The water loss might be sufficient to cause distress to the cells of the living layers so that some of them die and signal their plight by releasing *histamine* which causes *irritation* and *reddening*. The irritation process is fully described in chapter 23.

The more mobile parts of the skin such as the angles of the mouth or exposed parts like the ears may even *crack* (see figure 12.4). The fingers of hard-working hands can become crazed with cracks. Should a crack extend down through the living layers of the epidermis it will become painfully sore. If it reaches the blood capillaries of the dermis, it will bleed.

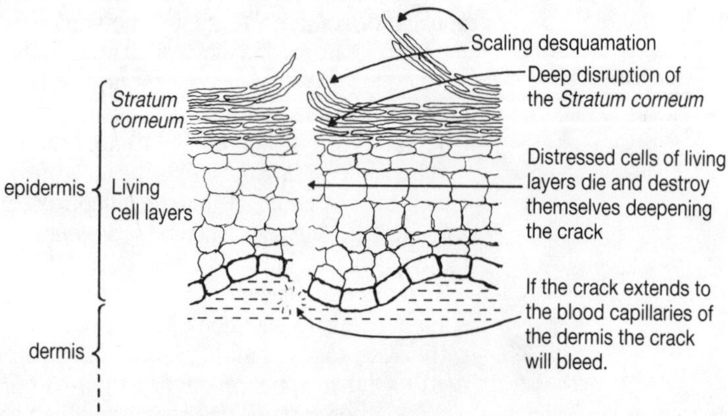

Figure 12.4 A crack develops in a dry and chapped skin

Caring for a dry skin

Many products are available for dry skins. They tackle the problem in one or more of three ways:

1. They may coat the skin with a greasy, waxy or oily film to supplement the waterproofing action of the sebum.
2. They may replace the lost moisture and attempt to hold it there by the *moisturising* action of a *humectant.*
3. They may attempt to replace the Natural Moisturising Factor of the squames. There is however no evidence to show that artificial 'NMF' applied to the surface of the skin actually finds its way into the squames.

Overall, dry skin care products impart upon the skin a smooth feel. The term *emollient* is used rather loosely for any substance which when applied to the skin gives it a smooth feel.

Emollient creams for dry skins

Coating the skin with a greasy, waxy or oily film may be done by using a cream with a relatively high oil content:

cold creams   *night creams*
nourishing creams   *sports creams*

A similar benefit may be had from an oil treatment:

hot oil treatment   *oil mask*

The effect of such a treatment will though be no longer-lasting than an application of cold cream. Using an oil coating alone does not however put back the lost moisture; the oil is being put on a still very dry skin.

Moisturising

A *moisturising* cream or lotion contains a *humectant.* This is a substance which is able to hold moisture in the upper layers of the epidermis and prevent it evaporating.

Humectants used in moisturisers include 'oily' water-soluble substances such as *glycerol*, *propylene glycol* or *sorbitol.*

Many of the 'natural' ingredients used in skin creams such as *soluble collagen*, *soluble elastin*, *vitamin* E or *oestrogen*, have a humectant action too. Indeed it could quite well be the only action they have.

If a humectant is used, a much lighter film of oil will now adequately waterproof the skin against water loss. Moisturising creams have a relatively *low* oil content.

The benefits of pH balanced creams and lotions

A skin deficient in sebum has little in the way of a protective *'acid mantle'* because the natural acids of the skin are part of sebum. It is therefore more likely to suffer a dryness aggravated by use of *alkalis* such as the humble *soap* and water (see chapter 2).

An acidic ingredient such as *citric acid* in 'Lemon' creams or *lactic acid* in 'Buttermilk' cream will restore the skin's acidity and combat the dryness aggravated by the alkaline soap. Such creams are often called *'pH balancing'* creams.

Greasy skins

It is the excessive sebum from overactive sebaceous glands which causes the problems of a greasy skin. The use of unnecessary excesses of oily and greasy cosmetics can produce the same effects. At least this will result in a greasy *'shine'*. More likely the complexion will become rather *'muddy'* as

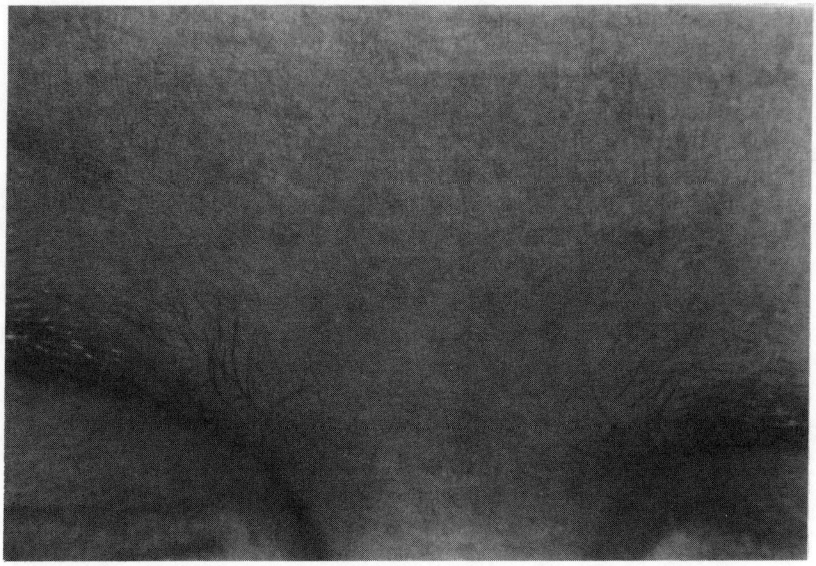

Figure 12.5 Greasy skin on the forehead

sloughed-off skin squames, instead of falling away, mix to a pulp in the excess sebum. Figure 12.5 shows the skin of a greasy forehead.

An unfortunate side effect of the greasiness is to encourage the development of the blackheads, spots and pimples of *acne*. An increase in sebaceous activity accompanies the general increase in glandular activity at puberty. The previously *normal* skin of childhood can become the greasy, acne-prone skin of adolescence. Thankfully, the sebaceous activity subsides again during one's twenties and the acne dies away.

Acne

The blackheads or *comedones* which characterise acne are plugs of a mixture of *keratin* and *sebum* which block the pores of the follicles (see figure 12.6). Often that is all that happens, resulting in a complexion punctuated by tiny black dots.

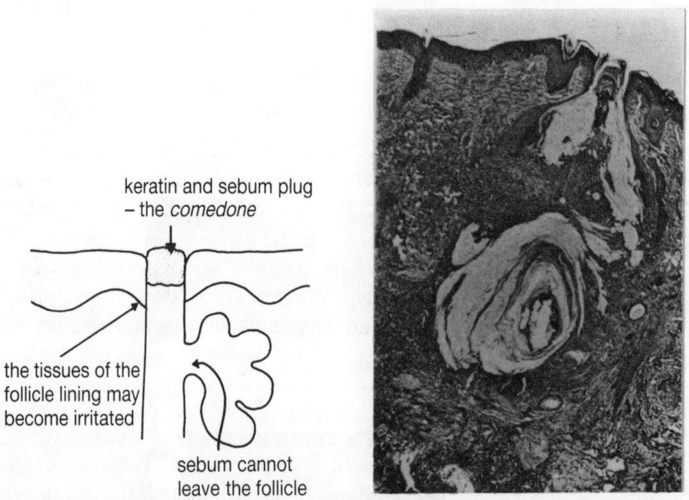

Figure 12.6 An acne comedone in section

The pressure of the sebum which cannot leave the follicle may push up a small mound, a small white pimple. The accumulated sebum might be forced into the living tissues of the skin. It could then become *irritant* and cause the eruption of the acne pustule.

Acne is *not* considered to be an infection but it is possible that *staphylococcus* bacteria could enter the follicle either as a result of squeezing the comedones or after the eruption of the pustule. Infection may then set in producing a *boil*.

If the acne pustules are particularly large, and this can happen if they become infected, the skin might become permanently pock-marked by their scars.

Caring for a greasy skin

Caring for a greasy skin involves regularly removing the excess sebum without stimulating the skin to produce even more. Effective and regular cleansing is the order of the day.

1 **Soap and water**
Washing with soap and water does tend to 'dry' the skin but it also tends to encourage bacteria.

2 **Intensive care cleansing lotions**
These soapless surfactant lotions often contain alcohol to act as astringents to reduce sebum output and skin disinfectants.

3 **Oil-absorbent face masks**
While these absorb and remove the excess oil, in doing so they can stimulate the production of more.

4 **Astringent lotions**
These can temporarily slow the production of sebum.

5 **Cathiodermy**
This is an electrical method (see volume 2) to remove excess grease from the skin and loosen the comedones but it, too, can stimulate sebaceous activity.

6 **High frequency electrotherapy**
This electrical treatment is both astringent and bactericidal (see volume 2).

The aging skin

A person does not have to be old in years to show the 'tell-tale' signs of an aging skin. Aging of the skin is more likely to be a product of *abuse* by the environment than of the advance of time.

How does one tell if those wrinkles are due to 'natural' aging or environmental abuse? Look at an area of the skin that is *not* normally exposed to the great outdoors. Any wrinkles there? If not, those on the face, the neck and the backs of the hands were caused by the environment. The skin is suffering from *premature aging*.

Natural aging of the skin

The *natural aging* of the skin is quite closely dependent on the levels of *hormone* activity in the body. Hormones are chemical substances produced in the body by the glands of the *endocrine system* to control the level of body activities, and this includes control of the processes of growth and replacement of the tissues. As one gets older the hormone levels decline with the result that the skin becomes less well maintained.

The *sebaceous glands* become less active. The sebum output is reduced and the skin becomes *drier*.

The *protein fibre network* of the dermis starts to break up and the skin *loses* its *firmness* and *elasticity*.

The *rate of growth* of the epidermis slows, resulting in a *thinning* of the *epidermis*.

Women at the *menopause* often experience a sudden and drastic reduction in hormone activity accompanied by an equally sudden deterioration in the skin.

In *men*, the reduction in hormone activity is usually more gradual and so the natural aging is spread over a much longer period.

A really *senile* skin has a papery thin epidermis over an inelastic and easily wrinkled dermis. Its blood vessels are easily ruptured by the slightest scratch or graze, and even minor bumps and knocks cause bruising.

Delaying natural aging

Nothing in the way of applied cosmetics can have much effect on natural aging. Those *rejuvenating* creams with their soluble collagen, natural elastin, mucopolysaccharides, natural moisturising factor and so on are unlikely to bring about any miracles. However most of these substances are *humectants* or moisturisers. They can be made to penetrate into the epidermis where they can help the aging skin 'plump up' with retained moisture.

There has been some interest in recent years in *hormone replacement therapy*. This is the use of pills, injections, or implants of hormones to boost the failing natural ones and delay the natural aging process.

Facelifts and other *plastic surgery* are of some help but it can only be temporary. 'Excess' skin is taken away so the remaining skin fits snuggly and those wrinkles disappear. But the old skin is *inelastic*; it will soon stretch again and the wrinkles will be back!

Premature aging – the effects of the environment

In the Sun's life-giving radiation are *ultra-violet* rays. In small doses, ultra-violet is beneficial. It is invigorating: it gives a feeling of 'well-being' and helps the body to make its own supplies of *vitamin D*.

In excess, however, ultra-violet is lethal to the living tissues and it is a prime function of the skin to screen the body within from these excesses. This it attempts to do by its three natural lines of defence:

1 The *sebum* – Grease absorbs ultra-violet.

2 The *stratum corneum* – The scale-like squames reflect back much of the ultra-violet.

3 The *melanin pigment* – The development of a tan absorbs much of the ultra-violet.

The skin of some people is able to respond quite quickly to excesses of ultra-violet by developing a *tan*. To do so the skin has to be in a state of readiness. It must have in it a supply of uncoloured *melanin* granules. Ultra-violet then develops the colour in the melanin which can then screen against the rays penetrating deeper.

Many people's skin is *not* ready. Instead of the golden tan they develop the reddening, the irritation and the pain of *sunburn*: a cry for help from the tissues of the skin damaged by the ultra-violet. Quite likely this will trigger off the development of a tan eventually, but in the meantime there may be several days of discomfort or even agony.

Prolonged exposure to the sun is likely to produce less immediate but much longer-lasting effects. A major defence against the penetration of excess ultra-violet is *reflection* by the layers of squames of the *Stratum corneum* of the epidermis. It tends to adjust its thickness according to the *usual* amount of ultra-violet to which it is exposed. As a result, the much exposed skins of 'outdoor' people become much thicker and much less supple; more easily lined and wrinkled.

Despite the screening action, prolonged exposure to really *high intensities* of ultra-violet will allow sufficient to penetrate to the *dermis* to do damage to the collagen and elastic fibre network. The regularly exposed skin of the face, the neck and the backs of the hands will be sufficiently damaged to lose its resilience and elasticity and become deeply *wrinkled* long before its natural time. Outdoor people *beware!* A sportsman or a farmer may look *rugged*, but a lady looks, dare one say, *old!*

Remember too it is not just excesses of summer sunshine which can do the damage. The winter sunshine reflecting back off the snow and excessive use of sunbeds and solaria can be as bad if not worse.

Victorian and Edwardian society ladies would pride themselves on their *fair complexions.* Tanning was not for them. They shaded the skin from the sun with hats and bonnets, parasols, sleeves and gloves. They used light coloured opaque make-up to mask any tendency to darkness in the skin. But sadly even this was not without hazard. The *lead* and *mercury* based pigments they used were, unbeknown to them, extremely poisonous. So too were the doses of *arsenic* taken by some ladies in pursuit of a fair skin. This killed red blood cells and deliberately induced *anaemia.*

The modern day Mediterranean sun-seeker and the Californian beach girl pride themselves on their *deep golden tan.* It will not become evident for some years to come but they could have *already done the damage* which will show as *premature aging.*

All may not be lost. If a damaged skin is *screened* from further exposure to ultra-violet for a long time, it may well gradually recover. The collagen/elastin fibre network of the dermis has remarkable powers of recovery provided that the assault by ultra-violet is stopped. Cut out sunbathing and suntanning sessions on sunbeds; use a skin cream with a *sunscreen* and a prematurely aged skin may recover its youthfulness.

Do not be too alarmed if your only sunbathing is your annual fortnight in Spain, your skin has the next 50 weeks in which to recover.

(a) (b)

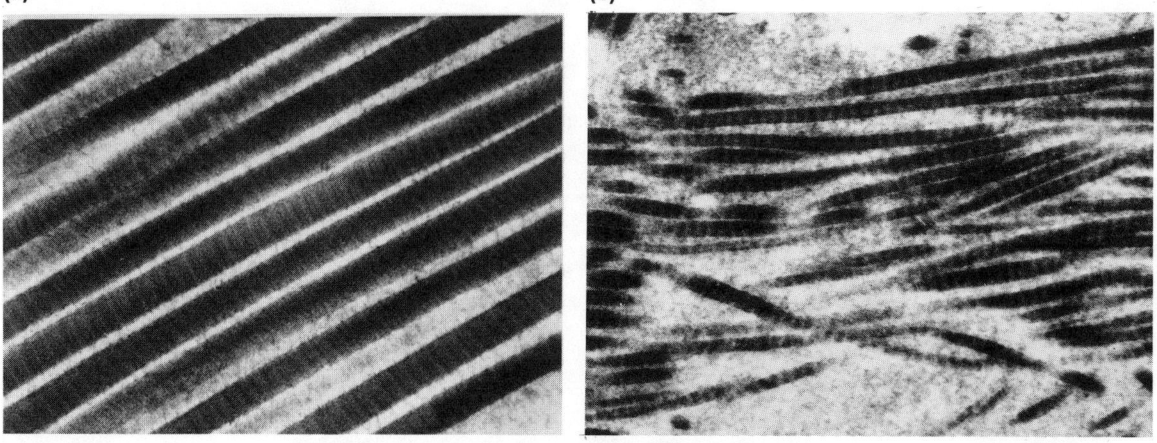

Figure 12.7 The collagen fibre network of undamaged and sun-damaged skins compared (courtesy of Professor R. Marks, University of Wales School of Medicine, Cardiff)

Suntan lotions and other aids to safe and painless sunbathing are the subject of chapter 15. More about the effects of ultra-violet and the use of ultra-violet lamps in beauty therapy may be found in Volume 2.

Things to do

Get into the habit of mentally diagnosing people's skin type and condition and suggesting to yourself the treatments you would prescribe were they to be your clients.

Self-assessment questions

1 Why are the forehead, nose and chin often greasy whereas the cheeks tend to be dry?

2 What is the cause of cracking of the skin?

3 What is meant by the term 'emollient'?

4 What is the skin's 'acid mantle'?

5 What kind of skin is prone to acne?

6 What are the features of a senile skin?

7 What is happening within the dermis of a prematurely aged skin?

8 What kind of skin cream or lotion could reverse the effects of premature aging?

13 Skin care cosmetics

High oil content creams for dry skins; moisturising creams and lotions; pH balanced creams and lotions; face packs and masks; natural materials in skin care; essential oils and herbal extracts as active materials in skin care products

Formulation of skin care products

In chapter 12 some of the problems of skin care were considered together with the types of product available to help overcome them. This chapter deals with the formulation of skin care products. All the creams and lotions may be made by the method detailed in chapter 6.

High oil content skin creams

For the care of dry skin, there are available several types of high oil content creams:

Cold cream	*Nourishing cream*	*Sports cream*
Emollient cream	*Night cream*	*Massage cream*

The physical difference between one and another is not always clear. Quite possibly it could be little more than the name of the label. Many users *do* like to have a product for each purpose; they cannot believe that one product can serve all purposes. For those who can and do not want the hassle or confusion of many products there are *general-purpose creams*.

All these creams have in common a high oil phase content. There is a very wide choice of oil phase materials. Table 13.1 lists some of the main ones.

In skin creams, various oil phase materials are made into either oil-in-water or water-in-oil emulsions. Often there is a moisturising ingredient such as glycerol included in the water phase.

Table 13.1 Oil Phase Materials for Skin Creams

Material type	*Oil phase material*	*Physical appearance*
Hydrocarbons	Mineral oil	Oily liquid
	Soft paraffin or Petroleum jelly	Greasy 'semi-solid'
	Paraffin wax	Waxy solid
	Microcrystalline wax	'Fudge-like' wax
	Ceresin wax	Waxy solid
	Osokerite wax	Waxy solid
Alcohols	Cetyl alcohol	Waxy solid
Fatty acids	Stearic acid	Waxy solid
	Myristic acid	Waxy solid
Esters	Isopropyl myristate	Light oily liquid
	Isopropyl palmitate	Light oily liquid
	Spermaceti wax	Waxy solid
	Vegetable oils	Oily liquids
Complex materials	Beeswax	Waxy solid
	Lanolin	Greasy 'semi-solid'
	Carnauba wax	Very hard wax

There are hundreds of formulations to be found in the specialist text-books and the technical literature. Listed in chapter 10 are some formulations for *cleansing/cold creams* and in chapter 6 are two formulations for *general-purpose creams*.

The choice of *oil phase* materials does affect the character of the cream. For a *massage cream* or *cleansing cream* a high content of actual *oils* will leave a mobile *lubricant* film on the skin. For a *dry* skin treatment the *matt* effect of waxy materials or the 'rub-in' property of the very light oils avoids leaving a greasy shine on the skin.

One could start with a basic cold cream formulation in which the oil phase is mainly mineral oil and try experimenting with it. Try including a little vegetable oil, a little isopropyl myristate or a little soft paraffin in place of part of the mineral oil. Try including a little lanolin, but if you do be aware that some people are allergic to it. In commercial creams its presence *must* be stated on the label. See how each variation affects the texture of the cream and the way it behaves on the skin. Be careful not to change the oil/water balance drastically, and mind that in your modifications you do not omit the emulsifier!

Moisturising creams and lotions

If a *humectant* or moisturiser is included in a skin cream then the oil content may be considerably reduced, resulting in a much lighter cream. Commonly used humectants include:

Glycerol or *glycerin*
Propylene glycol or *propan-1,2-diol*
Sorbitol – usually as a 70 per cent syrup

The humectant is usually included at between 5 and 10 per cent in a formulation. If used at a *much* higher level, it will draw moisture from deep in the skin and aggravate the dryness problem rather than remedy it.

Here are some formulations for moisturising creams and lotions. The first is *soap emulsified.* The cholesterol is another useful emollient for the skin.

Cetyl alcohol	– 2	Oil phase	Mix at 70°C
Cholesterol	– 1		
Olive oil	– 5		
Stearic acid	– 15		
Potassium hydroxide	– 0.8	Water phase	
Glycerol	– 16		
Water	– 60.2		
Perfume, preservative	– q.s.		

Use the normal cream-making method but mix these lighter creams with higher-speed stirring. As this cream employs the alkali potassium hydroxide, do not forget a pH check on the finished cream.

The next formulation uses as its emulsifiers two polyoxyethylene sorbitan esters, Arlacel 60 and Tween 60 by Atlas Chemicals. Both are non-ionic.

Mineral oil	7.5	Oil phase	Mix at 70°C
Isopropyl myristate	1		
Cetyl alcohol	2		
Glycerol monostearate	7.5		
Arlacel 60	6		
Tween 60	6		
Sodium lauryl sulphate	0.2	Water phase	
Glycerol	8		
Water	61.8		
Perfume, preservative	q.s.		

This 'complexion cream' uses a non-ionic self-emulsifying wax Lanbritol wax N21:

Lanbritol wax N21	5	Oil phase	Mix at 70°C
Lanolin	1		
Mineral oil	10		
Glycerol	5	Water phase	
Water	79		
Perfume, preservative	q.s.		

A *cationic* self-emulsifying wax is used in this cream. The acidic nature of the cationic surfactant in the emulsifying wax has an additional 'conditioning' effect on the skin:

Lanette wax CAT	7	Melt together and stir until cool
Glycerol	8	
Water	85	
Perfume, preservative	q.s.	

As written, these formulations produce light creams. A thinner more 'milky' cream can be produced by increasing the amount of water in the formulation. Again, be free to experiment with the formulations. Hand creams, too, are moisturising creams. Turn to chapter 16 for more formulations.

pH balanced creams and lotions

These, too, are moisturising creams and lotions, with the addition of an *acid* ingredient to help maintain or restore the '*acid balance*' of the skin. *Citric acid*, the lemon juice acid, and *lactic acid*, the milk acid, are both suitable.

The first formulation is a 'Buttermilk cream' with lactic acid. No perfume is necessary: the lactic acid gives the characteristic buttermilk odour.

Lanette wax SX	10	Oil phase
Cetyl alcohol	4	
Mineral oil	4	
Glycerol	6	Water phase
Water	75	
Lactic acid BP	1	
Preservative	q.s.	

This 'Lemon cream' can be made either with lemon juice or with a 7 per cent solution of citric acid in water.

Lanette wax SX	– 12	Oil phase
Cetyl alcohol	– 5	Oil phase
Glycerol	– 6	Water phase
Water	– 57	Water phase
Lemon juice or 7 per cent citric acid solution	– 20	Water phase
Lemon perfume, preservative	– q.s.	
Yellow colour	– optional	

Both these creams are made initially *without* the acid to avoid the possibility of it affecting the *anionic* Lanette wax emulsifier. In the first, part of the water is kept back to dilute the lactic acid; the acid solution is then added to the emulsified cream.

If desired, the *non-ionic* Lanbritol Wax N21 could be substituted for the Lanette SX. Then the acid need not be added separately but can go in with the rest of the water phase.

The next formulation is for a 'Lemon lotion'. Pectin is used as a thickener.

Lemon juice or 7 per cent citric acid	– 10
Glycerol	– 10
Water	– 78.5
Pectin (250 grade)	– 1.5
Lemon perfume, yellow colour and preservative	– q.s.

Mix the glycerol and pectin. Add the water. Heat to dissolve, then cool. Add the lemon juice or citric acid solution, the colour, the perfume and the preservative.

Moisturisers with sunscreens

Since screening the skin from the ultra-violet rays of the sun is a major factor in delaying premature aging, a small proportion, say one or two per cent of a *sunscreen* may be incorporated in the *oil phase* of any of the formulations for moisturising creams and lotions.

Sunscreens include a wide variety of materials. Mostly they are quite complex esters. Here are some examples:

Aminobenzoates	– for example, ethyl aminobenzoate
Cinnamates	– for example, benzyl cinnamate
Salicylates	– for example, benzyl salicylate

You may read further about sunscreen creams and lotions in chapter 15.

Face masks and packs

Face masks and packs are of three main types:

1 **Plastic masks** – wax-based, latex-based or vinyl-based.
2 **Hydrocolloid masks** – gel masks.
3 **Argillaceous masks** – clay-based or earth-based masks.

Wax masks

The main effect of a plastic mask is its *deep-cleansing* action. In addition, wax masks are somewhat *emollient*: they leave a film of wax on the skin, making it feel soft and smooth.

The wax is melted in a 'double vessel'. This has a water jacket round the wax pot and preferably a thermostat so that wax cannot be overheated. After checking the temperature of the wax by trying a little on the therapist's own skin, the molten wax is painted on to the skin. It sets to form a continuous occlusive film which prevents the loss of both heat and moisture from the skin. The heat beneath the wax film encourages perspiration and sebaceous activity. It flushes out the pores of the skin. In addition, contraction as the wax cools has a 'drawing' or suction effect which helps to clear blocked pores.

A *paraffin wax* with a melting point of around 43°C could be used but it is often difficult to remove without the film crumbling.

Ideally, a plastic mask should peel off in one piece. This *plastic wax mask* is designed to do this. The microcrystalline wax adds the plasticity.

Microcrystalline wax	– 13	Melt together Stir to mix
Paraffin wax – 43°C	– 60	
Cetyl alcohol	– 5	
Mineral oil	– 20	
Bentonite	– 1.4	
Propan-2-ol (isopropanol)	– 0.6	

Wet the bentonite, a volcanic clay, with the propan-2-ol and add it to the molten waxes. It may be omitted if desired.

Also available commercially are masks based on *rubber latex* and *vinyl plastics*. These are supplied as a liquid emulsion which when painted on the skin sets to form the mask. When finished with, the mask may be pulled off in one piece.

Hydrocolloid masks

When applied, these are of a soft spreadable jelly consistency. On the skin they lose water and set to a gel film, shrinking as they do so giving a feeling of *tightening* the skin. They are particularly *soothing* to inflamed and delicate skins.

A variety of *gelling agents* can be used to form the gel:

Vegetable gums	– *tragacanth, acacia*
Cellulose derivatives	– *methyl cellulose*
Proteins	– *casein, gelatin, egg white*
Water soluble plastics	– *polyvinyl pyrollidone*

A *humectant* such as glycerol prevents the film drying to become hard and brittle on the skin. A small proportion of a powder ingredient may be incorporated if desired such as *kaolin*, an oil-absorbent clay, to absorb grease from the skin, or *calamine*, a mild astringent to soothe an inflamed skin. Here are some formulations:

Tragacanth jelly mask

Tragacanth powder	5
Calamine	0.5
Water	75
Witch hazel	q.s.

Add water slowly to the tragacanth. Stir to form a porridge, then a clear gel. Sieve through muslin. Add the calamine and enough witch hazel to make a brushable consistency. This makes a cooling, soothing mask for an inflamed skin. This formulation could be made using acacia gum instead.

Tragacanth and gelatin mask

This is the '*gelanthum mask*' suggested by Janistyn. He also suggested the '*gelanthum mask with honey*' in which 4–5 per cent of the water is replaced by honey. To apply, the mask is warmed to make it spreadable and sets to form the mask as it cools on the skin.

Tragacanth powder	2.2
Glycerol	2.5
Gelatin	2.3
Water	90.5
Zinc oxide	2.5
Preservative (methyl-4-hydroxybenzoate)	q.s.

Dissolve the gelatin in water with heat. Wet the gum with the glycerol and add it to the gelatin solution. Moisten the zinc oxide with a little glycerol and mix in.

Gelatin mask

Gelatin	15
Water	70
Zinc oxide	5
Kaolin	7
Titanium dioxide	3
Camphor in alcohol	a few drops
Preservative	q.s.

Dissolve the gelatin in water with heat. Moisten the powders with a little glycerol and stir in. To apply, warm the mask to make it spreadable.

A protein mask

Casein powder	16
Glycerol	4
Borax	0.4
Water	79.6
Preservative	q.s.

Dissolve the borax and the preservative in water with gentle heat. Moisten the casein powder with the glycerol and stir in. Casein is widely available as 'Sanatogen' nerve tonic. Albumen may be used instead of casein.

Argillaceous masks

A variety of clays and other mineral ingredients can be made into face packs. The materials are able to absorb both water and oil and grease. Frequently used materials include:

Kaolin	– a white clay, China clay
Fuller's earth	– a green-brown clay
Bentonite	– a greyish volcanic clay which makes fine gels
Light magnesium carbonate	– a refined limestone mineral known to therapists as 'magnesium'
Zinc carbonate	– the mild astringent 'Calamine'.

For *cleansing* and for *greasy skins*, the masks can be made up ready-to-use or presented in 'dry' form to be mixed with water or rose water just before use.

To make a *kaolin mask*, mix kaolin with sufficient water or rose water to make a workable consistency. A kaolin mask is a smooth white gel.

A *Fuller's earth* mask is made similarly. The smooth khaki green gel is not so attractive but it is a remarkably good grease absorbent.

A *bentonite mask* needs more time to make. The bentonite is sprinkled a little at a time into the water or rose water while stirring it constantly and briskly, until a workable gel is obtained. It makes a beautifully smooth cooling gel. Unlike kaolin and Fuller's earth gels, it does not dry out quickly in storage so it can be made in ready-to-use form.

Mixed earth masks

Mixtures of clays and other absorbent materials can be made into masks. Here are some examples:

1	Magnesium carbonate	– 50	Mix dry then add water
	Kaolin	– 33	
	Fuller's earth	– 17	
	Water, rose water	– to make workable	
2	Kaolin	– 80	Mix dry, then add water
	Magnesium carbonate	– 14	
	Starch	– 5	
	Tragacanth powder	– 1	
	Water	– to make workable	

Astringent masks

Alum, calamine and witch hazel are astringents. They help close the pores of a greasy skin to reduce the sebum output. In this formulation, they combine to produce an astringent mask:

Magnesium carbonate	– 80
Zinc carbonate (calamine)	– 13
Potassium alum	– 7
Witch hazel (or water)	– to make a workable paste

Masks for dry skins

For dry skins, masks can be used as the basis of an oil treatment by mixing the clays with vegetable oils instead of water. Simple masks can be made by mixing kaolin or Fuller's earth to a creamy paste with a vegetable oil such as olive or groundnut oil. Mixtures of clay ingredients could be used too as in this example:

Magnesium carbonate	– 50
Kaolin	– 33
Fuller's earth	– 17
Vegetable oil	– to make workable

In using these oil masks for an oil treatment, it is an advantage to apply the mask warm and keep it warm while on the skin with the heat from a facial steamer or an infra-red lamp.

Natural materials in skin care products

There is a great deal of interest nowadays in the use of '*natural*' materials in skin care. These materials fall into two groups:

1 Materials which are similar to those found naturally in skin; materials which are part of its structure or possibly are concerned with its metabolism.

2 Materials such as *herbal extracts* and *essential oils* which have, or are *thought to have* an active beneficial effect on the skin.

Natural skin materials

The dermis is composed of collagen and elastic fibres in a jelly-matrix of muco-polysaccharides. *Soluble collagen*, *soluble elastin* and *mucopolysaccharides* are sometimes included in skin creams in the hope that they will penetrate to the dermis to repair and rejuvenate an aging skin.

There is *no real evidence* to show that any of these substances finds it way to its 'natural' place. Even if soluble collagen and elastin should penetrate to the dermis, there is no known mechanism by which they could reform into fibres. Remember though, that if the damaging effects of ultra-violet are removed then the fibre network is able to recover on its own. Perhaps these additional materials could assist the process?

Materials which are thought to be the '*natural moisturising factor*' might be included in creams for treating a *dry skin* in the hope that they will find their way into the horny layer squames to attract moisture back into the dry epidermis. There is no real evidence of their effectiveness at any depth in the epidermis but, even if they do not penetrate, they are *humectants* and can serve a useful moisturising function.

Vitamins and hormones in skin creams

It is widely believed among users that skin creams 'with vitamins' or 'with oestrogen' have special value. Vitamins *are* good for you but there is nothing to be gained by applying them in skin creams rather than taking them in food even though the fat-soluble vitamins A, D and E can be absorbed percutaneously.

Oestrogen is a 'female' hormone. The implication in its use in skin creams is that it will make the user's skin 'more feminine' by counteracting the effects of natural aging as the user's own oestrogen level declines with age. Oestrogen too does have humectant or moisturising properties, but the possibility that it might encourage the development of malignant growths on the skin has led to a wane in interest in its use.

Herbal extracts and essential oils in skin care

In recent years there has been a revival in the use of herbal extracts and essential oils in both skin care and in health care generally. Until the advent of the modern synthetic drugs, herbal medicines were the only medicines, but the new 'wonder' drugs took their place and the use of medicinal herbs declined.

Recently, however, the press has carried a number of 'scare stories' regarding certain synthetic drugs and other synthetic additives in both foods and cosmetics. Some like thalidomide and the colourant tartrazine have been substantiated, others have not. Even so, many people are turning once again to the old-fashioned herbal remedies.

Even if they have no other effect, the juices of most plants have a content of acids, sugars and proteins, all of which have a general conditioning effect on the hair and skin. The acidity contracts and 'tightens' the keratin of the skin and hair, while the gum-like residues of the sugars and proteins impart a smoothness to the skin and a shine to the hair.

Many plant extracts, though, also contain materials of a more active nature. To assist plants in the constant battle against attack by bacteria and moulds, many contain antimicrobial substances. These substances will have a similar effect on the skin. Many essential oils have antimicrobial properties. They are the 'healthy' smelling ones such as the oils of pine, cedar, lavender or rosemary.

Many plant substances have a drug action. Indeed the analysis of the plant extracts has shown, in many of them, substances very like the synthetic drugs. Often they can be quite easily absorbed percutaneously, so when applied in creams or lotions they can act on the underlying tissues. They often act by affecting various features of the nervous system.

For instance, oil of wintergreen, that pungent smelling ingredient of embrocations and liniments, contains methyl salicylate. Absorbed through the skin, this acts as a painkiller to soothe damaged muscles. At the same time it acts as a *vasodilator*. By creating a feeling of intense warmth in the area, it causes the blood vessels to dilate and increase the blood flow through the damaged tissues to aid the healing process. The painkiller aspirin is also a salicylate.

On the other hand, oils like peppermint, eucalyptus and lavender are *vasoconstrictors*. Their cool sensation causes the blood vessels in the area to contract, cutting down the flow of blood. Their use on the skin produces a refreshing astringent effect.

Things to do

1 Make up a selection of the skin creams and lotions. Compare their effectiveness by performing an evaluation exercise (see chapter 23).

2 Make up and use the face mask formulations in your treatments.

3 Find out more about the use of herbal extracts and aromatic oils in beauty therapy by referring to the many books on herbal medicine and aroma therapy.

Self-assessment questions

1 Name any five oil phase ingredients suitable for use in skin creams and lotions.

2 What is an humectant?

3 Name two humectant ingredients used in skin creams and lotions.

4 What is a 'pH balanced' cream or lotion?

5 Of what advantage is the inclusion of a sunscreen ingredient in a face cream or lotion?

6 What are the three main types of face masks?

7 What is the specific purpose of (a) kaolin and (b) calamine in a face mask?

8 Name two essential oils which have an antibacterial effect.

9 Name an essential oil which acts as a painkiller when absorbed through the skin.

10 How does oil of eucalyptus act to clear a blocked-up nose?

14 Decorative Cosmetics

Colour in cosmetics; legislation and the choice of safe dyes and pigments for cosmetics; pigments for decorative cosmetics; vanishing and foundation creams; face powders, compacts and tinted foundations; rouges and blushers; eye make-up; lipsticks

Social trends in the use of make-up

In any department store, any chain store or any large chemist's, without fail your attention will be drawn by the colourful displays of make-up products on the cosmetics counters: foundations and face powders, eyeshadows and mascaras, eyeliners, blushers and lipsticks.

A prime function of cosmetics is to enhance the appearance of the wearer and a major part of this function is the *colour* contributed by the *decorative cosmetics*.

To put in perspective the many formulations for decorative cosmetics which appear in this chapter, one must be aware of the changing social scene and fashions, particularly during the last thirty years. This has been particularly dramatic in the sixties and seventies with the upsurge in youthful expression and spending power.

Before the sixties, fashion progressed slowly and its wearers *conformed*. They were in the main the more mature members of the middle and upper social classes. Make-up was a mask of uniform colour which obliterated the natural complexion. For day wear a coloured foundation was punctuated by a dense red lipstick and perhaps rouge (blusher) on the cheeks. Only for evening social events did eyeshadow and mascara complete the picture.

With the sixties came an explosion in the expression of youth and youthful ideas. The young led the way in fashions both in clothes and make-up. No foundation, or at most a translucent foundation to complement rather than obliterate the natural complexion, and most of all a shift of emphasis from the lips to the eyes. Heavy eyeshadow and even heavier mascara were the norm for all day, not just for evenings.

In more recent times, fashion has become almost a free-for-all. Literally anything goes so long as you conform to your peer group. Many girls prefer a 'no-make-up' look for the skin and a more delicate colour for the lips. Still the accent is on the eyes but much more restrained than the sixties look. Others though, have reverted to the mask, the artificial face. They take it to the extreme with their fantasy make-up – and for day wear too! Make-up is now no longer just for girls and ladies. Many young men, too, quite openly wear make-up.

Trends in make-up products

With the changing fashions in the use of make-up, so the make-up products themselves have changed. Whether the technology has developed in response to fashion or vice versa is difficult to say.

Prior to the sixties, make-up for the face was either a non-pigmented foundation for either loose or compact face powder or an opaque tinted foundation such as the famous 'Pancake' and 'Panstick'. Nowadays liquid or cream-pigmented foundations and translucent powders are the norm, though there is renewed interest in the more opaque products for the fantasy make-ups and of course for camouflage make-up to cover skin blemishes.

For the eyes, compressed powder eyeshadows in palettes have largely replaced the cream and stick eyeshadows which did tend to 'crease' as the eyelids moved. Eye-colour pencils have moved on from just eyebrow pencils to include eyeliners, kohl pencils and eyeshadow crayons.

The original mascaras were soap-based block mascaras: all very well for indoor evening wear, but absolute disaster in the rain which caused it to run in black streaks down the face. For day wear, the breakthrough was liquid mascara in a gum base and more recently the adhesive-resin-based waterproof mascaras.

The sixties also saw the demise, for a while, of the very heavily pigmented lipsticks with their *eosin* stains. These stains not only conferred a certain permanence of colour on the lips but caused irritant or allergic reactions on quite a number of users. Paler colours took their place and are still in fashion today, though the stronger colours have made a comeback in recent years. The use of the eosin stains is, though, much reduced and they are omitted altogether from 'hypoallergenic' ranges.

Colour in cosmetics

The use of colour in cosmetics and toiletries has two functions:

1 To colour the products themselves to make them more attractive for the user.

2 To impart colour to the skin.

Colour in cosmetics is contributed by an extensive range of *dyes* and *pigments*.

A *dye* is a soluble colouring agent. It colours a product by dissolving in it. It colours the skin by penetrating the surface and staining it.

A *pigment* is an insoluble powder colour. Most make-up colours the skin by coating it with a film of pigment. Because the pigments are not actually absorbed by the skin, the colours of most make-up can be easily cleansed away.

Only a very limited use is made of dyes for staining the skin: the eosin stains which were so commonly used to give 'staying power' to lipsticks and the brown dyes used as fake suntans.

Legislation and cosmetic colours

All the dyes and pigments used in cosmetics and toiletries must be *safe*. They must not be poisonous, allergenic or carcinogenic. To this end the choice of colours is controlled by legislation. Most countries have such legislation. Tests are continually being done on colours with the result that the lists of permitted colours are frequently amended.

The United Kingdom and much of Europe is controlled by the *EEC Cosmetics Directive of 1976*. This contains 'positive lists' of the colours which may be used in cosmetics and toiletries. It also indicates any limitations to the ways in which they are used. Basically, permitted colours are in three groups:

1 Colours for use in *all* cosmetics. Many of these have E numbers of the *EEC Directive of 1962* regarding food colours, which means they are permitted food colours.

2 Provisionally allowed for use in cosmetics which only briefly contact the skin *including* mucous membranes such as the lips.

3 Provisionally allowed for use in cosmetics which only briefly contact the skin and *not* allowed to contact mucous membranes.

Ideally, only colours from the first group should be used but there are not suitable colours in this group for all requirements. Colours from the other groups are therefore frequently used, bearing in mind the limitations to their use.

In the USA, the Food and Drugs Administration lists colours in three categories which differ slightly from the EEC groups. Because this listing was done long before the *EEC Directive*, it formed the basis for selection of colours in many countries with the result that many colours are known by their 'F, D and C' numbers rather than by name. The USA groupings are:

1 F, D and C – are colours for general use in Foods, Drugs and Cosmetics
2 D and C – may be used in Drugs and Cosmetics including those for use on mucous membranes
3 Ext. D and C – may be used in Drugs and Cosmetics but *not* in those for use on mucous membranes.

Any colour intended for use in a cosmetic product *must* comply with the requirements of the legislation in the country where it is to be sold.

Dyes suitable for cosmetic creams and lotions

The appearance of many cosmetics is enhanced by the judicious use of a little colour. To colour your experimental samples, readily available *food colours* may be used or solutions of permitted dyes may be made up. Make up a solution of each dye in water no stronger than 5 per cent. Dyes colour very strongly so even then only a *small amount* of the 5 per cent solution is required to colour a product. Take *care* or you will ruin the product.

When selecting dyes from a scientific chemical catalogue, there is no indication of whether they are permitted cosmetic colours or not. Those in table 14.1 are permitted colours.

Table 14.1 Some Permitted Colours for Cosmetics and Toiletries

Reds	Amaranth	E 183	F D and C – Red 2
	Erythrosine	E 127	F D and C – Red 3
Blues	Brilliant Blue FCF		F D and C – Blue 1
	Indigo Carmine	E 132	F D and C – Blue 2
Yellow	Tartrazine	E 102	F D and C – Yellow 5
Green	Fast Green FCF		F D and C – Green 1

Pigments for use in decorative cosmetics

Pigments for use as colourants in make-up come from a variety of sources:

Natural Iron Oxides – These are the 'earth pigments'. The coloured earths are crushed and washed. They may be used 'raw' or 'burned'. The main examples are:

Ochres – Yellows
Siennas – Yellows, buffs and browns
Umbers – Buffs and browns
Red iron oxides – Reds

Synthetic Iron Oxides

Ferrite yellow
Indian red
Black iron oxide

Ultramarines – China clay is reacted in kilns with deliberately introduced 'impurities' to produce a range of:

Greens and blues
Pink

Laked Colours – The metal salts of many of the organic dyes are insoluble. They can be used to indelibly dye a suitable powder to produce *lake pigments* in a full range of colours and shades. Just two examples are:

Carmine
Rose pink

These pigments are used in the full range of colour cosmetics: face powders, eye colours, lipsticks, nail enamels. Care is needed in the use of lakes in nail enamels – the solvents used may be powerful enough to dissolve the dye from the pigment and cause it actually to stain the nails. The colour is said to 'bleed'.

Vanishing and foundation creams

The descriptions *'vanishing'* and *'foundation'* are given to emollient moisturising face creams intended to be worn on the face during the day, probably under make-up. Nowadays foundation creams are pigmented, so the cream provides the basic colour for the make-up. These *tinted foundations* are considered later in the chapter.

The oil phase of such a *'day cream'* is traditionally largely *stearic acid* which, because of its crystalline nature, leaves the skin *matt* and *smooth*: hence 'vanishing'.

The cream acts as an *adhesive base* for powder make-up. Being non-oily, it does not spoil the make-up by being absorbed by it.

Traditional day creams are 'soap-emulsified' by reacting part of the stearic acid with an alkali such as potassium hydroxide. Three such formulations are listed in table 14.2. If you make samples of these do not forget to check the pH of the cream.

Table 14.2 Formulations for Soap-emulsified Vanishing Creams

	(1)	*(2)*	*(3)*		
Stearic acid	15	18	18	Oil phase	Mix at 70°C
Isopropyl myristate	–	–	2		
Cetyl alcohol	–	0.5	0.5		
Potassium hydroxide	0.7	1.	1	Water phase	
Glycerol	8	5	8		
Water	76.3	75.5	70.5		
Perfume, preservative	q.s.	q.s.	q.s		

More modern creams are emulsified by self-emulsifying waxes. Table 14.3 shows two examples.

Vanishing and foundation creams should be very lightly perfumed so as not to obtrude on the wearer's skin perfume.

Table 14.3 Vanishing Creams with Self-emulsifying Wax

	(4)	*(5)*		
Stearic acid	5	15	Oil phase	Mix at 70°C
Lanette wax SX	15	5		
Glycerol	7	7	Water phase	
Water	73	73		
Perfume, preservative	q.s.	q.s.		

Face powders

Face powders and other powder make-up – *powder eye shadow, powder rouge* or *blusher, camouflage make-up* – consist of a *powder base* and *pigments.*

Powder bases for powder make-up

A good powder make-up should have several attributes:

Covering power   Slip   Adhesion
Absorbency   Bloom

Covering power is desirable to mask skin defects: blemishes, broken veins, enlarged pores, greasy shine, high colour or even, in the case of camouflage make-up, scars, birthmarks and pigment defects. For a 'perfect skin' or for the 'less-made-up' look, modern fashion demands a lesser covering power so the natural colour of the skin will show through. Camouflage make-up, on the other hand, needs to be *opaque* to obliterate the underlying skin colour. Covering ingredients in the powder base range embrace:

the highly opaque	*titanium dioxide*
the almost as opaque	*zinc oxide*
the not so opaque	*chalk – calcium carbonate*
the translucent	*talc*

Absorbency is contributed by, for instance *kaolin* to absorb both the watery and greasy shine of the skin.

Slip is contributed by the lubricant property of *talc.*

Bloom is the matt, silky appearance conferred on the skin by *chalk* or *starch* or even *powdered silk* in the powder.

Adhesion is to enable the powder to cling to the skin. Apart from the adhesive property of talc, adhesion is contributed by insoluble soaps such as *magnesium stearate* or *zinc stearate.*

Table 14.4 lists formulations for translucent, medium and opaque powder make-up bases.

Table 14.4 Formulations for Powder Make-up Bases

	Light/ translucent	*Medium*	*Opaque*
Talc	65	40	15
Kaolin – light	20	40	60
Calcium carbonate – chalk	5	5	10
Titanium dioxide	–	–	3
Zinc oxide	5	8	5
Zinc stearate	5	7	7

The methods for mixing these powder bases are described in chapter 6. Whether you use a tumbler mixer or the polythene bag method, make sure the mixing is *thorough.*

A suitable perfume, again light and unobtrusive, may either be sprayed in or absorbed on to a little *light magnesium carbonate* before being added to the main mix.

Colour for face powder

The pigments are mixed in the powder base by methods which are also described in chapter 6. The fine pigment particles must coat the particles of the powder base. The pigment colours the powder not the skin, so here too the mixing must be *thorough*.

The *natural colour* of skin is the result of the combination of

brown – of melanin
yellow – of subcutaneous fat
red – of blood

The main pigments used are *red*, *pink*, *black*, *brown* and *yellow* plus some green and blue. The traditional shades for face powder for white persons' skins used to be:

'Naturelle' – a clear pink for blondes, particularly if their skin has a bluishness
'Rachel' – a cream-yellow for brunettes

Modern powders are coloured on a cream–yellow–brown theme. For highly coloured complexions, the redness may be toned down with a bluish-green powder.

For black skins a translucent base must be used and the pigments be selected to complement and modify the natural colour of the skin. An opaque powder based on the 'covering' ingredients listed earlier would produce a ghostly mask effect on a black skin.

Experimenting with colour

When doing colour work, *good daylight* is essential to be able to see and match colours properly. A work bench in front of a north-facing window is ideal.

Protect both yourself and the worktop: working with pigments can be *very* messy. Wear an overall and cover the worktop with disposable paper. Newspaper could be used.

To make experimental samples of face powders, use the 'test-tube and rod' method described in chapter 6. Half-fill a test tube with the chosen powder base. Add colour 'one spatula-tip-full' at a time using one of those long slim metal spatulas with an angled tip. *Note down* each addition of colour and *thoroughly* mix in each addition with the glass rod using a rotating motion against the side of the tube (see figure 14.1).

Start with, say *brown* or *red* and *black* to give the required degree of 'brown-ness'. Then modify with *pink* and *yellow* until the desired colour is obtained.

Try your powder on the skin. The colour on the skin, known as the '*undertone*' might be quite different from the colour of the bulk powder in the

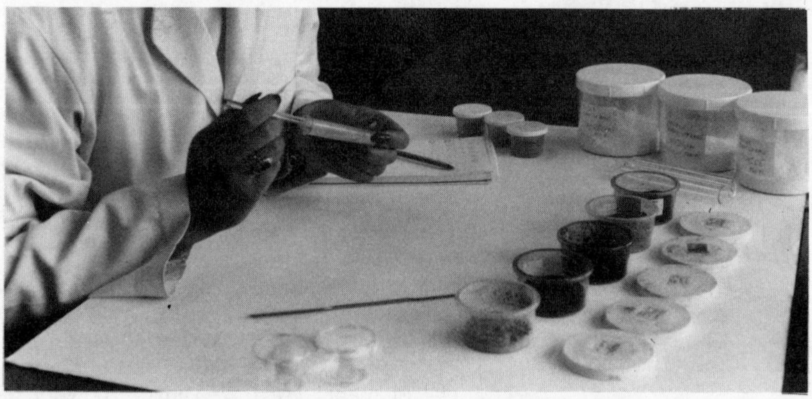

Figure 14.1 Making a sample of face powder in the laboratory

tube, the *'mass-tone'*. Trying it out on the skin will also reveal any shortcomings in your mixing – as streaks! If so, mix again – more *thoroughly* this time.

Having noted the proportions of the pigments in each of your experimental mixes, a larger batch of any 'successful' formulation may be made.

Compact face powders

Most modern powder make-up is in *compact* form. This is much more convenient and portable and it is easy to produce palettes of several colours in one container as with eye make-up.

Compact powders are formulated in much the same way as loose powder although increasing the proportions of the kaolin, the zinc oxide or the zinc stearate, or including some rice starch, will make the powder more compressible. A *binder* is necessary to form the compact. This may be a *gum* or a *wax mixture:*

A gum binder – Carboxy methyl cellulose – equal to 3 per cent of the dry weight of the powder – is made into a 10 per cent solution in water. This solution and the powder are thoroughly mixed to form a paste which when almost dry is pressed into shallow metal trays called *godets* on a *press.*

A wax binder –

Beeswax	– 12	Melt together
Lanolin	– 2	
Mineral oil	– 86	

The powder and molten wax mixture are mixed together. It can then be pressed into the *godets* on the *press.*

You will notice that to make compact make-up requires a *press*. Also required will be a supply of the shallow metal trays called *godets* and a set of suitable *dies* for the press: one to locate the godet and one to compress the powder into it.

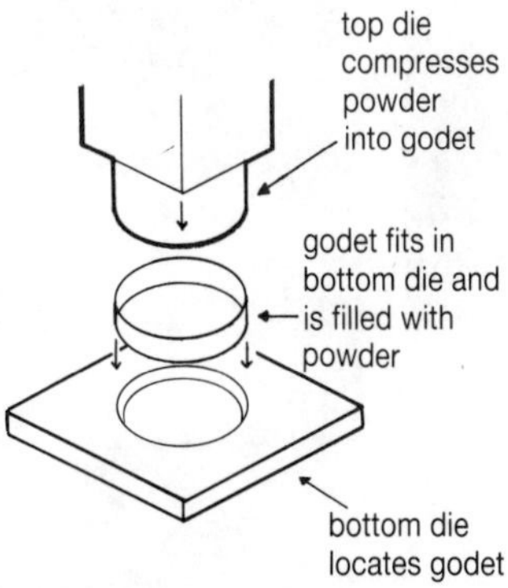

Figure 14.2 The dies of a compact powder press

Figure 14.3 Filling compact powder godets (courtesy of the Kemwall Engineering Company)

Cream make-up – tinted foundation

This is a complete make-up for the face made by combining a face powder and a vanishing–foundation cream. *Cream eye shadow*, *cream mascara* and *cream blusher* may be made in a similar way.

The foundation cream formulation is made up *without* its glycerol. The face powder is then dispersed in the glycerol before mixing it with the cream. Here are three formulations.

	Ingredient	Amount	Phase	
1	Lanette wax SX	8	Oil phase	Mix at 70°C
	Stearic acid	8	Oil phase	
	Water	64	Water phase	
	Perfume, preservative	q.s.		
	Face powder, powder eye colour, etc.	10		
	Glycerol	10		
2	Glycerol monostearate – self-emulsifying	16	Oil phase	Mix at 70°C
	Water	44	Water phase	
	Perfume, preservative	q.s.		
	Face powder, powder eye colour, etc.	15		
	Glycerol	25		
3	Lanbritol wax N21	10	Oil phase	Mix at 70°C
	Paraffin wax 55°C	5	Oil phase	
	Lanolin	1	Oil phase	
	Mineral oil	15	Oil phase	
	Water	54	Water phase	
	Perfume, preservative	q.s.		
	Face powder, powder eye colour, etc.	10		
	Glycerol	5		

In each case, make up the cream by the usual method. Make the face powder. Mix the face powder with the glycerol; then mix it into the cream (see figures 14.4 and 14.5).

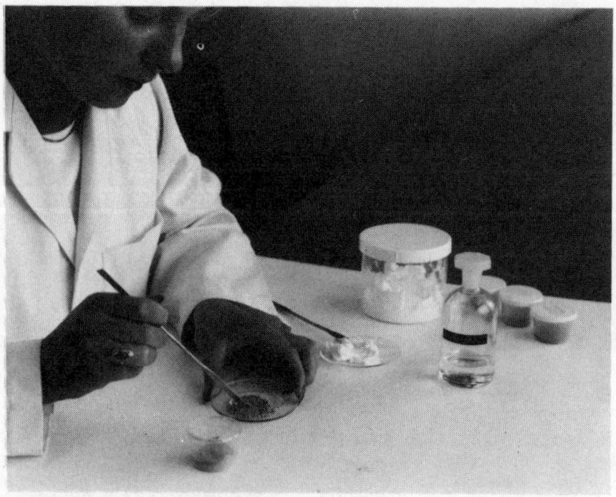

Figure 14.4 Cream make up. Mixing the powder with the glycerol

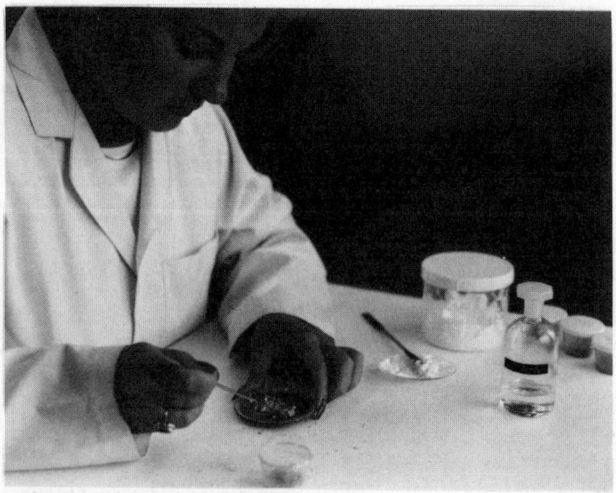

Figure 14.5 Cream make up. Mixing the powder and glycerol into the cream base

Liquid foundation

A liquid foundation is basically a 'thinner' tinted foundation cream. The same method is used to make it. Here is the formulation:

Ingredient		Amount	Phase	
Lanbritol wax N21	–	5	Oil phase	Mix at 70°C
Mineral oil	–	15		
Water	–	65	Water phase	
Perfume, preservative	–	q.s.		
Face powder	–	10		
Glycerol	–	5		

Liquid face powder

From time to time, interest is shown in 'liquid face powder'. This is basically a face powder dispersed in water and glycerol. Here are two possible formulations. The proportions may require adjusting to produce the required result. To make them, mix the powder base and pigments. Incorporate the powder mix into the glycerol then mix with the water.

	Ingredient		Amount	
1	Zinc oxide	–	3	Powder base
	Chalk	–	15	
	Kaolin	–	2	
	Pigments	–	q.s.	
	Glycerol	–	15	
	Water	–	65	
	Perfume, preservative	–	q.s.	
2	Zinc oxide	–	10	Powder base
	Titanium dioxide	–	10	
	Talc	–	10	
	Pigments	–	q.s.	
	Tragacanth 0.5 per cent solution	–	25	
	Glycerol	–	15	
	Water	–	30	
	Perfume, preservative	–	q.s.	

Stick make-up

Blends of pigments in a wax or grease base have long been used as *grease paint* for the theatre. In the 1930s came the wax-based stick make-up for everyday use: a product which still enjoys a certain popularity and has replaced grease paint for much stage make-up.

The blend of powder base and pigments in a wax base is cast into sticks and applied to the skin like a fat wax crayon.

Ingredient		Amount	
Mineral oil	–	47.5	Wax base
Paraffin wax 55°C	–	3.5	
Beeswax	–	1.5	
Carnauba wax	–	4	
Kaolin	–	9	Pigment blend
Titanium dioxide	–	30	
Pigments	–	4.5	

Melt and blend together the materials for the wax base. Mix the pigment blend to give the desired shade. Thoroughly mix the pigment blend into the molten wax base. Cast into sticks using a method similar to that for lipsticks but make the stick much thicker.

Rouges and blushers

Once called *rouge* but now usually called *blusher*, this product is to highlight the colour of the cheeks. Nowadays most blusher is produced in compact powder form, but rouges have been produced as loose powder, cream, wax stick or liquid.

A *powder rouge* might be made by incorporating predominantly red pigments into a translucent face powder base. See the methods used for face powders.

To produce a *compact blusher*, the following powder base suitably coloured is mixed with either a gum or wax-based binder and pressed into godets. See compact face powder methods.

Talc	– 48
Kaolin	– 10
Zinc stearate	– 6
Zinc oxide	– 5
Magnesium carbonate	– 5
Rice starch	– 10
Titanium dioxide	– 4
Pigments	– 6
Binder	– 6

A *cream rouge* may be made in the same way as cream make-up by dispersing suitable pigments into glycerol and blending the mixture into the cream base.

A non-aqueous cream rouge is virtually a grease paint. Here are two possible formulations:

Soft paraffin	– 70
Kaolin	– 30
Pigments	– q.s.

Blend the pigments and kaolin and disperse the mixture into the soft paraffin.

White beeswax	– 5
Stearic acid	– 7
Cetyl alcohol	– 3.5
Soft paraffin	– 77
Mineral oil	– 7.5
Pigments	– q.s.

Melt the oils and waxes together and blend in the pigments.

A *liquid rouge* might be made by dissolving a red dye in a gum solution. Glycerol helps it to spread evenly.

Methyl cellulose	– 2
Water	– 98
Water-soluble red dye	– q.s.
Glycerol	– q.s.
Preservative	– q.s.

Eye make-up

Huge dark eyes have long been a mark of beauty. For centuries all cultures have made up the eyes. The ancient Egyptians used *kohl*, a black cosmetic containing as its black pigment stibium or *antimony trisulphide*. Tsocco used by Indian women is similarly pigmented.

But *user beware!* Antimony trisulphide is a *poison* and is now banned by Western cosmetic products regulations. Despite this, antimony trisulphide kohl is still occasionally imported and might be offered for sale in 'Oriental' shops.

Modern eye make-up comprises:

Mascara	– to colour and accentuate the eyelashes
Eyeshadow	– for the eyelids
Eyeliner	– to highlight close to the eyelashes
Eyebrow pencil	– to colour the eyebrow area
Kohl	– to line the inner edge of the eyelids (modern kohl contains safe pigments

For a longer lasting colour for the eyelashes, there are also:

Eyelash dyes

Pigments for eye make-up

Choosing *safe colours* is particularly important for the eye area. Colour manufacturers produce colours of specially safe specification for eye cosmetics. Use *only* these in your eye cosmetics.

Coal tar dyes are *not* allowed. *Do not* be tempted to save a little hair dye to colour your brows and lashes to match your hair! Please note too: in some quite recently published formulations you may see *carbon black* – lamp black or bone black – given as the black pigment for eye colours. *Carbon black* has been '*delisted*' by the regulations and should not be used. Use *black iron oxide* – eye quality – instead.

The *irridescent* or '*glitter*' effect so popular in make-up is produced by:

1. Fine aluminium powder, suitably dyed.
2. Bismuth oxychloride.
3. Mica coated with titanium dioxide.

Guanine and powdered fish scales have also been used as glitter in make-up. All consist of flat shiny particles which 'catch' and reflect the light.

Mascara

At one time, mascara was frequently made as a *block* or *cake* to be applied with a moistened brush or sponge applicator. The pigments were mixed in a *soap* or *wax* base:

Stearic acid	– 27	Carnauba wax	– 50
Triethanolamine	– 12	Pigments	– 25
Beeswax	– 30		

Melt the materials together and mill in the pigments as it cools. Cast into blocks.

Also available were cream mascara and grease-based mascara. Cream mascara is made in the same way as cream make-up. Grease-based mascara is made in the same way as the non-aqueous cream rouge already described.

A constant problem with these older mascaras was their lack of permanence, particularly in the wet – rain or tears! – which meant they were not really suitable for day wear.

This all changed with the invention of *liquid mascara* and the 'tube' pack with its built-in brush. The '*automatic mascara*' has now become popular, virtually to the exclusion of the older types.

Liquid mascara is a solution of a gum in alcohol and water in which the pigments are dispersed. Sometimes very short, fine, filamentous flock is included to thicken and lengthen the lashes. The gum base is still water-soluble so even liquid mascara can smudge and 'run'. Here is a formulation:

Gum tragacanth powder	– 0.2	Pigments	– 8
Alcohol	– 8	Preservative	– q.s.
Water	– 83.8		

Disperse the gum in the alcohol. Add the water. Stir to dissolve, then add the pigments.

To make a mascara which is less likely to run, an *alcohol* solution of a gum is preferable. Industrial alcohol is irritating to the eyes, so pure ethanol should be used.

Ethyl cellulose (a synthetic 'gum')	– 0.3
Castor oil	– 3
Ethanol	– 86.7
Pigments	– 10

The latest development in mascara is *indelible mascara.* This too is a liquid product, but it employs an acrylic resin instead of a gum as its adhesive. This product will defy the efforts of any amount of rain or tears to make it run. Indeed it often defies the efforts of cleansers to remove it, and attempts to do so might dislodge the lashes too!

Figure 14.6 Block (left) and automatic mascaras

Eyeshadow

Eyeshadow these days almost always is in *compact powder* form. A number of small godets, each containing a different shade, are assembled together into a *palette* together with brushes and a mirror in the lid.

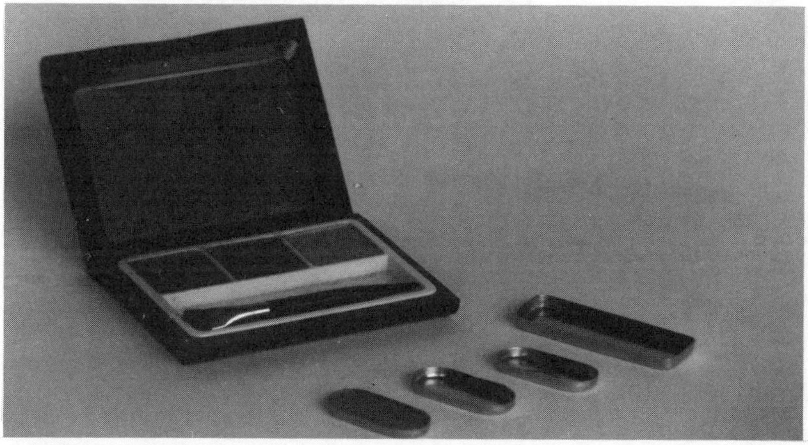

Figure 14.7 Eye colour palette and godets

Here are two formulations for compact eye shadow. The second is for an irridescent type employing titanium-dioxide-coated mica pigments:

1	Talc	– 82.5	**2**	Talc	– 42
	Zinc stearate	– 6		Zinc stearate	– 7
	Pigments	– 7.5		Mica–titanium dioxide	– 40
	Wax-based binder	– 4		Pigments	– 2
				Wax-based binder	– 9

The wax-based binder:

Beeswax	– 12	Melt and blend together
Lanolin	– 2	
Mineral oil	– 86	

The powder base ingredients are blended together and coloured as required. The completed powder is then thoroughly mixed in the molten wax base, and then pressed or hot filled into godets (see figures 14.8 and 14.9).

Figure 14.8 Pressing eye colour into godets (courtesy of the Kemwall Engineering Company)

Figure 14.9 Hot-filling eye shadow (courtesy of the Kemwall Engineering Company)

In the laboratory, where pressing compacts might not be possible, a *powder eyeshadow* may be made by colouring a translucent face powder type base with suitably coloured pigments.

Despite their tendency to 'crease' during wear, there is still occasional interest shown in cream eyeshadow and grease-based eyeshadow. A *cream eyeshadow* is made by blending the required pigments with glycerol and incorporating them into the foundation cream base as described for tinted foundation cream.

A *grease-based eyeshadow* may be made by making the following wax mixture and blending the pigments into it:

White soft paraffin	– 58	Melt and blend together
Glycerol monostearate	– 18	
Lanolin	– 4	
Beeswax	– 8	
Candelilla wax	– 4	
Pigments	– 8	

Eyeliner

Eyeliner is intended to highlight the eye make-up close to the eyelashes. Both liquid and 'dry' eyeliners are available. A *liquid eyeliner* is a gum solution with pigments dispersed in it. Here is a formulation:

Carboxymethyl cellulose	– 2.5
Polyvinyl pyrrolidone	– 2
Water	– 85.5
Preservative	– q.s.
Pigments	– 10

Dissolve the gums in the water. Add the preservative. Incorporate the pigments.

A *dry eyeliner* is powder-based and 'bound' with a little mineral oil, as in this formulation:

Talc	– 60	Pigments	– 30
Titanium dioxide	– 5	Mineral oil	– 5

Eyebrow pencil

The eyebrow area may be accentuated by the use of *wax crayons* or *pencils*. This formulation may be used to make crayons or pencils:

Beeswax	– 21	White soft paraffin	– 18
Carnauba wax	– 5	Lanolin	– 9
Paraffin wax	– 29	Pigments	– 10
Cetyl alcohol	– 8		

The waxes are melted together and blended. The pigments are mixed in. The mixture is cast into sticks similar to lipstick or made into 'leads' to be incorporated into pencils by a pencil manufacturer.

Eyelash dyes

Dyeing the eyelashes is fraught with potential danger: physical injury from applicators and the entry of what could be harmful chemicals into the eye. While the process must be as safe as possible in this very sensitive area, to be effective there are certain risks involved.

The preparation of the dye mixture for use is very similar to preparing a permanent hair dye: mixing with hydrogen peroxide solution. Despite this, the dyes involved are *not* the coal tar dyes used for scalp hair. They are dyes of *vegetable* origin. Scalp hair dyes are *dangerous* to the eyes and could cause blindness.

The hydrogen peroxide used too is only 5 or 6 volume strength (1.5 – 1.75 per cent). *Do not confuse* this with 6 per cent (20 volume) peroxide used for hair colouring.

Formulations for eyelash tints have been omitted deliberately. Only factory made and tested products from a *reputable* manufacturer should be used.

Lipsticks

Lipstick must not only be able to impart an attractive colour and gloss to the lips, but must also be dense enough to modify the outline of the lip area.

Traditionally, the colour in lipstick is derived from a combination of *pigments* which confer the main colour and dyestuffs which *stain* the skin to give a certain *indelibility* after the main colour pigments have been licked away.

In recent times the stains have gradually been dropped. They have been found to cause *sensitisation* or *photo sensitisation* in quite a number of users, leading to an inflammation of the lips called *cheilitis*. The stains also *fluoresce* under ultra-violet light, giving a strange green glow under the lights in discotheques.

Lipstick pigments

The choice of colours is very dependent on current fashion. This can demand anything from garish oranges, scarlets and 'shocking' pinks to the most delicate of pinks. Sometimes the 'un-made up' look requires an unpigmented '*lipgloss*' just to give gloss and prevent cracking.

The pigments used include a variety of red, pink and orange *lakes*. They *must* be safe because much of it will probably be *swallowed!* Titanium dioxide white is used to 'let down' the lake pigments to produce the pastel shades.

Glitter and irridescent effects are popular. Titanium-dioxide-coated mica, bismuth oxychloride and dyed aluminium powder confer these effects.

Lipstick stains

While they are little-used these days, mention must be made of the stains. They are '*fluorescein*' or '*eosin*' dyes such as:

Eosin – tetrabromo fluorescein	– purplish red
Tetrachlorobromo fluorescein	– bluish red
Dibromo fluorescein	– orange red

For lipstick formulation, the stains are soluble in fats and oils. Castor oil was commonly used as the solvent for this purpose.

Lipstick bases

A lipstick base is a mixture of fats, waxes and oils carefully chosen so that it has a 'softening point' at around lip-surface temperature, and also so that it is *thixotropic:* it will spread easily over the lips when being applied yet will remain a firm stick in its case. In addition, it should not easily smudge or transfer on to cups, glasses and shirt collars!

Lipstick formulations

There are many, many published formulations for lipstick bases. Those which follow are but a few examples. In each listing the ingredients of the wax base total 100 parts. The pigments are extra to this. As grades of materials differ it might be necessary to vary the proportions slightly to produce lipsticks which are not too soft or too firm.

1
Carnauba wax – 18
Ozokerite – 18
Lanolin – 27
Mineral oil – 27
Castor oil – 10

Stains/pigments – q.s. up to 10
Flavour/perfume – q.s.

2
Castor oil – 30
Mineral oil – 15
Beeswax – 15
Paraffin wax – 10
Carnauba wax – 10
Ceresin wax – 10
Silicone fluid – 10
1000 cs viscosity

Stains/pigments – q.s. up to 7.5
Flavour/perfume – q.s.

3
Beeswax – 36
Lanolin – 8
White soft paraffin – 36
Cetyl alcohol – 6
Castor oil – 8
Carnauba wax – 6

Stains/pigments – q.s. up to 10
Flavour/perfume – q.s.

4
Beeswax – 17
Ceresin wax – 33.5
Lanolin – 5.5
White soft paraffin – 27
Cetyl alcohol – 6
Olive oil – 11

Stains/pigments – q.s. up to 10
Flavour/perfume – q.s.

5 A creamy lipstick formulation:
Castor oil – 65
Lanolin – 10
Isopropyl myristate – 5
Beeswax – 7
Candelilla wax – 7
Carnauba wax – 3
Ozokerite – 3

Pigments/stains – q.s. up to 15
Perfume/flavour – q.s.

Industrial manufacture of lipsticks

The manufacture of lipsticks is not an easy process. In industry the waxy–fatty materials are melted together. The stain is dissolved in the castor oil or other solvent. The pigments are often 'wetted' by milling them with some of the castor oil. The components are mixed, then thoroughly milled together using a roller mill or similar machine.

The molten lipstick is cast into sticks by pouring it into special moulds. When set the sticks are removed and *'flamed'* by passing them quickly through a gas flame. This removes surface imperfections and imparts a high gloss (see figures 14.10 and 14.11).

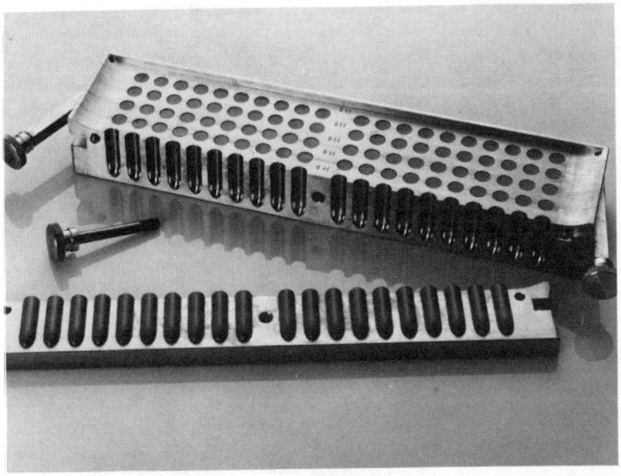

Figure 14.10 A lipstick mould (courtesy of the Kemwall Engineering Company)

Figure 14.11 Lipstick mould with lipstick cases being fitted (courtesy of the Kemwall Engineering Company)

Making lipstick in the laboratory

Samples of lipstick formulations may be made in the laboratory but *be prepared for a mess* and, because the task is not easy, be prepared for disappointment with your early efforts.

To minimise the clearing up:

1 Protect all work surfaces with disposable covering.

2 Heat wax mixtures over a waterbath.

3 Heat the formulations in disposable vessels; round individual *foil* pie dishes are ideal.

4 Take care not to get lipstick stains or the coloured lipstick on your hands. *It will stain your skin.* Wear rubber gloves if possible.

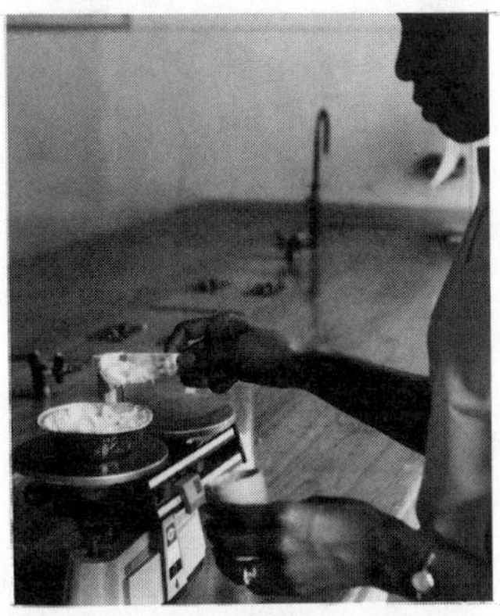

Figure 14.12 Making lipstick in the laboratory. Weighing the ingredients for the lipstick base

Weigh out the waxy and fatty materials and melt them together over the waterbath. Keep out the castor or olive oil at this stage (see figures 14.12 and 14.13).

Dissolve the stain in some of the oil. Mix the pigments on a white tile to the required shade and mill them thoroughly into some more of the oil. Incorporate the stain solution and pigment suspension into the molten wax mixture (see figures 14.14 and 14.15).

Note – Some lipstick stains and pigments are obtainable already mixed in castor oil. If these are used, this castor oil must be allowed for in the formulation.

Figure 14.13 Melting and mixing the lipstick base over a waterbath

Figure 14.14 Mixing the lipstick pigments on a tile

Figure 14.15 Adding the lipstick base to the pigments and oil

Lipstick moulds for laboratory use are obtainable but they are expensive. For occasional use, simple moulds can be made from aluminium foil. To do this you need some test-tubes of 10–12 mm in diameter. Cut pieces of aluminium kitchen foil about 8 cm square. Roll a piece round the test tube and press it closed round the bottom of the test tube. Repeat until enough moulds are made.

Fill a large beaker with talc or flour and tamp it down. Push the foil moulds vertically into the talc or flour and *carefully* withdraw the test tubes (see figure 14.16).

Pour the molten lipstick into the moulds (see figure 14.17). Save a little to 'top-up' because lipstick contracts as it sets. When the sticks are set, remove the foil and 'flame' the sticks in a gas flame (see figure 14.18). Fit them into cases or rewrap with fresh foil.

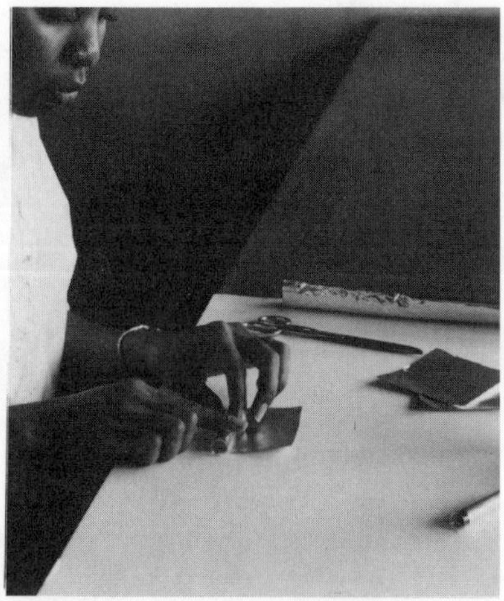

Figure 14.16 Making simple lipstick moulds from kitchen foil

Figure 14.17 Pouring the molten lipstick into the moulds

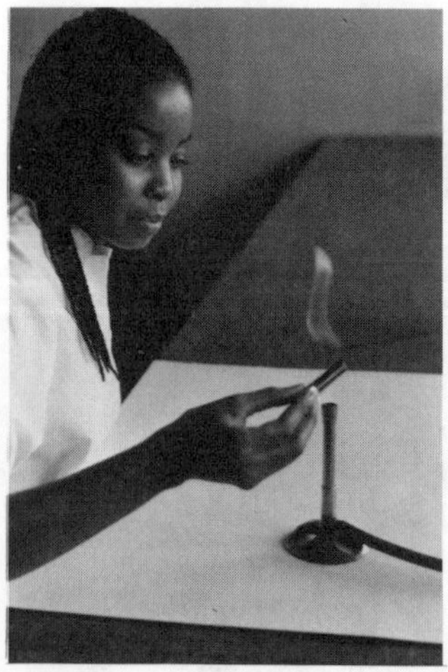

Figure 14.18 Flaming the lipsticks with a gas flame

Things to do

1 You may make up samples of any of the products described in this chapter but, if they are to be used on the person, pay very strict attention to the quality of the raw materials and to the hygiene of the workplace. The methods are detailed in chapter 6.

2 Make up stocks of powder, cream and wax bases and use them to experiment with colour. Colour pigments for cosmetics may be obtainable from the manufacturers, or from certain laboratory chemical suppliers: for example, Scientific and Chemical Supplies Ltd of Sedgley, West Midlands.

3 Study the history of make-up. Books on the subject include:

Angeloglou, M. [1970]. *A History of Make-up*, Macmillan, London.
Corson, R. [1972]. *Fashion in Make-up*, P. Owen, London.
Garland, M. [1957]. *The Changing Face of Beauty*, Weidenfield and Nicolson, London.
Haweis, M. [1978]. *The Art of Beauty*, London.
Williams, N. [1957]. *Powder and Paint*, London.

Self-assessment questions

1 In the UK, what legislation governs the choice of colours for cosmetics?

2 What is meant by 'F, D and C' colours?

3 What is a laked pigment?

4 List the five desirable physical properties of a face powder.

5 What is the purpose in make up of titanium dioxide?

6 What is the function of magnesium stearate in a face powder?

7 Name two substances used to produce a glitter effect in cosmetics.

8 What hazard is sometimes associated with the stains in lipstick?

15 Sunshine, suntan, sunburn

Suntanning products; sunscreens; fake tans; melanogenics; treatments for sunburn; skin bleaches

Suntanning products

In chapter 12 we saw the effects, both beneficial and harmful, that the *ultra-violet rays* of the sun have on the skin. During the holiday season in particular, there is a vast market for a variety of products to make the gaining of a tan a much more rapid and a much less painful and damaging experience. These products fall into four categories:

Sunscreens	– mostly to protect against sunburn
Melanogenics	– to speed the tan with or without sunshine
Fake tans	– to simulate a tan
Palliatives	– to alleviate the discomfort of sunburn

Sunscreens

Ultra-violet is a wide-ranging band of radiation. Different parts of the ultra-violet band have different effects. The two important bands as far as the skin is concerned are known as UV-A and UV-B.

UV-A is the band which develops a *rapid tan* in a skin which is ready. It will not tan a skin which does not have in it the necessary uncoloured melanin granules. It is this band which also causes the damage to the elastic fibres which results in premature aging.

UV-B is the band which causes *sunburn*. It also initiates the production of melanin in the skin to give a *lasting tan* and stimulates epidermal growth to *thicken* the *Stratum corneum*.

The short-term aim of the *sunbather* is a *rapid* tan with *no* sunburn. The *sunscreen* they require is one which ideally would let through UV-A but not UV-B. No sunscreen is perfect in this respect, but this is fortunate because without UV-B no lasting tan would develop and the 'slow' tanner would not tan at all. Even the quick-tanning sunworshipper needs protection from the excesses of UV-A which bring on premature aging.

Unlike most other cosmetics which have an active effect on the skin, where there are only one or two universally used active ingredients, there is a very wide selection of *sunscreen* materials to choose from. They come from several chemical 'families'. Some examples are:

Aminobenzoates *Hydroxybenzoates*
Cinnamates *Salicylates*

They have varying degrees of sunscreening ability. By careful choice of the sunscreen and by careful adjustment of the proportion of it used, it is possible to formulate a range of sunscreen products for different skin sensitivities.

Sun Protection Factor – SPF

The Sun Protection Factor is a measure of the effectiveness of a sunscreen product. In simple terms, the SPF of a product is the number of times longer a person can stay exposed to the sun without getting sunburn when using the product.

For instance, if, without a sunscreen, a person could sunbathe for *one* hour before suffering sunburn, then with a sunscreen with SPF-2 he could sunbathe for *two* hours.

Users should be aware that there is, as yet, no agreed standard method for measuring SPFs. Each company has its own method, so SPF numbers are only truly comparable within one company's range of products. From one range to another they are only a general guide.

As to which SPF you should choose, this depends on the sensitivity of your skin. For convenience, people are divided into four groups:

1 Quick tan – no burn
Safe unprotected time 40+ mins

2 Tan fairly easily – may burn a little initially
Safe unprotected time 20–30 mins

3 Burn easily – but tan eventually
Safe unprotected time 10–20 mins

4 Very sensitive – burn very easily – little likelihood of tanning
Safe unprotected time 5–10 mins

Having established the sensitivity of the skin, the choice of SPF is:

Group 1 – need minimum protection	– SPF	2–3
Group 2 – need 'average' protection	– SPF	4–6
Group 3 – need extra protection	– SPF	7–8
Group 4 – need 'total block'	– SPF	10–20 or more

Table 15.1 shows the sunscreen content of a product range and the amount of burning rays each still allows through.

Table 15.1 Sunscreen Content of a Range of Suntan Lotions

		Percentage of UV-B let through	*Percentage of sunscreen – p-N,N-dimethylaminobenzoate*
Quick tan	SPF 2	Up to 15	0.8
Average	SPF 5	8–10	1.0–1.1
Extra protection	SPF 8	3–5	1.3–1.5
Total block	SPF 12	1	2.0

In practice, the SPF depends not only on the sunscreen ingredient but also on the product in which it is incorporated. Paraffin waxes, soft paraffins and mineral oils all confer a degree of ultra-violet protection of their own, so obviously cream-based products will be more effective than water-based or alcohol-based lotions.

When sunbathing on the beach, one must also consider if the sunscreen will stay on in the sea. Oil-based lotions will – the others wash off. The user must also bear in mind that ultra-violet rays penetrate through water. You can sunburn *under the water*.

On the other hand, if you prefer to sunbathe lying on the beach, the sand will stick to your oily lotion. You cannot win! Here are formulations for a sunscreen oil and a sunscreen cream.

Sunscreen oil

Liquid lanolin	– 5
Isopropyl myristate	– 43
Mineral oil	– 50
Sunscreen	up to – 2

Blend the ingredients together. Note that the proportion of sunscreen should be adjusted to suit the SPF required.

Sunscreen cream

Moisturising cream		– 98
Sunscreen	up to	– 2

Make the moisturising cream using any of the formulations listed in chapter 13, but include the required amount of the sunscreen in the oil phase before adding the water phase.

Melanogenics

There are those who have neither the time nor the patience to await the development of a natural tan. There are those too who dare not make their first sortie to the beach in all their pinkness. Their wish is to speed up nature's process with a *melanogenic* or by-pass it altogether with a *fake tan*.

Melanogenics work by deliberately making the skin more sensitive to ultraviolet. It has long been known that many perfumes *photosensitise*. A liberal application of your favourite splash-on cologne before sunbathing and you could tan in random dark and light patches: dark where the cologne has splashed and light where it has not.

If this should happen then it is quite likely that the cologne contained a raw material such as *bergamot oil* or *celery oil*. These oils contain *photosensitising* materials called *psoralens*. In bergamot oil it is 5-methoxy-psoralen or 'Bergaptan'. This is frequently employed in suntan products to speed up the development of the tan by making the *melanocytes* more active. But beware, the high-speed tan is often yellowish rather than brown.

As an alternative to applying it in a suntan lotion, one could instead take a psoralen *orally* as a course of tablets or capsules. These need to be formulated with great care. Some of the early ventures were withdrawn rather hurriedly when it was found that they not only produced a faster tan but also faster and much more serious sunburn!

Fake tans

Another way to produce an 'instant' tan is to simulate it with a fake tan. These products produce the effect of a tan by *dyeing* the skin brown.

This might be done with a vegetable dye such as henna, or perhaps with a substance which reacts with the keratin protein of the skin turning it brown.

When you bite into an apple and it turns brown, it is because proteins and sugars in the exposed apple flesh have been mixed then *oxidised* by the air.

If suitable sugar-type substances such as *dihydroxyacetone* or *erythrolose* are applied to the skin, they react with keratin in the outer layers, and then oxidise to a tan colour. These products colour only the surface of the skin so their effect soon wears off and is lost. They are, however, frequently included in suntan lotions to colour the skin quickly while the real tan develops.

To show the tan simulation of dihydroxyacetone, make up this lotion and apply it to an area of skin:

1,3-dihydroxyacetone	– 4
Alcohol	– 30
Water	– 66

To make it, dissolve the dihydroxyacetone in the alcohol, and then add the water. This makes a colourless lotion. The colour on the skin takes several hours to develop. Only then will you find out whether or not you have applied it evenly.

Palliatives

Should the worst happen and you suffer *sunburn* with its reddened, itching, possibly painful and peeling skin, the pain can be lessened by using a soother or *palliative* such as *calamine lotion*. The mildly astringent calamine (zinc carbonate) soothes away the pain. Here are two formulations for calamine lotions:

1			2		
	Calamine	– 20		Calamine	– 15
	Glycerol	– 5		Zinc oxide	– 5
	Water or rose water	– 75		Glycerol	– 5
				Water or rose water	– 75

Skin bleaches

Not everyone wants a deeply bronzed skin. There are those who consider their skin to be too dark already and would dearly like it to be fairer.

For many dark races in Africa, a fair skin is highly desirable. In some tribes, young girls approaching marriageable age are sheltered indoors for several months for their skin to fade. Later they may resort to very drastic means to maintain a fair skin. They may use *oxidising skin bleaches* based on *hypochlorites* or *peroxides*, or they may take *drugs* which inhibit the formation of melanin in the skin. Such drugs include *hydroquinone* and *ammoniated mercury*.

Things to do

1 Collect information literature on suntan products which could be useful in advising clients on their choice of products when visiting any part of the world.

2 Find out which sunscreen products also contain fake tan dyes and which contain melanogenic substances.

Self-assessment questions

1 What is meant by SPF-4?

2 Name two classes of chemicals which are sunscreens.

3 How does dihydroxyacetone colour the skin?

4 What is the chemical name for calamine?

5 What is Bergaptan and how does it assist the attainment of a tan?

6 In what type of cosmetic product might hydroquinone be the active ingredient?

16 The hands, the feet, the nails

Hand care problems; hand creams and lotions; protective hand creams; hand cleansers; care of the feet; foot care products; the nails; nail disorders; nail care products; nail enamels and varnishes

Hands

Hands that do dishes, that wash clothes, that scrub floors, that weed gardens, that mend cars . . . .

Hands must be the most assaulted parts of the body, yet they are the *least protected*. The palms and finger 'pads' have *no follicles* and therefore *no sebum* of their own, though they do pick up some from other parts of the skin.

They do, however, have a vast number of sweat glands which go a long way to keeping the skin moist and supple.

The hands are very vulnerable to attack, particularly by the repeated wetting with detergent solutions which solubilise and remove grease and the lipid substances even from the living cells deep in the epidermis. This results in a *dry, flaking skin*. Add to this the dry cold of of a winter's day and you have the recipe for *cracking* and *splitting* of the skin.

Hand creams

Any good *moisturising* or *emollient* (skin-softening) cream will do so long as it is quick and easy to apply and does not leave the skin obviously greasy. Hand creams are usually lightly coloured and perfumed to make them pleasant to use.

The only constraint is that the cream should not leave a sticky greasiness on the hands which would 'fingerprint' everything one touched. Very greasy emollients, therefore, cannot be used, at least not in large proportions. There are many, many formulations for hand creams in the technical literature. Here are just four examples. Each may be made by the 'standard' method described in chapter 6. The oil and water phases are heated separately to 70°C, mixed and stirred until cool.

Formulations for hand creams

	Ingredient	Amount	Phase
1	Mineral oil	– 3	Oil phase
	Lanolin	– 3	
	Spermaceti wax	– 3	
	Glycerol monostearate S.E.	– 12	
	Sorbitol 70 per cent syrup	– 5	Water phase
	Water	– 74	
	Colour, perfume, preservative	– q.s.	
2	Iso-propyl myristate	– 2	Oil phase
	Cetyl alcohol	– 2	
	Stearic acid	– 15	
	Lanolin	– 2	

(*cont.*)

Formulations for hand creams (*cont.*)

No.	Ingredient	Amount	Phase
	Glycerol	– 3	Water phase
	Sorbitol 70 per cent syrup	– 3	Water phase
	Triethanolamine	– 1.4	Water phase
	Water	– 71.6	Water phase
	Colour, perfume, preservative	– q.s.	
3	Mineral oil	– 1	Oil phase
	Iso-propyl myristate	– 1.5	Oil phase
	Cetyl alcohol	– 8	Oil phase
	Lanolin	– 3	Oil phase
	Lanbritol wax N21	– 4	Oil phase
	Triethanolamine	– 1.65	Water phase
	Methyl cellulose	– 1.25	Water phase
	Glycerol	– 5	Water phase
	Water	– 74.6	Water phase
	Colour, perfume, preservative	– q.s.	
4	Glycerol monostearate S.E.	– 4	Oil phase
	Lanolin	– 4	Oil phase
	Stearic acid	– 4	Oil phase
	Cetyl alcohol	– 2	Oil phase
	Propylene glycol	– 3	Water phase
	Triethanolamine	– 1	Water phase
	Water	– 82	Water phase
	Colour, perfume, preservative	– q.s.	

Hand lotions

Many prefer a more liquid product easily dispensed from a bottle, plastic tube or pump dispenser and easily spread and rubbed in. Here are three formulations for hand lotions:

No.	Ingredient	Amount	Phase
5	Lanolin	– 2	Oil phase
	Lanbritol wax N21	– 2	Oil phase
	Mineral oil	– 3	Oil phase
	Glycerol	– 3	Water phase
	Triethanolamine	– 0.3	Water phase
	Water	– 89.7	Water phase
	Colour, perfume, preservative	– q.s.	
6	Lanolin	– 1.3	Oil phase
	Cetyl alcohol	– 0.5	Oil phase
	Mineral oil	– 10	Oil phase
	Stearic acid	– 5	Oil phase
	Triethanolamine	– 2.5	Water phase
	Water	– 80.7	Water phase
	Colour, perfume, preservative	– q.s.	
7	Lanette wax CAT	– 7	Melt together. Stir until cool
	Glycerol	– 8	Melt together. Stir until cool
	Water	– 85	Melt together. Stir until cool
	Colour, perfume, preservative	– q.s.	

Can you identify the *emulsifier* in each of these creams and lotions? There may be more than one. Do you know the function of the other materials? Turn to skin creams in chapters 10 and 13.

An old favourite hand lotion is *glycerin and rosewater*. In the original formulation they were used 50:50. That concentration of glycerol may actually aggravate the dryness of the hands. A modern glycerin and rosewater contains much less glycerol and needs to be thickened with, in this instance, a methyl cellulose:

Glycerol	– 10	Methyl cellulose	– 1–2
Rosewater	– 90	Colour, preservative	– q.s.

Protective and barrier creams

Before doing work with strong detergents or other harmful substances it is advisable to *protect* the hands. Wearing work gloves is not always feasible and a *barrier cream* is a useful alternative. Here are two formulations. In the first the barrier is provided by lanolin, soft paraffin, and kaolin.

Ingredient	Amount	Phase
Stearic acid	– 6	Oil phase
Cetyl alcohol	– 3	Oil phase
Lanolin	– 3	Oil phase
Soft paraffin	– 2	Oil phase
Sodium hydroxide	– 0.65	Water phase
Water	– 67.35	Water phase
Kaolin	– 18	
Colour, perfume, preservative	– q.s.	

The oil and water phases are made into a cream by the 'standard' method, then the kaolin is milled into it.

Silicones are intensely water-repellent substances. The silicone in the second formulation waterproofs the skin to prevent the entry of water-based harmful substances.

Ingredient	Amount	Phase
Lanbritol wax N21	– 15	Oil phase
Lanolin	– 5	Oil phase
Mineral oil	– 20	Oil phase
Silicone fluid 200 c/s viscosity	– 5 to 10	Oil phase
Water	– to 100	– Water phase
Colour, perfume, preservative	– q.s.	

Hand cleanser gels

Some kinds of work such as painting or motor mechanics so ingrain dirt into the hands that it is very difficult to remove with soap and water. It can be removed with a *strong* detergent such as 'neat' wash-up liquid but better still by using a special hand cleanser. Here is an example:

Ingredient	Amount	Phase
Deodorised Kerosene	– 35	Oil phase
Lanolin	– 10	Oil phase
Coconut diethanolamide	– 4	Oil phase
Stearic acid	– 2.43	Oil phase
Oleic acid	– 3.64	Oil phase
Sodium hydroxide	– 0.38	Water phase
Water	– 44.55	Water phase
Perfume, colour, preservative	– q.s.	

Feet

The feet are probably the hardest worked parts of the body but at the same time they could well be the most abused and neglected.

'Everyday' foot problems, *sweat* and possibly *odour* stem directly from enclosing the feet in shoes. Like the palms of the hands, the *soles* of the feet have a very high population of sweat glands but unlike the hands the sweat *cannot evaporate* to cool the feet. They become hot, tired and ache.

With today's *nylon* socks and stockings and *plastic* shoes, there is nothing absorbent to absorb the perspiration. The atmosphere inside the shoe is *warm* and *moist*: ideal conditions for the growth of *bacteria* and *fungi* and ideal for generating *foot odour*.

Besides the 'routine' problems, there are a number of diseases and disorders of the foot which are important.

Hyperidrosis

Hyperidrosis is over-activity of the sweat glands. Excessively sweaty feet produce very 'soggy' conditions inside the shoes which could cause swelling, redness and *maceration* (a pulpy flaking) between the toes, looking very like Athlete's foot.

Athlete's foot – *tinea pedis*

Athlete's foot is by no means confined to athletes. In fact a quarter of the population could be suffering from it. It is a *fungal* infection which almost always starts in the 'web' between the small toe and the one next to it. If it becomes severe, the flaking, cracking and blistering of the *Stratum corneum* could spread between the other toes and even to the sole of the foot. Among the fungi that can cause it are *Trichophyton* and *Epidermophyton*.

Corns

A corn is a small patch of thick hard skin. A small area of pressure from an ill-fitting shoe might prevent the proper exfoliation of the epidermis which builds up in thickness and pushes down into the dermis below.

Callus

A callus is a larger accumulation of hard, thickened skin caused by pressure and friction over a larger area. Calluses often occur on the pads of the toes and the heels.

Bunion

A bunion is a misaligned toe joint which has become swollen and painful having been pushed out of line by ill-fitting shoes.

Verruca

A verruca is a corn-like growth consisting of a mass of *keratin* which forms a 'core' or 'plug' extending down through the dermis. It is the result of a *virus* infection traditionally transmitted by walking barefoot on changing-room floors. It is not a disease for the beauty therapist to treat.

Ingrowing toenails

If the toenails are trimmed too short, particularly at the corners where they rest in the nail grooves, the nail may dig into the groove causing an injury which often turns septic.

Foot care and foot care products

Much of the routine care of the feet is easy to do. Wash the feet at least once a day. Dry them well and apply a *foot powder*. Choose sensible shoes and socks.

Bathing the feet in warm water improves the circulation. This is particularly valuable if they get little exercise or if the shoes, socks or tights grip the feet or legs too tightly thus restricting the circulation.

The use of *foot bath salts* helps to ease swelling and aching feet by drawing out moisture by osmosis. One can use *epsom salt* (magnesium sulphate), *sea salt* or *foot bath salts*.

Foot bath salts

Ingredient	Amount
Sodium sesquicarbonate	– 99.5
Sodium lauryl sulphate	– 0.5
Perfume	– q.s.
Colour – soluble-powder type	– q.s.

Mix the powders together. Absorb the perfume on to a little light magnesium carbonate and then add it to the main mixture.

Artificial sea salt

The relaxing effect of bathing the feet in sea water can be had even if one is not near the sea by using artificial sea salt. This is available from health food stores but it can be made by mixing the following salts in the stated proportions:

Ingredient	Amount
Sodium chloride	– 57
Sodium sulphate	– 19
Magnesium sulphate	– 9.5
Calcium chloride	– 4.8
Magnesium chloride	– 9.5
Potassium bromide	– 0.15
Potassium iodide	– 0.05

Foot powder

A foot powder is basically a talcum or dusting powder usually with the addition of a *fungicide*. Suitable fungicides include:

Bronopol
Chlorphenisin
Dichlorophen

Here is a formulation. It may be made by the method described in chapter 6.

Ingredient	Amount
Talc	– 79.8
Kaolin	– 20.0
Fungicide	– 0.2

Foot cream

A foot cream has a similar formulation to a hand cream. Here is a formulation. Foot cream, too, often contains a fungicide. Mix 1 per cent into the finished cream.

Ingredient	Amount	Phase
Glycerol monostearate	– 15	Oil phase
Lanolin	– 1	Oil phase
Sorbitol 70 per cent syrup	– 2.5	Water phase
Glycerol	– 2.5	Water phase
Water	– 79	Water phase
Perfume, colour, preservative	– q.s.	

Foot spray

Deodorant and antiperspirant sprays are available for use on the feet. They are virtually the same as those for underarms. *Aluminium chlorohydrate* is the usual antiperspirant raw material.

Corn and callus remover

Corns, calluses and even verrucas can be removed by putting on them a *keratolytic* or keratin-dissolving substance. In this 'paint-on' lotion, *salicylic acid* is the keratolytic material. The collodion solution sets on the skin like a nail varnish yet it is permeable to let the skin 'breathe'.

Ingredient	Amount
Salicylic acid	– 10
Lactic acid	– 10
Collodion solution	– 80

This *alkaline* lotion can be used to soften calluses. As will be seen later, it is very like a cuticle remover.

Ingredient	Amount
Potassium hydroxide	– 0.5
Glycerol	– 15
Water	– 84.5

Chilblains and chilblain ointments

Chilblains are areas of inflammation of the skin and the underlying tissues which tend to result from exposure to cold and damp. Particularly affected are the toes but the fingers, ears and nose may also be affected. The symptoms are an itching or burning sensation with reddening and swelling as a result of localised poor circulation.

The cure for chilblains is to keep the affected parts warm and dry. To improve the circulation an ointment may be applied. Often the ointments consist of *aromatic oils* such as oil of wintergreen or its synthetic equivalent, methyl salicylate mixed into a base of soft paraffin. The oil acts as a *vasodilator*: it dilates the blood vessels to improve the circulation.

The nails

A nail grows from a fold in the skin near the end of the finger or the toe. In some ways it behaves like a wide flat hair follicle (see figure 16.1).

There is still some doubt as to the function of the *nail bed*. It is not clear whether it just 'sticks' the nail to the finger or toe or actually adds further growth to the underside of the nail-plate.

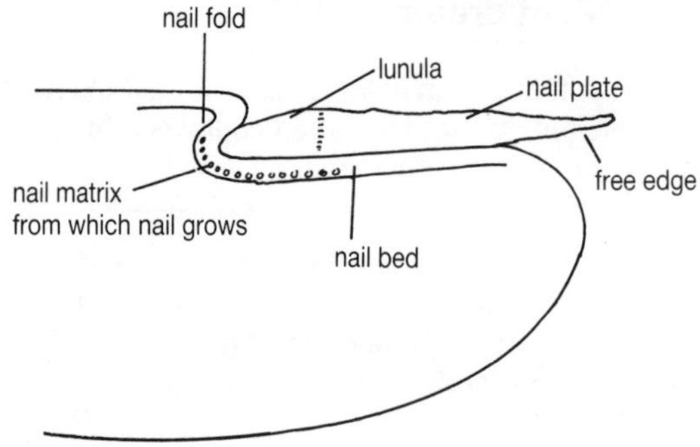

Figure 16.1 Section through a nail

The nails grow at a rate of 0.5 to 1.3 mm each week. Their growth is basically like that of a hair except that it is *continuous*. There is no cycle of shedding and regrowth as there is with the hair. If, though, a nail is lost through accident or disease, it will regrow. A fingernail takes 5½ months to reach its full length, a toenail 12–18 months.

The *nailplate* is made of the skin protein, *keratin*. Unlike the hair in which the keratin is fibrous, in the nail plate it is in the form of sheets or *lamellae*.

Disorders of the nails

A variety of disorders of the nails are recognised by beauticians and manicurists.

In rare instances a nail might be shed as a result of severe illness or injury to the nail. The absence of the nail is *anonychia*.

Onycholysis is when the nail separates from the nail bed and hangs free from the nail fold. This could be the result of using nail hardeners, particularly those containing formalin which might penetrate through the nail and damage the tissues of the nail bed.

Women in particular might suffer from *brittle nails*. Brittleness is caused by dehydration of the nail plate, possibly by nail enamel solvents or strong detergents. The nails may break, split or flake.

Marks and ridges on the nails are a common occurrence. *Longitudinal* or lengthways ridges are common on otherwise perfectly healthy nails but they do tend to spoil the appearance, particularly of enamelled nails. *Buffing* with an abrasive nail polish will remove minor ridges but deeper 'furrows' might require filling with a special 'filler' base-coat before applying nail enamel.

Transverse or crossways lines and ridges do indicate abnormal nail growth. Furrows across the nails indicate periods of poor growth such as might accompany disease or distress. Really deep depressions associated with severe illness are called *Beau's lines*.

A number of factors might result in *pitting of the nails*. Substances which cause dermatitis of the hands might also pit the nails. Psoriasis, the condition of abnormal skin growth, can produce deformed and pitted nails. Ringworm and Athlete's foot fungi can spread to the nails, causing pitting.

Whitening of the nails is called *leuconychia*. *Leuconychia punctata* are those white flecks on the nails. They are *not* due to calcium deficiency; more likely they arise as a result of damage to the nail during manicure.

Discoloured nails can result from tobacco staining or by the 'bleeding' of colour from nail enamel. The latter can be prevented by using a base-coat before applying the nail enamel.

Nail biting can be an extremely disfiguring habit. Some people bite their nails right back to the nail fold.

Nail care products

Manicure products are of two types: those for the care of the nails and those for decorating the nails.

Cuticle remover

The cuticle of the nail is skin scales shed from within the nail fold which adhere to the nail as an unsightly 'growth'. An alkaline lotion will remove them. Here is a formulation:

Potassium hydroxide	– 2
Glycerol	– 25
Water	– 73

Alkalis such as potassium hydroxide are very 'drying' to the nails. This basic cuticle remover can be made into a *milk* cuticle remover which will be less damaging to the nails. To do this mix together equal parts of mineral oil and oleic acid. Add sufficient of the mixture to the cuticle remover to give the required effect.

Cuticle cream

Cuticle cream softens the cuticle by *macerating* it in oil so it can then be pushed back. Here are two formulations. The first is a simple wax/oil mixture: the second is a cold cream:

1	White soft paraffin	– 40	Melt together	
	Spermaceti wax	– 20		
	Lanolin	– 40		
	Perfume	– q.s.		
2	Lanolin	– 4	Oil phase	Mix at 70°C
	Mineral oil	– 50		
	Beeswax	– 16		
	Borax	– 1	Water phase	
	Water	– 29		
	Perfume, preservative	– q.s.		

Nail creams

A nail cream for brittle nails is also virtually a cold cream or a moisturising cream. Any of the *cold creams*, *vanishing creams* or *moisturising creams* described in previous chapters will do, especially if it contains a little *lanolin* and an humectant such as *glycerol*.

Nail bleaches

Those stains caused by tobacco, vegetable preparation, ink or nail enamel can be removed with a nail *bleach*. A simple bleaching action is achieved by using 20 volume (6 per cent) hydrogen peroxide. Alternatively, an abrasive cleanser for the nails can be made by milling *pumice* powder into a *cold cream*:

Cold cream	– 92
Pumice powder	– 8

Nail polish

Also of an *abrasive* nature are *nail polishes*. To remove ridges from the nails a variety of abrasives can be used. *Stannic oxide* is probably the best, but talc, silica, kaolin and precipitated chalk are also suitable. Formerly these would be available in powder form:

Ingredient	Amount	Method
Stannic oxide	– 90	Mill together in mortar with pestle
Silica powder	– 8	
Oleic acid	– 2	
Colour pigment	– q.s.	
Perfume	– q.s.	

A 'wax polish' can be made by milling the abrasive into a wax mixture. For example, make the liquefying cleansing cream described in chapter 10:

Ingredient	Amount	Method
Isopropyl myristate	– 25	Melt together
Mineral oil	– 25	
White soft paraffin	– 30	
Paraffin wax (55°C)	– 20	
Perfume	– q.s.	

Then mill together the cream and stannic oxide:

Ingredient	Amount
Stannic oxide	– 70
The cream	– 30

Nail hardener

Splitting nails are the curse of many women. It has been suggested that applying a lotion containing one of the 'metal-salt' astringents such as *aluminium potassium sulphate (alum)* or *zirconium chloride* might help to strengthen them. The lotion has to be painted on the nails and left on for several minutes, so glycerol is included to prevent it drying out.

Ingredient	Amount	Ingredient	Amount
Alum	– 3	Menthol	– trace
Glycerol	– 10	Water	– 87

Nail white

Commercial 'Nail White' is usually made as a *pencil* which is moistened and drawn beneath the free-edge of the nails to whiten them. These pencils are normally made by pencil manufacturers. Cosmetic houses do not usually have their own equipment.

A simple nail white cream is easily made by milling together a white pigment such as titanium dioxide and white soft paraffin:

Ingredient	Amount
Titanium dioxide	– 38
White soft paraffin	– 62

Nail enamels and varnishes

Almost any 'paint on' coating for the nails, whether coloured or not, tends to be called *'nail varnish'*. Strictly speaking, a varnish is a clear, non-pigmented product such as 'base-coat' or 'top-coat'. A pigmented colour-coat should be called *nail enamel*.

Colour pigment apart, nail enamel, base-coat and top-coat all have basically the same formulation. They are solutions of a 'film-forming' plastic in a suitable solvent. The main components of a nail enamel are:

A *film-forming plastic*	– usually nitrocellulose
A *plastic resin*	– usually aryl sulphonamide formaldehyde to give gloss
A *plasticiser*	– traditionally castor oil to give flexibility to the plastic film
A *solvent*	– a mixture of volatile organic solvents selected to give rapid but not too rapid drying. Solvents used include: Ethyl acetate Butyl acetate Amyl acetate Toluene Alcohol
Pigments	– to provide the colour

A nail enamel might be made to this formulation:

Nitrocellulose	– 10	Ethyl acetate	– 20
Resin	– 10	Butyl acetate	– 15
Plasticiser	– 5	Toluene	– 35
Alcohol	– 5	Pigments	– q.s.

WARNING – DO NOT MAKE YOUR OWN NAIL ENAMELS.

Nitrocellulose is very highly flammable. The solvents are all highly flammable.

For safety reasons most cosmetic houses do not make their own nail enamel bases. They buy them in bulk from specialist manufacturers either to colour themselves or even ready coloured.

You could try experimenting with colouring your own nail enamels. An unpigmented base might be obtainable from a specialist manufacturer, or you could try using 'top-coat'.

Nail lacquers are coloured with *pigments*. The more brilliant colours are *lake* pigments – dyed aluminium oxide powder. There is a risk of colour being 'leaked' from these by the very strong organic solvents. This is why a base-coat should be used to prevent staining the nails.

White is better supplied by *titanium-dioxide-coated mica*. This suspends better in the enamel-base than ordinary titanium dioxide.

Pearlescent effects are produced either by *guanine* or by *bismuth oxychloride*.

The shortcomings of nail enamels

Applying nail enamel properly is a skilled and time-consuming task. After the time and effort one would hope the finished result would last a week or more, but what usually happens is that the enamel either wears off or chips.

In formulating a nail enamel there has to be a compromise in the proportion of *plasticiser*: use a little and the enamel is hard wearing but chips easily; using more prevents chipping but the enamel wears off quickly.

Nail enamel removers

To remove nail enamel, the same sort of organic solvents must be used to re-dissolve it so it may be wiped away. The most frequently used solvent is *acetone*.

Used alone this is very effective, but it is also very harsh and drying to the nails. The inclusion of 2 per cent of glycerol with the acetone will counteract this, as also will the addition of a little olive oil. About 1 per cent of olive oil added to the acetone produces an *'oily'* nail enamel remover. The inclusion of oil makes nail enamel remover unsuitable as 'thinners' for nail enamels.

'Acetone-free' nail enamel removers are popular. They are mixtures of other nail enamel solvents such as ethyl, butyl and amyl acetates and toluene.

Cream nail enamel removers are also available. In this example the enamel solvents replace part of the water phase in what is otherwise a vanishing cream formulation:

Ingredient	Amount	Phase
Stearic acid	9.5	Oil phase
Mineral oil	10	
Triethanolamine	3.5	Water phase
Water	17	
Butyl acetate	50	Nail enamel solvents
Butyl stearate	5	
Carbitol	5	

Make the cream by the usual method (see chapter 6) and then incorporate the solvent mixture into it.

Nail strengtheners and thickeners

Poor or damaged nails can be thickened and strengthened by applying a liquid plastic coating which sets hard on them. This is usually an *acrylic* plastic coating which is not damaged by subsequent applications of nail enamel or removed by nail enamel remover.

These *acrylic nail hardeners* often have to be mixed from the components just before they are applied. One is the liquid plastic; the other is the hardener.

Repairing broken or torn nails

A temporary repair to a broken nail can be done by sticking nail-repairing tissue to the nail with what is virtually a clear nail varnish. A more permanent repair can be done using one of the *acrylic* strengtheners to which has been added a *reinforcing* material such as *rayon* fibres.

Nail elongaters

Nail elongaters, too, are *acrylic* strengtheners with added *rayon* fibres. Several coats painted on to the nail and drawn towards the free edge will gradually elongate the nail.

False nails

Modern false nails are shaped from *plastic sheet*. They are fixed over the existing nails with an *adhesive* which is basically a clear nail varnish.

When finished with, plastic false nails are removed by applying a *removing solvent* (virtually nail enamel remover) to the edges and rocking the false nail gently until it comes away.

Self-assessment questions

1 List reasons why the skin of the hands is particularly susceptible to dryness and cracking.

2 List reasons why the feet tend to suffer from sweatiness.

3 What is hyperidrosis?

4 Briefly describe the appearance of *Tinea pedis*.

5 What is callus on the hands and feet? How might it be caused?

6 What is an ingrowing toenail? What is frequently its cause?

7 Name two substances which might be used as active materials in corn and callus removers.

8 What is *Leuconychia punctata*?

9 What manicure product might contain potassium hydroxide as its active material?

10 Name two substances which are suitable ingredients for abrasive nail polishes.

11 List the five main constituents of a nail enamel.

12 How does one prevent a nail enamel from staining the nails?

13 Name the solvent commonly used as a nail enamel remover.

14 Why cannot nail enamel remover be used as 'thinners' for nail enamel?

17 Hair

Types of hair; the hair follicle; hair growth; the growth cycle of a terminal hair; the hair shaft; strength of the hair; the structure of the hair shaft; the chemistry of keratin – the hair protein; hair colour

Do you know?

A head has between 100 000 and 150 000 hairs. Oriental heads have most hairs; redheads have least. Even a bald head is covered with tiny downy hairs.

Each hair grows up to 0.4 mm a day. Multiply that by the number of hairs and that gives a total hair growth of 50 metres or more each day.

A head hair will grow for up to *seven* years and if not trimmed it might reach over *one metre* in length. A few people can grow hair down to the floor; each of their hairs grows for ten or more years.

Types of hairs and their distribution

Apart from the palms of the hands and the soles of the feet, almost *all* the skin has *follicles* from which hairs could grow. Obviously not all the follicles contain hairs and not all hairs grow as quickly or as long as those of the scalp. It would cause great embarrassment if the eyelashes grew to one metre long!

Over much of the body are tiny hairs which grow very slowly but continuously. On some parts of the body they may wear away as fast as they grow. Where they do not suffer so much wear, they will gradually get longer and as one gets older the body will gradually become more hairy. These continuously slow-growing hairs are *vellus hairs.*

On certain parts, hairs grow more rapidly but for a shorter, more definite period of time, and then fall out, hopefully to be replaced by new ones. These are *terminal hairs.* From infancy we have *scalp hair* on our heads and *eyebrows* and *eyelashes*. From our mid-teens onwards, follicles in other parts change from growing vellus to terminal hairs as *underarm* and *pubic hair* and in men *beard* and *chest hair* appear. Many men will find as their hairline recedes, that many of the follicles on their heads are changing from growing terminal hairs to tiny vellus hairs.

Table 17.1 lists the types of terminal hairs, the length they could reach and the duration of the growth cycle of the hairs.

Table 17.1 Types of Terminal Hair

Type of Hair	*Maximum Length*	*Duration of Growth Cycle*
Scalp hair	Up to 100 cm	Up to 7 years
Eyebrows	Up to 1.25 cm	Up to 4 months
Eyelashes	Up to 1.25 cm	Up to 4 months
Beard, moustache	Up to 30 cm	Up to 1 year
Chest hair	Up to 6 cm	Up to 5 months
Underarm hair	Up to 6 cm	Up to 1 year
Pubic hair	Up to 6 cm	Up to 3 years

The hair follicle

Each hair grows from a *hair follicle.* Although a follicle extends well down through the dermis, it originates as an intucking of the epidermis. Hairs originate from the *epidermis.* Figure 17.1 is a drawing of a hair follicle.

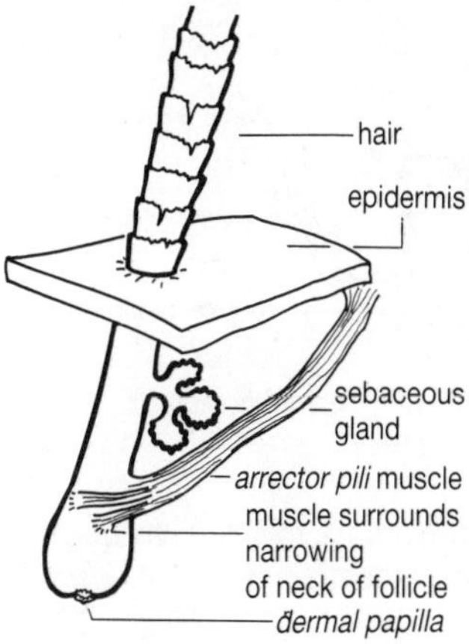

Figure 17.1 Vertical section of a hair follicle with hair

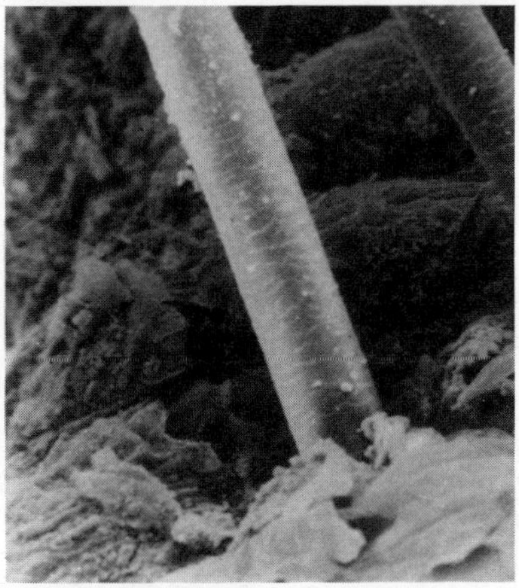

Figure 17.2 Scanning electron micrograph of a single hair follicle (photo – Hugh Rushton, courtesy of the Philip Kingsley Trichology Clinic)

Figure 17.3 A multiple hair follicle (photo – Hugh Rushton, courtesy of the Philip Kingsley Trichology Clinic)

Usually a hair follicle grows a single hair at a time (see figure 17.2). Sometimes one might encounter *multiple* follicles which grow more than one hair at a time (see figure 17.3). Multiple follicles are a problem in electrical epilation. The electrolysist may think she has removed the hair from the follicle, only to find a regrowth as another of the hairs becomes the main hair in the follicle.

The growth of a hair in a follicle

Figures 17.4 and 17.5 show respectively a vertical and a transverse section through a follicle containing a hair. The hair is held in the follicle by the interlocking of the scales of the cuticle with the scales of the inner root sheath.

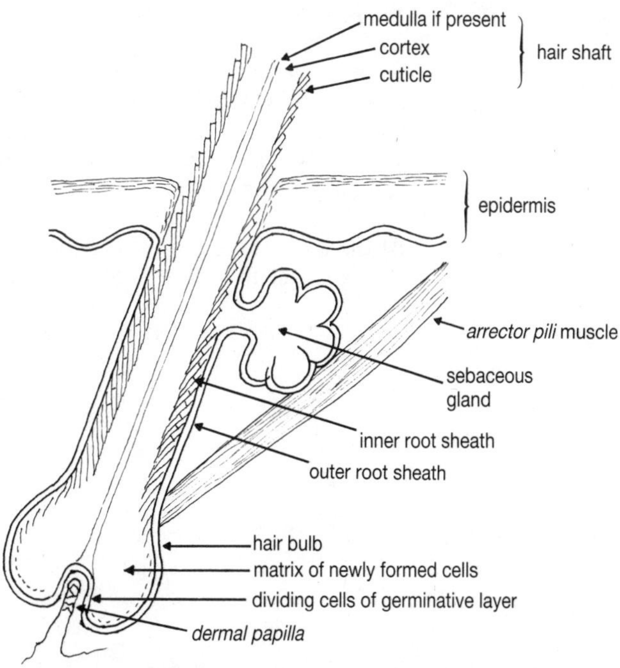

Figure 17.4 Vertical section diagram of a hair follicle

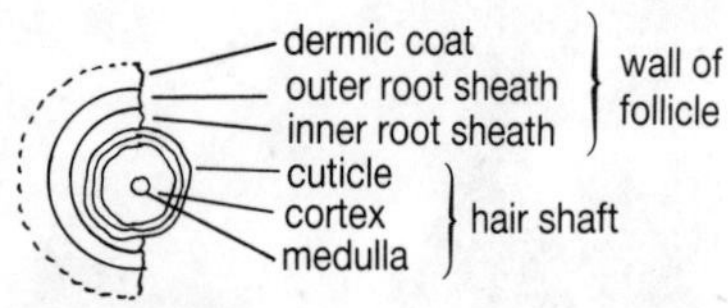

Figure 17.5 Cross-section of hair follicle and hair

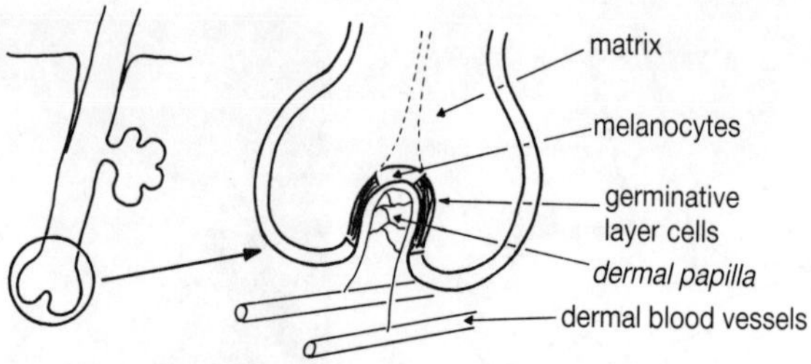

Figure 17.6 The hair bulb and dermal papilla

It is not 'rooted' at the bulb. If a hair is plucked from its follicle it frequently breaks off just above the bulb and brings the root sheath out with it. That is the white speck at the end of a plucked hair.

When, long before one is born, the epidermis tucks in to make a hair follicle, the whole follicle is lined with the *germinative layer* of the epidermis. At the bottom of the follicle, the hair grows from a dome of this germinative layer which covers a cluster of blood capillaries, the *dermal papilla*, which provide its nourishment (see figure 17.6).

The cells of the germinative layer divide by *mitosis* to produce new cells for the hair. Initially these new cells are roundish and constitute the *matrix* of the hair bulb. Those cells which are to form the *cortex* of the hair shaft receive an injection of *melanin* pigment granules from the *melanocytes*. The presence of the melanocytes on the top of the papilla leaves a 'gap' in the matrix of cells which in coarse and medium texture hairs may result in a hollow centre to the hair shaft – the *medulla.*

As new cells are added to the matrix, cells are forced through the narrowing of the neck of the follicle. Those destined to become the cortex become long and narrow with pointed ends – *spindle cells*. The cells closest to the outside become squashed to form the overlapping and interlocking scales of the *inner root sheath* and *cuticle.* It is this interlocking which holds the hair in its follicle (see figure 17.7).

At this stage, the living cells of the hair produce inside them the hair *protein* called *keratin.* Once this has happened the cells have finished their purpose and they die. The mature hairshaft is *dead.* There is little remaining sign of the cells. The spindle-shaped cells of the cortex have given way to bundles of keratin fibres and the cuticle cells have become overlapping keratin scales which encircle the hair (see later in chapter).

At the level of the *sebaceous gland,* the inner root sheath is sloughed off, probably to fall into the sebaceous gland and be absorbed by it, leaving the mature hair shaft to grow to the surface.

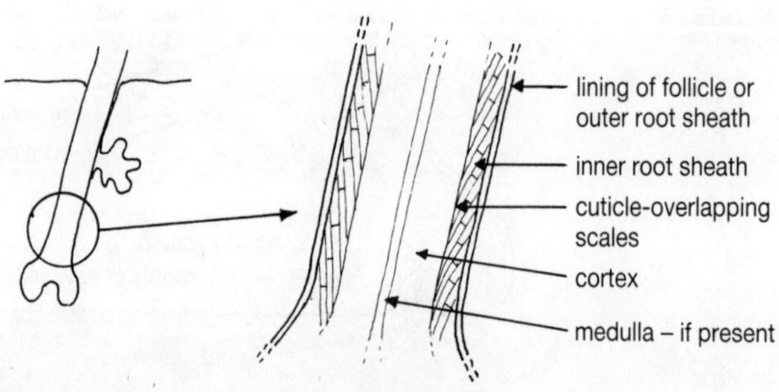

Figure 17.7 How a hair is held in its follicle

The hair growth cycle

A terminal hair does not grow continuously for ever. It eventually stops growing and falls out, to be replaced by a new one.

The hair goes through *three* distinct growth phases during its growth cycle: the active growth stage or *anagen*, the 'preparation for rest' stage or *catagen*, and the resting stage or *telogen*.

Anagen

In the anagen stage the hair is in the actively growing state already described. Early in anagen the growth rate is at its greatest. As anagen comes to its close, the rate gradually decreases until it stops altogether. This is why a neatly trimmed head of hair soon loses the neat, just-trimmed look.

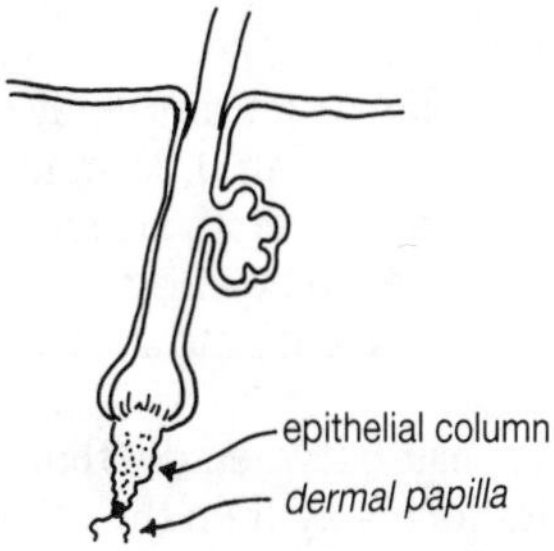

Figure 17.8 A hair in the catagen phase of the growth cycle

Catagen

In catagen, although no new growth is added to the base of the hair, the germinative cells continue to divide for some time producing a column of tissue, the *epithelial column* (see figure 17.8) as the failing papilla retracts down into the dermis.

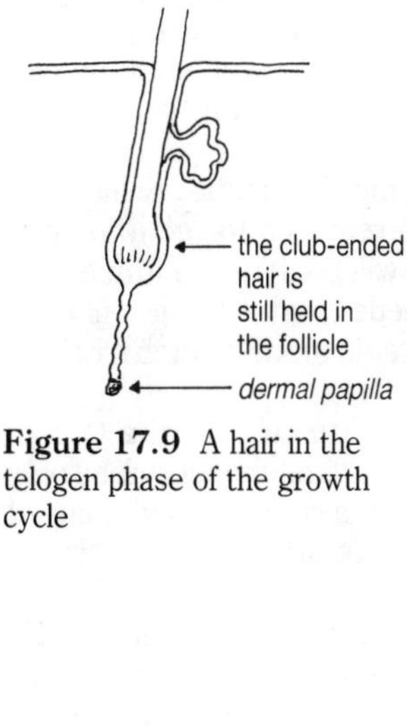

Figure 17.9 A hair in the telogen phase of the growth cycle

Telogen

As the hair enters the telogen phase all growth of the germinative cells has stopped and the papilla degenerates. The base of the hair takes on a brush-like appearance. It is called a *club-hair* (see figure 17.9).

Early anagen – the start of a new hair

In the earliest stage of the next anagen phase, an entirely new lower section of the follicle will form, complete with a regenerated *dermal papilla* and new germinative cells. This will start to grow a new hair in the follicle. It is only at this stage that the old hair becomes dislodged and will fall out (see figure 17.10).

On an 'average' head, around 100 hairs will be at this stage each day. Each day about 100 hairs will fall out. This is much more noticeable for a person who wears the hair long than for someone who wears it cut short. Normally the new hair growing in the follicle will be another terminal hair but it need not be the same colour. A man with male-pattern alopecia (baldness) will find only the downy vellus hairs will replace the fallen ones.

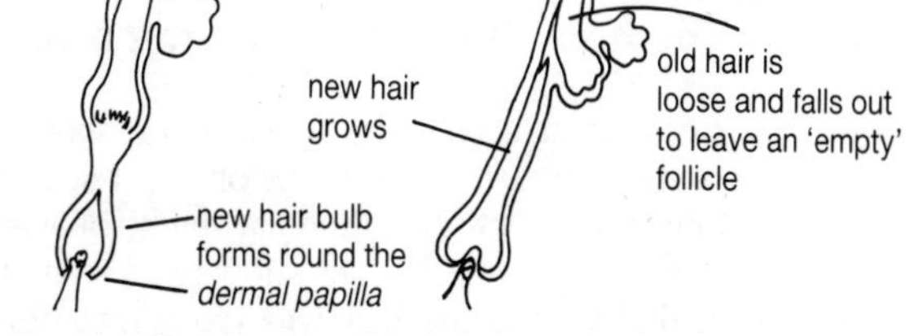

Figure 17.10 Early anagen – a new hair grows, the old one falls out

Women who have recently given birth to babies will often be alarmed by the tremendous amount of hair loss they suffer. They may not have noticed though that during pregnancy the normal hair loss had all but ceased and by the time the baby was due they had a much more luxurious head of hair. The extra loss after the birth is simply the follicles catching up with their growth cycle.

The hair shaft

Although a hair may grow up to one metre long it is too fine to see any detail of its structure with the naked eye. A fine hair may be less than 0.05 mm in diameter; even a coarse hair will be no more than 0.15 mm. Yet its structure gives it tremendous strength and hard-wearing properties. The ends of long hair may be up to *seven* years old, worn day and night for all that time and even then not worn out.

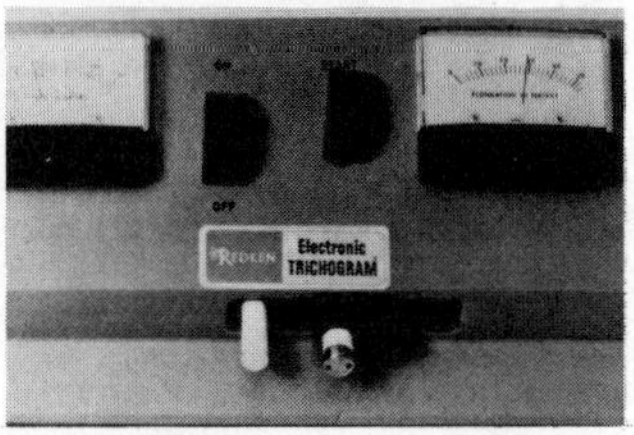

Figure 17.11 A tensometer designed specifically to measure the strength and elasticity of hair (courtesy of Redken)

Try the strength of hair for yourself. Hold a single hair between the thumb and finger of each hand. Gently slide the fingers first one way then the other along the hair. Because of the overlapping scales of the cuticle, this is easier from root to point than from point to root. Now pull gently and note the springiness or *elasticity* of the hair. Finally pull until the hair breaks and note the quite considerable force required to break it.

The *strength* of a hair may be measured in a number of ways. It may be accurately measured with a fibre *tensometer* (see figure 17.11). This gradually stretches the hair and measures the pull on it, and it does so until the hair breaks. A less accurate test may be done with simple apparatus such as that shown in figure 17.12.

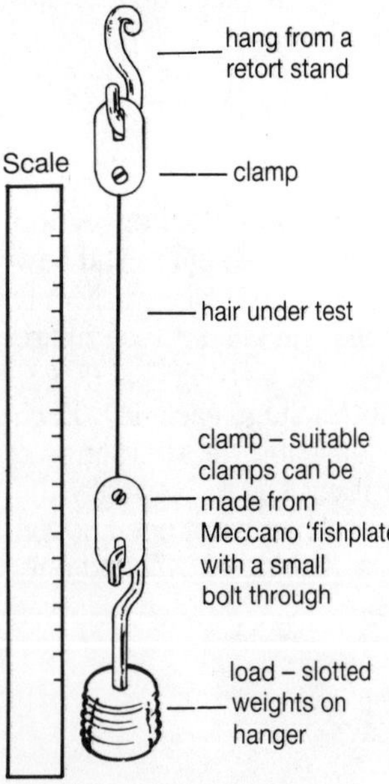

Figure 17.12 A simple apparatus for measuring the strength of a hair

The load is increased by steps of, say, 5 g at a time. Each time the increase in length of the hair is noted. Then the weight is removed to see if the hair returns to its original length. Eventually a point will come when it does not fully return. Its *elastic limit* will have been exceeded and the hair will have been damaged. It will however carry a much greater load and stretch far more before it eventually breaks.

Depending on its diameter and its condition, a hair will carry a load of between 50 and 150 grams before it breaks. Its elastic limit though will be only *half* its breaking force. it is all too easy when pulling a comb through tangled hair to overstretch and damage it even if it does not break. It goes 'frizzy' instead.

The *diameter* of hair may be measured in one of two ways. An engineer's *micrometer* might be used. Alternatively it may be done with a *microscope* fitted with a measuring scale in its eyepiece. The hair is mounted in a drop of water on a microscope slide and covered with a cover glass. The eyepiece scale is calibrated using a *micrometer slide.* It can then be used to measure the diameter of hairs. It will then be possible to relate the strength of a sample hair to its diameter.

The hair shaft under the microscope

Looking at a hair through a microscope will reveal incredibly little detail of its structure. The most one can see are the scales of the cuticle and if one is present, the medulla might be visible. For this reason, most early textbooks about the hair showed its structure in very little detail. Even some of that was as the hair was *thought* to be, and turned out to be wrong (see figure 17.13).

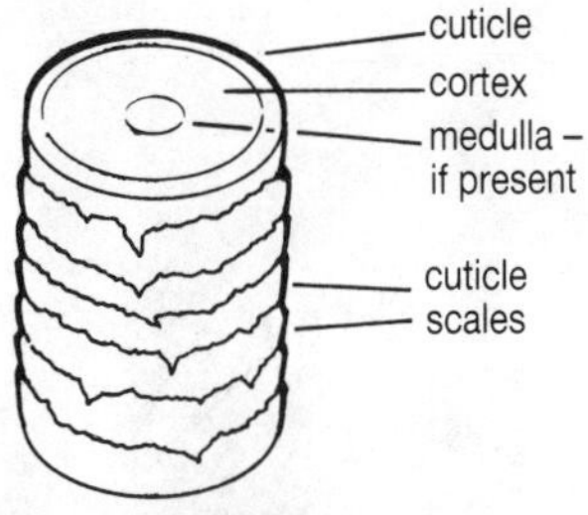

Figure 17.13 Part of a hairshaft

It is only in quite recent times that the development of the *electron microscope*, and more recently the *scanning electron microscope*, has let the hair reveal the secrets of its very complex structure.

The scanning electron microscope is particularly useful because it is able to show incredibly fine detail with tremendous clarity. Such an instrument is very expensive, so rather than spend hours sitting at the microscope it is usual to take photographs of features of interest. These may then be studied in detail at leisure. The photographs always give an incredible illusion of depth, an almost three-dimensional effect.

The cuticle of the hair

The fine detail of the surface of the cuticle is shown well by the scanning electron microscope. Figure 17.14 shows how the cuticle scales overlap each other. It also shows that each scale extends a long way round the hair, perhaps even right round. The series of photographs in figures 17.14 to 17.19 were taken at intervals along the length of one long hair. Figure 17.14 was taken at a point close to the scalp and shows the newly emerged cuticle in pristine condition. Figures 17.15, 17.16 and 17.17 were taken at points further along the hairshaft and show how, subject to wear and tear, the cuticle gradually erodes away to reveal the underlying cortex. When this happens, the cortex, too, rapidly deteriorates and tends to split. This happens particularly at the ends of the hairs, the famous 'split-ends' (figures 17.18 and 17.19).

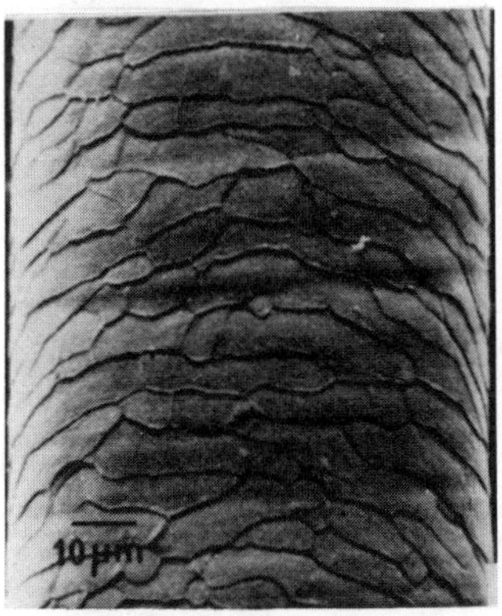

Figure 17.14 Scanning electron micrograph of the hair cuticle close to the scalp (reproduced from the *Journal of the Society of Cosmetic Chemists* by permission of the Editor)

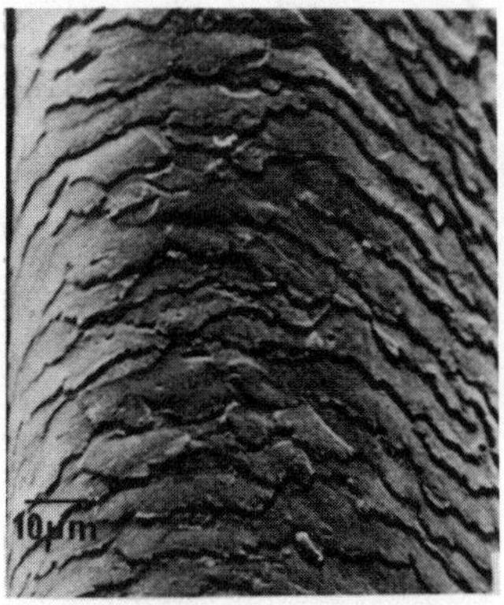

Figure 17.15 The cuticle of the same hair about 10 cm from the scalp (reproduced from the *Journal of the Society of Cosmetic Chemists* by permission of the Editor)

Figure 17.16 The cuticle about 25 cm from the scalp (reproduced from the *Journal of the Society of Cosmetic Chemists* by permission of the Editor)

What is strange is that the deterioration in the cuticle could be the result of modern hair care! Hair from people who lived long before the age of modern hair care products remained in much better condition right along its length. It might be though that the wearing of hats, caps and bonnets protected the hair from damage by the sun's ultra-violet rays.

The cuticle of newly grown hair is actually several scales thick. The scales are quite long and overlap considerably to build up a cuticle up to fifteen scales thick. This shows in the broken hair in figure 17.20 and the lengthways section in figure 17.21.

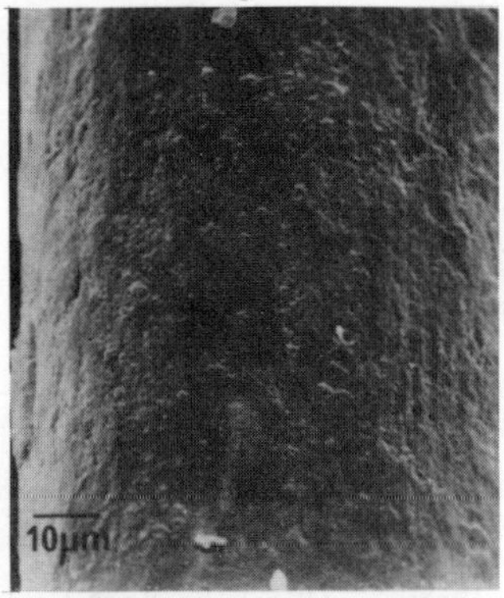

Figure 17.17 The same hair 30 cm from the scalp and devoid of cuticle (reproduced from the *Journal of the Society of Cosmetic Chemists* by permission of the Editor)

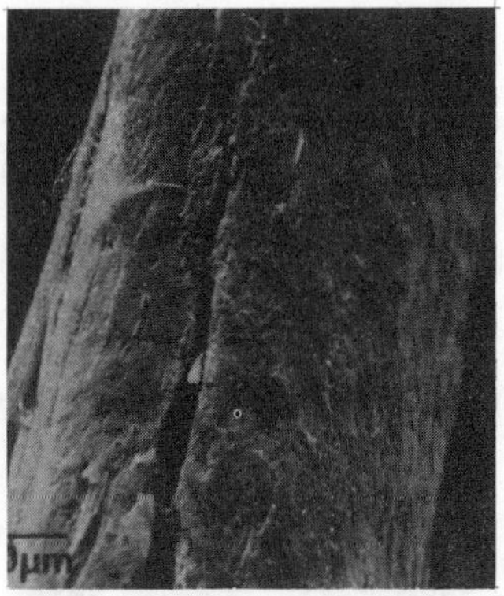

Figure 17.18 Splits in the cortex near the end of the 40 cm long hair (reproduced from the *Journal of the Society of Cosmetic Chemists* by permission of the Editor)

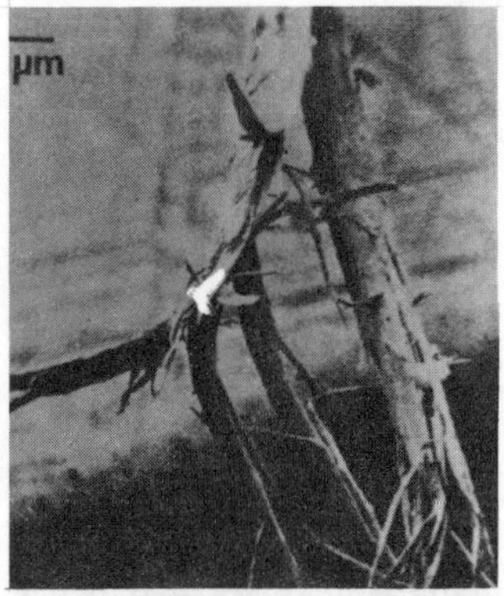

Figure 17.19 Split end of the 40 cm long hair (reproduced from the *Journal of the Society of Cosmetic Chemists* by permission of the Editor)

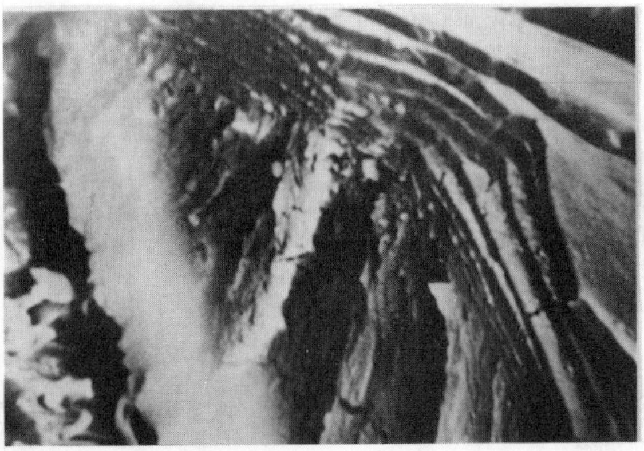

Figure 17.20 Scanning electron micrograph of a broken hair showing the layers of cuticle scales (courtesy of Wella International)

Figure 17.21 Electron micrograph – longitudinal section of hair showing overlapping of the cuticle scales (photo – Hugh Rushton, courtesy of the Philip Kingsley Trichology Clinic)

The cortex

To study the *cortex*, a hair is best split apart rather than sliced. Cutting across the hair smears the cut surface with a putty-like infilling of the cortex which obliterates much of the detail. This putty-like material is a form of the protein *keratin* which binds the hair structure together. Loss of the cuticle allows this to be lost too, making the hair prone to split. Figure 17.22 shows how the scanning electron microscope 'sees' the cortex in a hair that has been split in half.

The cortex is seen to consist of rope-like *fibres* which seem to branch and rejoin. The fibres are called *fibre bundles* and each corresponds to what in the immature hair low in the follicle was one of the spindle-shaped cortical cells. A closer look at the fibre bundles (figure 17.23 shows just three) shows why they are called fibre bundles. Each consists of a bundle of smaller fibres called *macrofibrils*. A closer look at a macrofibril (see figure 17.24) shows it, too, consists of still smaller fibres called *microfibrils*.

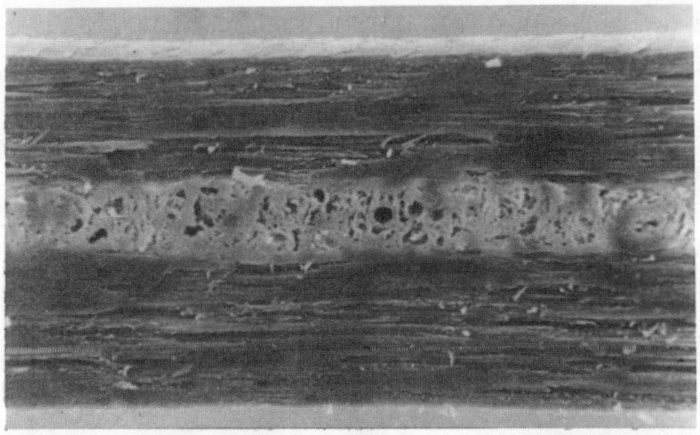

Figure 17.22 Hair split in half showing the cortex (photo – Hugh Rushton, courtesy of the Philip Kingsley Trichology Clinic)

Figure 17.23 Fibre bundles of the hair cortex showing the macrofibrils (courtesy of Wella International)

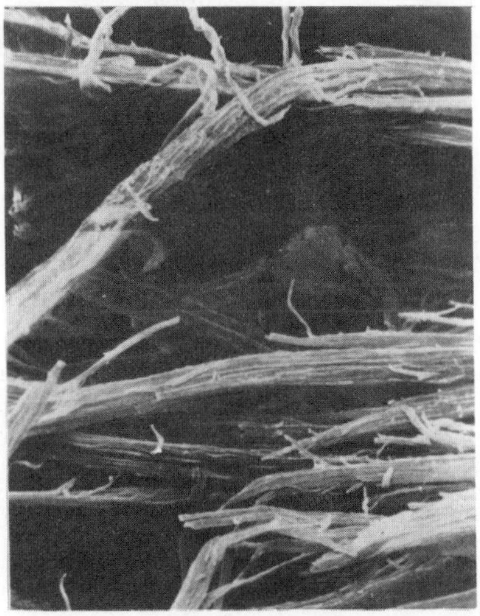

Figure 17.24 Close-up of the macrofibril showing the microfibrils (courtesy of Wella International)

This is the limit of the detail which can be shown by the scanning electron microscope. To find out about the structure of the microfibrils, it is necessary to turn now to the *chemistry* of the hair and particularly the chemical structure of the hair protein, *keratin*.

The chemistry of the hair and of keratin

A basic chemical analysis of hair would show it to consist of just *five* chemical elements. All five are *non-metals*. They are:

carbon hydrogen oxygen nitrogen sulphur

Table 17.2 shows the relative percentage of each. However stirring together this mixture of elements would *not* produce hair. Its structure is much too complex.

Table 17.2 The Elements in the Hair Protein, Keratin

Element	*Percentage by Weight in Keratin*
Carbon	50–51
Hydrogen	6– 7
Oxygen	19–23
Nitrogen	17–18
Sulphur	4– 5

Proteins

The *keratin* of the hair is a *protein*, just one of thousands in the body. The *molecules* of proteins are often *huge*. The keratin molecules of the *cortex* probably extend the full length of the hair, being added to as the hair grows and shortened when it is trimmed.

Protein molecules are assembled in the body from smaller units called *amino acids*. More than *twenty* different amino acids are the 'building bricks' for all the proteins in the body. *Eighteen* of these are present in keratin.

Figure 17.25 shows three of the amino acids (see also chapter 4). Note how part of each is *identical*. This forms a connecting arrangement so the amino acids may be joined to each other.

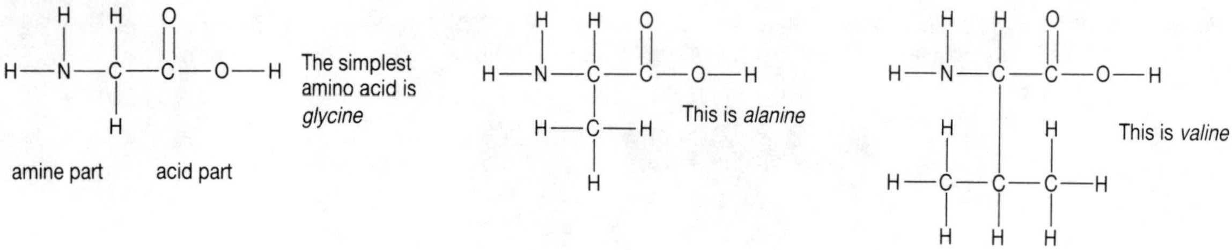

Figure 17.25 The molecules of three amino acids

The 'different' part of each amino acid is called its *side chain*.

To form a protein such as keratin, amino acids join together in the correct order to produce a long chain, a *polypeptide chain*. The 'amine part' of one amino acid joins to the 'acid part' of the next, forming a *peptide bond* as shown in figure 17.26.

The order or sequence of amino acids in a particular protein is dictated by information encoded on the *chromosomes* found in the nucleus of each living cell of an organism.

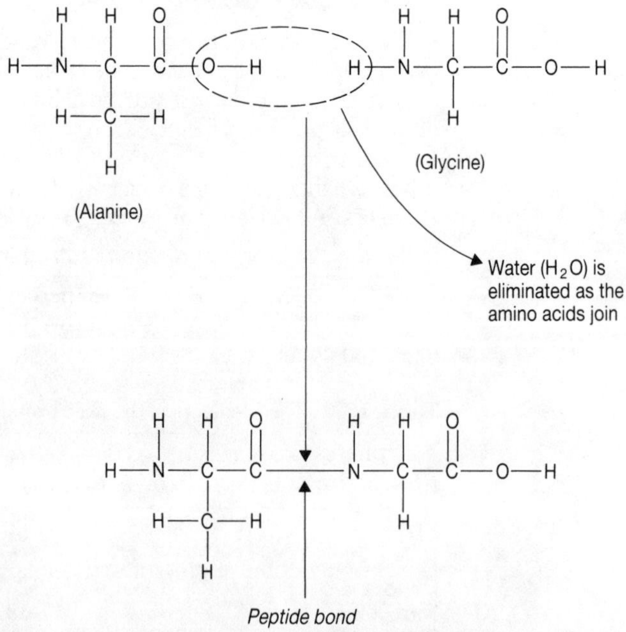

Figure 17.26 The formation of a peptide bond

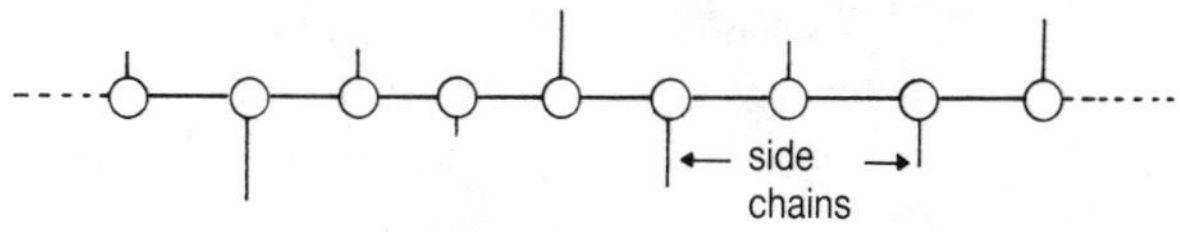

Figure 17.27 The amino acids join to form a polypeptide chain

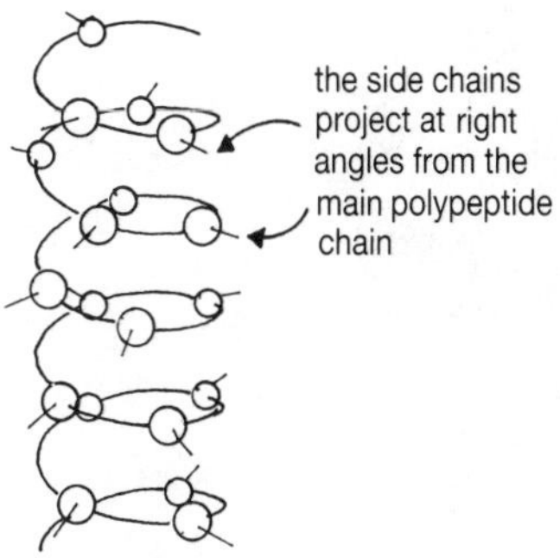

Figure 17.28 The polypeptide chain forms a helix

In *keratin*, the amino acids initially are joined end-to-end in a *polypeptide chain*, shown diagrammatically in figure 17.27. The chain, however, quite automatically coils itself into a spiral or *helix* (see figure 17.28). Notice how the 'side chains' project out from the chain and from the helix. As will be seen later, the side chains of certain of the amino acids form the *cross linkages* which in the hair hold the keratin molecules together to form a firm structure.

The structure is reminiscent of a spring and indeed it confers on the hair tremendous 'stretchability' and *elasticity* – but *only* when the hair is *wet.* The reason is that in *dry hair* weak chemical links form to join one turn of the helix to the next (see figure 17.29). These weak links are *hydrogen bonds.* Individually they may be quite weak, but there are so many of them that they prevent the hair from stretching much *when it is dry.*

If the hair is *wet,* the hydrogen bonds break and the hair can be stretched considerably until the spiral keratin molecules pull out *straight.* If the stretched hair is then *dried,* the hydrogen bonds will reform to lock or *set* the hair in the stretched form. It will stay stretched until it gets wet again which will break the hydrogen bonds once more and let the hair spring back to its natural length. It is this property of keratin that allows hair to be *set* by wetting it, curling it and drying it such as in a 'shampoo and set' or a 'blow-style'.

The coiled form of keratin in the relaxed hair is called *alpha-keratin.*

The straight form of keratin in a fully stretched hair is *beta-keratin.*

The effect of water on the stretching properties of the hair can be shown using the same simple apparatus shown in figure 17.12 for measuring the strength of a hair. A hair is mounted between the clamps and hung from the stand. A weight just less than the elastic limit is hung from the hair and the small amount the hair stretches is noted. The hair is now wetted by playing steam on to it from the spout of a boiling kettle (*take care*). The hair will now stretch tremendously; up to half as long again as its natural length.

Let the hair dry, then remove the weight. The hair contracts back only a little; it retains most of its *set.* Now steam the hair again and watch it shrink back to its original length!

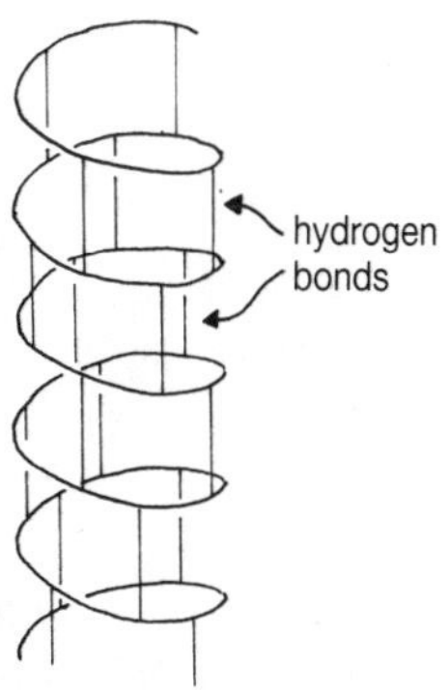

Figure 17.29 Hydrogen bonds link the turns of the helix

The keratin molecules and the cortex fibres

In the *microfibrils* of the *cortex* of the hair, the keratin molecules are arranged side-by-side in ordered bundles. It is thought that initially the keratin molecules are twisted together in *threes.* Then the 'threes' are twisted together in bundles of *eleven* (nine around two) to form the microfibril. This is shown in figure 17.30.

The microfibrils are then bundled together to form the *macrofibrils* and the macrofibrils are bundled together to form the fibre-bundles of the hair *cortex* (see figure 17.30).

As the keratin molecules lie side-by-side in the fibrils, they join to each other by *cross linkages* formed from the *side chains* of many of the amino acids. Many of these cross linkages are *hydrogen bonds* which when broken will allow a *wet* hair to swell. But there are also two types of much stronger linkages, *salt linkages* and *disulphide bonds,* which hold the structure of the keratin together.

Filling all the spaces between the fibrils of the *cortex* of the hair is another form of keratin called *amorphous keratin.* This is a putty-like material which helps to bond the fibrils to each other to form a strong and rigid structure.

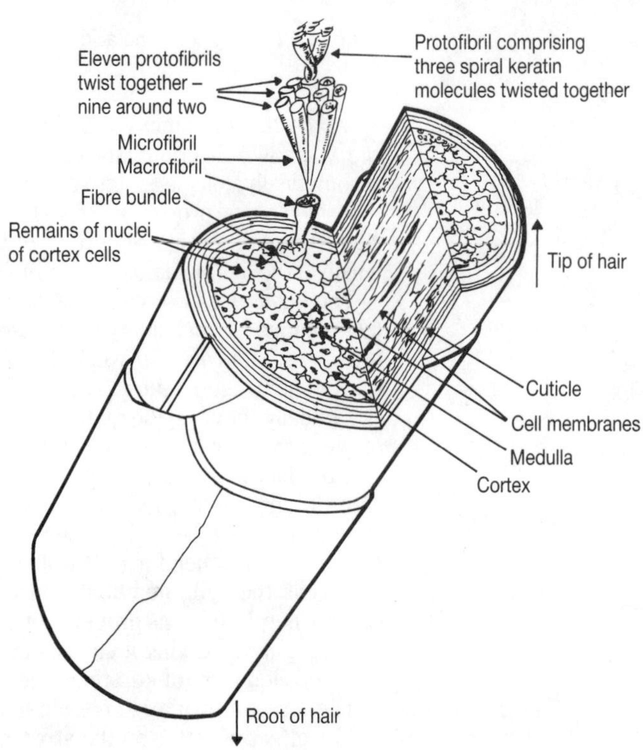

Figure 17.30 The hair structure (based on the diagrams of Unilever and Ryder and Stevenson)

The cross linkages

The *salt linkages* are formed from amino acids which have acidic and basic (alkaline) side chains. Figure 17.31 shows two such amino acids: aspartic acid which has an acidic side chain, and lysine, a basic side chain. An acidic side chain in one keratin molecule will join to its basic opposite number in the neighbouring keratin molecule provided the hair is dry and cool enough to form a salt linkage. This happens best at between pH 4.5 and pH 6 – that is,

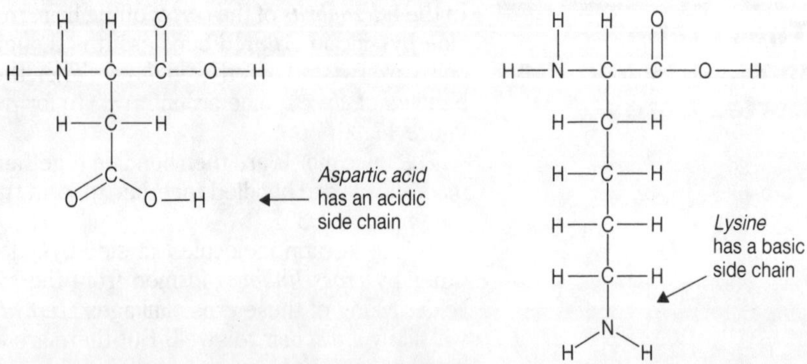

Figure 17.31 The amino acids – aspartic acid and lysine

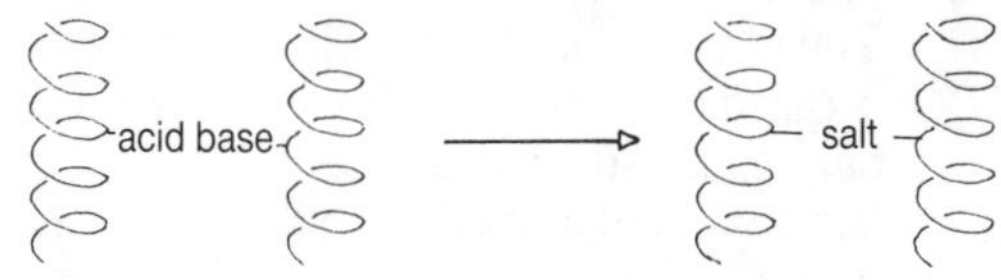

Figure 17.32 Acidic and basic side chains form a salt linkage

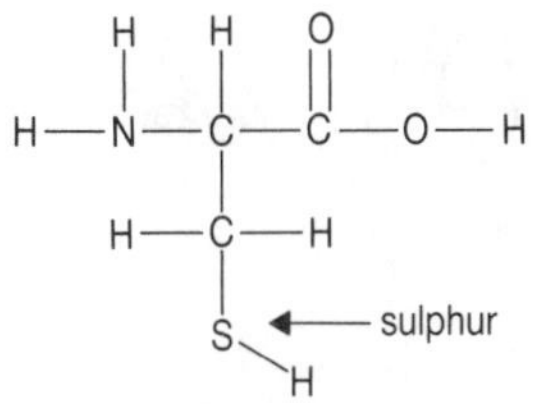

Figure 17.33 The amino acid cystein

slightly acidic (see figure 17.32). Wetting the hair with something of higher pH, such as most shampoos and hair processing lotions, will break the salt linkages, as also will modest warmth. Salt linkages too are broken and reformed in setting the hair (see chapter 19).

The *disulphide bonds* are formed from the side chains of a very special amino acid called *cystein* (see figure 17.33). This contains the element sulphur. Where cystein occurs in two adjoining keratin molecules, the hydrogen atom is lost off the end of each side chain; the process is called *oxidation.* The two *sulphur* atoms then join to form the *disulphide bond*, or cystine linkage (see figure 17.34).

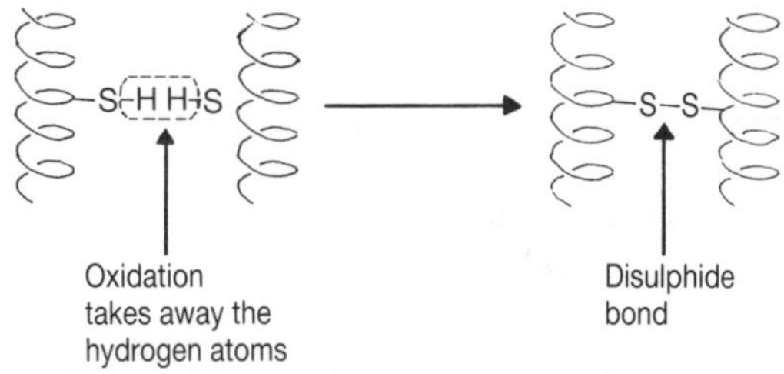

Figure 17.34 Formation of a disulphide bond

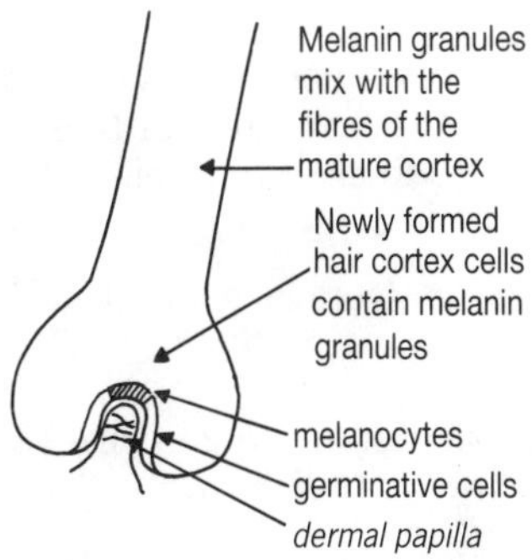

Figure 17.35 Production of melanin pigments to colour the hair

Disulphide bonds are the strongest and most resistant of the cross linkages. If they all were to break, the hair structure would collapse and dissolve. This is what happens with a *depilatory cream* (see chapter 20).

In *permanent waving*, the disulphide bonds are made to break and reform *a few at a time* to allow the hair to *relax* into the curl (see chapter 19).

Breaking disulphide bonds is done with a *reducing agent* such as *ammonium thioglycollate* in *perm lotion.* This parts the sulphur atoms and attaches hydrogen atoms to hold them apart. Then the action of the *'neutraliser'*, actually an *oxidising agent*, removes the hydrogen again so the linkage can reform.

Hair colour

Hair colour is due to the presence of granules of *melanin* pigments. These granules are produced by a group of *melanocyte* cells situated on the top of the *dermal papilla* in the follicle (see figure 17.35). They inject the granules into new hair cortex cells as they are produced from the germinative cells. As the hair cortex matures and cells give way to the fibrous structure, the melanin granules remain mixed among the fibres.

Melanin pigments of the hair

The wide variety of hair colour is the result of the presence of different amounts of pigments in the hair. There are *two* melanin pigments:

Melanin itself or *eumelanin* is brown to black
Pheomelanin is yellowish to reddish

The intense *red* of redheads is due to a third pigment which contains iron and is called *trichosiderin.* This pigment is also often present in Negroid and Asian hair, as these peoples find out when they attempt to bleach their hair and it turns orange! Table 17.3 indicates the pigments present in different colours of hair.

Table 17.3 Naturally Occuring Hair Pigments

Hair Colour	*Pigments Present*
Intense black	Much melanin (+ trichosiderin in some races)
Dark brown	Mostly melanin
Light brown	Mostly pheomelanin
Blonde	A little pheomelanin
Auburn	Melanin and trichosiderin
Redhead	Mostly trichosiderin
White	Almost no pigment
Albino	No pigment
'Grey'	Mixed pigmented and white hairs

Things to do

1 Survey the comparative strength and texture of people's hair. Measure the strength and diameter of several hairs from each volunteer using the methods described in the chapter. See if there are any noticeable correlations with natural hair colour or with the racial origin of the hair samples.

2 Many of the major hair products companies produce booklets and other literature on hair structure and hair care. Make a collection of these. Notable examples are the publications by Wella, Redken and Unilever.

Self-assessment questions

1 Approximately how many hairs are there on an 'average' human head?

2 What are vellus hairs?

3 On a sketch of a hair follicle label the dermal papilla, the germinative cells, the melanocytes, the matrix and the *arrector pili* muscle.

4 What is mitosis?

5 Briefly describe the growth cycle of a terminal hair.

6 What is meant by the elastic limit of hair?

7 What is the purpose of the cuticle of the hair?

8 What are macrofibrils and microfibrils?

9 Name the five chemical elements which make up the hair.

10 Which is the most abundant element in the hair?

11 What is the importance of the amino acid cystein in the hair structure?

12 Which type of chemical bond prevents dry hair from stretching much?

13 Why is wet hair able to stretch far more than dry hair?

14 What is the difference between alpha-keratin and beta-keratin?

15 What is trichosiderin?

18 Hair Care

Shampoos; hair condition and conditioners; setting lotions; hairsprays; hair creams and oily dressings

Clean hair

Like dirt on the skin, dirt on the hair is held on by a film of greasy *sebum* and maybe also by adhesive or greasy hair dressings. So cleaning the hair presents the same problem as cleaning the skin: the grease must be removed to loosen the dirt. As explained in chapter 10, there are three ways to remove grease:

1. *Dissolve* it with a grease solvent.
2. *Absorb* it with a grease absorbent powder.
3. *Emulsify* it with a detergent.

To cleanse the hair, there are products which work in each of the three ways.

To clean a *wig* or *hairpiece* without damaging its base, it is dipped into a dish of a dry-cleaning fluid such as *trichlorethylene*. This fluid *must* be used in a well-ventilated place. It is one of the 'glue-sniffing' solvents and inhaling the fumes is *dangerous*. Inhaled through a lighted cigarette the fumes are *lethal*. An alternative solvent is *petroleum spirit* but, being poisonous and highly flammable, it is equally dangerous.

To clean hair without getting it wet, a *dry shampoo* may be used. A grease-absorbent powder such as *talc* or *kaolin* is sprinkled on the hair, massaged in and brushed out, taking most of the grease and dirt with it. This is useful for invalids whose hair would be difficult to wash, or as an 'in-between' shampoo for people with very greasy hair.

For the majority of people, cleaning the hair means *shampooing* the hair with a *detergent*. The word 'shampoo' is an Indian word meaning 'massage'. The detergent shampoo emulsifies the grease so the dirt may be rinsed away.

Shampoos

Most of the *four hundred plus* shampoos on the market are *detergent* products and almost all of these are based on *soapless* detergents rather than *soaps*. You only have to wash your hair using ordinary soap to realise why, particularly in a *hard water area*. The alkaline soap will leave the hair dry and coarse and, with hard water, the sticky soap *scum* will be difficult to rinse away.

A basic formulation for a *soapless shampoo* is described in chapter 8. Also described there is the method for making up shampoo formulations.

Most manufacturers produce a *range* of shampoos for *dry*, *normal* and *greasy* hair. It is important when cleaning the hair that *not all* the grease is removed. A film of sebum must be left on the hair that is thick enough to give a healthy shine and to prevent the hair becoming dry and unmanageable. It must not be so thick that dirt is left on the hair. A shampoo must be formulated with just sufficient 'detergent power' to do this. A shampoo for *dry hair* may contain as little as 8 per cent of actual detergent whereas one for *greasy hair* might have 25 per cent or more.

Some shampoo formulations are shown in tables 18.1 and 18.2. The proportion of detergent in them might look a lot, but remember that the available triethanolamine lauryl sulphate is only 40 per cent actual detergent and sodium lauryl ether sulphate is only 30 per cent detergent.

These formulations are all transparent liquid shampoos. A more luxurious appearance may be obtained in a *cream* or *lotion* shampoo. Any of the formulations may be made into a *lotion* shampoo by including an *opacifier* or *pearlising agent* such as *magnesium stearate* or *ethylene glycol monostearate*.

Table 18.1 Shampoos based on Triethanolamine lauryl sulphate

	Dry Hair	*Normal Hair*	*Greasy Hair*
Triethanolamine lauryl sulphate (40 per cent)	30	35	40
Coconut diethanolamide	4	3	2
Water	66	62	58
Ammonium chloride – sufficient to thicken	q.s.	q.s.	q.s.
Perfume, colour, preservative	q.s.	q.s.	q.s.

Table 18.2 Shampoos based on Sodium lauryl ether sulphate

	Dry Hair	*Normal Hair*	*Greasy Hair*
Sodium lauryl ether sulphate (30 per cent)	45	52	58
Coconut diethanolamide	3	2.5	2
N-alkyl betaine	4	3	2
Water	48	42.5	38
Sodium chloride – sufficient to thicken	q.s.	q.s.	q.s.
Perfume, colour, preservative	q.s.	q.s.	q.s.

For each 100 g of shampoo, one or two grams of one of the pearlising agents is melted and the warmed shampoo is stirred into it. As it cools, the pearlising agent forms tiny flake-like crystals which give the pearlescent effect.

Because of its wax and lanolin content, the *cream shampoo* in the next formulation has a conditioning action on dry hair. It may be made by the cream method described in chapter 6.

Ingredient	Amount	Phase	
Lanette wax S.X.	– 13.5	Oil phase	Mix at 65°C
Lanolin	– 3.5	Oil phase	Mix at 65°C
Sodium lauryl sulphate	– 33	Water phase	Mix at 65°C
Water	– 50	Water phase	Mix at 65°C
Perfume, colour, preservative	– q.s.		

Shampoo additives

Many additives are included in shampoos, mostly for conditioning the hair, though the effect of some of them may be more psychological than physical! Additives include:

Various plant extracts	in *herbal shampoos*
Skin disinfectants	in *medicated shampoos*
Protein materials	in *protein shampoos*

The smell of a shampoo is psychologically important. All must smell *clean*, but herbal shampoos must smell 'herbal' and medicated shampoos must smell 'medicated'. Perfumes for shampoos must be chosen bearing this in mind.

Dandruff shampoos

One of the more valuable additives to shampoos is an *anti-dandruff* agent. This is a substance which reduces the rate of shedding of the horny layer of the scalp and thereby avoids those socially unacceptable flakes on the collar!

For moderate dandruff conditions a shampoo with *zinc pyridine thione* or ZPT, will suffice. This type of shampoo is not unpleasant to use as one's regular shampoo, but sufferers from severe dandruff may not find their shampoo so pleasant to use. It contains *selenium sulphide* which has a not too attractive sulphurous odour.

Shampoos for babies and young children

Nothing is guaranteed to put little ones off having their hair washed than the 'smarting' of shampoo in the eyes. Babies' hair does not get very dirty or greasy so very low detergent levels are used, and special detergents such as '*sulphosuccinnates*' and amphoterics have very low eye-irritancy.

For other people who do not like the sting of shampoo in the eyes, the eye-irritancy of most shampoos can be reduced by including sufficient citric acid in the formulation to reduce the pH to about 6.

Hair condition

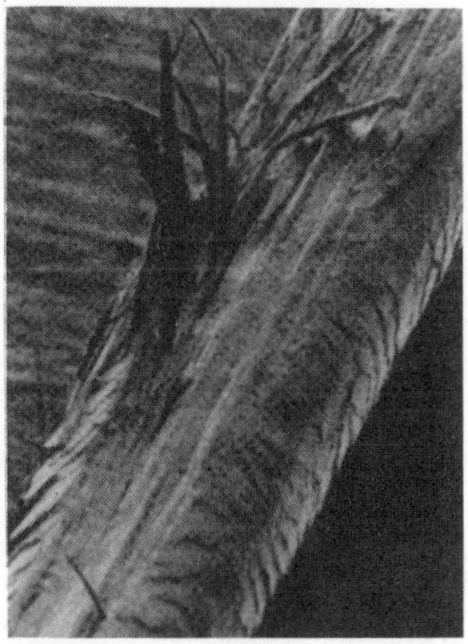

Figure 18.1 Razor cutting damage to the hair (reproduced from the *Journal of the Society of Cosmetic Chemists* by permission of the Editor)

Apart from the effects of 'natural' wear and tear as shown in chapter 17, the hair may suffer *self-inflicted* factors which might result in a deterioration of its condition.

Combing with cheap moulded plastic combs and brushing with poor-quality, sharp-bristled brushes can gouge pieces out of the hairs, as also can the once-popular *razor-cutting* (see figure 18.1).

Hair in poor condition tangles easily. Careless and rough combing out of tangles, particularly when the hair is *wet*, can overstretch or break hairs or carve pieces out of each other. Figure 18.2 shows two hairs parting as the comb passes through, and the groove cut in one of them as a result is shown in figure 18.3.

Shampooing with too strong or too harsh a shampoo can excessively *degrease* the hair, leaving it *dry* and rough to the touch. A good shampoo leaves a little grease still on the hair to make it smooth and looking good.

Worst of all are the effects of *chemical processing* of the hair: perm, bleach and oxidation dyes. To work, these must open the cuticle to penetrate to the cortex. To do this they usually have to be quite *alkaline*. Once opened in this way, the cuticle scales will never lie properly flat again. The alkalis will also dissolve out some of the keratin of the cortex, thereby reducing the strength of the hair. Over-processed hair is characteristically dry and rough to the touch. It becomes easily charged with static electricity when combed, making it very difficult to manage.

Figure 18.2 One hair cuts deeply into another while combing out a tangle (reproduced from the *Journal of the Society of Cosmetic Chemists* by permission of the Editor)

Figure 18.3 The groove cut in the hair (reproduced from the *Journal of the Society of Cosmetic Chemists* by permission of the Editor)

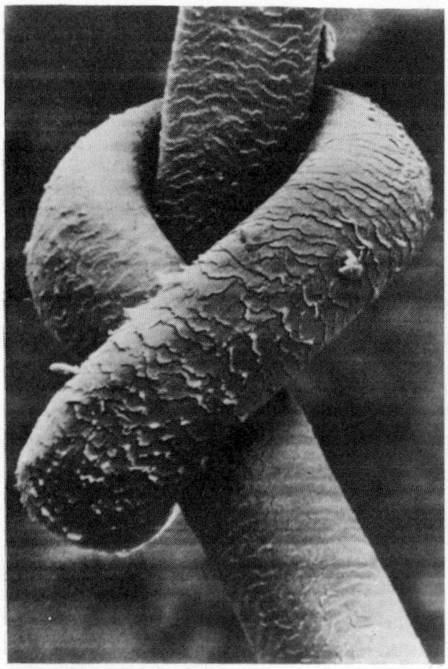

Figure 18.4 A knotted hair in good condition (courtesy of Wella International)

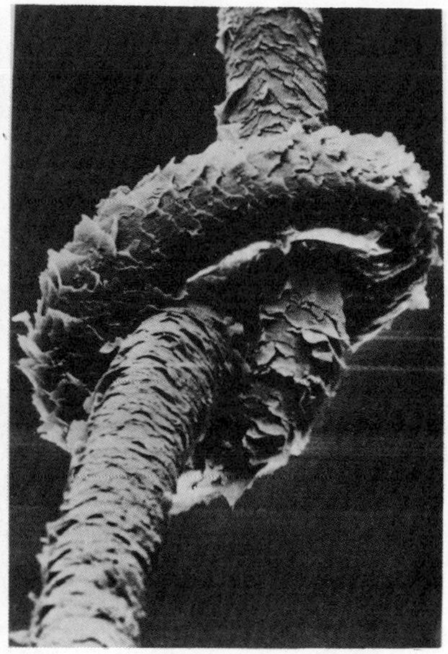

Figure 18.5 Knotted hair which has been chemically processed (courtesy of Wella International)

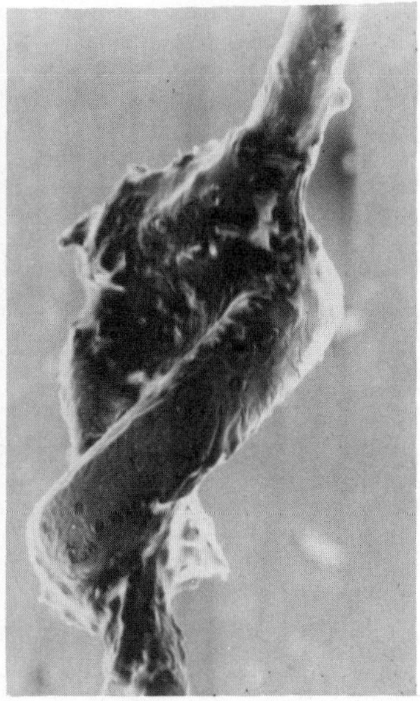

Figure 18.6 A severely overprocessed hair (photo – Hugh Rushton, courtesy of the Philip Kingsley Trichology Clinic)

The effects on the cuticle can be shown by looking at knotted hairs using the scanning electron microscope (see figures 18.4, 18.5 and 18.6).

It is not always necessary to tie the hair in a knot to see the effects of chemical processing. Figures 18.7(a) and (b) show the same part of the same hair before and after it has been permed.

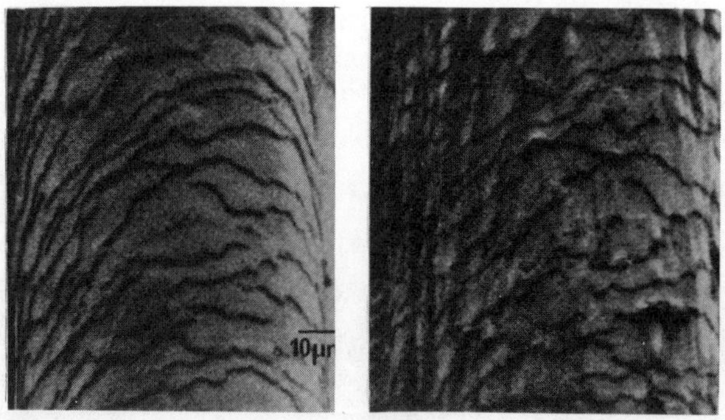

(a) **(b)**

Figure 18.7 The hair (a) before and (b) after perming (reproduced from the *Journal of the Society of Cosmetic Chemists* by permission of the Editor)

Conditioners for the hair

Damaged hair can *never* be fully restored to its original condition, but conditioners can make the hair look glossy and feel smooth again. Some can even glue down the splayed out cuticle scales and stick together the split-ends.

To perform their function, conditioners might contain:

1 *Oils*, *waxes* and *silicones* to lubricate and smooth the hair.

2 *Mild acids* and *cationic surfactants*. In acid conditions the cuticle scales contract and close.
3 *Plastics* and *proteins* which glue together the damaged parts of the hair.

Here are two formulations for hair conditioning creams. The first contains a wax and an acid as conditioning agents; in the second the cationic self-emulsifying wax has the conditioning action.

1	Lanbritol wax N21	– 15	– Oil phase	Mix at 65°C
	Sodium lauryl sulphate	– 0.5	Water phase	
	Citric acid crystals	– 2		
	Water	– 82.5		
	Perfume, colour, preservative	– q.s.		
2	Lanette wax CAT	– 5	Melt together and stir until cool.	
	Water	– 95		
	Perfume, colour, preservative	– q.s.		

Controlling the hairstyle

There are a number of products designed to assist with styling the hair and holding the finished style in place. A *setting lotion*, *styling gel* or *styling mousse* is to put on the wet hair before it is set into a style. A *hairspray* is sprayed on to the finished style. A *cream* or *oil* dressing is to put on the dry hair before combing it into the style.

Setting lotions and hairsprays

Both setting lotions and hairsprays hold the hairstyle in place by coating the hair with a film of an adhesive plastic or resin. In a *setting lotion*, the adhesive is made into a *water-based* product to be applied to the wet hair, and then to be dried with it. In a *hairspray* the adhesive is dissolved in *alcohol* which will evaporate quickly when the product is sprayed on to the finished hairstyle.

At one time, *natural gums* and *resins* were used in these products. A setting lotion was a solution of a vegetable gum in water. Such gums include *tragacanth*, *acacia* and *karaya*. Here is a typical formulation:

Gum tragacanth powder or Gum acacia or Gum Karaya	– 1.2
Alcohol	– 10
Glycerol	– 5
Water	– 84
Perfume (solubilised)	– q.s.
Preservative	– q.s.

To make the setting lotion, the gum and the alcohol are shaken together. The water and glycerol are added and the mixture is shaken again. It is then allowed to stand for 24 hours before adding the other materials.

Hairspray or *hair lacquer* was originally made from *shellac*, a natural resin which encrusts the bodies of lacquer beetles. This hair lacquer gave all sorts of problems. It was stiff; the hairstyle set like a crust; there was no 'natural' swing to the hair. It tended to flake off like dandruff, yet it could only be cleansed from the hair with special lacquer-removing shampoos which contained *borax* or *ammonia* to dissolve away the shellac. Here is a formulation for hair lacquer. The *propylene glycol* acts as a *plasticiser*. This takes away some of the stiffness and flaking of the shellac.

Bleached shellac	– 2.5
Propylene glycol	– 2
Alcohol	– 100

Dissolve the shellac in the alcohol with continuous stirring for 24 hours. Decant the solution to leave behind any sediment. Make up any losses of alcohol, then add the propylene glycol and a suitable perfume. Pack the product in a squeeze bottle or pump spray.

Nowadays a variety of *synthetic resins* is available for use in setting lotions and hairsprays. These are some examples:

Polyvinyl acetate	– PVA
Polyvinyl pyrrolidone	– PVP
Dimethyl hydantoin formaldehyde	– DMHF

Development of these resins continues all the time. The consumer demands a 'natural hold' that controls the hair but allows it freedom of movement. They want it to wash out of the air easily, yet not get tacky in damp weather.

Many *co-polymers* have been produced. These are combination plastics; for example, vinyl acetate and vinyl pyrrolidone have been combined in 'PVP/VA' and both vinyl acetate and vinyl pyrrolidone have been made into co-polymers with acrylic materials. Here is a simple formulation for a *'plastic' setting lotion*:

Polyvinyl pyrrolidone or PVP/VA	– 2
Alcohol	– 45
Water	– 53
Perfume	– q.s.

Dissolve the resin in the alcohol, it dissolves very quickly. Then add the water and perfume.

Here is a simple PVP hairspray. This particular formulation is for a squeeze bottle spray or a pump spray:

Polyvinyl pyrrolidone	– 5
Glycerol triacetate (plasticiser)	– 1.5
Alcohol	– 100
Perfume	– q.s.

Dissolve the polyvinyl pyrrolidone in the alcohol. Add the glycerol triacetate and a suitable perfume.

Currently very popular with those who style their own hair at home is the *styling mousse*. The modern plastic setting lotion is a very mobile liquid product which is not easy to apply to one's own hair. In a styling mousse, a basic setting lotion has added to it a special surfactant and it is packed in an aerosol with a foam button. The product discharges from the aerosol as an easily applied foam which breaks down on the hair to become a normal liquid. This is an example of a '*quick breaking*' foam product.

Haircreams and oily dressings

Haircream, brilliantine, spray-gloss and styling gel all use a film of *oil* to control the hair.

A brilliantine is a straightforward oily dressing. Liquid brilliantine is usually mineral oil or isopropyl myristate or a mixture of both with colour and perfume added. While intended as a men's hairdressing, an aerosol brilliantine or *spray-gloss* has found favour with both sexes.

Haircream is an emulsified oily dressing. In an emulsified form the oil is much easier to apply to the hair. Here is an example. It can be made by the 'cream method' described in chapter 6.

Ingredient	Amount	Phase	
Mineral oil	– 45	Oil phase	Mix at 70°C
Stearic acid	– 3.5	Oil phase	
Cetyl alcohol	– 1–3 parts	Oil phase	
Triethanolamine	– 1.5	Water phase	
Water	– 50	Water phase	

A styling gel is also an emulsified oily dressing but the emulsion has such tiny droplets in it that the product is a crystal clear gel called a *micro-emulsion*. This formulation is by the Atlas Chemical Company and uses as emulsifiers two of their non-ionic polyoxyethylene surfactants (see chapter 8).

Polyoxyethylene (10) oleyl ether	– 15.5	Part A
Polyoxyethylene fatty glyceride	– 15.5	Part A
Mineral oil	– 13.7	Part A
Propylene glycol	– 8.6	Part A
Sorbitol syrup (70 per cent)	– 6.9	Part A
Water	– 38.8	Part B
Perfume	– q.s.	

To make it, heat part A to 90°C. Heat the water (part B) to 95°C. Add B to A. Stir until mixture cools to 60°C, adding the perfume at 70°C. Pour into tubs. When cool it sets to a clear gel.

Things to do

1 The formulations for hair care products in this chapter can be made up and should be quite safe to use on one's hair.

2 If you make up several of the shampoo formulations (see also those in chapter 8), they could form the basis of a product evaluation exercise (see chapter 23).

3 With so many brands of hair care products available, finding out what products and what brands people actually buy could form the basis of an interesting market research survey.

Self-assessment questions

1 What is a dry shampoo? When might one be used and what might it consist of?

2 Why are shampoos based on soapless detergents rather than soaps?

3 For what reason might a shampoo contain zinc pyridine thione?

4 Most shampoos contain salt. Why?

5 List three different kinds of hair conditioning agents that might be in hair conditioning creams.

6 In what kind of hair care products might polyvinyl pyrrolidone be used?

7 What is the purpose of a plasticiser in a hairspray formulation?

8 What type of material in a brilliantine controls the hair?

19 Hair Waving & Hair Colouring

Temporary hair waving; permanent waving; perm lotions and neutralisers; old-fashioned perms; bleaching the hair; dyeing the hair; temporary, semi-permanent and permanent hair colours

Waving the hair

Waving the hair involves reshaping it and 'locking' it in the reshaped state. In hair waving processes, certain of the chemical linkages within the cortex of the hair have to be broken and reformed in new positions. How this happens is described in chapter 17.

Temporary hair waving

Hair waving might be *temporary* or *permanent*. Temporary waving or *setting* the hair involves breaking and reforming the *hydrogen bonds* and the *salt linkages*. The *disulphide bonds* are not broken but are distended, as also are the spring-like keratin molecules. This means that temporarily set hair is under quite considerable tension and should the hydrogen bonds and salt linkages be broken again while the hair is *not* being held in the curl, the set will *fall out*.

Because the hydrogen bonds and salt linkages are broken by water, a temporary set will last only until the hair gets wet again. This does not have to wait until the next shampoo. Hair is *hygroscopic*: it absorbs moisture from the air. Part of the action of a *setting lotion* (see chapter 18) in prolonging the 'life' of a set is by slowing down the absorption of atmospheric moisture.

How the hydrogen bonds are broken is described in chapter 17. The part played by the *salt linkages* in temporary waving is shown in figure 19.1. The drawings show just two of the thousands of spiral keratin molecules in the cortex of a hair. The salt linkages are represented by the – +– – symbols, the disulphide bonds by –S–S–.

In roller setting and blow styling wet hair, the hydrogen bonds and salt linkages broken by wetting the hair reform in new positions as the hair is dried.

Curling irons, styling brushes and heated rollers used on dry hair break only the salt linkages by their heat. They reform in new positions as the hair cools. The heat of a hairdryer will break the salt linkages too. Always *let the hair cool* before releasing the curl.

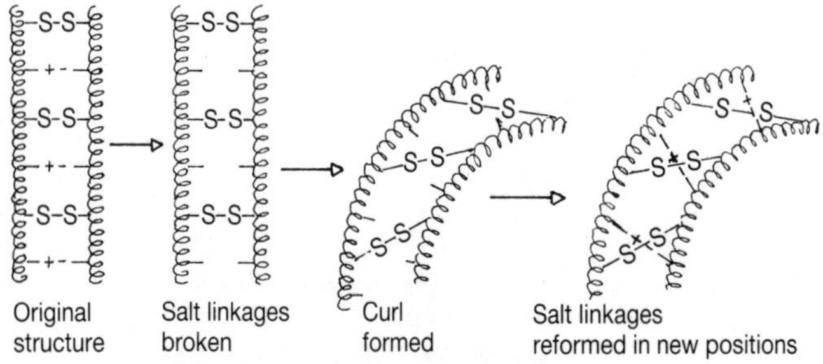

Figure 19.1 The breaking and reforming of salt linkages in temporary hair setting

Permanent waving the hair

When the hair has been *set* into a curl, it has a tendency to straighten itself out again because both the *tension* due to the 'stretching' of the disulphide bonds and *gravity* are acting to pull the hair out straight.

In applying a *permanent wave* to the hair, the idea is to make the hair *relax* into a tighter curl than is required in the final hairstyle. When the hair has been *set*, the perm will tend to pull the hair *into* the curl while gravity tries to pull it out of the curl. The result is the hair set lasts a lot longer.

In the *permanent waving process*, relaxing the hair into the curl involves breaking the *disulphide bonds* in the hair and reforming them in new positions. It is important that these bonds break and reform *a few at a time*. Were they all to be broken at once, the hair would collapse and dissolve. Figure 19.2 shows how breaking and reforming the disulphide bonds between the keratin molecules allows the hair to *relax* into the curl.

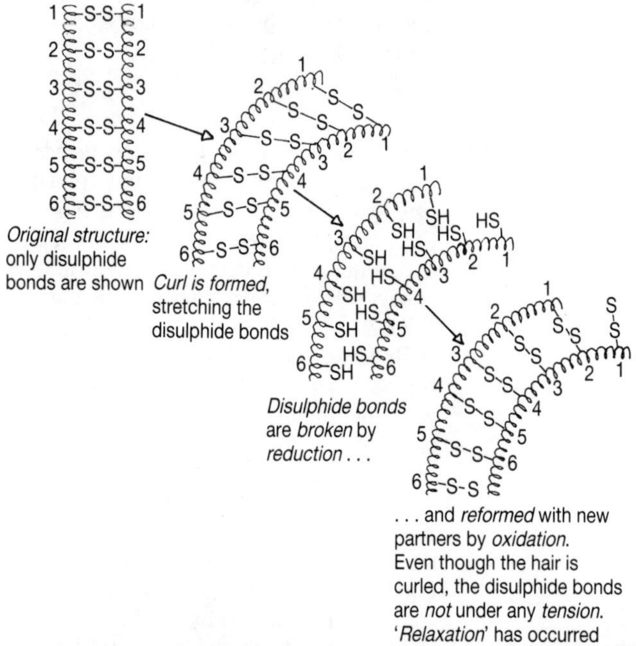

Figure 19.2 The breaking and reforming of the disulphide bonds during a perm

The cold permanent wave process

In the modern permanent waving process, sections of hair are wetted with a *cold waving lotion* and carefully wound on to special polythene perm curlers. When all the hair has been wound on to curlers, the remaining lotion is sponged over the curls. The client is then left for up to 40 minutes for *relaxation* to take place.

Although it is called a *cold* waving process, like any other chemical reaction, it proceeds *faster* if *warmth* is provided. It is usual to cover the head with a plastic cap to prevent the lotion from drying out, then apply gentle heat from a hairdryer. If water evaporates from the lotion it actually gets *stronger*. The strength of a perm lotion is critical. If it gets too strong the hair will break.

After processing, but *before* removing the perm curlers, a '*neutraliser*' must be applied to *stop* any further action of the perm lotion and repair any disulphide bonds which are still broken. Despite its name, it does *not* neutralise in the acid–alkali sense, but actually *oxidises*.

Formulation of cold wave lotions

The active ingredient of a cold wave lotion is a *reducing agent*. In salon lotions this is usually *ammonium thioglycollate* or sometimes *monoethanolamine thioglycollate*. In home perms, sodium bisulphite is more often used.

A thioglycollate lotion contains the equivalent of between five and eight per cent of *thioglycollic acid* (mercaptoethanoic acid) reacted with sufficient 0.880 ammonia or monoethanolamine to give a pH no higher than 9.5. That is moderately alkaline. The maximum strength and pH of thioglycollate lotions are laid down in the *EEC Cosmetics Directive* and the *Cosmetic Product Regulations*.

To improve its performance and acceptability, a professional lotion will also contain:

An anionic or non-ionic surfactant as a foaming agent

A conditioner such as polyvinyl pyrrolidone

A dye – This must be a basic dye such as Rhodamine B (pink)

A perfume

Thioglycollates have a rather unpleasant smell which cannot be masked by perfume, though 'orange' perfumes can make it more acceptable.

Often salon lotions are made from a commercially available 40 per cent solution of ammonium thioglycollate. This experimental lotion can be made by carefully measuring the following materials:

Ammonium thioglycollate (40 per cent)	– 19.3 cm^3
0.880 Ammonia solution	– 1.4 cm^3
Water	– 82.3 cm^3

Work in a fume cupboard. Measure the materials with graduated pipettes fitted with safety fillers (see chapter 1). Test the pH of the lotion with a pH meter or pH sticks (see chapter 2) and adjust the amount of ammonia solution to give a pH no higher than pH 9.5.

CAUTION. 'Home-made' perm lotion must not be used on a person's head of hair. It can though be tried out on swatches of hair.

Perm neutralisers

Perm neutralisers are of two types. One type uses *hydrogen peroxide* as its *oxidiser*; the other type uses sodium or potassium *bromate*.

Hydrogen peroxide neutralisers are made by mixing the hydrogen peroxide with a *conditioning cream*. A suitable example might be:

Monoethanolamine lauryl sulphate (27 per cent active)	– 18.5
Sodium lauryl sulphate (100 per cent powder)	– 10.0
Stearic acid	– 5.0
Water	– 66.5
Perfume, colour, preservative	– q.s.

To make it, the first three items are melted together over a water bath. The water is stirred in followed by the preservative. The perfume and colour can be added when cool.

Just before use on the hair, mix:

1 part Hydrogen peroxide (20 volume or 6 per cent)
1 part Conditioning cream
2 parts Water

Work the mixture into a foam and sponge well on to the perm curls. This mixture gives an effective hydrogen peroxide strength of 5 volumes or 1.5 per cent. This is too weak to bleach hair noticeably, although the perm lotion itself will cause loss of colour from tinted hair. Rapidly gaining popularity are 'ready-mixed' *cream peroxide* neutralisers.

Also supplied in 'ready-to-use' form and therefore popular are the *bromate* neutralisers. The sodium or potassium bromate is formulated either into a *shampoo* base or a *conditioning cream* base. Here are two formulations. The first is shampoo-based; the second is cream-based.

1	Sodium or potassium bromate	– 5 to 10		
	Monoethanolamine lauryl sulphate (27 per cent)	– 6		
	Water	– to make 100		
	Perfume, colour, preservative	– q.s.		
	Warm the materials together and stir until mixed.			
2	Lanbritol wax N21	– 5	Oil phase	Mix at 70°C
	Mineral oil	– 10	Oil phase	Mix at 70°C
	Sodium bromate	– 10	Water phase	Mix at 70°C
	Water	– 85	Water phase	Mix at 70°C
	Perfume, colour, preservative	– q.s.		
	This may be made by the cream-method described in chapter 6.			

CAUTION. Should you have thioglycollic acid and sodium or potassium bromate in your chemical store, make sure they are kept well apart. Should they accidentally mix, they will *explode*.

Tepid waves

An alternative perm process uses a more *dilute* thioglycollate lotion – 4 per cent thioglycollic acid as opposed to 8 per cent. The process *must* be assisted by *heat*. This heat is provided either by special heating clips, pre-heated on a machine or by a *hot* hairdryer. No neutraliser is required.

Hair straighteners or relaxers

While it is possible to use ordinary perm lotion to straighten a white person's hair, it is not easy to control by just combing it through the hair.

Black people's hair though cannot be straightened with normal perm lotion. This is because the hair cortex has a different structure. There is much less of the infilling putty-like *amorphous keratin* and, to bind the structure, there is another type of cross linkage called a *peptide bond*. These are the same bonds that join the amino acids to each other to make a protein (see chapter 17). They are not broken by the perm lotion so before a perm, they have to be pretreated with a '*relaxer*'. This is basically a solution of sodium hydroxide with a maximum of pH of 12.5. Having broken the peptide bonds, a black person's hair is much more fragile so the following permanent wave must use much milder lotions and lots of conditioner.

Old-fashioned heat perms

In the 1930s and 1940s, before the introduction of the modern thioglycollate perms, perming the hair involved applying quite considerable *heat* to the hair while it was in the curlers.

After sliding on to it a rubber insulating pad to protect the scalp, each section was wetted with a *strongly alkaline lotion* and carefully wound on a heat-resistant curler. *Heat* was then applied by one of three methods.

The 'machine' perm used electric heating elements clipped over each curl and supplied with current through wires from an overhead machine. In the 'wireless' perm, metal clips were pre-heated on a machine before clipping them over the curls (see figure 19.3).

Figure 19.3 The Callinan 'wireless' perm machine

The 'machineless' perm used sachets containing *calcium oxide* to provide the heat. The sachets, about the size of teabags, were made of blotting paper on one side and aluminium foil on the other. They were dipped in water and clipped, foil side inwards, over the curls. The calcium oxide reacts with the water producing considerable heat: an *exothermic reaction*.

Should a perm machine be available, it could be tried out on swatches of hair, but check first that it is in *safe working order*. A waving lotion suitable for use with a machine can be made to this formulation. The sodium sulphite is the reducing agent:

0.880 Ammonia solution	– 20
Sodium carbonate	– 4
Sodium sulphite – the reducing agent	– 2
Water	– 74

Checking with a pH stick will show that the lotion is quite strongly alkaline with a pH of around 11.

Bleaching the hair

In *bleaching* the hair, the pigments which give it its colour (see chapter 17) are changed to a *colourless* form by *oxidation*. In sunny weather, hair often *fades* because of the oxidising action of the ultra-violet rays of the sun. In hair bleaching, the oxidising is done more rapidly by the oxidising agent, *hydrogen peroxide*.

The ease of bleaching the various hair pigments varies. *Eumelanin*, the true brown-black melanin, bleaches relatively easily to a light brown but then the *pheomelanin* is quite difficult to bleach colourless to leave the hair a white 'platinum blonde'. The hair might be quite badly damaged in the process.

The *trichosiderin* of red and very black hair is almost impossible to bleach. Negroid and Asian hair will often bleach only to a reddish-brassy shade and no further, because of its trichosiderin content.

The usual strengths of hydrogen peroxide used for hair bleaching are:

Normal bleach	– 20 volume,	6 per cent
Strong bleach	– 30 volume,	9 per cent
Fierce bleach	– 40 volume,	12 per cent.

Just before use, the hydrogen peroxide is made *alkaline* by mixing it with either an '*oil bleach*' or '*powder bleach*'. Both contain *ammonia* such that when mixed according to the instructions, the mixture contains the equivalent of *one* part of 0.880 *ammonia* to 40 parts of 20 volume *hydrogen peroxide* and has a pH of between 10 and 11 – quite strongly alkaline.

An *oil bleach* contains 0.880 ammonia solution in a shampoo-base. A *powder bleach* contains ammonium carbonate as its source of ammonia. The remaining bulk of the powder is usually magnesium carbonate plus a powder detergent such as sodium lauryl sulphate to give a foaming action.

When applied to the hair, the alkaline mixture penetrates between the cuticle scales to reach the pigment granules in the *cortex*. In the alkaline conditions, the *hydrogen peroxide* decomposes:

$$\underset{\text{(Hydrogen peroxide)}}{H_2O_2} \rightarrow \underset{\text{(Water)}}{H_2O} + \underset{\text{(Oxygen)}}{O}$$

The oxygen is '*active oxygen*'. It is momentarily in the form of single atoms and is *very reactive*. It is able to *oxidise* the hair pigments, gradually rendering them colourless.

When first mixed the bleach is quite active, but its activity gradually diminishes. To take over and maintain the bleaching action as the hydrogen peroxide expires, *bleach boosters* are often added. These are tablets or powders containing a second bleach such as *urea peroxide* which being initially solid is slower to act.

Dyeing the hair

Hair dyes are of three main categories: temporary, semi-permanent and permanent. A *temporary* hair dye colours just the outside of the cuticle and should be removed by the next shampoo. Modern *semi-permanent* hair colours penetrate to the cortex of the hair but they are not colour-fast and last only through six or eight shampoos. *Permanent* 'tints' are colour-fast and are not removed by shampooing.

Temporary hair colours

Most temporary hair colours are based on *water-soluble dyes*. Almost 150 different dyes have been submitted for EEC approval. They come from a wide variety of chemical families. The dyes are used singly or in combinations to produce a full range of colours.

At one time the dyes were made into *colour rinses*. Concentrated solutions of a range of dyes were available in dropper bottles. Colours were mixed by adding a certain number of drops of each to a pint of water which was then poured through the hair. A famous example is the *blue rinse* used to take away the yellowishness of white or bleached hair. This is based on *methylene blue* dye.

One per cent solutions in water of each of the following dyes will be suitable concentrated colours to use in colour rinses:

Red	– Erythrosine B	(Colour index 45430)
Yellow	– Tartrazine	(Colour index 19140)
Blue	– Erioglaucine	(Colour index 42045)

Add the concentrated colours to beakers of water to produce a variety of colours and use them to dye swatches of blonde hair. Note that careful mixing of all three colours will produce *browns*.

Modern temporary colours are usually presented as *tinted setting lotions* and *colour mousses*. The concentrated colours as above could be included in a plastic setting lotion (see chapter 18). This example is an *auburn* tinted setting lotion. Try experimenting with different colour combinations.

Polyvinylpyrrolidone or PVP/VA	– 2
Alcohol	– 45
Tartrazine 1 per cent solution	– 10
Erythrosine 1 per cent solution	– 2.5
Erioglaucine 1 per cent solution	– 0.75
Water	– to make 100
Perfume	– q.s.

Of novelty interest are *coloured hairsprays*. These are hairsprays to which have been added alcohol-soluble dyes or to give a glitter effect dyed *aluminium powder*.

Semi-permanent hair colours

Around fifty dyestuffs have been submitted for EEC approval for use as *semi-permanent* hair colours. They include:

Nitro-phenylene diamines
Nitro-aminophenols
Amino-anthroquinones

They are of a variety of reds, yellows, oranges, pinks, blues and violets. The blue colours tend to be less fast than the others, so brown semi-permanents tend to become gradually reddish on the hair.

There are *two* main types of semi-permanent hair dye products. In one type the dyes are dissolved in a shampoo base to produce *colour shampoos*. In the other type the dyes are dissolved in a carefully selected solvent mixture to produce *liquid* semi-permanents.

In both types, when applied to the hair, the dyes penetrate to the *cortex* of the hair to become lightly bonded to the cortex fibres.

Permanent hair dyes

The *oxidation dyes* are the most frequently used permanent hair colours. Apart from their permanence, they differ in two other respects from temporary and semi-permanent colours.

Temporary and semi-permanent colours use ready-coloured dyes which *add* to the existing colour of the hair. The existing colour must be taken into account when using them.

Oxidation colours contain materials which have to develop their colour on the hair by being *oxidised* with *hydrogen peroxide*. The final colour can be darker or *lighter* than the original hair colour. To produce a lighter result the products are actually using the *bleaching* action of the hydrogen peroxide. Their colour then *replaces* the natural colour.

The main *oxidation bases* used in these dyes are:

Paraphenylene diamine
Paratoluylene diamine

When oxidised, both of these will colour the hair *black*; but by mixing with them other substances as *modifiers* a whole range of hair colours can be produced. The modifiers include:

Metaphenylene diamine
Resorcinol
4-amino-phenol

An added complication in formulating oxidation dyes is that the substances do not possess the final colour, nor is the colour predictable according to the rules of conventional colour mixing. Formulation is therefore initially a matter of try-and-see.

Commercial oxidation dyes are made in a variety of bases. Some are liquid products, some are creams, some are gels, others are shampoo-based. They contain *ammonia* to 'open' the cuticle. This gives them a pH of around 10. An antioxidant such as sodium sulphite prevents them oxidising in storage.

Just before use, the dye product is mixed with an equal amount of 20 volume (6 per cent) hydrogen peroxide. When applied to the hair some of the mixture penetrates to the *cortex* of the hair where the dye molecules become *oxidised* to develop their colour and make them group together to form granules of colour too large to wash out of the hair. Hence the colour is permanent.

The lighter colours in the range are usually mixed with 30 volume (9 per cent) hydrogen peroxide to boost their bleaching action.

An important problem with oxidation dyes is a quite high incidence of *allergic reactions*. About one person in five thousand is allergic to them. This makes a *skin test* necessary before any new user tries these dyes. A small amount of a dark colour placed behind the ear is left for 48 hours to see if any reaction occurs.

Here is a formulation for a simple oxidation hair dye. Try it on a swatch of hair, *not* on anyone's head.

Paraphenylene diamine	– 1
Alcohol	– 50
Water	– 49

Dissolve the dye in the alcohol. Add the water. Divide the solution into two parts. Set one aside and watch it gradually darken by *air oxidation*. Mix the other part with an equal amount of 20 volume hydrogen peroxide. Put in a swatch of blonde hair and see the colour develop. This will produce *black*.

Try experimenting with a lesser amount of paraphenylene diamine and include a little of one of the modifiers. Try your formulations out on swatches of hair.

Vegetable-based hair dyes

Despite the fact that oxidation dyes are well established as permanent hair colourants, from time to time there is a revival of interest in *vegetable hair dyes*.

The most frequently used vegetable dye is *henna*, the powdered leaves of Egyptian Privet. It contains a red-orange stain called 'Lawsone' or 2-hydroxy-1,4-naphthoquinone. Henna dyes white hair a reddish orange; on darker hair it gives a red tone.

Henna powder is quite easily obtainable. Mix some into a paste in very hot water and smear it on a swatch of blonde hair. Cover it so it does not dry out and keep it warm for, say, half an hour. Rinse it off and note the effect.

By mixing other substances with henna, the resulting colour can be changed. These *compound hennas* can produce a wide variety of colours, all with the *red* tone of henna! Acids will accentuate the red (vinegar could be used); alkalis such as borax subdue the red. Metallic dyes and earth pigments may also be used with henna.

Another famous vegetable colourant is *chamomile*. The flowers yield a yellowish stain called 4,5,7-trihydroxyflavone. Mix 2 parts of powdered *chamomile flowers* and 1 part of kaolin to a paste in hot water. Smear on hair, cover and keep warm. A 15-minute treatment 'brightens' fair hair; a 1-hour treatment dyes it a warm golden blonde.

Metallic hair dyes

Another old-fashioned group of hair dyes are the *metallic hair dyes*. These are of *two* types: *sulphide dyes* and *reduction dyes*.

In the former a solution of a *metal salt* and a solution of *sodium sulphide* are combed alternately through the hair, gradually building up a coating of dark-coloured metal sulphide.

Try a 4 per cent solution of sodium sulphide and a 2 per cent solution of a metal salt on swatches of hair;

Silver and Lead salts	give Black
Iron salts	give Chestnut
Copper salts	give Dark brown

The only present-day metallic hair dye is a well-known 'colour restorer' for greying hair which relies on the sulphur content of the hair to develop its dark colour. Lead salts *are* allowed for this purpose.

Reduction dyes use pyrogallol or pyrogallic acid to *reduce* a metal salt to its *metal*. Soak a swatch of hair in 2 per cent copper sulphate solution. Then apply a *freshly made* 2 per cent solution of pyrogallol. With luck, a reddish coating of *copper* should form on the hair!

Incompatibility with bleaches and perms is a problem with metallic dyes. Metals and hydrogen peroxide do *not* agree with each other. In a test-tube, put a little copper salt solution and then *carefully* add a little hydrogen peroxide. The mixture reacts quite violently and turns black. Imagine that happening on your head if you tried to bleach out a metallic dye!

Try also adding a few drops of an iron salt such as ferric chloride solution to some cold wave lotion and watch it turn a deep pinkish red: all very well if you *want* your hair that colour!

Things to do

1 Should you decide to make up samples of the perm lotions and permanent hair dyes described in this chapter, be sure to use them only on swatches of hair, not on anyone's head.

2 Test the pH of the perm lotions, the hair bleach mixture and the oxidation hair dyes using the methods described in chapter 2.

Self-assessment questions

1 Which types of chemical bonds in the hair are broken and reformed during a temporary hair set?

2 Which bonds are also broken during a permanent wave?

3 What additional bonds in a black person's hair must be broken by the relaxer before the hair is permed?

4 What is meant by the term 'hygroscopic'?

5 What is the main active ingredient of a professional perm lotion?

6 Name two substances that are used as the active materials in neutralisers.

7 What is the true chemical action of a perm 'neutraliser'?

8 What is the chemical action of a hair bleach?

9 What type of hair dyes contain nitrophenylene diamines?

10 What is the main active ingredient in permanent oxidation hair dyes?

11 Why is it advisable to perform a skin test prior to using an oxidation hair dye?

12 What actually is henna?

20 Unwanted hair

Depilation; wax depilatories; depilatory creams; shaving; shaving creams and foams; after-shave lotions

The problem of unwanted hair

With some minor exceptions, hair grows on almost all of the skin. Mostly the hairs are fine and downy and unless particularly dark coloured, they are not too obvious. However, if they are dark, they might be very noticeable indeed. Certain other areas bear the faster growing and more luxuriant *terminal hairs*: the scalp, the underarms, the pubic region and, for men, the moustache, the beard and possibly the chest.

Fashion dictates that certain hairy parts shall not be hairy. It is not fashionable to have underarm hair. Hairs on the legs do not look well through sheer nylon tights or stockings. The 'bikini-line' might require attention. A visible growth in the 'moustache area' is considered rather masculine. A stronger growth here and perhaps in the beard area is common as women approach middle age.

Depilation and epilation

Growths of unwanted hair may be tackled in a variety of ways. The electrical methods for *permanent* removal of hair are called *epilation*. Electrical epilation is dealt with in Volume 2.

Depilation refers to the methods of hair removal which allow regrowth: plucking, cutting or dissolving away the hairs.

Wax depilatories

In shaping of the eyebrows, unwanted hairs are removed one at a time by plucking with tweezers. This would be far too tedious and discomforting for removing all the hairs from the legs or even the upper-lip. For the 'mass-plucking' of these areas, '*waxing*' is employed.

The term 'waxing' actually covers a number of techniques: 'hot wax', 'cool wax', 'cold wax', 'organic wax'. Not all of them actually use wax.

Hot wax

In a hot wax treatment, molten wax is painted on to the area in a long, narrow band. When it cools it sets to form a cohesive plastic strip embedding the hairs. When lifted and pulled smartly it should come away in one piece, bringing the embedded hairs with it.

Most waxes are too brittle and crumbly when they set to form a flexible plastic film. Careful blending of waxes is necessary to produce a suitably cohesive mixture. Here are some possible blends. To make them, simply stir together the molten ingredients:

1	Beeswax	– 25	**3**	Rosin	– 53
	Rosin	– 75		Beeswax	– 25
2	Beeswax	– 50		Paraffin wax	– 17
	Paraffin wax	– 50		Soft paraffin	– 5

For use, the wax mixture must be melted in a suitable wax heater. Most wax heaters are electrically heated double vessels. Often the wax-pot rests in an outer water jacket and the electric element heats the *water*. The temperature

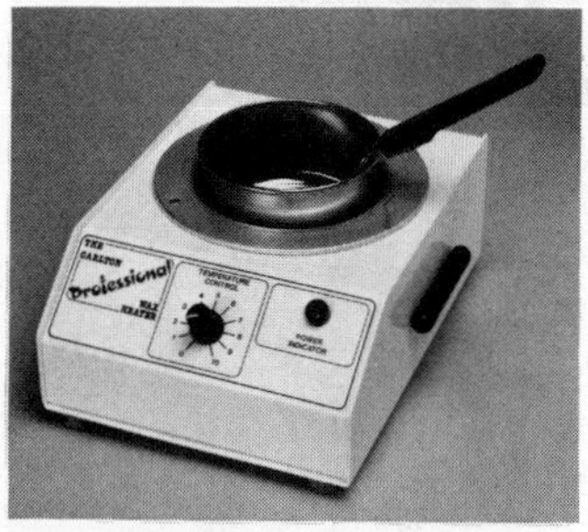

Figure 20.1 A depilatory wax heater (courtesy of Taylor Reeson Laboratories Ltd)

is controlled by a *thermostat*. In this way the wax cannot be dangerously overheated. Even so, the therapist must check that the wax heater is set to the correct temperature and test it by painting a little on her own skin before painting it on to the client.

Some wax heaters can be switched to a higher temperature setting to sterilise the wax. Make sure it has cooled sufficiently before using the wax again. Many heaters too have two pots: one for fresh wax and one with a filter to clean the hairs from the used wax. There are, though, signs that in the interests of hygiene it might become illegal to reuse wax on other clients.

Hair removal by waxing can leave the skin sore and open to infection. A soothing lotion containing a local anaesthetic, such as benzocaine, and an antibacterial agent, such as hexachlorophane, will reduce the soreness and risk of infection.

Cool and cold waxes

Cool and cold depilatory waxes are not waxes at all. They are basically a rubber latex solution in a volatile solvent. Some require warming before painting on the skin, others are painted on cold. The solvent evaporates to leave a rubber latex film on the skin with the hairs embedded in it, ready to be pulled smartly away. The used film is then discarded. It cannot be melted down for further use.

Another 'cold' or 'organic wax' is an adhesive based on a glucose syrup and zinc oxide mixture. Honey, which is basically a fructose syrup, is very similar to glucose and can be used instead.

The mixture may need warming before use. It is then painted on to the skin and a fabric strip is pressed on to it then pulled sharply away, bringing with it the adhesive and the hairs. Alternatively, the adhesive may be impregnated on to fabric backing strips. The strip is pressed down on the skin and pulled away repeatedly until the area is clear of hairs or the strip is clogged with hairs and ceases to be sticky.

The advantages of the cool, cold and organic waxes are:

1 More hygienic – as they are used only once there is no risk of cross-infection.
2 Safety – there is no dangerous heating of the wax and no danger of burning a client's skin with a wax which is too hot.
3 Convenience – hot wax needs a heater and time to heat up. It is not easy for the 'mobile' therapist to use.

Cream depilatories

Plucking out unwanted hairs by waxing is a painful business. The hair follicles are damaged and left open to the possible entry of infection. Many women therefore prefer to either *shave* off unwanted hair or *dissolve* it away with a *cream depilatory*.

However, because shaving and creams remove the hairs at or just below skin surface level and do not take out the entire hair from the follicle, regrowth will show much sooner making more frequent treatments necessary.

The active ingredient of a depilatory is a *keratolytic* or keratin-dissolving substance. Remember though that the skin also is made of keratin so it too will be subject to attack by the depilatory. This precludes the use of such a cream by a man as a daily alternative to shaving. He would soon have no skin on his face!

The usual keratolytic substances used are soluble metallic sulphides such as *calcium sulphide* or thioglycollates: *ammonium thioglycollate* and *calcium thioglycollate*.

The sulphides are fairly satisfactory for use on the legs or underarms but are too drastic for use on facial hair.

A perm lotion allows hair to be curled by first softening it. Take the softening a little further and the hair will easily collapse and wipe away. The thioglycollate creams are in effect 'over strength' perm lotions. They are not so severe in their action as the sulphides so they are suitable for use on the face. However, being milder in action perhaps renders them less able to cope effectively with the stronger hair growth on some skins.

In recent years, some work has been done on the use of *protein-digesting enzymes* in depilatories. *Papain*, well known as a 'tenderiser' for meat, has been tried with some success.

Formulations for cream depilatories

Note: In view of their activity and possibly damaging effects, it is *NOT RECOMMENDED* that samples of cream depilatories be made to use on the person.

1 A Sulphide Depilatory

Ingredient	Amount
Calcium sulphide	– 20
Talc	– 20
Methyl cellulose	– 3
Glycerol	– 15
Water	– 42

2 A Thioglycollate Depilatory

Ingredient	Amount
Calcium thioglycollate	– 7
Calcium hydroxide	– 7
Calcium carbonate (chalk)	– 20
Cetyl alcohol	– 5
Sodium lauryl sulphate	– 1
Sodium silicate	– 2.5
Water	– 57.5

Shaving

Shaving off unwanted hair may be done either with a *razor* or an *electric shaver*. When a razor is used, the blade slides over the skin, cutting the hairs at skin surface level. By lightly *stretching* the skin, the hairs can be made to 'pop out' of their follicles a little so the blade then cuts them *below* normal skin surface level, resulting in a closer smoother shave (see figure 20.2).

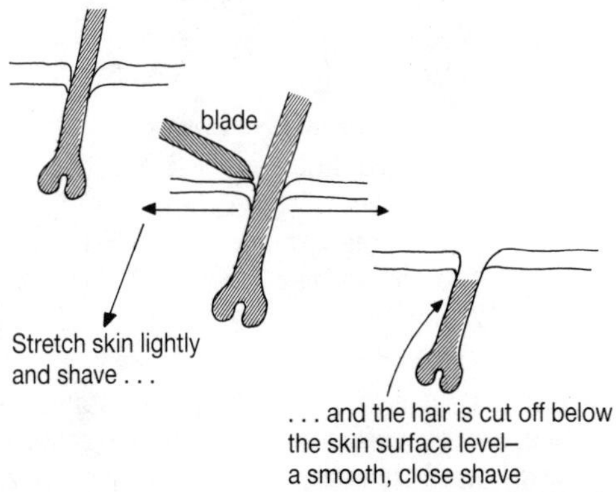

Figure 20.2 Stretching the skin allows a closer shave

Shaving soaps and creams

Fine hair growth, as usually occurs on a woman's skin, can be cut 'dry' – perhaps dusting the skin first with a little *talc* to lubricate the passage of the blade. A man's moustache and beard hairs though are far too tough. They tend to bend over in front of the blade, causing it to 'dig in' and cut the skin.

A shaving soap, foam or cream contributes to a more comfortable shave in three ways:

1 It *softens* the hairs so they may be cut more easily.
2 It *holds* the hairs upright so they do not fall over in front of the blade.
3 It *lubricates* the skin so the blade glides more easily over it.

Shaving *soap* is basically similar to toilet soap though it is often in the form of a *shaving stick*. Alternatively it could be a soft soap or *lather cream*. Either product is worked into a fairly firm lather with a shaving brush and is brushed into the beard. The *alkaline* soap softens the hairs, the lather holds them erect and the extra oils in the soap lubricate the passage of the blade.

Working up a lather from a solid *shaving stick* or a *lather cream* is a somewhat time-consuming chore in the split-second timing of a busy man's morning routine, so a '*brushless*' product is preferred by many men.

Brushless shaving cream does not foam. It is spread on the skin as a rather greasy cream which tends to clog the razor blade. *Aerosol foams* on the other hand are very easy to use, producing an *instant* lather at the touch of a button – ready to smooth into the beard.

Formulations for shaving creams and foams

Ingredient	Amount	Phase	
1 Lather Shaving Cream			
Stearic acid	30	Oil phase	Mix at 75°C
Coconut oil	10	Oil phase	
Palm kernel oil	5	Oil phase	
Potassium hydroxide	7	Water phase	
Sodium hydroxide	1.5	Water phase	
Glycerol	10	Water phase	
Water	36.5	Water phase	
2 Brushless Shaving Cream			
Stearic acid	20	Oil phase	Mix at 75°C
Mineral oil	2	Oil phase	
Cetyl alcohol	0.5	Oil phase	
Potassium hydroxide	1	Water phase	
Glycerol	7	Water phase	
Water	69.5	Water phase	
3 Aerosol Shaving Foam			
Lauryl alcohol	2	Oil phase	Mix at 75°C
Stearic acid	9	Oil phase	
Coconut fatty acids	1.5	Oil phase	
Triethanolamine	5	Water phase	
Water	82.5	Water phase	

Each of these may be made by the standard cream method (see chapter 6) but because *saponification* (soap making) has to take place, mixing must be done slowly and thoroughly. The products must be tested for any residual uncombined alkali. Perfume and preservative are added as required.

The aerosol foam is designed to be packed in an aerosol container (see chapter 24). It should be packed and propellant injected in the following proportions:

Aerosol foam formulation	– 93
Propellant 11/114 (60:40)	– 7

The product can be packed in one of the 'pump-up' type refillable aerosols provided it is fitted with a foam button.

After-shave lotions and pre-electric lotions

Washing in hot water followed by a cover of insulating and alkaline lather leaves the skin thoroughly wet and the pores wide open. The razor blade skims away the surface layers of the *Stratum corneum* along with the whiskers. Just drying with a towel can leave the skin rather sore.

Splashing on an astringent *after-shave lotion* closes the pores. It has an antiseptic action against possible infection. It assists the drying of residual moisture. It has a *styptic* action to speedily stem the bleeding from any small cuts or 'beheaded' spots and pimples.

A traditional after-shave lotion, the sort that barbers used to make up to use on their clients, might have been made to this formulation:

Witch hazel	– 15	(astringent)
Alcohol	– 10	(astringent, cooling)
Alum	– 0.5	(astringent, styptic)
Menthol	– trace	(cool sensation)
Boric acid	– 1	(antiseptic)
Glycerol	– 5	(moisturiser)
Water	– 68.5	(astringent, cooling)
Colour, perfume	– q.s.	

A modern after-shave lotion is basically a perfume cologne; a suitable 'masculine' perfume diluted with alcohol and perhaps water. Alcohol is quite effective as an astringent, an antiseptic and a styptic. It does however tend to sting a sore skin; hence the inclusion of some water in formulations. Formulations may be found in chapter 22.

A *pre-electric* lotion is an essentially similar formulation but with the addition of some oil to lubricate the skin so the shaver glides more easily.

A cut with a sharp razor is a very clean cut which gives the body's blood-clotting system very little to grip on. Any but the most minor cuts tend therefore to bleed for quite a time. Many a man emerges from the bathroom with a dab of tissue on his face to help heal a cut. An old-fashioned alternative was to use a *styptic pencil*. This is a stick of *alum* or aluminium potassium sulphate, a very effective astringent which heals these minor cuts quite quickly. Styptic pencils were once common in barber shops but their use is nowadays frowned upon as most unhygienic. There is the possibility that the use of a styptic pencil on different clients could transfer a blood-borne disease such as *hepatitis* or even *AIDS*.

Self-assessment questions

1 Distinguish between epilation and depilation.

2 What device on a depilatory wax heater ensures that the wax does not overheat?

3 Name two substances which might be used as active materials in cream depilatories.

4 List the three functions of a shaving soap.

5 What is a styptic?

6 Describe briefly each of the methods for removal of superfluous hair. Indicate the type of hair and the parts of the body for which each method is most appropriate.

21 The Teeth & Oral Hygiene

Dentition; tooth structure; dental hygiene problems; tooth decay; toothpaste; mouthwashes

Teeth

We arrive in this world without teeth. Until recently it was quite likely we would depart it without teeth too: our own natural ones anyway. It was more or less expected that sooner or later all the teeth would have to be extracted and a set of *dentures* fitted to take their place. Modern dental care is trying to change all that.

We each grow *two* sets of teeth, both in early life. The *milk teeth* see us through early childhood while beneath them the *adult teeth* are developing. From around six years old, one by one the adult teeth grow dislodging the milk teeth as they do so. The final adult teeth, the *wisdom teeth*, will not arrive until the late teens or twenties.

The problem with teeth is that once full grown, they have virtually no ability to repair themselves so they *need looking after*. With proper modern care they have a much better chance of lasting a lifetime.

Dentition

When all the adult teeth have grown, a full set is 32 teeth: 16 in the upper jaw and 16 in the lower. Each jaw has:

4 *cutting teeth* or *incisors*
2 *tearing teeth* or *canines*
10 *grinding teeth* – 4 *pre-molars* + 6 *molars*

Each tooth has a basically similar construction as shown by the diagram of an incisor tooth in figure 21.1.

The incisors have a chisel point and a single root. The canines have a pointed crown and a single root. The grinding teeth have two grinding edges and multiple roots.

The main structure of the tooth is *dentine*: a hard yet elastic material made of mineral materials and collagen fibres. The *crown* is covered with *enamel*. This is highly-crystalline *calcium phosphate* and is the *hardest* substance in the body.

Inside the tooth is the *pulp cavity* containing its blood and nerve supplies. The tooth is rooted in the jawbone and held in place by the *cementum*. The flesh of the *gum*, or *gingiva*, covers the jaw up to the base of the enamelled part of the tooth.

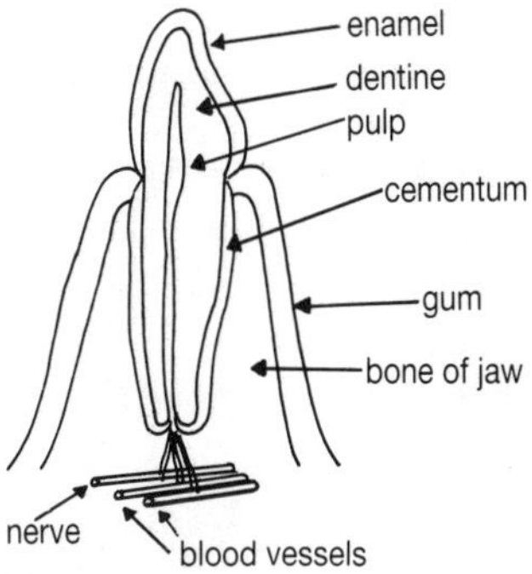

Figure 21.1 Vertical section of an incisor tooth

Tooth problems

Saliva is not just water. It contains many organic substances. A freshly cleaned tooth soon becomes coated with these substances, producing the '*acquired pellicle*'. This layer is soon occupied by *bacteria* and becomes *plaque*.

The plaque is easily removed by thorough brushing with a toothbrush and toothpaste. If the brushing is not thorough, the plaque may acquire crystals of a mineral deposit called *calculus* or '*tartar*'. This may become dark stained and unsightly due to staining by bacteria, blood or tobacco.

Dental decay or caries

Acids produced by the bacteria in plaque seek out any faults or cracks in the enamel and, should they penetrate through to the dentine, will cause it to soften and eventually break-up. Should the decay reach the pulp cavity the result will be *toothache*.

The build-up of bacteria in plaque is hastened by *much sugar* in the diet. It is no coincidence that *children* like sweets, and decay is greatest in children's teeth.

Fluoride

The connection between *fluoride* and reduced tooth decay was established about forty years ago. Since then, the inclusion of fluorides in some drinking water supplies, and nowadays its inclusion in virtually all brands of toothpaste, has reduced child tooth decay dramatically. There are now many young adults who must be thankful for fluorides.

Fluoride combines with the mineral structure of the tooth, making it less liable to acid attack, and thus less likely to decay. *But* because most of the growth of the teeth occurs in one's youth, fluoride can only be really effective if administered to children. It is much less advantageous to adults. The usual fluorides in toothpaste are:

Sodium fluoride
Stannous fluoride
Sodium mono fluoro phosphate or 'MFP'

Peridontal disease

More of an adult problem are diseases of the gums. Gums which are tender and inflamed are suffering from *gingivitis*. If poor oral hygiene allows bacteria to build up where the teeth meet the gums, if tartar accumulates and if the gums are not well-massaged by chewing fibrous food, then gingivitis could occur.

Should gingivitis occur and be neglected, the infection may penetrate deep into the gum and jaw, loosening the tooth. This is *pyorrhoea*. Should this stage be reached, the tooth may then have to be extracted.

The emphasis on fibre in the diet and more regular proper brushing of the teeth has already led to longer-lasting teeth.

Mouth odour

All ages can suffer *mouth odour*. The causes are various:

Bacterial action in the mouth
Strong-flavoured foods
Various diseases which upset the production of saliva

The 'freshness' of the mouth is enhanced by using mouth disinfectants and fresh-tasting flavours such as those included in toothpastes and mouthwashes.

Toothpaste

Proper use of the *toothbrush* alone is probably enough to clean the teeth of plaque, but the use of a *toothpaste* contributes greatly to the cleansing as well as making the brushing of teeth a pleasant and refreshing experience and one which is more likely to get done!

A *toothpaste* will contain:

An *abrasive* – to polish the teeth
Calcium carbonate – precipitated chalk
Calcium phosphate
Silica

A *detergent*	– to cleanse the teeth Sodium lauryl sulphate Sodium N-lauryl sarcosinate Sodium ricinoleate – castor oil soap (the 'S.R.' of SR toothpaste!)
A *humectant*	– to stop the toothpaste drying out and hardening Glycerol Sorbitol
A *binder* or *thickener*	– to make a paste rather than a runny cream; Tragacanth used to be used Cellulose products are used nowadays
A *flavour*	– most contain a 'minty' flavour peppermint or spearmint
A *sweetener*	– glycerol and sorbitol are both sweet tasting; Saccharin provides extra sweetness if required
A *bleach*	– to *whiten* the teeth is an optional extra Peroxides Perborates

Here is a general formulation. The cellulose material is dissolved in the water followed by the other water solubles, then the abrasive. If fluoride is to be included then chalk cannot be used as the abrasive inactivates the fluoride.

Precipitated chalk	– 40 to 50
Glycerol	– 15 to 25
Sodium lauryl sulphate	– 1 to 2
Carboxy methyl cellulose	– 0.5 to 2
Flavour	– 0.7 to 1.3
Saccharin	– q.s.
Preservative	– q.s.
Water	– to make 100

The toothbrush

Despite all the urging to brush our teeth, there is actually little concrete evidence to show that brushing as such reduces decay. Indeed, recent reports indicate that excessively hard brushes could have the opposite effect.

The main factor in reducing decay is the introduction of *fluoride* into the teeth. This is now an established *fact*.

The real value of *brushing* is that it *does* reduce the likelihood of *gum disease* This it does by removing food debris and *massaging* the gums. Make sure *your* brushing does massage the gums.

It is important that the brush is of good quality. The bristles should have rounded ends and *not* be left rough-cut, so they massage the gums and do not scratch.

The brush should be in good condition with its bristles standing erect and not splayed out. The brushing technique should include the up-and-down movements to dislodge food from *between* the teeth. Side-to-side brushing cannot do this.

Denture cleansers

Ordinary toothpaste is for cleaning natural teeth, not dentures. To clean these it is necessary to remove the salivary materials to dislodge food particles, to remove stains and reduce bacteria.

Salivary materials are removed by an *electrolyte*. Ordinary *salt*, sodium chloride, is most frequently used. Stains are removed by a mild bleach such as *sodium perborate* or *sodium percarbonate* working with an *alkali* such as sodium carbonate. This combination is also quite effective against bacteria.

A denture cleanser, whether powder, paste or tablets will contain:

an *oxidising bleach*	– sodium perborate or sodium percarbonate
an *electrolyte*	– salt
an *alkali*	– sodium carbonate or a sodium phosphate

Mouth washes

These are products to freshen the mouth and sweeten the breath. They contain a mild antiseptic, such as a phenol or cresol and a fresh-tasting flavour – peppermint, spearmint or cinnamon are popular. 'Glycerin of Thymol' is an example:

Thymol (isopropyl metacresol)	– 0.03
Alcohol	– 3
Borax – to make thymol soluble	– 2
Sodium bicarbonate	– 1
Glycerol	– 10
Water	– to 100
Flavour	– q.s.

Aerosol and pump spray mouth fresheners

These are simply solutions of fresh minty-type flavours to spray into the mouth to take away the smell of smoking or alcohol. They are a novel alternative to chewing-gum or strong-mints.

Things to do

Collect information leaflets and posters on tooth care and oral hygiene.

Self-assessment questions

1. What is the purpose of (a) the incisors, (b) the premolars and molars?
2. Of what substance is the main structure of a tooth composed?
3. What is the hard substance which forms the outer covering of the tooth?
4. What is (a) caries, (b) gingivitis, (c) pyrrhoea?
5. What is (a) plaque and (b) tartar? How does each occur?
6. Name two fluorides which can be included in toothpaste formulations.

22 Perfumery

The broad scope of perfumery; the sense of smell; raw materials for perfumery; essential oils and their extraction; animal products; synthetic perfumery materials; the perfumer; some simple formulations; skin perfumes and colognes; perfumes for consumer products

The importance of perfume

Have you ever wondered why the cosmetics department of a store is on the ground floor, just inside the entrance? The intermingling of a thousand scents is your welcome to the store, your invitation to come in and buy. It helps to put you in a buying frame of mind. Hopefully, the aroma will draw your attention to a display or a promotion. Perhaps a pack catches your eye. You stop to investigate. You try a little from the 'tester'. You *sniff* it gently. You like what you smell? You want to buy . . . *now*! The sales psychology has worked.

Top *perfumers* are the elite of the cosmetics business. Theirs is the world of essential oils and other exotic materials which make up a fragrance. However, perfumery is not just the creation of those magnificent and expensive couture perfumes. Mostly it is mundane tasks: fragrances for all the cosmetics, toiletries and household products right 'down' to the humble lavatory cleanser.

Whatever his task, a perfumer must 'get it right'. The success of a product hinges on the results of his work. The best hand cream, the best face powder, the best floor polish in the world are all doomed to failure if they do not smell 'right'.

The powerful sense of smell

The sense of smell is powerful, often uncontrollably so. Yet it is perhaps the least appreciated of the senses. In the *animal* world the sense of smell is all important, a matter of life and death. Do not forget that *we* are animals too!

The importance of the sense of smell can be summed up in the three 'S's:

Sustenance Sex Sociology

Sustenance is food. We all like our food. A large part of its appeal is its flavour and a major part of flavour is the smell or *aroma* of the food. The aroma attracts us to our food. It enables us to recognise it and lets us know that it is good to eat. It also stimulates the secretion of the digestive juices ready to digest it.

Sex is the continuation of the species. The chances of a tiny moth seeing his prospective mate in the big wide world are somewhat remote, but by scent he can detect her and home in on her from many miles away. The special scent she gives off is a *pheromone*. Pheromones are responsible for the mating attraction between male and female and also the displays of aggression between males to establish dominance. Humans have pheromones too. Many perfume oils contain traces of pheromone-like substances. Hence the sexual and sensual connotations of perfumes. Indeed, some fragrances are 'laced' with synthetic pheromones to increase their sensuality.

Sociology is the importance of smelling 'nice' or of being noticed. It is also the association of smells: the clean smell of a shampoo, the healthy smell of a disinfectant, the supporific effect of a 'heady' floral fragrance or the stimulant effect of a cool cologne.

The mechanism of smell

The word *perfume* is derived from the latin – *par fumum* which literally translates 'through smoke'. For anything to have an odour it must be *volatile* – that is, it must be able to *evaporate*. Molecules of it will then mingle with the air and may well be breathed in through the nose.

High in each nostril are the *smell organs* (see figure 22.1). This part of the lining of the nose is formed of special nerve cells whose fibres connect *directly* through the *olfactory nerves* to the brain.

This direct connection with the brain means the sense of smell is *always* active, even when you are fast asleep. It is a 'hot line' continuously monitoring the air that you breathe. You can 'turn a deaf ear' to a sound or close your eyes to what you do not want to see, but you *cannot* ignore smells, not even the barely detectable pheromones.

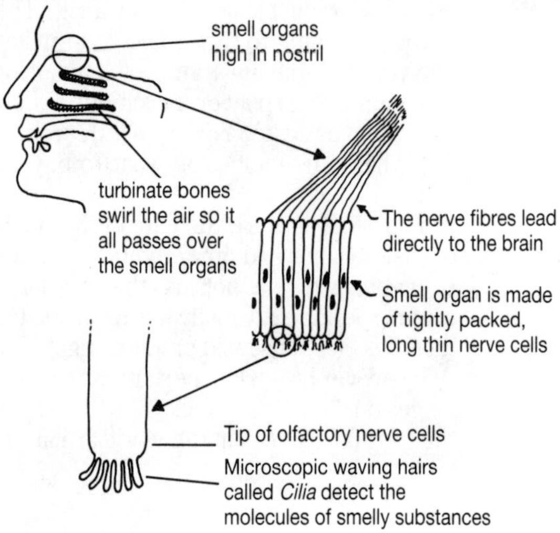

Figure 22.1 The mechanism of the sense of smell

The waving cilia of the olfactory nerve cells scour the passing air for the individual molecules of smelly substances. The molecule 'latches on' to a special protein on the surface of the cilia. This causes the nerve cell to 'fire' and send its signal to the brain to register the scent.

There are different nerve cells to register the different smells. The cell recognises the molecules of its smelly substance by their shape. This means that sometimes substances of a very different chemical nature, because their molecules are a similar shape, will have the same smell.

This can be of great value in perfumery. An alternative, much cheaper substance could replace a very expensive one or perhaps a synthetic material could replace a natural one. Musk-ketone, for instance, is a substitute for the rare and controversial natural musk.

Perfumery materials

A perfume is rarely, if ever, the product of a single aromatic substance. Even a modest fragrance is the result of a carefully balanced blend of perhaps dozens of different raw materials.

Perfumery materials are of three main categories:

Products of *plant* origin
Products of *animal* origin
Synthetic materials

Perfumery materials of plant origin

These are the traditional perfumery materials. There are many of them. In the main they are the *essential oils*.

An *essential oil* is a volatile plant oil. Being able to evaporate, it is able to have an odour. This distinguishes essential oils from the *fixed oils*. These are the *non-volatile* vegetable and mineral oils which in their pure state have no odour.

A great variety of plants can yield useful essential oils. By no means all come from flowers. The leaves, wood, bark and seeds of some plants often yield valuable oils. Here are some examples:

Flowers	– Rose, Jasmine, Violet, Orange flower
Leaves	– Bay, Thyme
Fruit	– Orange, Lemon, Bergamot
Seeds	– Almond, Celery
Wood	– Cedar, Sandalwood
Bark	– Cinnamon
Roots	– Orris (iris)
Moss	– Oak moss

In addition to the essential oils themselves, there are also *absolutes* and *concrètes*. These are solutions of the oils in the solvents used to extract them from the plant material.

Each essential oil is not a single substance but a complex mixture of many different substances. In rose oil, for instance, over 400 components have been discovered so far.

Frequently, the more abundant essential oils are separated into their components which can then be used as perfumery materials in their own right. These components are called *isolates*. Here are some examples:

Citronella is a grass which grows in the Far East. Isolates from its oil include:

Geraniol *Citronellal*

Both have a rose type floral odour.
Clove oil is a rather pungent smelling oil which yields

Eugenol

This has a very distinctive smell of carnation.

Figure 22.2 A field of roses for perfume oil in the Valley of Roses, Bulgaria (courtesy of the Bulgarian National Tourist Office)

Figure 22.3 A lavender field in Norfolk, England

Many of the gums and resins which ooze from plants contain a percentage of essential oils. These resinous odour materials are called *resinoids* and *balsams*. Examples are Peru Balsam and Pine Tar.

The cost of essential oils

While some essential oils are relatively abundant and therefore fairly cheap at a few pounds per kilogram, others are in very limited supply and hence very expensive, running to £1000s per kilogram:

Natural Oil of Rose – Annual Yield 3000 kg
Price £6000 per kg

The quality of certain oils varies depending on their country of origin and this is reflected in the price.

Oil of Jasmine – French (considered the best)
Price £6000 per kg

Italian – Price £3500 per kg
Egyptian – Price £4000 per kg

Because yields depend so much on the vagaries of the weather, yields can vary widely from year to year. This makes the low-yield, high-value oils ideal subjects for commodity speculators. In an abundant year, production 'excesses' may be bought up by speculators at relatively cheap prices. This creates an artificial shortage to keep prices up. Then in a year of real shortage the stored excess can be gradually released on the market to realise a handsome profit.

The extraction of essential oils

The method chosen to extract an essential oil depends on how stable the oil is to heat and on what kind of yield is likely. The extraction of some oils requires the handling of vast amounts of plant material to obtain just a few kilograms of oil. Methods used include:

Steam distillation   *Enfleurage*
Solvent extraction   *Maceration*
Expression

Steam distillation

Many oils such as Rose, Orange flower and Lavender are extracted by *steam distillation*. Essential oils have low boiling points and are volatile in steam. Steam is passed through the plant material and evaporates out the oil. When the steam and oil vapour is condensed it forms two layers (usually oil on top) which can be easily separated. A typical example of a yield: it takes 5 tonnes of rose petals to yield a single kilogram of Attar of Rose, the natural rose oil.

Figure 22.4 shows the steam stills at the Norfolk Lavender Farm. During the harvest period in July and August, the stills will be filled several times a day with spikes of lavender flowers cut by machine from the fields. Each 'fill' of about a tonne of flower spikes will within half an hour yield about a kilogram of lavender oil.

Lavender grown in the garden is an ideal material for steam distillation in the laboratory. Distillation does not have to be done immediately. If the lavender spikes are cut when in full flower then dried, the dried spikes can be distilled when convenient. Figure 22.5 shows the laboratory apparatus and process.

Figure 22.4 Steam still at the Norfolk Lavender Farm

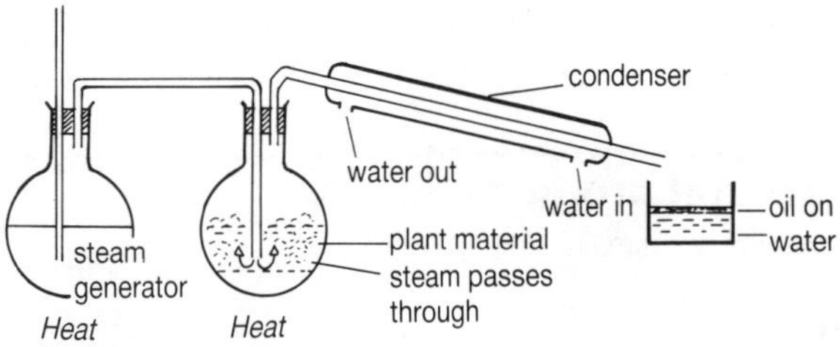

Figure 22.5 Steam distillation in the laboratory

Solvent extraction

Delicate oils such as Violet may be damaged by steam temperatures. Solvent extraction is one answer to the problem. A low-boiling point solvent such as a *petroleum ether* is repeatedly circulated through the plant material. Then the solvent is distilled off to leave the oil.

Enfleurage

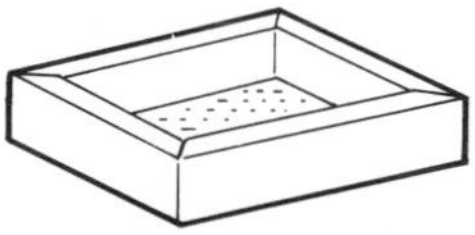

Figure 22.6 A wood and glass chassis for enfleurage

Have you noticed that if you keep an onion in the fridge its flavour is picked up by the butter and milk? The fact that essential oil vapour is easily absorbed by fats is used in *enfleurage* and *maceration*.

Jasmine oil is extracted by *enfleurage*. A thick wood and glass frame called a *chassis* is spread with fat (see figure 22.6). Flower petals are laid on the fat and a second chassis is inverted over the top. The flowers are changed daily through the three-month flowering period of the Jasmine. During this time, each tonne of fat will absorb the perfume of 3 to 3½ tonnes of flowers. The perfume-laden fat is called *pomade*.

The perfume is extracted from the fat by washing with alcohol. This yields 1000–1500 litres of dilute alcohol solution called *lavage*. This will be concentrated to reduce it to 150–180 kg of Jasmine *absolute*. An absolute is an alcohol solution of an essential oil. If the absolute is extracted with petroleum ether it will yield 10 kg of Jasmine *concrète*. If required, from the concrète can be separated just 1 kilogram of *Oil of Jasmine*.

Maceration

In maceration, the flower petals are immersed in *molten* fat to produce the pomade. After this, the process is similar to enfleurage.

Expression

When you peel an orange, the 'zest' which squirts from the peel is oil of orange. Citrus oils, orange, lemon, lime and bergamot, are extracted from the rind of the fruit by using a *press* to squeeze it out. This is *expression*. First the rind has to be grated from the fruit using a special grating machine.

A Bergamot, although a citrus fruit, is not edible but its rind yields *oil of bergamot* which is the basis of classic Eau de Cologne and the source of Bergaptan, the suntan promoter used in some suntan creams and lotions (see chapter 15).

Actually, nowadays much orange oil and lemon oil is obtained during the preparation of *comminuted* orange and lemon for the fruit drinks industry. The entire fruit, peel, pith, pulp and pips is liquidised. The oil floats to the top and is skimmed off.

Animal products in perfumery

Four animal products are of importance in perfumery. They are expensive and hence are used as dilute alcoholic solutions or *tinctures*. The four are:

Ambergris – a 'growth' from the stomach of the Cachelot Whale which can either be found on the beach or removed from the stomach of killed whales.

Musk – is in an internal pouch of the male Musk Deer from the Himalayas. This is supposed to be removed by a surgical operation, though all too often the local hunters kill the deer first.

Civet – is the secretion of the Civet – a cat-like animal of the Middle East. Aggravating the animal causes it to secrete.

Castoreum – is the secretion of the scent gland of the Beaver which is removed from killed animals.

Apart from expense, the use of these animal products is frowned upon by the conservation and animal welfare organisations. They are very largely replaced by synthetic alternatives.

Synthetic materials for perfumery

Although perfumery has been practised for thousands of years, its scope has been limited to a great extent by the availability of natural odour materials. Only in the last 70 to 80 years has it been possible to synthesise artificial perfume compounds. There are now literally thousands available. They have revolutionised perfumery, making a wide range of fragrances available for all manner of uses at quite modest cost. About 85 per cent of all perfumery materials are synthetics.

Synthetic organic odour chemicals are very important for four main reasons:

Wide range of odour types   Consistent quality
Reliable supplies   Modest cost

Synthetic materials are of three main types:

1 Derivatives of isolates from natural essential oils:
for example, from Citronella oil are obtained Geraniol (an alcohol) and Citronellal (an aldehyde – see chapter 4). From the latter another alcohol, Citronellol may be made. Both alcohols may then be reacted with organic acids to form esters such as Geranyl acetate. These all have rosy floral odours and are used to make synthetic rose-type perfumes at a fraction of the cost of the natural rose oil.

2 Isolates themselves can be synthesised from less expensive raw materials: for example, Geraniol can be made from Pinene which is isolated from Turpentine. Linalol (a lily odour) can be made from acetone.

3 Completely synthetic materials can be made as petrochemicals from oil-refining products. Some examples are:

Benzyl acetate – a fruity/jasmine odour
Bornyl acetate – a pine essence
Phenyl ethyl alcohol – a rose-type odour

The main chemical classes of synthetic aroma chemicals are

Alcohols – These have floral odours. Examples are Geraniol (rose), Linalol (lily) and Terpineol (lilac).

Aldehydes – These also are floral. Examples are Citronellal (rose) and Cyclamen aldehyde.

Acetals – An acetal is a combination of an alcohol and an aldehyde. They have a 'green' or leafy odour – for example, Phenylacetaldehyde dimethylacetal.

Ketones – These tend to have 'heavy' floral odours. An example is the intense violet smell of Ionone.

Esters – Esters are fruity or floral. Examples are Amyl acetate (banana, pear), Benzyl acetate (jasmine) and Benzyl propionate (pineapple).

There are also the synthetic 'animal' materials, muscone, musk-xylene, musk-ketone and civetone, which among others have largely replaced the natural materials.

Odour description – the language of perfumery

Take a gentle sniff from a perfume. Now try to describe *in words exactly what you smell* so someone reading them could recognise that smell. With some scents this is easy: you can relate to a well-known flower or fruit. But with many it is much more difficult. The words are just not there.

Perfumers recognise *seven* different odour types, although each can be further subdivided, qualifying it by the name of the flower, the name of the herb and so on:

Citrus – orange, lemon, bergamot
Floral – rose, jasmine, violet
Fruity – apple, pear
Herbal – mint, thyme
Green – leafy, mossy, fern
Animal – musk
Woody – cedar, sandalwood, pine

The perfumer

Creating a fragrance is a very highly skilled task and it is not the purpose of this chapter to show anyone how to become a perfumer.

The expertise demands a natural aptitude and lots of patience. A critical sense of smell, instant recognition of raw materials and how they will contribute to a formation come only after years of practice and expert guidance.

It is no use the novice 'throwing' a few oils together and hoping to create a classic perfume. The formulations shown later are but a starting point – they do not claim to be 'finished' perfumes by any means.

While every perfumer dreams of creating a classic fragrance which will survive to his everlasting memory, for the most part he will be performing much more mundane tasks.

He will receive a *brief* from a cosmetics or toiletry manufacturer for a perfume, for a face cream. . . , a soap. . . , a washing powder. . . , an air freshener. . . . He will then use his skill to create a selection of fragrances which the *applications laboratory* (see figure 22.8) will incorporate into samples of the product. In developing his formulations he will have to bear in mind the likely price of the product and also any effect the ingredients of the product such as acids or alkalis might have on the perfume ingredients.

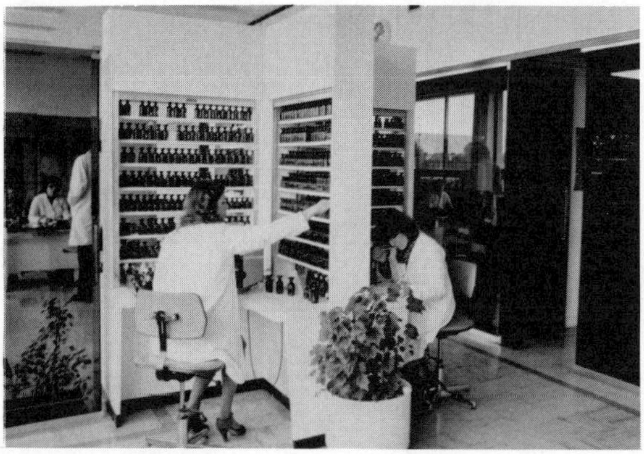

Figure 22.7 Perfumers working at their 'organs' (courtesy of Bush Boake Allen Limited)

Figure 22.8 A perfume applications laboratory (courtesy of Bush Boake Allen Limited)

A creative perfumer needs to have a wide range of raw materials close at hand. These are arranged on tiered shelves around his workbench. The arrangement looks like an organ console and indeed is called the *perfumer's organ* (see figure 22.7).

Some simple perfume formulations

Making up a perfume formulation is done in *two* stages:

1 Making the *concentrated base* from the raw materials.
2 Diluting the base for use.

In a formulation the materials are shown as parts by weight. In the laboratory aim to make around 10 g of a formulation in the first instance. This is an accurate weighing task and because the amounts of materials may be very small it is best to weigh them into the container 'on top of each other'. This demands great care. Add too much of a material and the batch is ruined. An accurate balance such as an electronic 'top-pan' (see chapter 1) is very suitable; the 'tare' control can be used to reset the balance to zero after each material has been added (see figure 22.9).

All glassware should be thoroughly clean. It should be give a final wash in alcohol and dried. Weigh the materials into a small beaker. Until you become

Figure 22.9 Making a perfume in the laboratory

skilled at pouring and 'dropping' from a bottle, dispense the materials into the beaker using a clean dropping pipette. Disposable Pasteur pipettes are ideal.

After mixing the materials with a clean glass rod, transfer the formulation to a clean glass bottle and store it in a cold, dark place (a refrigerator is ideal) for 3–4 weeks. This is to allow the materials to blend and the odour to develop.

Perfumes based on essential oils

This very basic *lavender* perfume is composed largely of essential oils. Two versions are given: the second containing Spike lavender oil, a rather 'sharper' oil distilled from the flower spikes of lavender in southern Europe, in addition to Lavender oil from the flowers of French or English lavender:

Lavender	I	II
Lavender oil – French	60	50
Lavender oil – Spike	—	10
Bergamot oil	40	40
Rose oil or synthetic	2	2
Clove oil	2	2

When mature, the concentrated base may then be diluted to produce a *lavender water*. This is basically a dilute alcohol solution of the perfume. These are the proportions of perfume base and alcohol:

Lavender base	– 5
Industrial alcohol	– 94
Diethyl phthalate	– 1

The diluted perfume must then be left to mature again for a further 3–4 weeks. During this time the diethyl phthalate will take away the smell of the alcohol. It may then be decanted if necessary and bottled. Lavender waters are one of the oldest perfumes. The earliest published reference is from 1615.

Although the term has come to refer to any dilute solution of a perfume, an *eau de cologne* was originally a perfume based largely on citrus oils. The original Eau de Cologne was devised about 1725 by Johann Maria-Farina and was based on Oil of Neroli. This is Orange-flower oil and was so called because Orange-flower water was originally invented by the Duchess of Neroli.

During the French Revolution, all premises in towns and cities were each given a number. Cologne was, at the time, part of France. In Cologne a famous Eau de Cologne house was given the number 4711 which survives to this day as the company trade-mark. Here are two Eau de Cologne formulations:

Eau de Cologne	I	II
Bergamot oil	33	30
Lemon oil	17	32
Neroli oil	17	—
Orange oil	17	19
Petitgrain oil, bigarade	—	15
Rosemary oil	8	3
Rose oil or synthetic	—	1
Lavender oil	8	—

Petitgrain oil is from the wood of a citrus tree. When mature, this concentrated base is then diluted to the required strength:

Cologne base	– 2–5 parts
Industrial alcohol	– 100 parts
Diethyl phthalate	– 1 part

After further maturing and, if necessary, filtering, it is ready for use.

There are many variations of the Eau de Cologne theme. In this example the orange is stressed:

Orange Cologne	
Bergamot oil	– 25
Neroli oil	– 35
Orange oil	– 25
Petitgrain oil	– 10
Rose oil or synthetic	– 2
Lavender oil	– 3

This is matured and diluted as above.

Perfumes based on synthetic materials

In the nineteenth century the emphasis in perfumery switched from colognes to florals. By the end of the century, synthetic organic fragrance chemicals were being developed and increasingly were used to produce less expensive imitations of the very expensive natural floral odours. Very simple synthetic rose, jasmine and violet fragrances are shown in the following formulations:

Rose	
Geraniol	– 30
Citronellol	– 10
Rhodinol or Geranium Bourbon oil	– 20
Phenyl ethyl alcohol	– 40

This is but a starting point. The formulation may be modified, for example by including ionone at 5 parts per 100. The violet odour of the ionone confers a much more 'velvety' effect on the basic rose fragrance.

Jasmine	
Amyl cinnamic aldehyde	– 45
Benzyl acetate	– 40
Hydroxycitronellal	– 6
Phenyl ethyl alcohol	– 5
Geraniol	– 2
Terpineol	– 2
Violet	
Ionone-α	– 60
Phenyl ethyl alcohol	– 20
Benzyl acetate	– 10
Hydroxycitronellal	– 5
Geraniol	– 4
Amyl cinnamic aldehyde	– 1

Dilution of perfume concentrates for use

If and how a concentrated base will be diluted will depend on its intended use. It may be for a skin perfume, for a cologne, for a splash-on aftershave or to perfume a skin cream.

The level of perfume in the product will depend on how strong is the odour of the concentrate and how strong an odour is required in the finished product.

Skin perfumes are normally solutions of the concentrate in alcohol. Glycerol is normally included to counteract the drying effect of alcohol on the skin. Concentrated skin perfumes or *extraits* contain up to 25 per cent of perfume concentrate. Here are shown three levels of dilution:

	Expensive	*Medium*	*Cheap*
Concentrated base	25	10	5
Alcohol	67	81	89
Diethyl phthalate	2	2	2
Glycerol	6	7	4

Dilute perfumes are variously referred to as *colognes* or *eau de toilette* or for men, *aftershave* or '*splash-on*'. They contain between two and five per cent of perfume in alcohol or alcohol and water. These are typical dilution proportions:

Concentrated base	– 2 to 5
Alcohol	– 100
Diethyl phthalate	– 1
Glycerol	– 0 to 6

When water is included in place of part of the alcohol, there may be solubility problems. A solubiliser will be required to stabilise the mixture (see chapter 7).

A *flower water* is basically a 'solution' of a perfume in water or water and alcohol. The best known are *rose water* and *orange-flower water*. Here are two formulations: one with alcohol, one without:

Rosewater

	With alcohol	*Without alcohol*
Rose oil or synthetic	1	1
Alcohol	40	—
Tween 20 – solubiliser	3	6
Water	56	93

Thoroughly mix the perfume and Tween 20, and then add the water or water and alcohol. Orange flower water is made similarly, substituting Neroli oil for rose.

Perfuming cosmetics and toiletries

When perfuming skin creams, any of the above concentrated bases can be used just as they are. About 6–8 drops in each 100 g of cream is sufficient. The perfume then forms about 0.5 per cent of the product.

It is possible to present a skin perfume as a cream, in which case the perfume forms up to 5 per cent of the product replacing that amount of the oil phase. A 'light' cold cream or a moisturising cream is a suitable base for a cream-perfume.

Perfume bases are also soluble as they are in alcohol-based products such as hairsprays, but in water-based products such as shampoos and setting lotions the perfume will need a solubiliser. In 'bought in' perfumes for water-based products, the solubiliser will already have been added so do not add it again!

Evaluating a perfume

Selecting a perfume is not to be undertaken lightly whether it be the vitally important selection of the perfume for a product, or the customer selecting at the perfume counter.

The professional will often be using concentrated bases. These must be diluted to their 'in-use' level with alcohol and allowed to mature before testing. He will use *smelling strips* or '*blotters*': narrow strips of blotting paper dipped in the perfume and allowed to dry before his critical smelling. Blotters must not be put down, so are held in clip-stands; menu stands are often used. The professional will not try to compare more than two or three fragrances at a time, nor should you. The nose quickly becomes fatigued and confused by too many odour samples at a time.

A fragrance produces its odour over a period of many hours, perhaps even several days. The effect is in three stages:

1 The *top note* is the initial impact created by the most volatile ingredients. This passes quite quickly.
2 The *body note* is the main odour of the fragrance which usually lasts several hours.
3 The *dry out* is the residual effect as the least volatile materials continue to evaporate. It could last for several days.

The perfumer will critically evaluate his samples at each stage. If you are going to make a choice of a perfume, so must you.

Figure 22.10 A perfume evaluation session in progress (courtesy of Bush Boake Allen Limited)

Choosing at the perfume counter

When as a customer you are selecting a perfume for yourself, you must be just as critical as the professional perfumer. A perfume cannot be chosen in a moment. Nor can it be chosen from dozens.

Select no more than *two* to try. Spray one on each wrist. Do you like the *top note*? Now go and do the rest of your shopping. Smell occasionally. Do you like the *body note*?

Go home and carry on smelling into the evening. Do you like the *dry out*? Only if at all three stages it pleases you, is that perfume for you.

Now you can go back and buy and you will not have wasted your money. After all a perfume is to give pleasure.

Things to do

1 Try extracting Lavender oil from Lavender spikes by the steam distillation method described in this chapter.

2 Try expressing Orange or Lemon oil by crushing the outer peel.

3 Make up samples of the perfume formulations described in this chapter. Try varying the proportions of some of the ingredients slightly and note the effect. Perfume oils are not normally supplied by the usual laboratory chemical suppliers. Perfume oil suppliers advertise in the 'trade press' journals such as *Soap, Perfumery and Cosmetics*. Many suppliers will be willing to supply oils and other perfume materials in the small quantities you require.

Self-assessment questions

1 What is meant by the term 'volatile'?

2 What is a pheromone?

3 Why is it not possible to ignore smell stimuli?

4 What is an essential oil?

5 How does an essential oil differ from a fixed oil?

6 Give examples of essential oils extracted from (a) leaves, (b) seeds, (c) wood.

7 What is (a) an absolute, (b) a concrète, (c) an isolate?

8 What is the source of (a) ambergris, (b) musk?

9 What is a perfumer's 'organ'?

10 Describe briefly each of the three stages in the evaporation of a perfume from the skin.

23 The Development & Testing of Cosmetic Products

The organisation of a cosmetic house; the development of new products; product testing; evaluating product performance; safety testing; microbiological safety; toxicity; allergy; irritation and sensitisation

The organisation of a cosmetic house

A cosmetic or toiletry does not just happen. A great deal of time and effort is involved in developing a product ready for the market-place in the first instance and a lot more is required if it is to maintain its market-share in a *very* competitive business.

Cosmetics and toiletries manufacturers range from large 'multinationals' down to small businesses. A multinational might even be part of a much larger organisation with interests in many fields. It could well have the full resources of the whole group at its disposal. The small business could literally be a 'one person' business where the one person has to perform all the tasks himself.

Every company, whatever its size will, in addition to manufacturing its products, need the wherewithal to market them and to develop and test them. In all but the smallest companies these will be the tasks of the *marketing department* and the *research and development department*.

The marketing department

The marketing department is responsible for:

market research
sales and distribution

Market research establishes how well the current range of products is being received by the public and finds out how the range might be developed or extended in the future.

Sales and distribution deals with the *promotion* and *advertising* of products and handles the *distribution* of supplies to the wholesale and retail trade.

Research and development department

'R and D' is the scientific department of a company. It has to perform a number of functions:

1 *Development* of *new products* from the 'good idea' stage to be ready for full-scale production.

2 *Improvement* of *existing products* in the light of recent research, new materials or changing fashions. In both these areas 'R and D' will be working closely with 'Market Research'.

3 *Trouble-shooting.* From time to time something goes wrong with a batch of a product. As a matter of urgency 'R and D' must find the cause of the problem, and then find a way to remedy it. To lose a production batch would be very costly.

4 *Cost-optimisation*. The costs of raw materials constantly fluctuate in response to world demand. In order to maintain the stability of its prices, a company may have to find alternative supplies of materials or even alternative materials to use in its products. The formulation will need to be adapted to suit the new materials.

5 *Quality control* ensures that a product always matches its specification in appearance, quality and performance. This will involve:

Checking the purity of raw materials
Checking the texture of the products
Colour matching colour cosmetics
Shelf tests for the stability and keeping qualities of products
Checking for microbiological safety

New products

It is very rarely that a truly new product is invented. Most so-called 'new products' are just up-dates of existing ones in response to market demands and recent scientific developments.

Occasionally there will be a marked improvement in product performance, but mostly it will be a range of new colours to complement the new season's fashions, a new perfume, or a new pack design.

From time to time a really big step forward in science or technology results in a *new product*. Some product milestones in recent years have been:

Automatic mascara. The liquid mascara in its applicator tube with built-in brush
Antiperspirants
Aerosols
Hairsprays which give 'natural control' of the hair
Soapless shampoos which have ousted soap as a hair cleanser

The development of a new product

The first stage in any new product is the *idea* for the product. The idea might arise from:

Public demand. Prospective customers might have asked for it
Market research might have revealed a *need* which no current product fulfilled
Original research might have shown that a new product could be effective or even that the existing product was not!
A *raw material supplier* might have a 'revolutionary' new ingredient

Having established an idea, there now follows the long, involved procedure of turning it into a successful finished product.

'R and D' will work with the idea to develop a possible formulation for the new product. This is known as the *product brief*.

Samples will be assessed in the *test salon* to see if the new product is effective for its purpose and whether or not it is an improvement on the existing products, both of that company and its competitors. If it is not, there is no point in taking it further. If it is, then a *perfume* and a *package* can be commissioned for it – usually from outside manufacturers – and it will go on to the next stage as a *modified product brief*.

Next will follow a period of thorough *testing*. Salon and *consumer panel* tests will check the new product's effectiveness and acceptability. *Safety* tests will make sure it complies with product safety legislation, particularly its microbiological (bacteriological) safety and level of toxicity. *Shelf tests* will check the stability of the product: the *pack* that is to contain the product will be sufficiently developed at this stage to be used in the shelf tests.

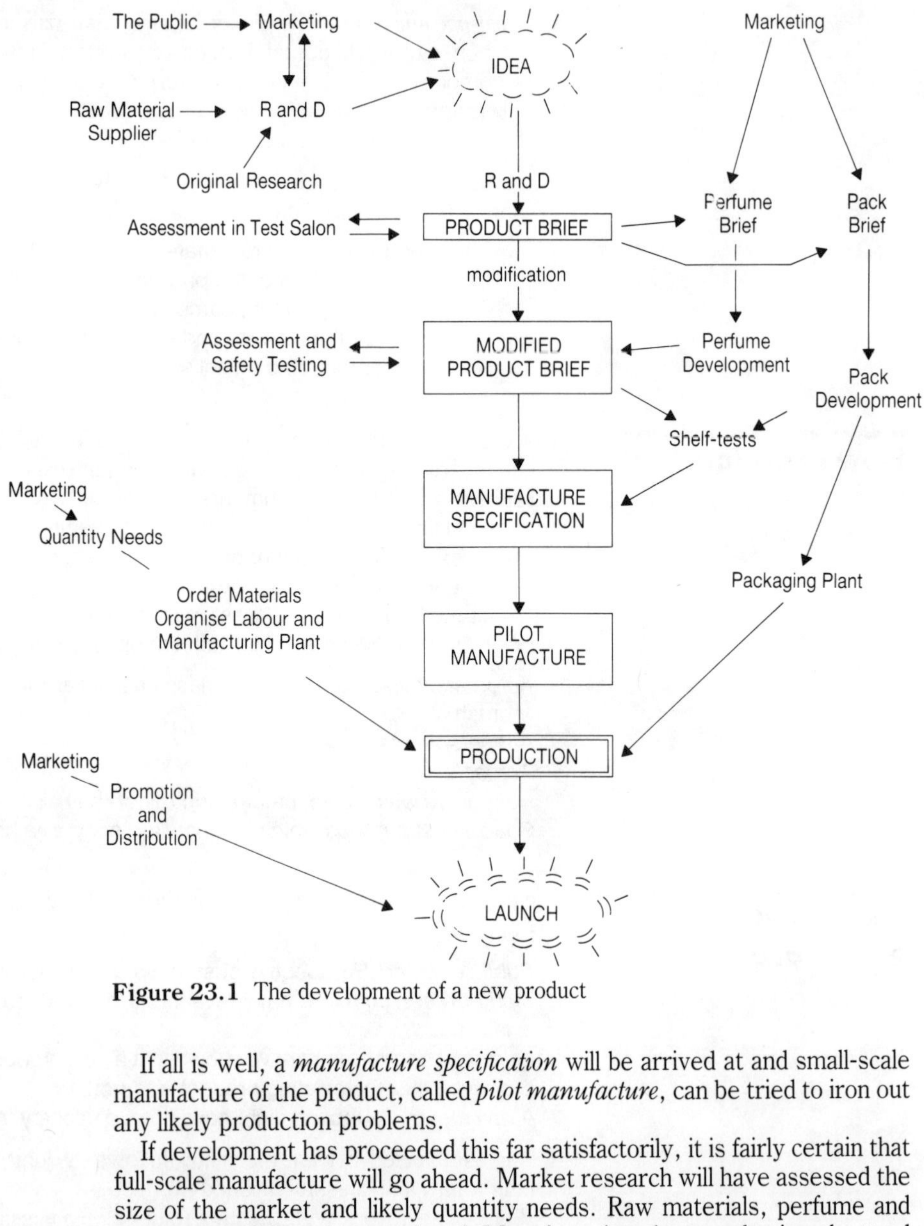

Figure 23.1 The development of a new product

If all is well, a *manufacture specification* will be arrived at and small-scale manufacture of the product, called *pilot manufacture*, can be tried to iron out any likely production problems.

If development has proceeded this far satisfactorily, it is fairly certain that full-scale manufacture will go ahead. Market research will have assessed the size of the market and likely quantity needs. Raw materials, perfume and containers will have been ordered. Manufacturing plant, packaging plant and labour will have been organised and *production* can commence.

The marketing department will have arranged *advertising* in magazines, on TV and radio; special *promotions* and *distribution* of supplies to retailers ready for the big day of the product *launch*.

Then it is a case of 'hope and pray' that the customers will buy and the product will be a success. After all, the development may have taken many months, even years, and cost perhaps millions of pounds.

Product testing

Before it is marketed, any new product must be thoroughly tested for both *performance* and *safety*. The programme of tests is *product evaluation*.

Testing must also be maintained right through the production run of a product to ensure that the quality is maintained. This is *quality control*.

Evaluation of product performance

During the development stages, the researchers will want to know:

Will the product work?
Will it justify the claims which are to be made for it?
Will it be 'better' than others of its type?
Will it be *more acceptable* to the customers?

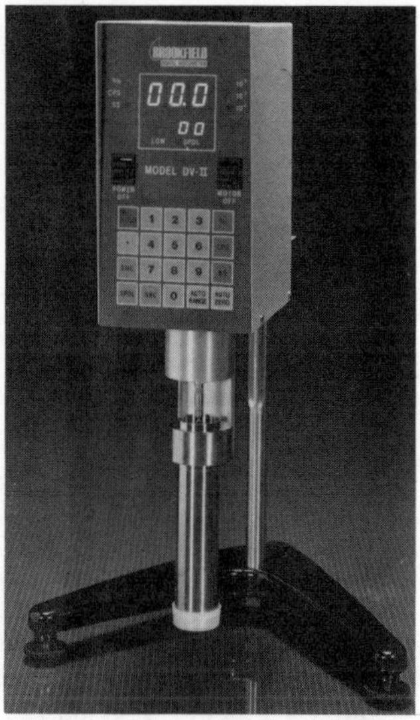

Figure 23.2 The Brookfield viscometer (courtesy of Baird and Tatlock Limited)

The evaluation of the performance of most cosmetics and toiletries is not easy because not all the evaluation criteria are measurable. Indeed many that are measurable vary considerably from user to user. This means that the results of performance tests are quite likely to be *subjective* or a matter of opinion, rather than *objective* or measured.

Some criteria *are* measurable, though the range of tests is as wide as the range of products. Here are some examples of objective tests.

The *covering power* of a colour-cosmetic can be both estimated visually and measured by light-analysing instruments.

The *output of sweat glands* is measurable by collecting and weighing the sweat. It is possible therefore to show the effectiveness of an *antiperspirant* by applying it to just *one* armpit and then comparing the output of the two.

The sebum, or other grease film on the skin, can be dissolved off and weighed. The effect of skin creams at applying a film or the effectiveness of detergents at removing it may be measured.

The *moisture content* of the *Stratum corneum* can be estimated (measuring its *conductivity* of electricity is one method) and hence the moisture-retaining ability of moisturisers can be compared.

The condition of the *collagen* fibres of the dermis may be seen by microscopic examination of small biopsy sections of skin. More easily it may be deduced from measurements of the *elasticity* or from the *surface appearance* of the skin. Whichever way is used, it is a measure of the degree of premature aging of the skin and the extent to which it is being arrested or reversed by the use of a cosmetic.

Product texture

Figure 23.3 A penetrometer for testing the firmness of a cream (courtesy of Baird and Tatlock Limited)

The actual performance of a cosmetic on the skin is not the only criterion on which it is judged. The physical properties and behaviour of the product are just as important.

A cream or lotion must have the right degree of *firmness* or *'runniness'* – that is, *viscosity*. A lotion must run easily from the bottle yet not run off the hand. A cream must 'pick up' nicely on the fingers or spatula; it must not slop around in its container; yet it must spread easily on the skin and not *'drag'*. The viscosity may be measured by one of a number of types of *viscometer*. The firmness is measured by a *penetrometer*. A weighted cone falls into the cream from a set height and its distance of penetration is measured; the less it penetrates the firmer the cream.

Shampoos and bubble baths are tested for their *foaming* characteristics. A bubble bath is tested for the sheer volume of its foam and its persistence. The *creaminess* of a shampoo foam is more important. This depends on the size of bubbles in the foam and the amount of water they retain.

Panel tests

Whether the properties and performance of a cosmetic are measurable or not, the acceptability of the product rests with the user. Panel tests are to judge *user-reaction*. Apart from the performance of a product, they will be used to determine:

Perfume preference *colour* preference *pack* design

These are *not* trivial matters. The best product in the world is no good if it does not sell, and it will not sell if it does not look right, smell right or feel right, or if the pack does not appeal to the customers.

Panel testing requires a substantial reserve of volunteers who can be called upon, for a small fee, to make up the test panels. These may be mixed or single sex, mixed or single age groups, mixed or specific social backgrounds as required.

The tests are usually conducted 'blind'. That is, only the researcher knows the identity of the samples given to each panellist who is then required to complete a questionnaire. Where the actual product is being evaluated, the samples will be in identical plain containers. Where a particular ingredient or additive is being tested, some panellists are given 'control' samples without the ingredient. Such are the opinions and judgements of people that on occasions the 'control' sample receives the top mark!

When you have made samples of some of the cosmetics described earlier in the book, why not try setting up a panel test to evaluate them. Make, for instance, a selection of cleansing creams and lotions. Ask your panellists to use them to remove a full make-up: foundation, eye make-up and lipstick. Ask them to comment on how effective each product is at removing each type of make-up. Ask them also to comment on the character of the product, its ease of application, whether it spreads easily or drags and if it leaves the skin dry, greasy or sticky. Each panellist could use two samples, one on each side of the face. Design a suitable questionnaire and work out a method of analysing the results.

Safety testing cosmetics and toiletries

The *EEC Cosmetics Directive* and its UK offshoot, the *Cosmetic Product Regulations* of the Consumer Protection Act require in effect that cosmetics and toiletries shall not do their users harm. To this end all products must be formulated so they are *safe* to use and tested to ensure that this is so.

The tests fall into three main areas:

Microbiological safety tests
Toxicity tests
Irritation and sensitisation tests

Microbiological safety

Bacteria, moulds and yeasts are everywhere. Most cosmetic products, particularly those with a water content, are potentially food and a growing place for these micro-organisms. If they should gain a foothold in a product they will quite likely *spoil* it and might even present a health hazard to the user.

Because no one wants to 'keep refrigerated' their cosmetics and 'use within two days of purchase' like food, most cosmetic products will require the addition of a *preservative*. Its function is to destroy any micro-organisms in the product. It is therefore a poison, so its proportion in the product needs to be as small as possible. One must ensure therefore that the *freshly manufactured* product is as free from micro-organisms as possible. The preservative will have enough to do killing all those which gain entry during the use of the product from fingers, from lips and from left-off tops.

Both raw materials and finished products are checked for microbial content.

This is done by diluting a sample of known volume with a known volume of sterile water, and using this to innoculate an agar-jelly plate. This is a shallow covered glass dish (a Petri-dish) containing a thin layer of agar-jelly to which a suitable nutrient medium has been added. If this is incubated by placing it in a warm place, within two days each viable micro-organism will have grown into a colony large enough to be seen and counted. From this count the number of viable micro-organisms in each cm^3 of the product can be calculated. This is the *total viable count* or TVC. The aim should be a TVC of less than 10 per cm^3.

A manufacturer not only wants to know if his products are of good microbiological quality but also that the preservative he has added will be effective. To check this a *challenge test* is performed. A sample of product is deliberately contaminated with a known mix of micro-organisms and is then tested by sampling as described to see how many survive. If no more than 10 micro-organisms survive in each cm^3 of product, the preservative has done its job.

Caution

Practical microbiology can be dangerous. It should be done only in a properly equipped microbiology laboratory under proper conditions and supervision.

Any micro-organisms which grow from samples will be 'wild types', not known laboratory strains; so once started, the culture must *not be opened* until killed by sterilisation. All cultures must be labelled with their source and the date.

Before embarking upon any practical microbiology in the school or college situation, one should consult the guidelines laid down by the Department of Education and Science, the Health and Safety at Work Act, and the *Cosmetic Products Regulations*. One should also use an *up-to-date* manual of practical microbiology.

Toxicity

A toxic substance is a *poisonous* substance. As far as possible, *no* toxic materials should be used in cosmetics. In well-controlled manufacturing countries this is the case.

There are however some materials which by the nature of their action must be potentially harmful. Each country's legislation lays down maximum limits on the proportion of these which may be in a product. Here are some examples from the *EEC Cosmetics Directive*:

Boric acid	in talcum powders: maximum 5 per cent – must state 'not to be used for babies'.
Thioglycollic acid	in permanent wave lotions: maximum 8 per cent, pH not to exceed 9.5.
	in hair straighteners: maximum 11 per cent, pH not to exceed 9.5.
	in depilatories: maximum 5 per cent, pH not to exceed 12.65.
Formaldehyde	in nail hardeners: maximum 5 per cent – must state percentage; must state 'protect cuticles with grease or oil'.

There have been instances where known poisons have been found in cosmetics. For example, antimony oxide or stibium has been used as a pigment in kohl sticks imported from Asia.

What can on occasions give rise to problems is the presence of *toxic impurities* or *contamination* in otherwise safe materials. For instance:

Carcinogenic asbestos in talc from certain sources
Tetanus contamination of talc or other minerals

For cosmetic purposes it is essential to use materials of a suitable standard of purity.

A long-term project in both the USA and EEC is the testing of *all* materials used in consumer products for their toxicity threshold. The so-called 'LD 50' test is a procedure in which batches of laboratory animals (rats or mice) are given increased doses of the test substance until it causes deaths among the test animals. From a statistical treatment of the results can be calculated the dose which should be lethal to 50 per cent of a batch of test animals – hence LD 50.

Allergic reactions

A much more difficult toxicity problem is that of *allergic* reactions. There are many substances which to the majority of users are completely safe but to a few they are, in effect, poisons: a case of 'one man's meat is another man's poison'.

The most usual effect of such substances is to bring about some kind of eruption of the skin or *dermatitis*, though it may be associated with a state of general illness throughout the body. This is because there are *two* main types of allergic reactions:

1 Primary irritation
2 Sensitisation

Primary irritation

Primary irritation is the result of the *direct* action of the offending substance. Its effects may be physical, chemical or physiological but they are usually confined to the area of application of the substance. The condition is called *contact irritant dermatitis* and the substance causing it is a *primary irritant*.

On occasions the irritant might gain entry to the body and travel elsewhere in the bloodstream, giving rise to more widespread symptoms as it goes. It may even gravitate to the feet and ankles, causing its reaction to occur there – a *gravitational* reaction.

Sensitisation – the true allergic reaction

Sensitisation involves the body's immune system of antigens and antibodies. It is a *rejection process* just like the rejection of a transplanted heart or a disease bacterium. The body recognises the offending substance as *alien* and reacts to expel it, causing as it does so the symptoms of a quite unpleasant general illness.

Irritants and sensitisers in cosmetics

Some known irritants and sensitisers are quite widely used in cosmetics. The answer to why they are used is either that there is no safer alternative or that a substance is so valuable as to make its use worth the risk; after all, it may adversely affect only very few people.

Substances in the first category where there is no safer alternative include para-phenylene diamine and para-tolylene diamine in hair dyes and thioglycollic acid in perm lotions. In the second category is lanolin. It is an excellent emollient and replacement for sebum. The reason is that it *is* sebum, but being sheep's sebum rather than human sebum, some peoples' bodies recognise it as alien and are allergic to it.

When a known irritant or sensitiser is included in a product, it must be stated on the label, together with any special instructions. Here are some examples:

Contains Lanolin
Contains Phenylene Diamines – skin test advised
Discontinue use if irritation occurs. Do not use on broken skin

Hypoallergenic and allergy-tested cosmetics

Many manufacturers produce a range of *hypoallergenic* or 'low-allergy' cosmetics either as their main speciality or as a supplementary range. They omit from them as many known allergens as possible. Usually, because something in a perfume is often the allergen, they are unperfumed.

It is, however, not possible to make completely 'allergy-free' cosmetics. There is always someone who is allergic to anything. In view of this, many countries are making it illegal to make low-allergy claims for products. Denmark is the first in Europe.

Testing for irritation and sensitisation

All products and materials must have been tested for *skin irritation*. Ingredients must have been tested for *sensitisation*. Products to be used around or near the eyes must be tested for *eye-irritation*.

The patch test for skin reaction

There is as yet no standard method laid down for patch testing, but the following is typical. The tests are performed on human volunteers. The samples to be tested are applied to a special adhesive patch-test strip (see figures 23.4 and 23.5). The strip is placed on the volunteer's back or arm (see figure 23.6). The test may be done '*open*' so air can get to the samples, or '*occluded*', to exclude air and prevent the sample drying on the skin, in which case a self-adhesive plastic film is used to cover the test area.

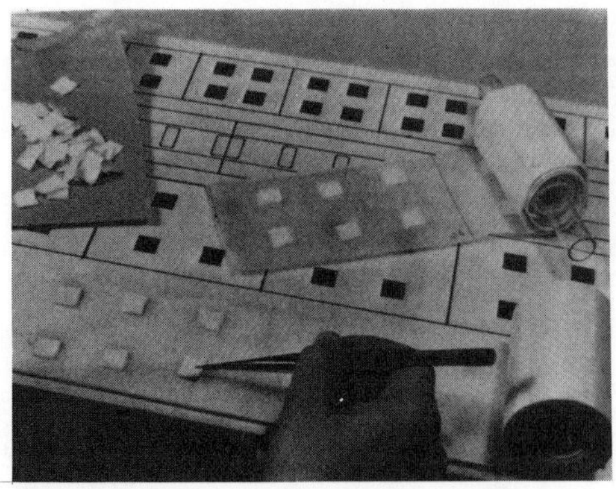

Figure 23.4 Preparing a patch test strip (reproduced from the *Journal of the Society of Cosmetic Chemists* by permission of the Editor)

Figure 23.5 Applying the samples to the patches (reproduced from the *Journal of the Society of Cosmetic Chemists* by permission of the Editor)

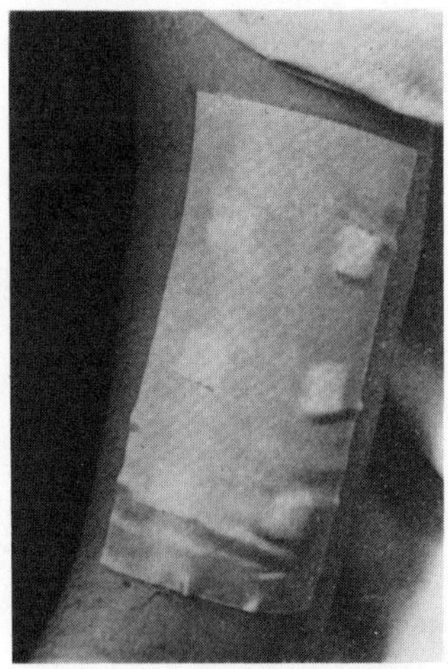

Figure 23.6 The patch test strip on the arm (reproduced from the *Journal of the Society of Cosmetic Chemists* by permission of the Editor)

The test samples will normally be left for no more than 48 hours. If a reaction is going to occur it will happen within this time. However, should a reaction occur, the test may have to be curtailed. When the patches are removed, the skin is inspected for signs of irritation, reddening, itching or blistering and any reaction is related to the sample placed over that area.

Eye-irritation test

The rabbit is used as the test animal in this instance because it does not shed tears, so a test sample placed in the eye is *not diluted*.

Cruelty to Animals Campaigners please note: a laboratory rabbit is an expensive beast and known eye-irritants are not applied just for the hell of it. Before a test of this nature is carried out, researchers are already fairly certain that no adverse reaction will occur.

By law, all shampoos and eye-make-up must be tested for eye-irritation. 0.1 cm^3 of the sample is put in the eye and left for 3 days. It is regularly inspected. If any reaction occurs such as irritation or reddening, the sample is flushed out of the eye. It has failed the test.

Testing for sensitisation

Tests for sensitisation are done either on human volunteers or on guinea pigs which react similarly to humans. A test sample is injected and the volunteer or guinea pig is observed regularly for any adverse reaction.

It may be that *photosensitisation* (ultra-violet sensitivity) is being investigated, in which case the animal or volunteer will be subjected to ultra-violet treatment. In this case, the researcher will be looking for any abnormal reaction to ultra-violet.

Many substances, particularly dyes, perfumes and medicinal drugs, are known photosensitisers: the eosin dyes sometimes used in lipsticks or bergamot and celery oils in perfumery.

Should a person intend undergoing an ultra-violet treatment, whether by natural sunlight or any kind of sun-lamp, they must be sure to remove all traces of make-up or perfume and be particularly careful if they are taking a course of medicinal drugs.

The mechanism of irritation

An irritant will cause a relatively rapid response. The severity of the response is more or less in proportion to the concentration of irritant on the skin.

To irritate the skin, a potential irritant must penetrate through to the living layers. Considering that the outer layers of the skin are supposed to be a barrier, it is amazing how many substances can penetrate through it.

To an irritant which penetrates easily, the reaction will be virtually immediate. To one which penetrates slowly, it may require use of the material over quite a long period before it builds up to an irritant level.

When irritation does occur, the symptoms follow a sequence. These are the symptoms of *contact dermatitis*:

1 *Irritation* – itch or pain.
2 *Erythema* – reddening.
3 *Oedema* – swelling, blistering.
4 *Eczema* – blisters burst, weep and scab over.

How far the symptoms advance will depend on the concentration of irritant in the skin and on the sensitivity of the person's skin to it.

The physiology of irritation

When an irritant penetrates through to the living layers of the skin, the live cells and particularly the *mast cells* of the dermis, may become so distressed that they die. When a cell dies, it releases internally special 'self-destruct' enzymes which will liquefy it so its remains may be dispersed. At the same time it releases *histamine*, a signalling substance whose functions are two-fold. On penetrating down to the dermis it will:

1 *Trigger pain nerve endings* to send impulses to the brain – triggering a few produces an *itch*, triggering many causes out-and-out *pain*. This is to bring the problem to one's attention.

2 *Cause dilation* of the *dermal capillaries*, allowing greater blood flow through the skin; hence the reddening or *erythema*. Its purpose is to speed the dispersal of the irritant and the remains of the damaged cells and to bring materials for repairs.

Should many cells be damaged and liquefy, the blood will deliver fluid to dilute the liquid remains and minimise the effects of the irritant. The damaged area will swell, producing the *oedema*. The nature of the swellings varies. They may be small pimples, larger blisters or widespread 'puffy' areas.

It is possible that the swellings may eventually subside, but frequently they burst, releasing fluid or pus, and then dry out to form scabs. This is the *eczema* reaction.

The physiology of sensitisation

At first sight a sensitisation reaction might closely resemble irritation. However, behind the scenes, it involves a series of much more complex physiological processes so a simple explanation is rather difficult.

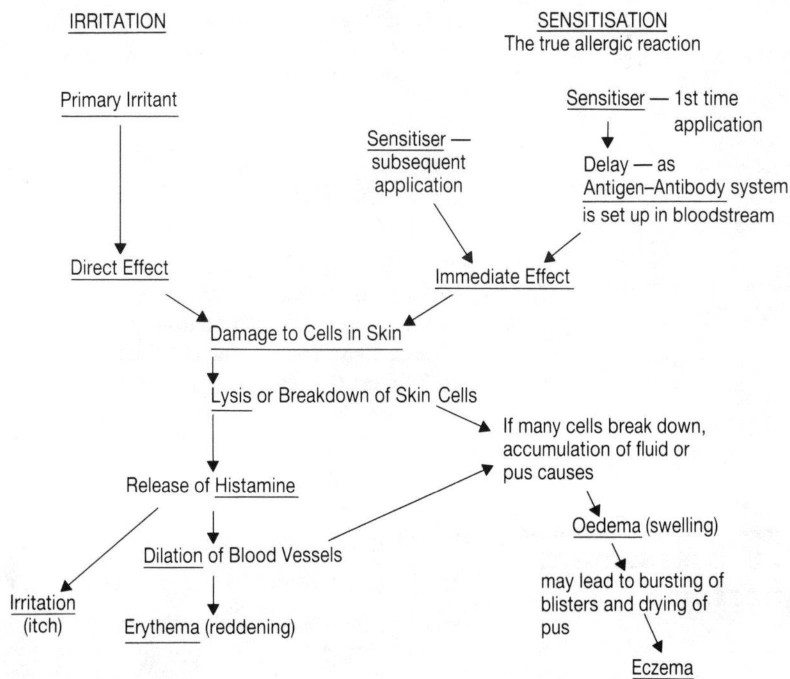

Figure 23.7 The mechanism of skin irritation and sensitisation

Basically what happens is that the body treats the invading substance as it would an infectious disease and brings into play its *immune-response* to fight the invasion and attempt to expel it.

But first it is a case of 'know your enemy'. The body must learn to recognise the invading substance as being potentially harmful. To recognise the substance at all, it must be *similar* to something the body already knows. A good example of this is in transplant surgery. The body will happily accept a stainless steel and nylon hip joint but will reject a heart from a human donor. Similarly it will accept the very foreign mineral oil but might reject the sebum-like lanolin.

The *first* time a sensitising substance is used there will probably be no outward signs but the harmful potential of the substance will have been realised and in the blood a fighting system of *antigens* and *antibodies* will be set up and will remain in readiness should another use of the substance occur in the future.

If a *repeat* application of the substance is made, then the *antigen–antibody* system will swing into action to fight it. If the sensitiser is in a product applied to the skin then the reaction will probably occur just there and will be very similar to the contact dermatitis caused by a primary irritant with the itching, the erythema, the blistering and the eczema; but this is *contact allergic dermatitis*. It is quite likely, though, that it will penetrate through the skin and circulate with the blood and cause a much more widespread illness.

Skin reactions and the dermatologist

Dermatology is the branch of medicine dealing specifically with the skin and its associated health problems. A *dermatologist* is a specialist doctor working in this field.

One of a dermatologist's more difficult tasks is the diagnosis and treatment of allergies. It is probably easy enough to recognise that a skin eruption is an allergy, but to what?

An allergic reaction might be held in check for a while by prescribing a *cortisone* cream, but it will not go away completely until the cause has been identified and removed.

Sometimes the cause is obvious, occurring beneath the sticky plaster or beneath the nickel-plated watch strap buckle. Other times it may be most elusive, defying the detective work, the patch testing and even the 'educated guesses' of the dermatologist.

Things to do

1 Set up product evaluation exercises for some of the products you have made from formulations in this book. For instance, you could compare the effectiveness of the cleansing products (chapter 10) or the shampoos (chapters 8 and 18).

2 In the library refer to textbooks of Dermatology for further details of irritant and allergic reactions of the skin to various products used on it.

Self-assessment questions

1 What is panel testing?

2 What is the reason for 'shelf-testing' a product?

3 Why does a cosmetic product need to contain a preservative when it has been made under strict standards of hygiene?

4 What is a 'challenge test'?

5 Distinguish between irritation and sensitisation.

6 What is the purpose of a patch test?

7 Describe briefly how a patch test is carried out.

8 What types of products must be tested for possible eye-irritancy?

24 Packaging Cosmetics & Toiletries

Psychology of packaging; product information; packaging materials; glass, plastics and metal containers; paper and board containers; caps and lids; specialised containers; pump dispensers and atomisers; aerosols; aerosol propellants; aerosol safety

The psychology of packaging

There is unlikely to be any real fundamental difference between different brands of a cosmetic or toiletry product; no manufacturer can afford to market products significantly worse than those of his competitors. So when you visit a store to buy a product, what factors influence your choice?

1 The conservative approach – 'The brand I had last time was alright. I'll have the same again'.
2 The 'me-too' syndrome – 'I'll have the same as my friend uses'.
3 Successful advertising – 'It was advertised on TV.'. 'I saw it in a magazine'. 'I like the boy/girl in the advert'.
4 Your own choice – 'I'd like to try something new – but which?'.

Looking round the large and confusing array of brands on offer, your attention is drawn to a particular brand by the design of the *pack*.

Pack design

Pack design is of prime importance to the success of any product. It is even more so for a cosmetic product. It is the pack which attracts your attention. It must stand out among the others. It must *sell* the product. This is far from easy when all the other packs have been designed to do the same thing for their products.

At the same time the pack must *identify* with the product. One *expects* to find a hairspray in an aerosol. One *expects* toothpaste to be in a collapsible tube in an individual cardboard box.

The pump-dispenser is an ideal pack for toothpaste, but those manufacturers who have offered toothpaste in them are having an uphill struggle. Toothpaste comes in tubes!

The pack must also express a *house identity* or a *range identity*. If a company's house-style is, say, brown and gold, the regular customer aims straight for the familiar brown and gold packs. Should the company decide to market a product in pink and purple, it would not be instantly recognised as being one of their products and as a result it could fail to sell.

Product information

Ever since commercial cosmetics began, they have been clouded in an air of mystery and secrecy. Manufacturers have tended to exaggerate the benefits of using their products or have been very reluctant to reveal the secrets of their contents: perhaps because there *are no real secrets* or their claims would not bear investigation.

Thanks to consumer pressure and the resulting national and international legislation this is gradually changing, though not as quickly as the consumer protection lobby would like.

Obviously the pack will show the product name and its purpose. It now has to show, if necessary, information as to the limitations to the use of the product, how it is to be applied, whether there could be potential danger in its use and if it contains any possibly harmful or allergenic ingredient. A skin cream with lanolin must say 'CONTAINS LANOLIN'. A hair dye must state 'CONTAINS PHENYLENE DIAMINES'. In the USA the pack has to show a listing of the ingredients in the product; the UK cosmetics industry has been able to resist this so far.

Packaging materials

As well as identifying the product
identifying the manufacturer
selling the product
informing the customer

the pack must *contain* the product
protect the product
allow the user to *use* the product

Not all packaging materials will do all these things. Some oil-based products such as perfume oils are very 'searching' and may penetrate certain plastic containers. Some products are quite corrosive to metals and will perhaps corrode through metal containers. Certain plastics are not 'gas-tight' and so are unsuitable for highly pressurised packs such as aerosols. They might also allow the ingress of air into non-pressurised packs which might spoil the product by oxidation. Then there is the problem of getting the product from certain containers; the 'tomato sauce' problem of a viscous product in a narrow-necked rigid bottle.

Glass containers

The great advantage of glass is that it is very good at containing products. Very few substances attack it – only strong caustic alkalis and hydrofluoric acid, neither of which is used in cosmetics. So glass is not likely to contaminate the product.

Glass is good-looking. The product inside is visible. Coloured products look good. For cream-pots, white opaque glass is often used. Using thick glass adds apparent bulk and weight to the product so the users think they are getting more product than they actually are!

On the other hand, being heavy makes bulk handling of glass containers more difficult and puts up transport costs. It is also *fragile* so it needs extra packing and extra care in transit.

Figure 24.1 A selection of glass containers

Plastic containers

In modern times all kinds of products are contained in plastic containers. There are three main types of containers:

1 *Rigid* – Cream-pots, Lipstick containers, Make-up palettes
2 *Semi-rigid* – Bottles, in particular 'squeeze' bottles.
3 *Flexible* – Collapsible tubes, Sachets

Rigid containers are made from either rigid unplasticised polyvinyl chloride (uPVC) or polystyrene, usually the toughened from which is not so prone to cracking.

Often cream-pots are double-walled with an inner liner separated by a space from the outer casing. This offers the same psychological effect of 'more for your money' as glass but without the weight and fragility.

Rigid plastics are also used to make lipstick and mascara containers and palettes for eye colours. For these uses the plastic may be metal-plated to give the effect of an expensive gold or silver container.

Semi-rigid bottles are usually made from polyethene (polythene) or polypropene (polypropylene). Their advantage is that they may be squeezed to assist the dispensing of viscous products.

There are two kinds of polyethene: low density and high density. A problem with the low density form in particular is that it is permeable to certain oils. Do not keep perfume oils in polythene bottles, they could gradually escape through the plastic. Water-based products present no problems in polythene because, being an oil-based material, it is water-repellant.

Sachets for shampoos are usually made of flexible polyvinyl chloride (PVC) sheet which is much less permeable to oils than polyethene. Again it must be toughened PVC so it does not split easily – and makes it a 'scissors job' to open the sachet.

Figure 24.2 A selection of plastic containers

Metal containers

Collapsible tubes are traditionally made of metal. Originally it was lead, now it is *aluminium*. One of the earliest uses of the tube was by Samuel Colgate for his 'Ribbon Dental Cream' toothpaste early in the century.

The real advantage of a metal collapsible tube is that it is always 'full'. There is no air space inside so no chance of oxidation damage to the product. This is very important for easily oxidised products like permanent hair tints. Having no air in the tube is equally important with toothpaste so it will emerge as a continuous 'ribbon' on to the brush.

The big problem with metal tubes is their appearance. A brand new tube looks fine but once handled it is likely to be dented and when squeezed and eventually rolled it is a most unattractive sight. This is why tube products are protected by their individual card cartoons.

Plastic tubes made of flexible PVC or polyethene are much better looking because they 'suck back' to their original shape. This does however have disadvantages. The sucked in air might damage the product. They also need to be stood opening-end downwards so the product is at this end when squeezed, otherwise they are likely to squirt out a mixture of product and air.

Most toothpastes are now being packed in laminated plastic and aluminium tubes. These are not so untidy when squeezed and only suck back slightly as the product is used.

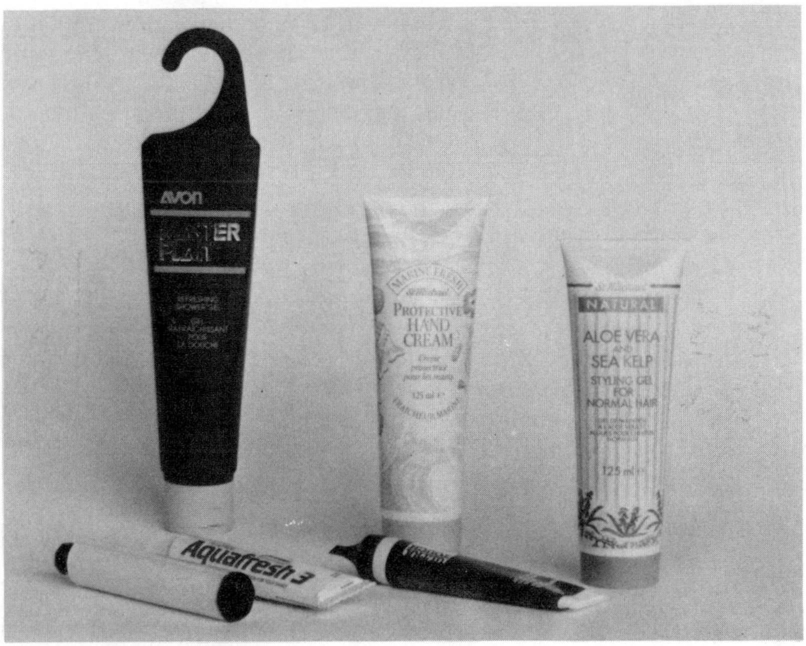

Figure 24.3 Metal, plastic and laminated collapsible tubes

Most aerosol containers are made of metal, usually tinplate steel or aluminium. Only a metal container can reliably and safely contain the product at pressures which may exceed 100 pounds per square inch. Metal containers are however susceptible to chemical attack by the product. To prevent corrosion, most must be lacquered internally.

Paper and board containers

As most cosmetics and toiletries are liquids, the opportunity to use cardboard containers is rare. However, *talcs* and *dusting powders* are frequently packed in card tubs, often with moulded plastic tops and bottoms.

Many products are packed in individual card boxes for a number of reasons.

Figure 24.4 Card packaging for cosmetics

The main container may be glass or a metal collapsible tube for which a box gives protection. The product may require an instruction leaflet, or the manufacturer may wish to bring to notice other products in the range. This literature is easily packed with the product in the outer box.

Bars of soap are often individually wrapped in paper. Apart from preventing physical 'bruising' of the soap, this also helps stop the bar losing moisture and cracking. It does however produce a moist atmosphere around the bar which could be conducive to mould growth. An inner wrapper impregnated with a safe fungicide prevents this.

Figure 24.5 Paper wrappers of a soap bar

Closures – caps and lids

Whether the container itself is made of glass, plastic or metal, the *closure*, the cap or lid, is most likely plastic bringing with it the *permeability* problems as well as the problem of forming a *leak-proof* seal.

This is most commonly dealt with by using a *cap-liner*. This is usually a disc or card coated with either *metal foil* or *plastic film*, depending on the product (see figure 24.6).

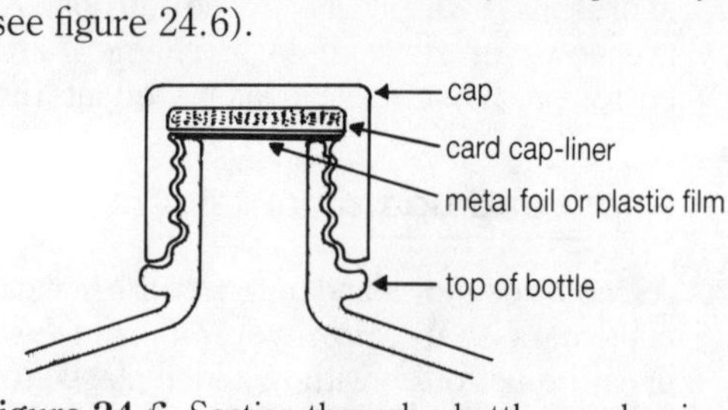

Figure 24.6 Section through a bottle cap showing the cap liner

Specialised packs

Certain products require containers designed specifically for holding and dispensing that type of product. Here are some examples of specialised containers:

Lipstick containers – with a 'screw-up' mechanism to advance the stick.
Mascara containers – a tube with a brush built into its cap to hold and dispense liquid mascara.
Compacts – to hold compressed face powder, with a mirror in the lid to aid one's make-up.
Palettes – to hold a selection of compressed powder colour cosmetics. Each colour is compacted into a small metal tray or *godet*. The palette holds a number of godets together with a brush.
Roll-on dispensers – for antiperspirants.
Pump dispensers – for lotions and perfumes.
Aerosols – for sprays and foams.

Figure 24.7 A selection of specialised containers

Roll-on dispenser

The armpit is not the easiest of places to apply a product. There are three possible solutions: the aerosol spray, the stick and the roll-on. In the latter a plastic ball takes the viscous product from the container and applies it to the skin (see figures 24.8 and 24.9).

Figure 24.8 Roll-on dispenser for antiperspirant

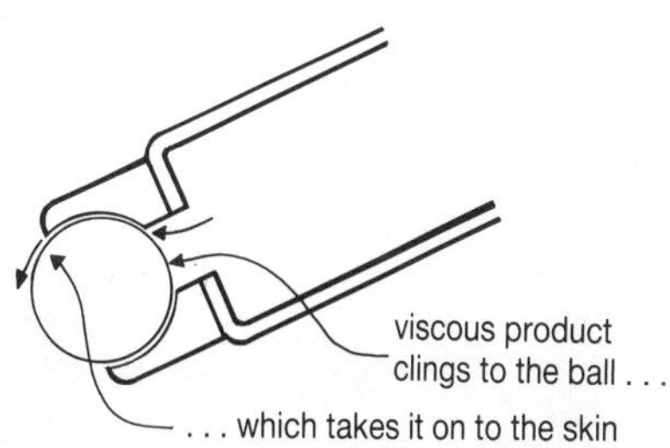

Figure 24.9 Section through the ball applicator of a roll-on antiperspirant

Figure 24.10 Pump atomisers for perfume (right) and pump dispenser for creams

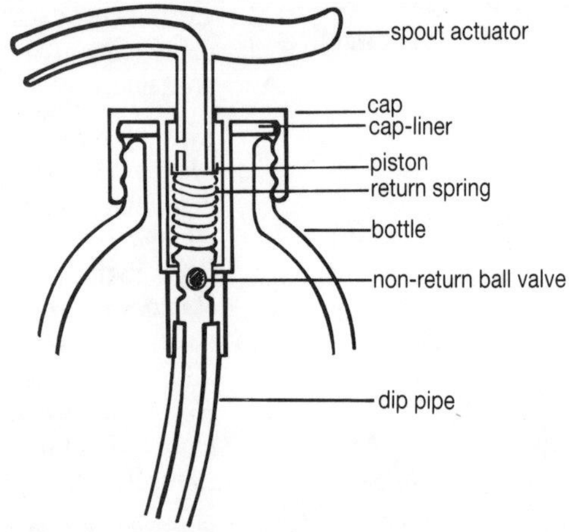

Figure 24.11 A pump dispenser

Pump dispensers and atomisers

A simple *pump* is built into the bottle cap. A press on its actuator dispenses the product: a spout dispenses a portion of hand cream or liquid soap on to the other hand or a spray head sprays a little perfume on to the wrist. Pump sprays are not really suitable for hairspray where a more sustained spray is required but they are ideal for 'dosing' skin creams, toothpaste or perfume. Figure 24.11 shows the components of the pump.

Aerosols

Spraying is the ideal way to apply products like hair lacquer and antiperspirant but it needs to be a *sustained* spray. For such products the *aerosol* is the ideal container.

At one time, having a shave meant working up a lather from a block or stick of soap with a shaving brush. Now at the touch of a button an *aerosol* will deliver an instant foam ready to smooth on to the beard.

Strictly speaking, the term 'aerosol' should not be used to describe the container. An *aerosol* is literally a suspension of fine droplets of liquid in air: a mist or fine spray. The container itself is a *pressurised pack*.

Pressurised packs have their origins early in the nineteenth century in the soda-water siphon and the 'champenoir' – a dispenser for champagne. Aerosols as such were patented at the turn of the century and some use was made of them in the 1920s and 1930s, but the valves were expensive so the products were not commercially viable.

The first big developments came during the Second World War as insecticide 'bombs' for use by United States troops in the Pacific where more servicemen were dying from insect-borne disease than were being killed in battle.

For consumer products, aerosols became widely used in the 1950s as their cost dropped as a result of valves being made from cheap yet precision moulded plastic components. Since then, despite more than their fair share of 'scaremongery' and as a result being banned in a number of countries, they are sold in vast numbers containing a huge variety of products. In the United Kingdom alone, around 500 million are sold annually.

Figure 24.12 A selection of aerosol containers

Aerosol products

At one time or another virtually every consumer product that can be, has been tried in an aerosol. By no means all have been lasting successes, but among the 'best sellers' are many cosmetics, toiletries and household products. Here are some examples:

Cosmetics and Toiletries	**Household Products**
Hairspray	Polishes
Setting lotion mousse	Oven cleaner
Antiperspirant	Air freshener
Foot spray	Fly spray
Shaving foam	Whipped cream
Suntan creams	Garden chemicals
Perfume	Paints

The aerosol pack

Figure 24.13 is a section through a pressurised pack to show its components.

The complete aerosol pack is pressurised with a propellant gas. When the actuator button is pressed, the *gas pressure* forces the product up the dip-tube, through the valve and out through the button. If a *liquefied gas propellant* is used, the product emerges mixed with liquefied gas. This *evaporates* as it emerges and serves to break up the product into a spray of fine droplets – the aerosol. For a foam product it instantly 'whips-up' the foam.

Although any aerosol *must* be designed as a coherent whole, it is made of distinct units:

The *container*	The *propellant*
The *valve*	The *product*
The *actuator button*	

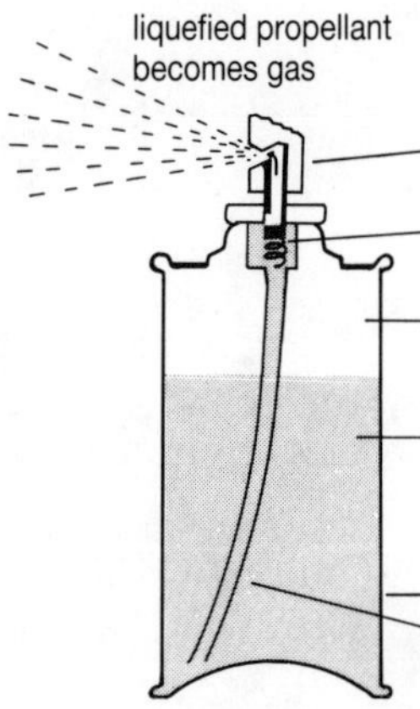

Figure 24.13 Section through a pressurised pack

Aerosol containers

Aerosols are in effect *pressure vessels* and as such they must have sufficient strength so they will not *burst* with 'normal' use or abuse.

The pressure of any confined gas rises dramatically as it is heated. After filling, all aerosols are tested in a water bath at 50°C. At this temperature, pressures approaching 200 lb/square inch are quite possible with some products. Containers must allow for at least a 50 per cent extra margin for safety above the 50°C pressure without deforming.

Containers may be made from:

tinplate aluminium glass

A tinplate container consists of three pieces of tinplated sheet steel: side, top and bottom. To withstand the pressure, the top and bottom are domed and the seams are rolled, and then welded or soldered together. Usually the inside of the can is lacquered to prevent corrosion.

Aluminium containers are formed from a single sheet of aluminium with *no* seams. They are much cleaner in appearance but much more expensive.

Glass looks good and it shows off the product inside, but to be strong enough it must be *thick* and therefore *heavy*. Often it is plastic coated to prevent flying fragments if it breaks. Its use is confined to small perfume aerosols where the working pressure is low and the cost is of less consequence.

The aerosol valve

An aerosol valve must be inexpensive yet utterly reliable. In fact it is very simple. Figure 24.14 shows a valve broken down into its components. Figure 24.15 shows how it works.

When closed, a tiny hole in the valve stem is covered by a small plastic ring – the gasket. Pressing the button pushes the stem down to uncover the hole and out comes the product. Lift the finger and a spring pushes up the stem so the hole is covered again and the flow stops. Valve failure is rarely the cause of a non-working aerosol. This is more likely due to a blocked button or loss of propellant. Both faults are usually caused by incorrect use.

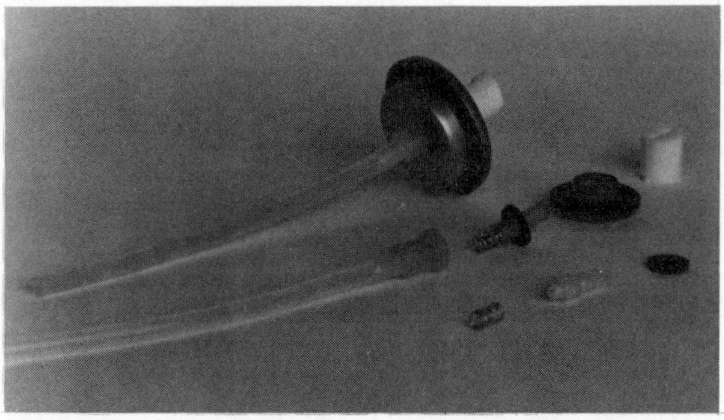
Figure 24.14 Aerosol valve and its component parts

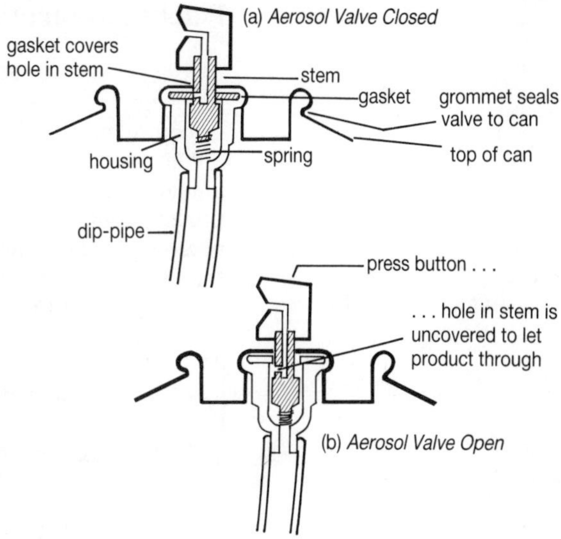

Figure 24.15 How an aerosol valve works

Figure 24.16 Aerosol actuator buttons

Actuator button

Buttons for aerosols are of many designs but there are only two kinds: spray and foam (see figure 24.16). There are, though, many types of spray buttons. The standard ones give a fairly fine spray with quite a wide spread. Others give a fine mist spray for hairspray or a paint, or more of a jet for mechanics' penetrating oil.

Aerosol propellants

After filling the product, the container is closed and *pressurised* with *propellant gas*. Closing is done by permanently crimping on the valve so the aerosol cannot be accidentally opened again.

Propellant gases are of *two* types:

compressed gases   *liquefied gases*

Compressed gases are not often used to propel aerosols. Air is not used because the oxygen in it is likely to oxidise the product and spoil it. *Nitrogen* and *carbon dioxide* are both innocuous and are used to propel food product aerosols such as whipped cream and tomato sauce.

Compressed gases do have a serious disadvantage. As the product is used and the volume of headspace increases, so the pressure *falls* in proportion: double the headspace, half the pressure. So what started as a vigorous spray from a full can will have deteriorated to a pathetic dribble when it is nearly empty.

With *liquefied gases* this pressure drop does not occur as the product is used. The reason is they work by *vapour pressure*. When compressed these gases quite easily turn to liquid and so long as the container contains liquefied 'gas' as well as gaseous 'gas', the gas will exert a certain pressure, the *vapour pressure*, however full or empty. Used in an aerosol, as the product is used and the headspace increases liquid propellant vaporises to *restore* the pressure. The pressure remains the same all through the use of the product.

Two groups of liquefied gases are used as propellants:

fluorocarbons   *hydrocarbons*

Fluorocarbon propellants

The big advantage of fluorocarbon propellants is their *non-flammability*, so products using them will not imitate flame throwers. They have however gained a tarnished image in the hands of the environmentalist lobby. A hitherto unproven theory that fluorocarbons discharged into the air would do untold harm to the ozone layers of the upper atmosphere has led some prudent countries – notably the USA – to ban them. In others their use has been reduced and much work is being done to find safe alternatives. Nevertheless they are still widely used, particularly where hydrocarbons would be too hazardous through fire risk.

The three main fluorocarbons used are:

Dichloro difluoro methane	– Propellant 12
Trichloro fluoro methane	– Propellant 11
Dichloro tetra fluoro ethane	– Propellant 114

The vapour pressures they exert at 20°C are:

Propellant 12	– 4.7 bar (68 lb per in.^{2})
Propellant 11	– 0.0 bar (it is liquid at 20°C)
Propellant 114	– 0.8 bar (12 lb per in.^{2})

Hydrocarbon propellants

Hydrocarbon propellants are now much used instead of fluorocarbons but their great disadvantage is their *flammability*. This does not mean that the product will burn or explode: there is no air in there. But it could mean that if the product is accidentally sprayed through a naked flame an alarming plume of flame several feet long could result. *Do not try it.*

It is not advisable to use these propellants in an alcohol-based product, such as hairspray, or kerosene-based product, such as insecticide, as in use it could imitate a welding torch!

The principal hydrocarbon propellants are:

Butane	– vapour pressure 1.1 bar (16 lb per in.^{2}) at 20°C
Isobutane	– vapour pressure 2.1 bar (30 lb per in.^{2}) at 20°C
Propane	– vapour pressure 7.3 bar (105 lb per in.^{2}) at 20°C

Selecting a propellant

Obviously the vapour pressures of some propellants are far too high for any product, others far too low. Usually propellants are used in combination. 12 and 11, 50/50 and 12 and 114, 60/40 are commonly used mixtures.

When they are incorporated in the product, the final working pressure will probably still be much less. This is because *all* the liquids in the product contribute in proportion to an *average* vapour pressure.

This is in accord with Dalton's Law of Partial Pressures which states that 'In a mixture of gases, the total pressure is equal to the sum of the partial pressures of the individual gases'. The partial pressure of a gas is the pressure that gas would exert if the same amount of it could occupy the whole space occupied by the mixture.

As many of the liquids present – water, alcohol, oils and Propellant 11 – are liquids at ordinary room temperatures, their share of the pressure will be zero, so they bring down the final average pressure. Table 24.1 lists the liquids in some products and shows their *working pressures*. Note that products must be specially formulated for aerosol packs. The proportions of the liquids are chosen to give the required pressure.

Table 24.1 Liquid Components and Working Pressures of Aerosol Products

Creams and Foams (such as Shaving Foam)	*Wet Spray (such as Perfume Cologne)*	*Spirit Sprays (such as Hairspray)*
Water	Water	Alcohol
Oils	Alcohol	Propellant 12
Propellant 12	Propellant 12	Propellant 11
Propellant 114	Propellant 114	
5lb/sq. in.	5 to 10 lb/sq. in.	35 to 40 lb/sq. in.

Figure 24.17 An aerosol filling line. The cans are filled (left), crimped closed (centre) and charged with propellant gas (right) (courtesy of Staffs Aerosols and Packaging Ltd)

Are aerosols safe?

An aerosol is safe provided one follows the *instructions*. As with anything else, to abuse an aerosol is dangerous. Here are answers to the most frequent questions concerning aerosol safety:

> An aerosol will not burst as such if punctured, but its contents will squirt out and could themselves be very messy or dangerous.
>
> An aerosol could explode if it gets *very hot*. Keep it in a cool place.
>
> An aerosol will explode if thrown on a fire, but so too will a closed bottle or a toothpaste tube.

Small aerosols are allowed on board in hand luggage by most airlines.

It is not wise to spray into the eyes or breathe the fumes. In normal use, breathing the fumes is not harmful.

Both fluorocarbon and hydrocarbon propellants can act as hallucinatory drugs if they are abused. While it requires a very deliberate effort to produce the effects, it is advisable to use aerosols in a well-ventilated place.

There is as yet no real evidence that fluorocarbons damage the atmosphere but surely it is wise to err on the side of safety.

Some useful hints with aerosols

If on a cold day an aerosol does not work, warm it by standing it in warm water.

Hold the aerosol the right way up or the propellant may run out before the product is all used.

After using a paint spray, hold it upside down and spray to clear the valve. It will then work next time.

If an antiperspirant spray fails to work, it could be that the fine hole in the button is blocked. Remove the button and wash it in hot water.

Things to do

1 Make a collection of well-designed packs. Some items, particularly early perfume bottles, have become collector's items.

2 Conduct a survey among your friends and colleagues to find out why they choose particular brands of products.

3 Where there is a choice of pack, survey people's preference. For example: roll-on, stick or aerosol antiperspirant or tube or pump-pack toothpaste.

4 One can obtain 'pump-up' aerosol containers. Make up a hairspray (chapter 18), shaving foam (chapter 20) or a perfume cologne (chapter 22) to pack in a pump-up container.

5 Look up the labelling requirements in the *Cosmetic Product Regulations*.

Self-assessment questions

1 What *must* be stated on the label of (a) a product which contains lanolin, (b) a permanent hair dye?

2 Why cannot perfumes be kept in polyethene containers?

3 Why is it frequently necessary to lacquer metal containers internally?

4 What is important about the inner paper wrapper on a soap bar?

5 What in its strict sense is an aerosol?

6 Why is it preferable to use a liquefied gas rather than a compressed gas to pressurise an aerosol?

7 What type of aerosol products *must* be pressurised with compressed gases such as carbon dioxide?

8 What hazard is now of much greater importance, now that more aerosols are pressurised with hydrocarbons rather than fluorocarbons?

Bibliography

More advanced reading in cosmetic science

Reference may be made to the cosmetic science textbooks. These include:

Balsam, M. S. and Sagarin, E. (Eds) (1972, 1974). *Cosmetic Science and Technology* (3 volumes), Wiley, New York.
Breuer, M. M. (Ed) (1978, 1980). *Cosmetic Science* (2 volumes), Academic Press, London.
Harry, R. G., Wilkinson, J. B. and Moore, R. J. (Eds) (1982). *Harry's Cosmeticology*, Godwin, London.
Hibbott, H. W. (Ed) (1963). *Handbook of Cosmetic Science*, Pergamon, London.
Poucher, W. A. (1974, 1975). *Perfumes, Cosmetics and Soaps* (3 volumes), Chapman and Hall, London.

Details of the full range of specialist publications in cosmetic science may be obtained from Micelle Press, Wellington House, Messeter Place, London SE9 5DF.

Up-to-date information of the formulation of cosmetics and toiletries may be found in the technical literature produced by the manufacturers and suppliers of raw materials. Names and addresses may be obtained from the professional journals.

Two series of booklets are available to teachers at nominal cost from Unilever Education Section. Titles in the 'Ordinary Series' include:

Detergents
Toilet Preparations
Vegetable Oils and Fats

Titles in the 'Advanced Series' include:

Carbohydrates
Chemical Engineering
The Chemistry of Glycerides
The Chemistry of Proteins
The Physics of Chemical Structure
Surface Activity
The Theory of Detergency
Water

Further study in theoretical chemistry and physics

Reference may be made to textbooks for 'O' Level/GCSE and 'A' Level Physics and Chemistry. Titles include:

Barker, A. L. and Knapp, K. A. (1986). *Work Out Chemistry, 'O' Level and GCSE*, Macmillan, London.
Critchlow, P. (1982). *Mastering Chemistry*, Macmillan, London.
Hicks, J. (1982). *Comprehensive Chemistry*, Macmillan, London.
Robinson, D. A. and Woollard, J. M. (1982). *Chemistry for Schools and Colleges*, Macmillan, London.
Selinger, B. (1980). *Chemistry in the Market Place*, John Murray, London.
Todley, P. (1971). *Chemistry in Industry* (4 volumes), John Murray, London.

Further reading in anatomy and physiology

The anatomy of the human body is detailed in:

Gray, H. (1980). *Gray's Anatomy*, Churchill-Livingstone, London.

General Human anatomy and physiology may be studied in the textbooks on: Anatomy and Physiology for Nurses. An example is

Ross, J. S. and Wilson, K. J. W. (1973). *Foundations of Anatomy and Physiology*, Longmans, London.

Human Biology for 'O', 'GCSE' and 'A' Level. These include:

Gadd, P. (1983). *Human and Social Biology*, Macmillan, London.
Soper, R. and Tyrell-Smith, S. (1982). *Modern Human and Social Biology*, Macmillan, London.

Biology for 'O', 'GCSE' and 'A' Level. Titles include:

Alderson, P. and Rowland, M. (1985). *Biology for GCSE*, Macmillan, London.
Kilgour, O. F, G. (1983). *Mastering Biology*, Macmillan, London.
Kilgour, O. F. G. (1986). *Work Out Biology, 'O' Level and GCSE*, Macmillan, London.
Kramer, L. M. J. (Ed) (1979). *Foundations of Biology* (5 volume series), Macmillan, London.
Stout, G. W. and Green, N. P. O. (1986). *Work Out Biology, 'A' Level*, Macmillan, London.

Some useful information on skin and hair is contained in books and booklets produced by some of the cosmetics houses. These include:

Toilet Preparations (Unilever)
On the Structure of Human Hair (Wella)
Hair Science and Beauty (Redken)
Through the Microscope (Redken)

Dermatology

Assistance for the beauty therapist in identifying skin problems can be found in the many clinical dermatology texts. Well illustrated examples include:

Fry, L. Wojnarowska, F. I. and Shahrad, P. (1985). *Illustrated Encyclopaedia of Dermatology*, MTP, London.
Levene, G. M. and Calnan, C. D. (1987). *A Colour Atlas of Dermatology*, Wolfe, London.
Rhodes, E. L. (1979). *Dermatology for the Physician*, Bailliere, London.

Professional journals

Scientific papers, review articles and news of the Cosmetics Industry and the Beauty Profession can be found in professional journals and periodicals which include:

International Journal of Cosmetic Science
Journal of the Society of Cosmetic Chemists
Soap, Perfumery and Cosmetics
The Manufacturing Chemist
Chemistry in Britain
Cosmetics World News
Les Nouvelles Aesthétiques

Glossary of Terms

Amphiphilic Having an affinity for both oils and water.
Amphoteric Depending on the pH, the active ion of an ionised amphoteric substance may be a cation or an anion.
Anionic The active ion of an ionised substance is its anion (negative).
Buffer Able to resist changes in acidity or alkalinity.
Cationic The active ion of an ionised substance is its cation (positive).
Detergent A cleanser which removes grease by emulsifying it.
Efflorescence Losing water to the atmosphere; causes the crystals of certain substances to collapse to powder.
Emollient To make soft; refers particularly to the softening of skin by cosmetic creams and lotions.
Emulsifier, Emulsifying agent An amphiphilic substance used to stabilise a mixture of oils and water to form an emulsion.
Emulsion A stabilised mixture of oils and water.
Homogenisation Splitting the disperse phase of an emulsion into minute droplets to improve its texture and its stability.
Humectant A substance able to attract and hold moisture; a moisturiser.
Hydrophilic Having an affinity or liking for water.
Hydrophobic Having a dislike of water; water-repellent.
Hygroscopic Able to absorb moisture from the atmosphere.
Immiscible Unable to mix as oil and water.
Ionic A substance which can ionise and is ionised in its active state.
Ionisation The splitting of the molecules of an ionic substance into electrically charged particles called ions.
Lipophilic Having an affinity or liking for oils, fats and waxes.
Miscible Able to mix.
Non-ionic A substance which does not ionise and is active in its non-ionised form.
Saponification Soap-making; the reaction of a fat or oil with an alkali to form a soap.
Solubilisation The 'dissolving' of oily substances in water with the aid of a surfactant to make a clear 'solution'.
Substantive The ability of one substance to be attracted and held by another; for example, dyes to the hair.
Surfactant A surface-active agent. A substance which by virtue of its amphiphilic properties is able to act at the surface of a liquid or at the interface between two liquids to reduce the surface tension and improve their miscibility.
Thixotropic Having variable viscosity. When undisturbed, the viscosity of a thixotropic liquid increases; when disturbed by stirring, the viscosity decreases and the liquid becomes more mobile.
Viscosity The 'runniness' or mobility of a liquid.

Index